Glaxo: A History to 1962

Glaxo is the world's second largest pharmaceutical corporation. This study of the company, from its beginnings to 1962, is based on unprecedented and unparalleled archival access to the company records. It gives a detailed account of the global operations of Glaxo, and describes not only the evolution of this international business, but studies its research and development programmes, its products, and its marketing and management. It is the first comprehensive study of a UK-based drugs company and one of the relatively few scholarly studies yet written of front-ranking world companies.

Portrait of Alec Nathan by Sir James Gunn. RA

Glaxo: A History to 1962

R. P. T. DAVENPORT-HINES and
JUDY SLINN

CAMBRIDGE
UNIVERSITY PRESS

CAMBRIDGE UNIVERSITY PRESS
Cambridge, New York, Melbourne, Madrid, Cape Town, Singapore,
São Paulo, Delhi, Dubai, Tokyo, Mexico City

Cambridge University Press
The Edinburgh Building, Cambridge CB2 8RU, UK

Published in the United States of America by Cambridge University Press, New York

www.cambridge.org
Information on this title: www.cambridge.org/9780521425599

First published 1992
First paperback edition 2010

A catalogue record for this publication is available from the British Library

Library of Congress Cataloguing in Publication Data

Davenport-Hines, R. P. T. (Richard Peter Treadwell), 1953-
Glaxo: a history to 1962 / R. P. T. Davenport-Hines and Judy Slinn.
    p. cm.
Includes bibliographical references and index.
1. Glaxo Laboratories - History. 2. Pharmaceutical industry - Great
Britain - History. I. Slinn, Judy. II. Title.
HD9667.9.G53D38 1992
338.4'76151'0941- dc20 91-42204 CIP

ISBN 978-0-521-41539-2 Hardback
ISBN 978-0-521-42559-9 Paperback

Additional resources for this publication at www.cambridge.org/9780521425599

Contents

Illustrations

Plates

These plates are available for download in colour from www.cambridge.org/9780521425599

Portrait of Alec Nathan by Sir James Gunn. RA   *Frontispiece*

I   An early tin of Glaxo powder. Cover of the Glaxo baby book using the Glaxo medallion. Postcards were a popular medium for Glaxo advertising in the interwar years.   *facing page* 210

II   Vitamin D was the Glaxo Department's first pharmaceutical product in 1924. It was added to Glaxo powder, presented as Ostelin Emulsion and then as Ostermilk.

III   Vitamin B_{12}, and the anti-pernicious anaemia factor was identified, isolated and crystallised at Greenford in 1948 after some years of work by a team led by Dr Lester Smith. The oil painting by Liam Breslin shows Dr Smith (on the left) with colleagues, Dr Parker and Dr Fantes in the laboratory. Below are crystals of vitamin B_{12}.

IV   Portrait of Sir Harry Jephcott by Sir Gerald Kelly.

Black and white

ix

Tables

Acknowledgements

The research for and writing of this history were financed by Glaxo Holdings plc at the Business History Unit in the London School of Economics. Glaxo gave us complete access to all the documents they have, but the loss of papers during enemy action in the Second World War is reflected in the gaps in the history of the early days of Joseph Nathan and of the Glaxo department. The contents of the book are, however, the responsibility of the authors and the views and judgements expressed in it are their own and not attributable to Glaxo.

During the research for the book we have had enthusiastic assistance from Betsy Bahr, Mark Dixon, Rachel Henry, Christine King, Helen Nicolson, Michael Robson, Jonathan Smith and Charlie Wilkinson. The last in particular made not only the most substantial contribution to the research but was of immeasurable benefit to the morale of the authors.

We have also been much helped by interviews and correspondence not only with numerous past and present Glaxo employees in Africa, Asia, Australasia and Europe but also with the late Doris, Lady Jephcott and with Sir Anthony Jephcott.

Earlier drafts of the manuscript have been read by Terry Gourvish, Leslie Hannah, Geoffrey Jones, Jonathan Liebenau and Mari Williams, to each of whom we are indebted for their comments and advice. Our thanks to Tony Hoskins and John Saxton of Glaxo for the illustrations.

We would particularly like to acknowledge the contribution both to the overall structure of the book and its detail made by the late Bill Reader. As always he gave most generously of his time, his knowledge and his experience, much to our benefit. We have had a great deal of secretarial help at the LSE, but special thanks must go to Gil Dixon of Eynsham for producing order out of chaos. Any mistakes of course are ours.

Introduction

In 1991 the Glaxo Group's turnover in its business, now wholly devoted to the discovery, development, manufacture and sales of prescription medicines, was £3,397m and profits (before tax) were £1,283m. Over the last two decades remarkable and mainly self-generated growth has made Glaxo the largest pharmaceutical company in Britain and taken the company to second place in the world league of the industry. Glaxo's operations and sales extend across the world with more than 80 per cent (87 per cent in fact, when the UK is included) of turnover arising in the developed countries of Western Europe and North America.

The group's competitors, the multinational pharmaceutical corporations, have varied origins but those of Glaxo must be among the most unusual. The entry into the dried milk business of the Nathans, a small Jewish family firm of merchants in New Zealand, came about by serendipity rather than deliberate intent. It was the determination of one member of that family, Alec Nathan, which kept and developed Glaxo babyfood as part of the Nathan business. In the two decades after 1918, the discoveries made by nutritional researchers took the Nathans into vitamin manufacture in order to strengthen the Glaxo range of products.

At the same time the company developed its international operations and Glaxo products were sold, and some manufactured, not only in the company's traditional spheres of interest, Australia and New Zealand, but also in India, Africa, Europe and North and South America. As the importance and profitability of the Nathans' traditional merchanting activities declined, the attractions of the new pharmaceutical industry were consistently urged on the company by Harry Jephcott; but the tendency to diversify rather into the food and associated industries remained strong in the business.

The Second World War, however, proved to be the turning point for the company. In the short-term there was an acute and urgent need to manufacture in Britain pharmaceutical products which had previously been

1

imported from Germany. In the long-term, and more significantly, Glaxo became involved with the development of penicillin and by the end of the war, the company was a pharmaceuticals manufacturer.

The post-war years were a period of rapid growth for the pharmaceutical industry internationally as new synthetic drug remedies for many previously untreatable diseases were found and launched on the market. Glaxo Laboratories, the name the Nathan company as a whole now took, participated in this growth and, as the period covered by this history drew to a close, a new generation of pharmaceutical products, the result of work done by the company's research and development scientists, were launched. Yet by comparison with the size of operations of Glaxo's main competitors in the 1950s, the US pharmaceutical corporations, Glaxo Laboratories, like most other British companies at the time, was small. It was, therefore, to strengthen and defend the British pharmaceutical industry as well as itself, that Glaxo merged with Allen & Hanburys and Evans Medical.

This history ends in the early 1960s, when Glaxo Laboratories, under the leadership of Harry Jephcott, was established as a leading British company with a strong, but not yet exclusive, attachment to the pharmaceutical industry. Its activities and interests overseas were, in the fashion typical of British business then, orientated principally towards the countries of the Commonwealth.

The subsequent transformation of Glaxo into a highly specialised transnational pharmaceutical company is another and different story.

I

Merchants and bonnie babies

1

The origins –
Joseph Nathan & Co

From London to Melbourne

Joseph Edward Nathan, founder of the company from which Glaxo
Laboratories grew, was born in London on 2 March 1835. He was the sixth
son of a wholesale tailor, Edward Nathan, and his wife Rachel. Family
tradition held that Nathan père was, or became, 'a charming old man with
very little brains', while the mother 'was a highly intelligent woman with not
a great deal of education'.[1] The Nathan family lived in Houndsditch, an area
of east London just outside the boundaries of the City and for many
centuries a centre of the clothing trade. By the early nineteenth century
Houndsditch had a large Jewish population – they built a synagogue there in
1809 – and there were many small factories, warehouses and businesses in
the area.[2] From the age of about twelve, Joseph Nathan helped his father in
his small business of making suits and clothes which he then sold in and
around London. Even at that early age Joseph showed signs of business
acumen and entrepreneurial zeal; from the travellers who sold cloth to his
father, he learned of the possibilities of an export trade and urged his father
to launch into this line. He succeeded in persuading the old man to buy a
tail-coat and silk hat to make himself more presentable, and sent him to
drum up connections for export business; but Edward Nathan had no heart
for expansion and nothing came of the venture. Disappointed at this, young
Joseph left his father's business and went to work for a Houndsditch
furniture store. At the same time he sought to improve his education in his
spare time.

In 1852 Rachel Nathan died. For Joseph, on whom she had been a strong
influence, her death was a shock which, combined with other factors, forced
a turning point in his life. In England he could see little prospect of realising
his ambitions and his health was poor, for he had always suffered from
asthma which was exacerbated by the filthy air of east London. Late in 1851
gold had been discovered in Australia, at Ballarat near Melbourne and, as

5

the news of the discovery reached Europe, many left to undertake the long journey to join the rush to riches. Joseph Nathan decided to seek his fortune and repair his health in Australia. With a few friends, including one who became a lifetime associate, Henry Isaacs, he embarked on the *William Ackers*, a 330-ton barque which left London in August 1853, bound for Melbourne and Sydney. As well as the passengers, the ship carried a mixed cargo of goods needed in Melbourne, including soap, currants and raisins, sugar, cheese, spices, brandy and gin.[3] It landed on 27 December 1853, at Melbourne, then in the process of dramatic growth. A small mainly pastoral settlement until the discovery of gold, Melbourne's population tripled between 1851 and 1854 with the influx of immigrants. Like many another, Joseph Nathan set off for the goldfields. However, according to family sources, on his way he met a policeman (or goldfields' warden) who warned him that the chances of making a fortune in gold prospecting were slim, but that a better 'goldmine' lay in starting a store supplying blankets, foodstuffs, picks, shovels and other such necessities required by the diggers. Young Nathan took this advice, returned to Melbourne and set up in business. Although nearly penniless on his arrival he was fortunate in his family and Jewish connections. The Moses brothers, owners of the Monkwell Street Warehouse Company, were kinsmen who dealt with his father's tailoring business and they had a policy of giving financial backing to Jewish boys of good character. They supported young Nathan in starting his business.

No record has survived of Joseph Nathan's early years of trading in Melbourne. By 1857, however, he was established in Collins Street, one of the main retailing streets of the city. There, too, lived the Marks family, who had also emigrated from England (from Stoke Newington in London), some months before Joseph Nathan, arriving in Melbourne in March 1853. Marks was a merchant and it was his daughter, Dinah, that Joseph Nathan decided that he wished to marry. Her mother, Jane, had been a Nathan before she married and possibly, therefore, the young couple were distantly related.[4] Meanwhile, back in London, Joseph Nathan's eldest sister, Kate had married in 1855. Her husband was Jacob Joseph, a merchant who, despite the handicap of blindness, had established his business in Wellington, New Zealand, during the previous decade. Soon after the couple returned to Wellington, Jacob Joseph, wishing to return to London again, asked his brother-in-law to come from Melbourne to Wellington to look after his business in his absence. Joseph Nathan seized the chance to negotiate a partnership and, when the bargain was struck, Joseph, then 22, and Dinah, aged 19, were married at her father's house in November 1857. The young couple left soon afterwards to sail to New Zealand.

1 Melbourne, the Yarra Yarra in 1853 as Joseph Nathan knew it.

Early days in New Zealand

The Nathans reached Wellington in December 1857. With a population then of less than 4,000, Wellington was much smaller than Melbourne and still more of a pioneer settlement. It was not, however, without some amenities; two theatres, a number of hotels, two newspapers and three fire-engines, the latter necessary because all the buildings were made of timber. Although the European population of New Zealand doubled between 1847 and 1860,[5] a transport infrastructure was largely undeveloped until the colony became more settled after the end of the Maori wars in 1869. The general merchant's business in which Joseph had arranged to participate depended largely on the arrival of a motley range of goods from England. The partners ordered from London anything for which they thought they might find a market and then apportioned the imports among their customers.

The partnership of Joseph and Nathan lasted until 1873. Never peaceful, for Jacob's blindness made him very suspicious, there were constant quarrels over sharing the profits and, in 1873, a final rupture led Joseph Nathan to sever the partnership and begin as a merchant trader on his own account. By that time he had a large family to support. Between 1858 and 1877 Dinah Nathan bore fourteen children, eleven of whom survived. Three of Joseph Nathan's brothers (David, Hyam and Lewis) emigrated to New Zealand, too, and established themselves, with varying success, as traders.

2 Cameo portraits of Joseph and Dinah Nathan taken about 1860.

There does not seem, however, to have been any involvement in business
between them and when Joseph Nathan decided, in 1876, to visit London to
see his father, then in ailing health, he left his young business in the hands of
two strangers. Messrs Watty and Roxburgh, despite a recommendation to
Nathan from a local bank, turned out to be an alcoholic and a rogue
respectively. Together they brought the business to the verge of bankruptcy.
On Joseph Nathan's return to New Zealand he had to make a renewed
effort to rebuild his business. In London his old friend, Henry Isaacs, acted
as his agent in offices in Sugar Loaf Court, off Leadenhall Street, while in
New Zealand, as his sons came of age, they joined him in developing the
business. The first to do so was the eldest, David, who was 22 at the start of
the 1880s – a decade which saw considerable changes and an expansion of
the family business.

Steamships were already changing the pattern of travel between Britain
and her colonies, but more slowly, because of the distance, as far as New
Zealand was concerned.[6] The introduction of steamships with refrigerated
holds made possible the transportation of meat and dairy products from
Australia and New Zealand to the increasing urban populations of Great
Britain. The first successful cargo of frozen beef and mutton travelled from
Melbourne to London in 1880 aboard the SS Strathleven. Two years later
the first cargo of meat went from New Zealand. Joseph Nathan helped to
pioneer New Zealand frozen meat and was an early chairman of the
Wellington Meat Export Company, formed in 1881 as a farmers' freezing
cooperative.[7] His commercial acumen made him realise that the improvement of transport was vital to the development of mercantile businesses like
his own. With Henry Isaacs he helped to organise a New Zealand freight

On Sale

JOSEPH NATHAN & CO,
LAMBTON QUAY,

HAVE ON SALE

GENERAL IRONMONGERY, comprising
—Copper rivets and burs, tower bolts,
drawer knobs, punches, braces, com-
passes, ship scrapers, wire gauges,
caulking irons, cutting plyers, dust and
furnace shovels, coopers' vices, foot
rules, beer and spirit cocks, cheese
tasters, lanterns, tinman's snips,
Scotch shears, gimlets, &c, &c
100 kegs Ewbank's nails
100 ditto wire nails
30 dozen galvanised buckets
20 ditto Parke's CS spades
20 ditto Foster's ditto ditto
10 ditto potato forks
4 casks Sorby's tools
2 cases Nixey's black lead
BRASS GOODS—Sash fasteners, rack pul-
lies, hat and coat hooks, hat hooks,
sash screws, sash lifts, cot swings, table
catches, roller ends, gun hooks, cup
hooks, jack chains, sash rollers, &c, &c
OILS AND PAINTS—Boiled and raw oil,
turpentine, white and red lead, sheet
lead, &c, &c
20 casks zinc
MARBLE MANTLEPIECES — A large
variety, in white, black, and other
marbles
PAPERHANGINGS—
30 bales of the newest French and English designs
20 cases Chance's sheet glass
100 boxes Belgium ditto
BRUSHWARE—Paint, oil, hair, scrubbing,
clothes, shoe, bannister, stove, whiting,
plate, hearth, and horse brushes, broom
heads, &c
CROCKERY—100 crates, assorted—Toilet
sets, ewers, jugs, chambers, white and
gold and blue and white cups and
saucers, basins, mugs, &c, &c
OILMEN'S STORES—
20 cases sulphuric acid
180 ditto Bell and Black's vestas, plaid,
250s, 500s, and 1000s
30 casks Day and Martin's blacking,
paste, 6d, and 1s

10 cases soap powder
5 casks carraway seeds
500 boxes Price's candles
20 cases Brown and Polson's corn flour
50 ditto Morton's pickles, mixed. Imperial hot, and West India
40 ditto salad oil, pints and half-pints
30 ditto herrings, kippered and red
6 casks ginger, bleached, unbleached, and
ground
3 cases essences
2 ditto mixed spice
20 ditto castor oil, half-pints and qr-pints
20 ditto hair oil, ditto ditto
5 ditto tartaric acid
80 ditto sardines, half and quarter
1 case cream of tartar
20 kegs saltpetre
40 cases Colman's Mustard, D.S.F. and
Durham
55 ditto Colman's starch, blue, white, and
glaze
40 ditto Colman's blue, indigo and Wind-
sor
20 ditto capers, C.&B. and Batty's
30 cases currie, C.&B., Batty's, and W y
brow's
10 cases Barcelona nuts
20 cases patent barley and groats
10 chests sago
2 cases West India arrowroot
3 ditto nutmegs and cloves
15 ditto cocoa, Epps', Taylor's, and Fry's
10 ditto chocolate, Barry's
3 ditto candied peel
10 ditto salt, in jars
10 ditto bath bricks
20 casks whiting
WINES AND SPIRITS—
Rum—Lemon Hart's, 14 o.p.
Rum do do 34 o.p.
Rum—Twiss and Browning's, 10 o.p.
Brandy, dark—Martell's, quarter casks
do pale do do
Port—quarter casks and cases
Sherry do do
Whisky do do
Brandy—Hennessy's
Old Tom—cases
Champagne and Moselle
Claret—St Julien
do St Estephe
Ginger Wine
Stout
Ale

3 The first advertisement by Joseph Nathan & Co, in the *Wellington Independent*, 26th June 1873.

shipping company, which chartered sailing ships from reputable London owners and ran cooperative freights all over New Zealand. In Wellington itself, Nathan proposed the formation of the Wellington Harbour Board. He was a member of the Board for some years and was instrumental in bringing in a high-grade engineer who re-modelled the whole harbour and designed the docks. He was also a director of the Wellington Patent Slip Company, which repaired small ships and coastal boats.

Nathan was not only involved in shipping. Railways opened up New Zealand for trading and settlement and between 1882 and 1886 Nathan was one of the chief promoters of the Wellington and Manawatu Railway Company. The policies of Sir Julius Vogel as Colonial Treasurer from 1869, and as Prime Minister from 1873 to 1875, involved heavy government borrowing, which had produced wild land speculation, in which Joseph Nathan participated. After the conclusion of the Maori wars, Vogel's government, which could not afford to pay off the British soldiers and sailors with cash, instead gave them 'Land Certificates' which were in effect allotments of pieces of land in Manawatu. Joseph Nathan used to buy these certificates at £25 each from the discharged soldiers, taking his chance whether the land allotted would prove to be swamp or mountain top in the hope that the value would be raised by railway connections, a hope eventually realised.

Sir Julius Vogel returned to England and was the New Zealand government's Agent in London until 1881 when he was forced to resign because the colonial government objected to his company-promotion activities; his help, however, was enlisted by Joseph Nathan, and Vogel arranged for the flotation of debentures worth £560,000 to finance the construction of the Manawatu railway. A London board was formed including Sir Penrose Julyan (Director of the London and Westminster Bank, and formerly Crown Agent) and Sir Edward Stafford (Prime Minister of New Zealand 1856–1861, 1865–1869 and 1872). Also a director was A. J. Mundella, the British radical politician who was later forced to resign as President of the Board of Trade in 1894 following the collapse of the New Zealand Loan Co, of which he had been a director. The completion of the Manawatu railway was celebrated with the ceremony of hammering in the last spike in November 1896, with the Governor doing the hammering; Joseph Nathan, as Chairman of the Board, gave a long address in which he spoke of the hopes and intentions that the railway would open up vast areas of New Zealand for development.[8]

The financial and other strains imposed on Joseph Nathan by the financing and building of the Manawatu railway during New Zealand's recession of the 1880s, depleted his strength, and his sons considered that he never fully recovered.[9] Indeed, although he was several times approached to stand for the New Zealand Parliament, he always declined, saying that his experience in lobbying for the railway had determined him 'never [to] be connected with such a set of Parliamentary blackguards again'.[10] Nevertheless, for the Nathan business the railway provided the immediate advantage of easier access to the store in Palmerston North, opened in the 1880s, as the 'Ready Money Stores', which was, from 1885, managed by Maurice Cohen, one of Joseph's sons-in-law.

By the early 1890s, the introduction of a regular fortnightly steamer service from Britain brought changes to merchanting activity. The Nathans found themselves facing increased competition in country districts: they began to be supplanted as wholesale import distributors by manufacturers' representatives selling direct to retailers. To widen his business, Joseph Nathan tried to diversify into the wool business, but found that the stock and station agents were too large and well established to challenge. Instead of wool and, at the prompting of his son David, he next turned to one of New Zealand's other great agricultural products, butter. The New Zealand government had already recognised the possibilities created by refrigerated ships, recruiting Danish experts on dairy product trade to advise on the development of these export lines. Around the same time, the perfection of the technique of Babcock's milk test enabled farmers to establish the butter-fat content of milk supplied to creameries so that they could be paid precisely in accordance with the butter-fat they delivered. This proved a further stimulus to New Zealand dairying. The refrigeration boom and Babcock's discovery resulted in the formation of farmers' cooperative associations to market and export butter.[11]

In the course of their commercial travelling tours through New Zealand, the Nathan family had built a good understanding with the many farmers' cooperatives which characterised the country's agriculture and, in 1891, David and Louis Nathan had discussions with the Cooperative Society at Palmerston North on the northern island of New Zealand. Two seasons earlier, the Society had lost its entire capital of £2,000 through buying butter, a loss it had recouped in subsequent years by doing business in groceries, locks and ironmongery. David, apparently without consulting his father, suggested that his family firm should take over the Society's butter marketing in London in return for a share allotment in the profits of the Society of about £500. David urged this scheme successfully on his father: 'It is the nucleus of a good business, and they sadly want more capital and a London office as now they must sell locally all produce.' Joseph Nathan & Company seized this opportunity and became the financial supporters, and distributors on commission, of the first dairy farmers' cooperative in Wellington province. After a few years the Nathans were succeeded as the Cooperative's agents by another firm and so they bought their own butter

4 Joseph Nathan's sons (a) David (b) Louis (c) Maurice (d) Phil (e) Fred (f) Alec.

factory at Makino. Within a short time the Nathans had seventeen little creameries in dairy districts.[12] Louis Nathan, Joseph's second son, was sent to Australia to study the creamery system supplying butter factories, which had been pioneered in Victoria, and by the end of the nineteenth century it was a solid element in the profits of the firm of Joseph Nathan & Company. These profits came not only from butter exports but also from specialised lines for which the firm was increasingly renowned throughout the colony, such as special brands of Union Teas.

Joseph Nathan's later years

By 1893 Joseph Nathan had spent nearly forty years in business in New Zealand, counting the time he spent in partnership with Jacob Joseph and his own years of independent trading. In his speech at the inauguration of the Wellington-Manawatu railway in 1886, he had referred to the 'feeling of self-reliance and thorough earnestness which, when directed towards a good purpose, invariably leads to success', and expressed his belief in 'well-directed energy and perseverance', and 'united action for the common good'. It was an outlook prevalent among New Zealand's prosperous merchants of the period, so that, for example, an Auckland newspaper in 1882 praised the business opportunities in a colony 'where the social disabilities, the exclusive taste, the over-strained competition and stereo-typed conventionalism of the Old World have not yet taken root – there is a clear field for men of talent, skill and energy to climb the social ladder, and to attain to a degree of wealth and social elevation that is possible only to the favoured few in older countries'.[13] This open and egalitarian spirit remained the hallmark of the Nathan (and later the Glaxo) way of business long after it had become mere cant in New Zealand society. For Joseph Nathan such a *credo* was not only to be applied in his own business, but also in service to the community, both to his own Jewish fellows and to society in a wider sense. For the former he had acted as Trustee of the Synagogue, built in Wellington in 1868, and for the latter he had been involved in many activities including shipping, railway development and the Wellington Gas Company, as well as the Chamber of Commerce of which he was Chairman. He had become 'as prominent as he was esteemed in the highest commercial and social circles' of what was a very small community.[14]

In 1893 Joseph Nathan's wife, Dinah, died of cancer (on board the *SS Kaikoura*). They had been a happy and devoted couple, and he always said that he owed much of his success to her sound advice. Her death, at the age of 53, was a severe blow. From 1887 the Nathans had divided their time between Wellington and London and after Dinah's death, Joseph spent an increasing amount of time in England, which by 1900 had become his home.

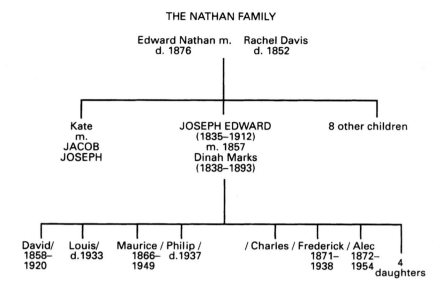

THE NATHAN FAMILY

Edward Nathan m.   Rachel Davis
      d. 1876   d. 1852

Kate	JOSEPH EDWARD	8 other children
m.	(1835–1912)	
JACOB	m. 1857	
JOSEPH	Dinah Marks	
	(1838–1893)	

David/	Louis/	Maurice / Philip /	/ Charles /	Frederick /	Alec
1858–	d.1933	1866– d.1937	1871–	1872–	
1920		1949	1938	1954	4 daughters

His house in London was 23 Pembridge Gardens, behind Notting Hill Gate. It was an area favoured by rich colonial Jews: Sir Julius Wernher's father-in-law, James Mankiewicz, was a resident, Sir Edmund Davis, the Rhodesian base-metals tycoon married from 8 Pembridge Square in 1889, and Sir Ernest Oppenheimer of De Beers Diamonds lived at 32 Pembridge Square in the mid-Edwardian period. Nor was it a coincidence that the house was only a minute's walk on the Sabbath from the St Petersburgh Place Synagogue, for Joseph Nathan's Judaism was precious to him, and he insisted that his children be meticulous in their practice of its rites. His outlook is well conveyed by a letter that he sent to his sons after making his final will in February 1903. With its precarious spelling, and indifference to punctuation, it gives a keen flavour of the man.

'My Dear Sons', he wrote:

I have today signed my will in it I have tried my best to be equitable towards all my dear children I feel the Great God of Israel has been pleased to bless me abundantly. He has blessed me in my children all of whom are good & loving.

After explaining the provisions that he had made for the future division of profits from the family firm, he continued:

we are only Trustees all is not given us for our own use to be used only for selfish pleasure all my life I have held these views & have done my best to carry same out sharing with others, seeking where help was wanted & acting according to the judgment vouchsaved to me, do you likewise you will find happiness in helping others – The possessions God places in your hands is not all for self I wanted to impress this on all of you I hope each and all of you will at all times feel as I have felt that it is a blessing to have been born a Jew be proud of your Birthright and all men will respect you of course you as well as I have learnt will be called upon to make sacrifices for your religion, do it with pleasure, & esteem it a privilege & God will bless you as he blessed your fathers at all times.

I need not tell my sons that Honour truth & integrity are sure roads to success because they are Thank God all Honourable Men.[15]

The *credo* had its effect on those of the Nathan sons who were to be most involved in the development of Glaxo Laboratories, notably his sixth son, Alec (1872–1954).

Before what can only be described as his semi-retirement in England – for Joseph Nathan did not find it easy to relinquish the reins – the family firm was converted in 1899 into a limited liability company, Joseph Nathan & Company. Even before this transaction there were divisions between the brothers, and misunderstandings between the Wellington and London Offices. In 1897 there was a serious row between David (1858–1920) in Wellington, and his brother Louis (*c.* 1860–1933), who was about to take over the running of the London office, now at 17 Fenchurch Street. Henry Isaacs, whose daughter had in 1894 married Maurice Nathan (1866–1949), retired in 1898. David opposed various financial proposals made in London, particularly the valuations put on stocks and on New Zealand properties in the accounts. As the eldest surviving son, David had been a great support to his father during difficult periods in the 1880s, and was accustomed to considerable responsibility. He felt threatened by the admission to the firm of his younger brothers – Maurice and Philip – with ideas of their own, and he was particularly apprehensive that Louis was seeking to cut him out. The breeze between them in 1897 was the precursor of many such storms in the next quarter-century.

The negotiations between father and sons took almost three years to settle the basis on which the company would be formed. Not only were there difficulties about the division of control between London and Wellington and the valuation of assets, but Joseph Nathan wanted to secure an income for his three unmarried daughters of £500 each a year. This was eventually achieved by an understanding that the managers (the brothers David, Louis and Maurice) whose own remuneration depended on the profits of the company should ensure a 5 per cent dividend on the Preference shares (£27,000). With a capital of £127,000 the company was registered in July 1899. Joseph wrote to his sons in November of that year:

I have I really believe made the Company a present of over £20,000 by under-estimating the value of my assets ... I hope to see Philip and Charlie become joint managers [Philip became a Managing Director in July 1900] with you, before placing either such position you will make them acquainted with the contents of this letter so that they become parties to it and take their share of responsibility. Let it be explained to them that their sisters portion was retained in the Company to give the Company more financial strength.[16]

In the absence of figures for the years before 1899, it is impossible to judge whether the company's performance improved in the five years 1899–1903. Profits were modest – they averaged £8,647 a year in that period – and the company was cautious in the dividends which it declared. It was to need such financial strength as it had husbanded for the new venture on which it embarked in 1903.

2

The Nathans and proprietary foods 1903–1918

Milk preservation and proprietary babyfoods

For more than fifty years the idea of preserving milk either by canning or drying had attracted the attention of chemists and manufacturers. The problem of supplying fresh milk to urban areas in England which, in the first half of the nineteenth century stimulated the search for a means of preservation, had to some extent been solved by the development of the railway network. But milk supplies in town remained of poor quality, frequently adulterated and, as was increasingly recognised towards the end of the century, the carrier of many diseases. At the same time breast-feeding of babies declined both among working-class mothers, who were employed in greater numbers in factories, and among middle- and upper-class mothers who were disinclined to feed their babies naturally.[1] Attempts to manufacture dried powdered milk failed to produce a form capable of satisfactory reconstitution before the end of the century, but improvements in the technique of 'condensing' milk led to the Borden patent, granted in the USA in 1856. It was not, however, until 1865 that American financial interests formed the Anglo-Swiss Condensed Milk Company (later Nestlé), based in Switzerland where it began operations the following year. By the early twentieth century Anglo-Swiss had opened further factories in Britain, Ireland, Denmark, Norway, Bavaria, the Netherlands, France, Austria and Italy, and a host of imitative competitors had arisen. The most reputable brands of condensed milk at that time were Ideal, First Swiss, Peacock, Viking and Hollandia, all containing about 10 per cent each of protein and fat, and 15 per cent of sugar.[2] Other condensed milks, of which the more respectable brands were Milkmaid and Nestlé (both made by the same company), had very large quantities of cane sugar added to prevent bacterial growth.

The use of canned condensed milk, particularly for feeding infants, increased rapidly after 1870; imports into Britain rose from 545,000 cwt in

1895 to 919,000 cwt in 1901 and 991,000 cwt in 1909. But although condensed milk was bacteriologically purer than fresh cow's milk, it had many
disadvantages. Its liability to contamination after tins had been opened
made it a dangerous infant food, especially during summer months; and its
nutritional value was low, both in the full-cream and the skimmed milk
versions. Because condensed milk was deficient in fat, low in protein,
lacking freshness and with excessive sugar content, babies overfed on it were
more vulnerable to a variety of diseases including epidemic diarrhoea,
anaemia, rickets and bronchitis. The excess sugar could also cause flatulent
distention of the intestines, leading to hernia; as Sir Arthur Newsholme,
Principal Medical Officer to the Local Government Board (forerunner of the
Ministry of Health), cautioned in 1911, 'there are serious drawbacks, except
as a temporary expedient, of full-cream sweetened condensed milk as an
infants' food, the most objectionable feature being the excess of sugar; but
the use of skimmed condensed milk for the same purpose implies a slow
process of partial starvation'.[3] Another authority wrote in 1909 that 'a
veritable holocaust of infants has been due to condensed milk, either directly
or indirectly, in consequence of the various ailments which they might have
escaped if they had been brought up on a proper diet'.[4] There was a
particular need for a milk suitable for infant feeding during the season of
summer diarrhoea (from July to September each year), when cow's milk was
'often dirty, lacking in freshness, kept from going sour by the addition of
preservatives, contaminated by faecal matter at the farm, by dust on its
journey to the retailer, and by flies while exposed in bowls on the shop
counter of a general dealer'.[5]

As well as condensed milk, there were various types of humanized and
desiccated (dried) milk available. Humanized milk was chiefly used for
nourishing bottle-fed infants, especially during epidemics of summer diarrhoea; comprised of milk modified by the addition of water, cream and
sugar, it was dispensed in separate bottles for each feed, the quantity and
strength varying with the age of the child. Although it secured 'uniformity
and regularity' in infant feeding, safeguarding the child 'against an ignorant
or careless mother, as well as against bacterial contamination', there were
many practical disadvantages. Its production required special machinery,
and hence a capital outlay at which many municipal authorities baulked
either because of parsimony or lack of resources. Even greater continuous
expenditure was entailed by washing bottles, bottling and replacing broken
bottles. Moreover, freshly humanized milk had to be supplied to infants
daily, so a municipal depot could only serve 'a comparatively small area in
its immediate vicinity'.[6]

Although desiccated milk had been in use since the 1870s, in making milk-
chocolate or malted drinks such as Horlicks, the process involved treating

skimmed milk which was markedly deficient in fat, and usually required the addition of preservatives. Moreover, these early types of dried milk were limited to factory processes, and could not be reconstituted as milk. Throughout the 1890s there had been attempts to develop a dried milk which would retain all the milk solids and become soluble on the addition of water. All the attempts were based on evaporation at moderate pressure, usually after the addition of sugar, and each one had failed: either because the product quickly went rancid, or because its albuminoid elements decomposed. Rancidity was the real problem. It seemed impossible to prevent butter-fat from going rancid if a full cream powder was sought and, without a full-cream content, the product would be too low in fat to use as a baby food.

The Nathans' acquisition of the Just-Hatmaker process

Early in 1903 Maurice Nathan called at Frank Debenham's department store in Wigmore Street, London. Debenhams at that time had a substantial drapery wholesale export trade and a piece of this business with Nathan's had gone awry. Maurice had a long interview with Debenham's elegant and supercilious managing director, Fred Oliver, who was the most powerful right-wing pamphleteer and polemicist of his day.[7] When this interview was concluded, Ernest Debenham took Maurice aside and displayed a parcel of skimmed milk powder. The powder had been made under a high temperature process for drying milk, the British patent for which was held by an American called James Robertson Hatmaker, with whom Oliver was discussing its possible exploitation in Britain. It is not clear how far Hatmaker and Debenham's had advanced in their negotiations, or when they had been introduced. Debenham's motives in showing the powder to Maurice Nathan are equally unclear and may have been casual. Whatever was intended, Maurice Nathan immediately recognised that the powder offered a solution to his firm's long-standing dilemma of utilising the surplus skimmed milk produced at their New Zealand creameries and butteries, by turning it to productive use as powdered milk. There is one tantalising reference to an earlier interest on the part of the Nathans in dried milk. In 1901 David Nathan had taken samples of dried milk made at the Makino butter factory to the Manawata Agricultural Show, in the hope of persuading farmers that it was a better business proposition than butter or cheese. Nothing further, however, seems to have come of it.[8]

The new process being touted by Hatmaker to Debenhams had been developed by two New York dairymen, John A. Just and Roy Bent and was known as the Just-Hatmaker method. Its use of high temperatures to dry the milk was a novel departure from the prevailing slow vacuum process and, in 1903, having only undergone laboratory testing, it remained unproven commercially. Just and Hatmaker had not then perfected their method of separating the dried milk power from the cylinders on which it had been heated (see page 23), and it was only later in 1903 that an English mechanical engineer, John Merrett, working for German paper machinery makers near Mannheim, devised a knife to remove the film of dried milk from the heated roller.[9]

Initially, when Maurice Nathan discussed the possibility of exploiting the Just-Hatmaker process in collaboration with the Debenhams, his father and brother Louis dismissed it as impractical. Maurice then left for Canada to deal with the firm's supply problems in tinned fish and flax, expecting his suggestion to recede into oblivion. In his absence, however, Joseph and Louis Nathan revived interest in the idea and resumed discussions with the Debenham family. 'At this time', so Alec Nathan and others recalled in later years, the London directors 'thought J.N. & Co had a gold mine in the Dried Milk business', and flung themselves into it with high enthusiasm.[10]

In the summer of 1903 Frank Debenham signed a series of agreements with Hatmaker, who held various international dried milk patents outside Canada and the USA, by which Debenham bought the manufacturing rights of the Just-Hatmaker process in Argentina, Brazil and Uruguay, and the right to import the product into Britain. The Dried Milk Company was registered in London in November 1903, with a nominal capital of £100,000. Frank Debenham and Louis Nathan were among the directors, the latter subscribing for 250 shares and Ernest Debenham for 2,500. Another company, the Dried Milk Company of Australasia, was registered in January 1904, to acquire the benefits of Hatmaker's dried milk patents in Australia and New Zealand, and again the Debenham and Nathan families were the main shareholders (the Nathans took 900 shares). In 1904 an additional 18,000 shares in the original company were issued to Hatmaker himself, and another 750 to Algernon Blackwood, the Marquess of Dufferin and Ava's literary kinsman, who was dabbling in the business.

The Nathans and Debenhams were not, however, the first in the United Kingdom to adopt the Just-Hatmaker process. Machines built under the patent had already been erected at the Cow & Gate Dairy at Sherborne in Dorset, while other machines were bought by firms at Edinburgh, Cheshire and Charleville in County Cork. From the outset this diversification was troubled. Hatmaker seems to have been greedy, sly, argumentative and peremptory. He received £8,000 for expenses from the London Dried Milk Company as well as £50,000 in shares credited as fully paid (although some were apparently issued for 'other considerations'). His contracts entitled him to £10,000 in cash and £18,750 in shares from the Australasian company. But in fact Hatmaker had merely acquired the foreign rights of the developers, Just and Bent, and Debenham's own agreements with Hatmaker were not ironclad. By August 1904 the latter was demanding a minimum guaranteed royalty from the Australasian subsidiary, which Nathans were not prepared to give. As Maurice recalled forty years later:

the old man and Louis were in such a state about the business . . . Eventually I got a shrieking telegram to come [back from Canada] at once. When I got back I saw father and Louis broken down: they had fallen in with a man named Hatmaker, who was one of the worst type of Americans I had come across. They wanted to chuck the whole business in and give up. My answer was NO! 'You sunk £5000 into it and we cannot afford to lose it.'

A complete breach between Hatmaker and his British associates occurred in 1905.

In January 1905 the Nathan family registered the Imperial Dried Milk Company in London, with Joseph, David, Louis, Maurice and Philip Nathan as the five shareholders, subscribing £4,000 each in cash.[11] Imperial acquired their rights in the previous two companies, which were voluntarily wound up later in the year as being unable to trade profitably. Joseph Nathan & Co also lent £20,000 to Imperial Dried Milk, secured by an overdraft from the Union Bank of Australia. Hatmaker did not, however, relinquish his legal vendetta against the Nathans and, following a petition by him, the Imperial Company was put into receivership in February 1909. On this liquidation, Joseph Nathan & Co were granted all Imperial's assets in settlement of its debt of £20,000 and in turn Hatmaker, in April 1909, terminated his licensing arrangements for the export of Australasian milk powder to Britain. The Nathans ignored this and continued with the business, although Hatmaker's legal action for infringement of his patents was not finally defeated until the case reached the House of Lords in 1919. Despite all this legal mischief, the Nathans were free to develop the business on a more sound and systematic basis.

Dried Milk, 1904–1908

Although it seems unlikely that they realized it at the time, the Nathans had, by the purchase of the Just-Hatmaker patents, moved into a wholly new area of business. It was one for which they were ill-equipped and ill-prepared. The first essential was to get the manufacture of dried milk started in New Zealand. For this the company turned to Joseph Nathan's two youngest sons; with five sons already in the business, they, it had seemed, were not needed and Frederick Nathan (1871–1938) and Alec Nathan (1872–1954) were farming together at Palmerston North. They responded to the call and Fred took charge of the creameries in 1904, while Alec was made responsible for the dried milk operations. Hatmaker's engineer, John

5 The Bunnythorpe factory *c*. 1904, showing the Defiance brand name.

Merrett (see page 20) was sent out to New Zealand, in January 1904, to supervise the erection of the new dried milk plant at the Nathan's butter factory at Makino. As Merrett later recalled, the New Zealand 'Nathans had not the slightest idea of what they were expected to do nor had they any policy or plans for the new venture'.[12] Production under the Just-Hatmaker process nevertheless made a faltering start in a small room at Makino in May 1904 and, in June, David Nathan arranged for a special train to bring more than 200 farmers and others to inspect the new process. It was soon realised, however, that the milk-drying at Makino could not be extended without disrupting butter production at the factory, and the decision was taken to erect a new dried milk factory at Bunnythorpe in the rich dairy farmland near Palmerston North. Merrett drew up the plans and supervised the erection of the timber and corrugated iron building, where operations began in October 1904. The first season's output amounted to some 200 tons of dried milk.

Under Hatmaker's original patent of 1903, two hollow metal cylinders were arranged to revolve in opposite directions, and mounted so as almost to touch one another. The cylinders were internally heated by steam until their surface temperature exceeded 100° centigrade and they were revolved between six and fourteen times a minute. Liquid milk was poured into the hollow between the two hot and revolving cylinders: the water content immediately evaporated, leaving a tissue-thin sheet of dried milk which after two-thirds of a revolution, was scraped off by knives. The resulting dried milk particles were then passed through a sieve to obtain a uniform, finely granular powder. The period of heating in this simple process was extremely short, and therefore altered the composition of the milk solids comparatively little. This was a matter of outstanding importance, for the dried milk retained all the benefits of humanized milk for the infant while destroying tubercle bacilli and other pathogenic organisms.

But there was still one major problem with the process, sufficient for Alec Nathan to consider that his family had been 'daft' to buy Hatmaker's process for £10,000 in cash. In later years he noted that 'they had bought a dud'. When the reconstituted milk was still hot it closely resembled milk, but when it had cooled, casein (the phosphoprotein precipitated) fell to the bottom of the glass while a sickly green whey rose to the top. 'If we had had sense enough to employ a first-class technical chemist, we might have got that right pretty shortly, but we did not', was Alec's retrospective verdict. Instead it took almost four years of continuous experiments by Alec and Fred Nathan to manufacture a milk powder that was soluble and did not separate into casein and whey. It also had to have keeping properties extending to some months. The initiative and technical expertise needed to refine and develop the manufacturing process came from John Merrett, aided by the Nathan brothers. Together they elaborated *ad hoc* improvements as their experience of output increased. The credit for the modifications to the original Just-Hatmaker drying process cannot be allotted with certainty, but largely belongs to Merrett and Alec Nathan; the London managers and directors had neither time nor inclination to offer suggestions.

The Nathans' refinements of the Just-Hatmaker process improved hygiene and produced a powder that would keep for longer than its competitors without a serious loss of flavour. They took their New Zealand milk supplies from tuberculin-tested cows farmed at close proximity to their factories. The cows were milked straight into closed vessels and the milk was delivered to the Nathans' factories within three hours. On receipt it was tested for acidity and, if found to be excessively acid, the farmer received a lower price and the milk was used for making cheese (a cheese-making factory was added at Bunnythorpe in 1906). Next, the milk was put through a special filter to remove dirt: it was then cooled and kept at a low temperature in insulated vats. Afterwards it was tested for its total solid content and standardised by the addition of lactose and butter fat. The drying process was done without delay, and the powder was then swiftly packed in hermetically sealed tins holding 50 lbs each.

Unfortunately there is no surviving account of this crucial period in which the Nathans were transformed from dairy distributors and exporters into manufacturers using a pioneering process, improved on by their own research and development. It can only be emphasised that the original drying plants were small, comparatively simple and geographically remote. It is not surprising that, in these circumstances, records of the technical improvisations and of other organisational arrangements do not exist. Some of the equipment was at first sent from England. The Board minutes of Joseph Nathan & Co reported on 1 January 1904 that four drying machines, two boilers, one chimney and one feeding pump had been purchased and shipped to New Zealand for the dried milk business.

According to the engineer, Merrett, the most troublesome part of the process in the pioneer days came in packing the finished product into tins. Originally twenty girls from Wellington were recruited for packing and labelling, to be replaced after a few years by American machinery which automatically weighed and packed the powder. Another difficulty was that local farmers possessed no coolers and needed persuasion to deliver their milk without delay after milking; for it was essential that the milk to be dried was completely fresh.

Nevertheless, despite all this technical ingenuity, the business only developed slowly as Alec later wrote:

It is a curious and interesting fact that the Nathans thought when they purchased that patent, that their fortune was made and that dried milk, with its convenience and adaptability would replace liquid milk, and their disillusionment was very costly. When first Dried Milk was put upon the New Zealand market, there was an enormous rush to purchase supplies, which confirmed the Nathans' idea that a fortune was waiting at their door to be picked up. However, they were too ignorant of Proprietary Article Trading in those days to realise that that was a 'curiosity' demand, and they waited impatiently and fruitlessly for the repeat orders to come. Again, they were not experienced enough or wise enough not to manufacture until those repeat orders did come, but they went full steam ahead on the basis of this 'curiosity' demand to manufacture, and when it did not materialise, they found themselves with a very substantial stock of dried milk that was unsaleable, nor was there any substantial sale for it in England. They did not know how to create a market for it as household milk, so they were forced to try to sell it to biscuit makers and confectioners. To them it was a novelty; they had no recipe for the incorporation of dried milk in their biscuits or sweets and in those days manufacturers were not as enterprising as they became later, nor had they chemists or research workers on their staff, so it was an extraordinarily slow process to get them to experiment and use any material quantity.[13]

Before considering in detail the Nathans' development of their dried powder milk business, which began so inauspiciously, it is worth looking at the British market at which they were aiming. An advertisement in the *Daily Express* of 16 March 1904 by the Galak Milk Products Company (probably, but not certainly, representing the Debenham and Nathan families) of 118

Fenchurch Street, using the Just-Hatmaker process, is explicit. It was headed:

LONDON'S MILK
"AN APPALLING STATE OF THINGS"

No Direct Control

We must not send any of our milk to old customers, since the place has been condemned. Never mind, there is a splendid market in London. It is good enough for London

The six million inhabitants of the metropolitan area will be startled to learn that this remark of a large provincial milk-seller expresses the almost general attitude towards the milk supply of London.

Quoting a Medical Officer of Health as saying that control over the London milk supply was 'terrible' and 'appalling' in its deficiencies, it warned that there 'was a disgraceful traffic' in diseased milk; as evidence a report was offered on Staffordshire dairy farms, which had said that 'most cowsheds are ill-lit, over-crowded, badly ventilated and badly drained'. The advertisement also condemned the 'pernicious effects' and 'curious facts' concerning the adulteration of milk and other food with preservatives. What was worse, according to Galak Milk Products, was that:

In many cases a large milk producer is one of the chief men on the local council, and the medical officer of health who fearlessly does his duty in protecting the health of the community may have to condemn that man's cowsheds and methods. He must often have to choose between winking at the evil and being dismissed . . . general tuberculosis affects more than 30 per cent of the milch cows in the country. Yet we go on allowing the children of today, the solidiers, inventors, thinkers, and workers of tomorrow – the British nation of a few years hence – to drink this milk. No wonder that there is a continuous battle against consumption and typhoid, diphtheria and scarlet fever.

The alternative, according to Galak, was obvious. 'By the Just-Hatmaker process of drying milk we produce Pure, Soluble Dry Milk, which is absolutely sterile and odourless', they declared; and a photograph of the process in action was captioned 'The wonderful machine which, in less than 30 seconds, reduces liquid milk to a fine sheet of dry powder'.[14] The Galak advertisement strengthened its case by publishing the tables showing the extent of the adulteration of milk, which was at its highest on Sundays. The position was worst in London where Galak's figures showed that nearly 16 per cent of milk was adulterated, a figure which came down to around 10 per cent in the twenty largest towns in the rest of England and Wales.

The advertisement suggests that at this stage, the Nathans were aiming to supplant household milk in its entirety, rather than marketing it specifically as baby food. The chronology is unclear, but Galak seems to have been

superseded later in the year by the Defiance dried milk brands which were
marketed by the Nathans from mid 1904 until 1908. The new Bunnythorpe
factory was named the Defiance Dried Milk factory and the product was
marketed as Defiance, the symbol a black rooster with a red comb, the trade
name already in use by Nathans for a brand of butter they marketed.[15]
Nathans' detailed claims for 'Defiance' dried milk are contained in a report
that they commissioned from a public analyst called Richard Woosnam and
subsequently printed and circulated in leaflet form as an advertisement.
Woosnam reported that the sample of Defiance Full Milk he examined in
1905 'was a pale yellow flocculent powder, possessing a very delicate
pleasant flavour'.

The original milk before concentration was of high quality, and contained
an above average percentage of fat and other solids. Woosnam concluded
that Defiance Dried Milk 'is one of the most natural and complete foods,
composed of those constituents most necessary for the building up and the
repair of waste of the human frame'. Unlike other Dried Milk powders
which he examined, 'Defiance mixed perfectly during stirring, did not
solidify and produced a thoroughly good emulsion. This was invaluable
where Dried Milk was fed to babies, for anything like heavy granular curdy
matter taken into an infant's stomach causes serious digestive trouble. This
Milk forms an excellent basis for an infant's diet, and for adults it is a food
of great nutritive value.' Its compact concentrated form made it convenient
and dependable for household use, Woosnam considered and, he noted:

that fever and sickness generally is far more often traceable to defects in the ordinary
milk supply than to any other cause.
   In reducing milk to a dry powder by what amounts to spontaneous evaporation of
its water, all disease-bearing germs are exterminated, even if any were likely to have
found their way into the milk in the short time which elapses between milking the
cows and passing the milk over the machines. Consumers of this Dried Milk have
therefore the satisfaction of knowing that in using it they are free from one of the
most common risks to be met with in everyday life.

An additional advantage was that dried milk kept fresh far longer than
either cows' or condensed milk: the tin could be opened, part of its content
used, the tin closed again, and the residue kept for months.

Nevertheless, the new product's sales were slow both in Britain and
overseas. Canvassers selling dried milk were sent over the southern island of
New Zealand in 1905, but they were largely unsuccessful. Curiosity about
the new product attracted some purchasers, but potential customers disliked
its fat separation and it proved unacceptable to household consumers as a
substitute for milk; in any case fresh milk was in plentiful supply in New
Zealand. In January 1906 when the Board of Joseph Nathan & Co
considered the accounts for the year 1905, they decided that after paying a

5 per cent dividend, the remaining £5,159 should be carried forward 'as provision against any loss on the Dried Milk Venture'. Even as that decision was being made in London, the factory at Bunnythorpe was destroyed by fire and, later in the same year, it was again badly damaged when a former employee, who had started his own butter factory, threw a stick of dynamite into the boiler. In view of these disasters it seems unlikely that 1906 was a good year for 'Defiance' dried milk.

The advent of Glaxo babyfood

The difficulties of the first few years, and the consumer resistance that 'Defiance' met, may have contributed to the decision in 1906 to relaunch dried milk under a new name, and directed to a specific rather than the general market. Alec Nathan recalled: 'We wanted to register the word "Lacto", but that was not accepted by the Trade Marks Office, so letters were put in front and behind the word "Lacto" until a euphonious word was arrived at; the result was the word "Glaxo".'[16] The Company applied to register this trade name in the autumn of 1906.

Louis Nathan had, meanwhile, arranged for infant feeding trials in London both by the Finsbury Health Department, and at Lewisham Infirmary, and was looking for other ways to propagate the gospel of dried milk. The Medical Officer at Finsbury, George Newman, was a childless Quaker with a passionate concern for infant health, whose views on infant mortality were held in the highest respect. It was largely owing to the evidence of Newman that in 1907 Sheffield City Council opened five depots to supply dried milk at cost-price for bottle-fed babies during the season of summer diarrhoea,[17] and Newman was equally influential elsewhere. In providing him with the data for his opinions, Louis Nathan and Glaxo were important; and they reaped the benefit as the consumption of dried milk rose. In Sheffield in the first year (1907) 445 babies attended the dried milk depots, where they were supplied not only with Glaxo, but also with Cow & Gate made by the West Surrey Central Dairy Company, and 'Universal', made by Universal Milk Powder Co. Of these 445 babies, thirty-five died, a mortality rate of 7.9 per cent which compared with a rate of 14.5 per cent in the first year of life in Sheffield as a whole in 1907.[18]

The comparative success of these early trials, together with the failure to establish dried milk for general household use, combined to force a marketing change for Glaxo powder. That there was still uncertainty about how to proceed is clear even from the scanty surviving records. Alec Nathan was called to England by his father and brothers, where he found as he recorded later:

the idea of running Dried Milk as a household article was exploded, though much work, time, energy and money had been spent in this direction, especially for use in the Army.

Glaxo as a business in itself did not exist – Mr L.J.N. used to put his spare time on Saturdays into it. No separate Glaxo books or staff – nobody's sole business, no defined policy or proper business organisation. No literature about Glaxo, though there was a booklet on Dried Milk.

At a Board Meeting in November 1907, attended by Alec 'by request', it was recorded that the company had accepted an offer from J. Lyons & Co to take Glaxo and market it as Lyons Baby Food.[19] The offer may well have been made through the Jewish business network of which both the Nathans and the Salmon and Gluckstein families, who owned J. Lyons & Co were prominent members. There is other evidence of a close relationship with Lyons & Co (see pages 31, 89, 93). Nothing further however was recorded of this agreement and, if it came into operation at all, it was short-lived for in 1908 Joseph Nathan & Co made a major launch of Glaxo powder on their own account.

Louis Nathan meanwhile had become involved with the Imperial Press Agency, then promoting the *Daily Mail's* 'Stocking-up Scheme', whereby each chemist who bought a specified amount of an advertised commodity had his name published on the front page of the *Daily Mail*. The Imperial Press Agency persuaded Louis to join the scheme, for which a special decorated patent tin was ordered by the Nathans for Glaxo powder from Edward Barlow, an East London manufacturer of tin boxes, whose son, Sir Robert Barlow, was later the principal architect of the Metal Box Company.

Edward Barlow 'was a tough, sometimes terrifying, Cockney, barely literate', based in Hackney and running 'one of the small businesses fighting for a living at the lower end of the market, many of his customers being Jewish firms in the East End'.[20] Barlow proved unable to deliver in time. The disaster did not ruin the Glaxo/Metal Box connection; the value of Glaxo orders for babyfood containers to Metal Box in 1938–1939 was £56,500. As Louis Nathan had already booked the *Daily Mail* space, and orders were in hand, Alec Nathan, in a rush, designed a coloured label for decorating the slip top tin which was quickly adopted.[21]

However, the Nathans had not distributed any Glaxo powder to retailers in advance. Their optimism about the advertisement, and their naivety about marketing were not uncommon at the time. They believed that, after the advertisement's appearance, Glaxo powder 'would be on the market, and all we would have to do would be to supply the demand'. This *Daily Mail* advertisement of 27 May 1908 cost £350 and was followed up in several other newspapers, 'but before they had a fair trial', so Alec wrote later, 'they were discontinued, on the score of expense'. Alec blamed Louis

6 *The Daily Mail* advertisement, 27 May 1908.

for this *debâcle*, which had serious long-term results for sales of Glaxo powder. Nine years later Alec recalled:

Great disillusionment and disappointment resulted . . . Everybody was keyed up to great enthusiasm and worked feverishly with the preparation to deal with the shoal of replies which we confidently expected – then came disillusionment. The page appeared ... it was well laid out, no technical fault could be found with it, but instead of thousands of replies as we expected, only 57 were received ... Money which would have been invaluable at a later stage of development was spent beyond recall. The latent optimism in the value of advertising was destroyed and much of the confidence and assurance of placing Glaxo successfully on the market disappeared.[22]

Despite the failure of the 1908 campaign to generate immediate results, two marketing devices developed at the time were retained and became the hallmark of Glaxo for many years. The sale of Glaxo powder to mothers brought many letters seeking advice about infant feeding and, to ensure that suitable answers were returned, a nurse, Margaret Kennedy, was engaged. Nurse Kennedy and her staff of trained nurses did invaluable work, especially in a period when infant welfare clinics were neither widespread nor necessarily well-staffed. In order to answer mothers' queries more adequately than was possible by correspondence, the *Glaxo Baby Book* was launched in 1908. Its object was to give sound advice on infant care and feeding, with Glaxo's sales only a secondary aim. The *Glaxo Baby Book* continuously reflected advances in medical and nutritional science affecting babies, and enjoyed far-reaching circulation and influence. With Nurse Kennedy as editorial supervisor, over a million copies were printed between 1908 and 1922, and sent either free, or in return for a trifling sum covering postage. The slogan in the *Daily Mail* advertisement: 'Glaxo – The Food that Builds Bonnie Babies' – its precise origin unknown but thought to be in the design studio – was also retained for many years.

The Company's financial problems

By 1908 when the Glaxo launch was made, Joseph Nathan & Co was facing financial problems. Since 1900 the Company had been struggling to expand its activities with inadequate working capital. Profits were low and the Company relied on overdraft facilities both in New Zealand and in Britain; the latter were provided by the Royal Bank of Scotland with whom a £15,000 facility was negotiated in October 1905, renewed in June 1906 and again in June 1907. By early in 1909 the debt had risen to £40,000. After carrying out an extensive review of the operations of the Company from 1900 to 1907, Louis Nathan reported to the Board in May 1908 that the 'expense of operating the business was considered excessive'. No doubt there were many reasons for the difficulties. For a trading and merchanting company there was always a time lag between purchasing goods and selling them. However, the Company was also supporting a number of Nathan families, some of whom clearly looked upon it as the family money box. In October 1909 the directors minuted that presents, donations and subscriptions had been charged to the Company, when there was no reason for them to be so, and queried expenditure in New Zealand on flowers, cigars and champagne for Fred Nathan's wedding (F. J. Nathan was made a director in 1908).

While Louis and Maurice had shouldered the major responsibility for the Company, Joseph Nathan remained as Chairman. Now in his seventies, he still exercised considerable control. Board meetings were held at his home at Pembridge Gardens, and the accounts had to be submitted to him first; in January 1909 he saw them before he departed to Monte Carlo. While some of the criticisms made by the youngest Nathan, Alec, about the mismanagement of the Glaxo business are valid, it should be noted that dried milk represented only a small part of the Nathans' commercial activity, and a part which had already consumed a large – perhaps too large – share of scarce resources, both money and time. Moreover, Alec clearly resented the fact that his father and his brothers, while making Fred a director, considered that *he* was too young and inexperienced to organise the Glaxo business on his own. Remuneration always caused the Nathan brothers to disagree and many of Alec's criticisms were written at a time when he was complaining bitterly on that score, and arguing his case for an increased share of the profits. It is, however, clear that the Nathans misunderstood both the importance of marketing for a proprietary article like Glaxo and the market characteristics with which they had to grapple. The co-ordination of product supplies with demand and the systematisation of the marketing organisation, were as lacking as a consistent advertising policy between 1907 and 1913. The poor sales performance of Glaxo in these years was a reflection of the uncertain handling by the Company.

Glaxo marketing and its competitors

There were already a large number of well-established products – in all some 300 infant and invalid foods – on the market in which Glaxo had to compete. The Edwardian period saw the increasing popularisation of many dried milk preparations in various formulations from many manufacturers including the Prideaux company and Allen & Hanburys. Horlicks offered condensed milks with malted flour and there was a wide variety of carbohydrate foods. There was also a range of pre-digested or peptonized milks marketed by Allen & Hanburys, Savory & Moore and others.[23] Glaxo then had been launched into a highly competitive market. At the beginning of 1909 the committee managing Glaxo was augmented by one Van Allen, who joined Nathans on the recommendation of Lyons. At the end of April he submitted a report on Glaxo's business, suggesting radical changes. During the previous thirteen months, Van Allen estimated that the Nathans

7 & 8 The first Glaxo Baby Book was launched in 1908.

had sunk £7,531 into Glaxo, comprising £1,918 for goodwill, £1,158 for
debtors and a loss of £4,454. The loss was running at £125 per week in April
1909, and Van Allen expected a further expenditure of £12,000 over three
years before Glaxo became profitable. He noted that, excluding wholesalers,
only thirty-one chemists had so far bought £10 or more worth of Glaxo. He
therefore urged a change of marketing policy to offer Glaxo as 'not only a
special food, but [as] . . . a household necessity'. He judged this would yield
an annual turnover of £1 million, compared with the predicted £200,000
turnover as an infant and invalid milk. To this end he had already 'quietly
but persistently done what I could, as occasion permitted, to influence the
introduction of a penny and sixpenny packet'. Van Allen wrote:

the cardinal points . . . for introducing . . . an article, such as ours to the masses, is
almost diametrically opposed to the policy we have been pursuing up to the present
and are roughly as follows:

(1)   Glaxo . . . is a milk in pure and convenient form, and, when reconstituted, can
        be used for all the purposes that ordinary milk is used. It is especially adapted
        for the rearing of the youngest children and to suit the weak digestion.
(2)   The article must be put up in small, cheap units for the public. Sold in small
        parcels for cash at a small profit and have a continued rapid sale.
(3)   No limit must be fixed as to where and by whom it is to be sold. Commencing
        with the smallest grocers and going to the largest people as the demand
        increases.
(4)   We, ourselves, must be the distributing medium, allowing intermediate profit
        and doing no advertising, above distributing a few units free with first orders
        and furnishing suitable show cards.
(5)   An organisation composed of a multitude of small men at small salaries.[24]

Although the committee did not wholly endorse Van Allen's recommendations, in the following month all advertising in the nursing papers was
abruptly stopped only to be resumed equally suddenly a fortnight later, for a
six-month period in the *Nursing Mirror* and the *Nursing Times*. But during
the hiatus, Nestlé had been able to buy the much desired front cover space
which it then retained for many years.

Similar vacillation occurred over the employment of travellers. The Glaxo
department of Nathans at this stage had one travelling representative,
Higgins, who boasted good connections with northern chemists, but 'after
his first trip to Newcastle [he] evidently thought he was on a losing horse
and resigned'. The Higgins fiasco was followed by the Gouldman *debacle*.
On 12 August 1909 Gouldman was appointed the agent for Glaxo in
Lancashire, but resigned on 20 September in protest at his terms of
engagement, demanding a payment of £5 instead of £1 per week. In the
course of the next fortnight he was, however, appointed Glaxo's wholesale
sole agent for three years for both Yorkshire and Lancashire, a decision that
so quickly proved undesirable that in December 1909 his agency was

rescinded, and he was paid off with £55. In October 1909, through the trade paper, *The Chemist and Druggist*, the Glaxo department contacted Frederick Harrison as a potential agent in South America. His personal finances were precarious and Louis Nathan had several interviews with Harrison and spent much time in trying to verify his claims. In December 1909, despite the ambiguities of Harrison's circumstances, he was appointed South American agent, with results that were as unsatisfactory as the Higgins and Gouldman agency appointments. There was however one small success in 1909. Glaxo donated a quantity of milk powder to the Lord Mayor of Sheffield for his Distress Fund, which was officially acknowledged in the *Sheffield Telegraph* of 5 February 1909, an issue which also carried a Glaxo advertisement. Alec recalled 'it may be argued that this coincidence went to show that the gift was not entirely disinterested, but it did, at any rate, give greater publicity to the name Glaxo, which was then far from universally known'.[25]

Throughout the summer of 1909, the committee debated whether to reduce the price of Glaxo, but their deliberations were hampered by the absence of proper figures from an accountant who was neither competent nor honest. It was, as Alec Nathan recorded, 'a record of procrastination and delay: showing ... want of clearly defined policy and tenacity of purpose'. The committee's meetings ceased in October 1909 and Van Allen was given notice. One of the committee's final decisions was to approach a suitable firm for assistance either in distributing Glaxo powder or in providing finance for the distribution and advertising. Despite Alec Nathan's optimism, the figures for Glaxo sales were not encouraging. In the year to September 1908, there was a loss of £2,930 rising in the following year to £5,166. By late 1909, Louis and Maurice Nathan, as the two managing directors of the family firm, had absolutely determined to transfer responsibility for the marketing of Glaxo powder to another firm and had already chosen Brands. As proprietary food manufacturers with a range of beef foods (Brands' beef tea; Brands' fibrous beef tea; Brands' beef bouillon; Brands' beef peptone; Brands' essence of the juice, without additives, of beef, mutton, veal or chicken), Brands competed with better-known meat extracts such as Bovril, Liebig's and Armour's.[26] Louis and Maurice Nathan were drawn to this course of action by their previous difficulties with agents, their own inability to give time and attention to developing the business, and by the expense and disappointing results of their sales campaigns of packeted Glaxo in London and Manchester during the summer of 1909.

Although Brands was one of the more reputable beef extract companies, its products were little esteemed by the medical profession, and were mostly sold through grocers. The association with Glaxo's marketing therefore did no good, and may have done positive harm, at a time when many doctors were rightly suspicious of quack-proprietary foods. As one Government report wrote:

People who have been taught to look upon such foods as objectionable, on seeing dried milk in the form of a fine powder bearing a proprietary name, are likely to say, 'Oh, another of these patent infants' foods. We will have nothing to do with it'. Even some medical men have taken this attitude with regard to certain proprietary brands of milk powder ... mothers had been taught to look upon patent infant foods as an evil, and to them dried milk seemed to be of the same class as those which had been condemned by the doctors and nurses of the [Infant Welfare] clinics.[27]

Alec Nathan opposed the agreement. In his view, Glaxo was at a turning point and he had hoped to be allowed to take sole responsibility for its development. In private notes written at the time (which he circulated in 1917), Alec wrote that Louis:

was so determined and so desirous to hastily [sic] get this Agency fixed, that he was not giving himself time to go deep enough to realise what he was doing.

On Dec 4th 1909 I pointed out to him that he was not making provision for Nathan's to have dual or single control over the money that we are to spend by way of advertising. I also told him, he and I would never agree about Brands, we were working on a different hypothesis.

In my opinion, the arrangement was a good one, except for the fact that he was handing the thing, lock, stock and barrel over to them and this was wrong in principle and in fact.

Brands are to supply a Foreman for Packing whom I am to instruct in the testing ... I am to allow ... Mr Dence and a confidential clerk to suck my brains and instruct them into the card system, the policy, the internal organisation – everything I know about the nature of the business – and there is no obligation on the part of Brands. When they reckon they know as much as I know – we can be of no further use to them, they will be the Boss of the situation.

Louis['s] answer to all this is, after Brands' have had me there six months, they will want to keep me there; this is nonsense, absolute nonsense ... Louis is too sanguine and optimistic, too confiding and trusting – he is reckoning all his troubles relative to Glaxo [will] cease as soon as he fixes this Agreement with Brands.

Brands enter into no guarantee as to Turnover. The motive that is causing Brands to take up Glaxo, stamps them as being old-fashioned, antiquated and fossilized.

Modern business necessitates system, push, energy, enterprise and personality. Brands are lacking in the first four qualities or they would be in a different position today.[28]

Alec also wrote to his father in December 1909:

Apparently we have not the money to advertise and though we are near, very near to the time of becoming self-supporting, it seems that Nathan's cannot stand the little extra strain necessary to bring this to a final issue. Beggars cannot be choosers, we have to take the best we can get.

Morry [Maurice] has no confidence in Glaxo – Wellington are always writing that they are up to stop Glaxo. If a man either will not or cannot see, and if he has not the sense to see from our repeat business in prospect, when the stuff is more universally known, then it is hopeless, absolutely hopeless, to get light into such darkness . . . the method by which the Nathans at present exert control over this branch of their business will never yield the best of desired results. They have not time to do anything thoroughly – they do not have a proper knowledge of any one thing – we have never yet had one uninterrupted meeting, and apparently they have never yet thought Glaxo of sufficient importance to give undivided attention or discussion.[29]

This letter alerted his father to the fact that Louis' proposed arrangement with Brands would transfer control of the Glaxo business to outsiders within three years, and the terms were modified to prevent the transfer. The one good result of the agreement so far as Alec was concerned was that after Brands began working in February 1910, Louis ceased any active part in running the Glaxo department in which Alec survived as export manager. 'From then on the Meetings ceased, and interferences from Gracechurch Street [where Louis was based] subsided, and I had complete charge of Glaxo with the exception of South American business'.[30]

Alec Nathan and Glaxo

Before he came to England in 1907, Alec Nathan (educated at Lincoln Agricultural College in New Zealand) had undertaken a correspondence course in advertising and marketing. Convinced that the way forward for Glaxo was as a high-class babyfood, he arrived bursting with ideas about how this should be achieved. After two years of frustration, the agreement with Brands, much as he disliked it, at least let him pursue some of his own ideas without fraternal impediment. From his office at St John's House, The Minories, leased by Nathans in 1908 for Glaxo, he put into operation his guiding principles, 'to protect and foster the individual as an individual', to win the potential customer's appreciation by personal attentiveness and cooperation. Because of the shortage of resources Alec Nathan relied on contacting doctors and potential customers by post. In later years he recalled how he got in touch with two doctors, one at the Chelsea Hospital and one at the Royal Waterloo Hospital, who were converted to the cause:

With Colonial courage and outspoken candour, I wrote and told them that whilst they were doubtless clever doctors and knew a lot about babies, they knew very little about Dried Milk. Apparently the quaint, but sincere tone of the letter made a favourable impression on both of them, for they both fixed up an appointment. Very interesting and fruitful interviews followed, as a result of which, both men started to use this Dried Milk and gave me much assistance in popularising its use amongst their colleagues.[31]

Between 1908 and 1913 Alec Nathan gave his meticulous attention to building up contacts and publicising Glaxo by means of mail. As he recalled:

For five long years I depended almost entirely upon the post, and I can pretty well claim that Glaxo is the only Baby Food in this country that has been built up on the principle of a mail order campaign. The[re] were five years of unremitting effort, close supervision and perpetual personal care. Slowly, but surely, the sales increased. Every letter delivered at the Glaxo offices received individual attention and each and every reply emphasised the vital message of service to the mother, the baby and to the trade. Form letters obviously had to be employed in many cases, but they were carefully selected and names and addresses matched in.

I have always held the view that when thousands of letters have to go out, and people say it is impossible to match the name and address with the body of the letter, they are just simply lazy and have a wrong conception of the true values. If it is worthwhile going to the trouble of sending a letter, preparing it and paying the postage, in spite of the fact that there are thousands of them to go out, each letter should be looked upon as an individual letter and have proper expert knowledge and painstaking care ... But in this machine age, having lost ... the true sense of values, placing too much importance upon numbers and not upon quality, they think they have done a job of work better by sending out thousands of bad letters than by sending out 100 good letters from the office ... the record number of replies that we used to get in those days justifies that statement. It was not unusual for us to get 30 or 40 per cent replies.[32]

This was highly innovative marketing at this period. Circulars were also sent to the parents of babies whose births were announced in the newspapers and replies were received from 19.6 per cent of the 240 circular letters despatched in the first three months of 1909. A modification of the letter then raised the percentage of replies to 29 per cent. When the circularising of doctors began, it was concentrated in special areas, such as Newcastle, so that the ultimate effect on sales could be seen. In the first circularisation of Newcastle doctors, of the 662 letters sent, 29 were returned through the dead letter office, leaving 633 delivered, from which 122 replies were received. Follow-up letters were prepared both for replies and non-replies, and elaborate records were kept by Alec Nathan to help devise further schemes. He analysed, for example, the best day for posting, the most successful length of letter, the best interval for a follow-up letter, the number of follow-ups that were economical, the desirable number of enclosures, and the value of reply cards, either stamped or unstamped. There was continuous scrutiny and investigation of the results of all propaganda, and the lessons were immediately applied to improve the methods in use. Alec recalled that in the Edwardian period special care was taken in sending individual letters to pharmacists, who in those days disliked being called chemists, preferring the second part of the Victorian trade name, chemist and druggist.

The Chemist in those days felt he lost caste by being associated with, or selling a proprietary article, and it was unfortunately more difficult then than now to get his interest in selling them ... Glaxo was fortunate in this respect because although it was a Patent Food, it was not a Patent Medicine, and it did not call forth wide wholesale condemnation like many of the Patent Medicines.[33]

While Brands held the agency the Glaxo business moved steadily, albeit slowly, into profit; a loss of £2,191 in the year to September 1910, a loss of only £225 in the nine months to June 1911 and a profit of £2,028 in the year to June 1912. Louis Nathan wrote to his younger brother in March 1912:

The success is well earned and richly deserved and I fail to find adequate words to express what I honestly feel. Then too it is due to you to tell you it means much more than a Departmental success – it will be far reaching in a larger direction – it will seriously affect the view of others when looking at the Balance Sheet. You have pulled the ship through and set her sailing in the smooth waters of prosperity.[34]

In September 1912, a year's notice was given to Brands to terminate the Glaxo agency and early in 1913 Alec Nathan took full responsibility for the Glaxo department. New premises were leased in February 1913 for Glaxo, part of the Idris drinks factory in King's Road, St Pancras and the department was poised for expansion.

Joseph Nathan & Co, 1913–1918

On 2 May 1912, Joseph Edward Nathan died at the age of seventy-seven. Nearly sixty years before, he had landed in Melbourne and established himself as a trader, and nearly fifty years before he had launched himself in New Zealand with the enterprise now owned and managed by his sons. In 1913 they increased the authorised capital of the Company to £250,000 and changed its status from a private to a public company. The outbreak of war prevented any major raising of capital, as presumably had been intended, but shares were sold to the directors and their acquaintances during those years and, by 1918, some £200,000 of the capital had been issued.

That money was needed not only to finance the merchanting business of Joseph Nathan & Co, but also the expansion of the Glaxo business. To meet the demand created both by Alec Nathan's marketing and, from August 1914, by a nation at war, increased supplies of milk powder were needed. Until the New Zealand dried milk factories could be expanded, the Company was forced to look elsewhere for its raw material. In November 1914 a contract was signed with Glaxo's competitor, Prideaux, to supply 10 tons a week of dried milk powder and, additionally, some milk powder was obtained from Australia. In London too the expansion was such that by 1916 the space at St Pancras was inadequate and Alec Nathan took new office accommodation at 155 Great Portland Street.[35] A year later the directors agreed that new premises for Glaxo should be built at Osnaburgh Street. Three new dried milk factories (Te Aroha, Matamata and Matangi) were opened by agreement with the dairy cooperatives in New Zealand.

9 Joseph Nathan in old age.

Glaxo sales from 1913–1918

The quantity of Glaxo sold had tripled in three years under Brands' management, rising to 300 tons, but Alec Nathan almost doubled this figure within a year, and pushed Glaxo's turnover up by nearly 50 per cent from £55,000 to £80,000 in the same period. Alec had studied the business for almost a decade, and resented the way in which both he and the Glaxo business had been treated by his elder brothers. His personal commitment, coloured by fraternal rivalry, gave him an edge over either Brands or anyone else in the Nathan firm. If this individual element was important in Glaxo's increasing success, the detailed marketing methods deployed by Alec Nathan were equally important.

Probably the paramount ingredient in Glaxo's success was Alec Nathan's resumption of national and local advertising. Jettisoning memories of the *debâcle* of Louis' *Daily Mail* advertisement of 1908 and, ignoring Louis' previous connection with the Imperial Agency, Alec approached the advertising consultant, Thomas Russell, of whom he wrote 'too much credit cannot be given to his splendid ability of analysis, shrewd commercial sense and wide experience backed by unrivalled judgement'. Russell introduced Alec Nathan to the Chancery Lane advertising agents, Saward, Baker & Co, which worked Glaxo's account from 1913. Saward himself supervised the account, assisted by Alexander Cox (who became Glaxo's advertising manager after the First World War) and Miss Woodyard.[36] Alec Nathan personally controlled Glaxo's advertising policy, even to the extent of writing much of the copy himself.

Some years later, in a speech to an advertising conference, he summarised his approach to selling Glaxo:

Advertising a Baby Food is about the easiest proposition. It is a human story that interests everyone. Advertising becomes just the simple question of telling this story in plain, easily understood words. Naturally there must be a good food that will substantiate the claims of the advertiser behind his story.

The copy permits a certain degree of emotion and sentiment handled with a degree of latitude which has to be determined personally by the judgement and good sense of the copywriter. The line where the permissible ends and objectionable familiarity begins is impossible to define in words, but is readily felt by a sensitive, decent copywriter.

This form of copy is capable of being extremely valuable but it is a dangerous and risky instrument in unskilful hands. The slightest facetiousness, any overstepping of the mark which defines the limits of good taste creates a bad impression immediately. Such copy, instead of gaining a sympathetic reception and making a favourable appeal to the reader, creates a feeling of antagonism that is often even aggressive and raises prejudice that is not soon or easily overcome.

Advertisements of the right class should build up prestige and goodwill as well as influence immediate sales. The copywriter must always be conscious of the fact that his readers are existing purchasers, prospective purchasers and anyone and everyone allied, however remotely, to one or the other.

The Glaxo copy originated a new application of sentiment which soon had its imitators in style. Such imitations lacked the red blood of sincerity, personality and enthusiasm of the original but were sufficiently similar to remind readers of them of a former advertisement for Glaxo.

Good original copy has no cause to fear the imitator. The copywriter should reflect the ethical standard and principles of the House behind the produce he is advertising. Selling the advertised goods is an incident which follows naturally from his efforts if the standard and principles benefit humanity and they are adhered to and form part and parcel of the everyday business methods of the House. The imitator is shut off from this invaluable aid, and so is more deserving of pity than contempt. Provided that a National distribution has been created, press advertising is undoubtedly the most effective and least expensive single means of selling that can be employed.

Glaxo's first big advertising campaign was started by Saward Baker in June 1913. Two years later *Advertising World* wrote 'seven years ago Glaxo was known among a very small section of the community – today it is not exaggeration to say that every mother at least knows about Glaxo. Alec Nathan . . . is responsible for one of the most successful forms of advertising of the present day.'[37]

Evidence of the association of Glaxo with babies, and the pervasiveness of its advertising, can be found in Virginia Woolf's novel, *Mrs Dalloway*, written in the early 1920s after a decade of Alec Nathan's promotions. The novel describes a mother, Mrs Coates, standing with her baby in St James' Park as an aeroplane flies overhead tracing an advertising slogan. 'Whatever it did, wherever it went, out fluttered behind it a thick ruffled bar of white smoke which curled and wreathed upon the sky in letters. But what letters? . . . "Blaxo", said Mrs Coates in a strained awe-stricken voice, gazing straight up, and her baby, lying stiff and white in her arms gazed straight up.' Glaxo had arrived, was a catchword, even in Bloomsbury.

In 1913 the Glaxo Department's expenditure on outdoor and general advertising was running at the rate of one shilling per pound of sales, proportionally about a penny more than was being spent on press advertising. Under Alec Nathan, this ratio changed immediately, drastically and permanently. By 1914 the outlay on outdoor and general advertising merely accounted for ninepence in every pound of sales, while the outlay on the press was over one shilling and five pence per pound of sales. The press figure soared even higher in 1915, but as war conditions temporarily transformed the business, providing new government and municipal demands which responded less to press advertising, it plummeted to its nadir, under fourpence, in 1917. Even so, in the war years from 1914 to 1918

10 Distribution of Red Cross parcels of Glaxo milk during the First World War: 1915.

between £15,000 and £20,000 was spent annually on advertising in the British press. Under the stimulus of war demand, Glaxo's total turnover rose from £50,000 in 1913 to £550,000 in 1918; increased demand from municipal authorities played a part in that remarkable rise.

The growth of municipal sales

One of the main developments during Alec's first decade in charge of Glaxo was the growth of sales to the health departments of local municipal authorities. In the early days of his association with Debenham and Hatmaker, Louis Nathan had arranged for infant feeding trials in London (see page 27) and Glaxo was later adopted as an infant food by the Public Health Departments of municipal authorities such as Barking (1907), Dewsbury (1909), Sheffield, Manchester, Salford (1911), Nottingham (1913) and Birmingham (1913). When in 1908 the Infant Welfare Centre at Rotherham began supplying Glaxo powder to mothers, 3,912 lbs was issued in the first sixteen months of the scheme. Glaxo was adopted at the instigation of the local Medical Officer of Health, who found that unsuitable patent foods (many of them too starchy) were being largely used by mothers for their infants. The Health Department supplied Glaxo powder to mothers at cost price, or occasionally *gratis* in cases where the parents were too poor to pay. Rotherham health visitors always advised mothers 'to do all in their power to feed their babies naturally on breast milk', but where mothers were unable to do this adequately, Glaxo was supplied to supplement or as a substitute for breast milk. All children thus supplied were at the outset considerably beneath normal weight, and often had diarrhoea. Records were kept of their progress: in 1911, for example, when there was a diarrhoea epidemic at Rotherham in September, the Medical Officer reported that of 240 babies fed on Glaxo, only one died; of 160 others, 37 died. By the end of the First World War, 20,000 lbs of Glaxo were being distributed annually by the Rotherham Infant Welfare Centres at almost no cost to the ratepayer: the Medical Officer there considered 'it is impossible to over-estimate the advantages which the Corporation depot offers to mothers of artificially fed babies ... its excellence as a food [is] proved beyond all doubt'.[38] Turnover on municipal sales from October 1910 to September 1911 had amounted to about £3,000, but for the same twelve months in 1915–1916 it was some £12,000. New municipal health authorities ordering Glaxo included Derby and Sunderland (1913), Bootle and South Shields (1915), Birkenhead, Stoke-on-Trent, Preston, Tynemouth and Hackney (1916).[39] Other Infant Centres offered Cow & Gate, or Lactogen.

When Lloyd George became Prime Minister in 1916, the Ministry of Food was created under Lord Devonport, a grocer and tea merchant from the firm of Kearley & Tonge.[40] This new government department was concerned to maintain the nutritional level of the population despite the dislocation of agricultural production and the loss of merchant shipping caused by the German U boats. Its success is indicated by the conclusion of a recent study of civilian health in 1914–1918, that British wartime demography shows an overall improvement in mortality rates. This divergence from the experience of Britain's continental allies and enemies is mainly attributable to the general rise in the working-class standard of living, coupled with increased wartime concern about public (and especially child), health, of which the formation of the Ministry of Food was only one manifestation.[41]

Later in 1917 the Ministry assumed responsibility for providing local authorities' infant welfare centres with Glaxo, and contracted with the company for supplies of their dried milk powder at $2\frac{1}{8}$ pence per lb, inclusive of packing and distribution. This price was far lower than the Nathans had originally envisaged, and was conceded in view of the large bulk of the orders involved, although the contract yielded no profit to the company.[42] As it was, Glaxo's turnover on municipal orders rose to £30,000 for the twelve months from October 1916; £102,000 for the same period in 1917–1918; and £237,000 for 1918–1919.

By 1918, thanks not only to Alec Nathan's painstaking cultivation of individuals, the keynote of his marketing policies, but also to the new demand created by war, Glaxo was firmly established both in the British market and in a number of overseas markets (see Chapter 5). In a highly competitive market, Glaxo held its own against Trumilk, Cow & Gate (which also used Hatmaker's methods), and products such as Lacta, Lacvitum (Prideaux), Lactogen (Nestlé), St Ivel and Vitalitas. Glaxo's predominance had been achieved, it seemed at times, against almost insuperable odds, not least the litigation with Hatmaker and the apathy of the Nathan family. In the years 1908–1913 the Glaxo business might well have vanished into oblivion. Instead, the child spawned so lightly was, by 1918, almost ready to outgrow its parent.

3

Boom and depression for Glaxo and the Nathans

Glaxo in the immediate post-war years

The rapid expansion of the Glaxo business during the First World War continued into 1919. After the Ministry of Food had relinquished its control of dried milk in April of that year, the Glaxo Department resumed direct trading with municipalities and in 1920–1921, turnover with them alone was £495,000. The end of the war presented an opportunity to recruit new staff, much needed by the business. Colonel E. A. Rose was a graduate engineer, trained and experienced, who gradually assumed responsibility for manufacturing operations. Archibald Sandercock, a Chief Inspector of Gunnery with the Royal Artillery during the First World War, was recruited as a director in 1919. On the marketing side, Hugo Wolff had assisted Alec Nathan during the war-time expansion and in 1919 he was appointed sales manager.

Alec himself was much exercised at that time by the problem of quality control of the supplies of dried milk sent from New Zealand. He warned the Wellington office in 1919 that although seven or eight years previously the Glaxo powder which they supplied was 'pre-eminent in quality', the distinction 'has largely been bridged by the added experience of other manufacturers and the lowering of the standard of quality of the N.Z. Glaxo'.[1] There were not enough skilled and experienced operatives to cope with the swift expansion of the Nathan milk drying operations in New Zealand. The original factory at Bunnythorpe, ably managed by Jack Robertson, maintained its high standards, but their newer factories at Matamata and Matangi were less reliable. In London there were intermittent complaints from customers and Alec Nathan noted that, 'although dried milk for infant feeding was made by the ton, it was used by the spoonful, and that there is no more critical customer than the mother of a young child'.[2]

It was both to remedy this problem and to set and maintain standards that in the spring of 1919 Alec recruited Harry Jephcott, a young man with chemical and pharmaceutical qualifications. Son of a Midlands train driver, Jephcott had been educated at the King Edward the Sixth Grammar School in Birmingham and at West Ham Technical College, and then had been apprenticed as a pharmacist at Redditch. Coming from a poor family and educated with financial help from his eldest brother, he had narrowly failed to win a scholarship from the Pharmaceutical Society in 1911, and so had joined the Customs and Excise Department of the Civil Service in 1912. There he specialised in the analysis of tobacco samples and, in 1914, after qualifying as a chemist and druggist, joined the Department of the Government Chemist. Continuing his special interest in tobacco, he took a first-class honours degree in chemistry at London University in 1915, and in the following four years received a diploma and silver medal from the Pharmaceutical Society and a fellowship of the Royal Institute of Chemistry. Jephcott was an austere, ambitious young man, who took pleasure and pains in everything he did, and his perfectionist character was well-suited to work in quality control.

Jephcott had no laboratory initially and was, according to his own account, given poky accommodation in a warehouse at Bravington Road off the Harrow Road in west London. His windowless room was twenty feet square and leaked when it rained. It was, he recorded, devoid of services of any kind, or of furniture, and in the early weeks Jephcott used packing-cases as his desk and chair. He married a distinguished fellow pharmacist, Doris Gregory, less than three weeks after starting work in the Glaxo Department and, even without her encouragement, had ample hardihood to withstand discouraging conditions. One day when the laboratory was still in the packing-case stage of furnishing, a well-dressed visitor, who it transpired was Maurice Nathan, peered round the door and asked who Jephcott was. The latter introduced himself, only to be devastated by the reply, 'Oh! Alec's bloody folly'.[3]

For six months Jephcott's only assistant was a boy of seventeen, Edward (Ted) Farmer, but in the autumn of 1919 they were joined by an experienced analyst, Norman Ratcliffe. In January 1920 the staff was further augmented by Alfred Bacharach, a Cambridge graduate from the analytical department of Burroughs Wellcome (see pages 71–2), and by another assistant, G. P. Dodds, from the public analyst's laboratory at Oxford. As Jephcott recalled,

The duties of the laboratory staff were never defined, but the members quickly realized the immediate problem – to ensure for Glaxo a uniform and high standard of quality. At this early and formative stage, working so closely together was an advantage; all became aware of the problems as they were identified, and all contributed to their solution. They were confronted by many thousands of tins, each

11 Glaxo staff (a) Colonel E. A. Rose, (b) Hugo Wolff and (c) Archibald Sandercock.

12 Early days in the laboratory – from left to right H. Jephcott, Alfred Bacharach, Edward (Ted) Farmer and G. P. Dodds around 1920.

containing 56 lb of dried milk, and a simple test was devised which could be applied to every tin and carried out quickly by unskilled but reliable persons. Within a few weeks every bulk tin was being examined at the packing factory before it was used. Two disabled ex-servicemen carried out these tests and after some training and experience, proved to be very reliable. Tins of powder which they did not pass were put aside and subjected to more critical examination and other tests by the laboratory staff.[4]

Each tin bore an indication of the New Zealand factory where its contents had been made, and it was soon clear that Bunnythorpe's milk powder was seldom, if ever, rejected. The samples from the Waikato factories, however, were poorly standardised and carelessly dried. When Alec sent Jephcott's laboratory reports to Wellington, they were forcefully rejected by Fred Nathan, then emerging as the new fraternal power in New Zealand. Fred retorted that his analyst examining samples in New Zealand did not confirm London's observations, and the impasse was only solved after the spring of 1920 when Alec sent Jephcott and (with characteristic generosity) Jephcott's young bride to New Zealand.

The journey, through the Panama Canal and the Pacific, took over two months and the ship was alive with cockroaches and packed with young women going out to New Zealand to marry demobilised soldiers who had just settled there. Cockroaches were not the only pests on board and, the story has it, that one of the passengers' main recreations was watching the weevily biscuits race one another. On arrival Jephcott (who was also accompanied by his assistant, Norman Ratcliffe who remained in New Zealand and ultimately became Managing Director of the company there) soon discovered the cause of the analytical discrepancies between Wellington and London. Whereas his laboratory tested samples from individual tins, the Wellington analyst employed occasionally by Fred, bulked the samples received daily from a factory, in order to save time and money by restricting the number of samples examined, and so missed the variations due to inadequate standardisation of individual vats of milk. The Bunnythorpe factory had benefitted from two outstanding managers, Charles Dunford and Jack Robertson. With the methods of Bunnythorpe, and the help of Robertson and Jephcott, the quality of the powder produced by the three Waikato factories was improved and standardised. The practical value of competent technical control was soon demonstrated by the reduction in the number of bulk tins rejected in London, and substantial savings in money and customers' goodwill accrued. Norman Ratcliffe remained in New Zealand after Jephcott's departure and supervised technical control for some years. Before he returned to Britain in 1921, Jephcott also visited Australia where a factory to manufacture Glaxo had started operations at Port Fairy (Victoria) in the previous year.

The solution of the problem of quality control, however, was followed by a new difficulty, less easy for the company to control – that of a surplus of dried milk powder. As the post-war boom turned to slump in the winter of 1920–1921, unemployment rose sharply. The price of and demand for Glaxo collapsed world-wide. Writing in 1947, Harry Jephcott recalled the Glaxo slump after 1921: 'Prices fell overnight and, as an example, products held by the Company which were worth £100 one day were worth £75 the next, and only £50 by the time they could be sold. Heavy losses were incurred: . . . one order for 2,000 cases of Glaxo monthly for the East cancelled just as it was about to be shipped, and remained on our hands until it went stale and had to be sold as pig-food.'[5]

Production of the dried milk powder in New Zealand scarcely diminished, for the good reason that it was difficult to restrict. Glaxo had contracted with its dairy farmers to take, at a premium, *all* the milk they supplied to its factories and the cows of course continued to produce milk, yielding a higher price to the farmers than they would get from their milk being processed into butter or cheese. The company therefore had to sustain losses from paying the dried milk premium price, and then selling the cream elsewhere to butter factories. In 1923 they finally extracted an agreement from the New Zealand Farmers' Cooperative Dairy Company which reduced the guaranteed milk supply at the Waikato factories and, with a sizeable capital loss to the Nathans, the Cooperative Dairy acquired the Waiho and Matamata factories in 1925 to run on their own account. The total tonnage of Glaxo milk powder produced in New Zealand fell from 5,147 in 1921, to 4,700 in 1922 and 2,247 in 1923, reaching a nadir during 1924 of 1,610 tons.

It was not, however, only the surplus supply of milk in the 1920s which created problems for the company. In 1921 when turnover of Glaxo powder was over £1.5 million, net profit was only £7,700; rising operating expenses were caused by the recruitment of additional staff after 1919, the development of export markets and increases in sales promotion through advertising, exhibitions and other marketing schemes. The cost of running the Glaxo business which had accounted for 29.3 per cent of turnover in 1914, fell to 11.5 per cent in 1917; but it started to rise again, reaching 19.5 per cent in 1921 and an all-time high of 29.5 per cent by 1925. Against this background of increasing operating costs, Glaxo also had to meet new competition from supplies of other brands of milk powder, which made further inroads into their command of the market. Net profit fell to less than 6 per cent on Glaxo turnover in 1922 and just over 2 per cent in 1923. Over 4,900 tons of Glaxo were sold in 1921, but by 1923 tonnage sold had dropped to under 2,900 tons. The decline in the demand for Glaxo powder was the result of British and world economic conditions as much as any deficiency in Nathan's business policy. As the Wellington office informed Port Fairy (the Australian factory) in July 1922:

we are in the position (should we work all the Factories to their capacity) of making such a quantity of Powder that would be impossible to dispose of . . . the demand for 'Glaxo', like everything else, has its limits, and is governed to a certain extent by such things as employment or unemployment in Great Britain or elsewhere – by foreign exchanges, which make the price so high in some cases as to prevent those foreign Countries purchasing – and so by the value of fresh milk in Great Britain. Fresh milk in England today is being sold at 6d per gallon.

The exchange in Belgium, France and Germany is such as to preclude the possibility of doing any business with these Countries.

The unemployment in Great Britain and elsewhere is so great, and the purchasing power of the public has been reduced to such an extent, as to seriously affect the turnover of the business.[6]

Nevertheless, it is clear that the Nathans in London lacked foresight and flexibility in letting this recession of demand overwhelm them. The difficulties of the dual responsibility between Britain and New Zealand, the personal antagonisms between the partner-brothers, and the organisational and strategic difficulties of marketing a proprietary article from a general merchandising firm must all have contributed to this failure.

SERVICE BULLETIN

Published Monthly by Glaxo Sales Department.

VOL. I. No. 2.   OCTOBER, 1920.   *Price 3d.*

In 1912—

In 1920—

Getting quite a big boy, now!

13 The Glaxo Bulletin celebrated the department's growth between 1912 and 1920.

Joseph Nathan & Co

The losses on the dried milk business of the Glaxo Department came at an unfortunate time for the company. Joseph Nathan & Co had undergone a complicated financial reconstruction in 1919–1922 which increased the pressure on the directors when the trading difficulties described above were encountered. In 1913, Joseph Nathan & Co had become a British public company with authorised capital of £473,000 of which £439,315 was issued. From then until the summer of 1919, all the capital was provided by the Nathan family and their connections and friends. However, in April 1919, 223,000 A preference shares were created. They were issued in June 1919, at which time the auditors certified the company's previous total profits as follows:

		£
15 months ended 30 September	1913	19,328
12 ,, ,, ,, ,,	1914	22,427
12 ,, ,, ,, ,,	1915	22,106
12 ,, ,, ,, ,,	1916	34,984
12 ,, ,, ,, ,,	1917	47,592
12 ,, ,, ,, ,,	1918	55,590

These figures were obtained after making provision for depreciation, but before taxation or charging interest on loans or overdrafts; they differed quite widely – and showed higher profits – from the company's previously published accounts. One financial journalist commented drily that it was 'curious how earnings can be made elastic according to the purpose to be served', but classed the issue as 'a fair industrial risk'.[7] The preference shares were well subscribed, as they were issued at the height of the euphoric post-war Stock Exchange boom and were later consolidated with the preference shares that had been issued in 1913. In May 1921, Nathans issued a further £300,000 preferred ordinary shares at par, but trading returns sank into a deeper morass and, in June 1922, another £250,000 shares were issued as A Preference. The A Preference shareholders ranked first for cumulative dividends of 7 per cent, and held a priority as to capital and any arrears of dividend over the preferred ordinary and ordinary shares. The preferred ordinary shares were next entitled to cumulative dividends of 8 per cent (increased from 6.5 by resolution of May 1921), and to a further 4 per cent *pari passu* with the ordinary shares. This complex capital structure was conceived in the post-war boom, and was found to entail trouble during a period of business depression. In the event, while an ordinary share dividend was managed for 1921–1922, in the next financial year and until 1926 Nathans could only cover their 7 per cent preference dividends. In

14 The 1920 dinner-dance for Nathan's London staff at the Trocadero Restaurant.

November 1923 the directors were obliged to declare that they were passing payment of the 8 per cent dividend on their preferred ordinary shares issued in their most sanguine mood in 1921, and the future looked threatening.

An attempt to revive their fortunes by developing in 1923 a new chocolate-flavoured milk beverage, Glax-ovo, was not a success, despite meticulous attention to its marketing by Alec Nathan, and the product was soon discontinued. The company also tried to diversify its food interests. Nathans had for many years been associated with the London firm of Henry Trengrouse & Company, importers of produce, who had acted as English distributors of Nathans' dairy produce from New Zealand. In 1925 the two firms amalgamated their butter and cheese interests to form a new subsidiary, Trengrouse & Nathan. Its capital of £50,000 was subscribed equally by both parties at par. Under the agreement Nathans were to assist the new company to procure contracts for the supply of butter and cheese, especially in New Zealand, while the Trengrouses were to do the same in South America, where they had connections, particularly with Waldron & Wood in Argentina. Trengrouse & Nathan had a chequered career in the interwar years, a fact reflected in the book value of its shares, written down in successive years until ultimately they stood in the Nathans' books valued only at £3,000. A very large debit balance had accumulated in Trengrouse & Nathan's profit and loss account by 1934, when Nathans advanced £30,000 against security as part of a financial reorganisation. A small recovery occurred in 1934–1938, when there was a further financial restructuring more favourable to the Nathan and Glaxo interests. But altogether the Nathans' attempt to strengthen and rationalise their marketing position in butter and cheese, whether in Britain or export markets, was not a success and, indeed, led to considerable anxiety and financial loss.

The financial crisis of 1921–1923 resulted in an enforced capital reconstruction in July 1926 in which the Preferred Ordinary shareholders lost one-half of their preferred capital and received in compensation nearly two-thirds of the equity. The share capital was reduced from £1.5 million to £1,231,341, first by writing nine shillings off each issued £1 preferred ordinary share and, secondly, eighteen shillings off each issued £1 ordinary share. Preferred ordinary shareholders then received 1 new preferred share of ten shillings and an ordinary share of one shilling in place of the reduced eleven shilling share, the reduced ordinary shares being subdivided into one shilling shares and increased to £1.5 million by creation of 286,686 shares of £1. The arrears of dividend to September 1926 on the 8 per cent preferred ordinary shares and the 4 per cent participatory rights of the preferred ordinary shares were cancelled. These reductions left many investors feeling aggrieved, the Nathan family humiliated and the Nathan directors financially traumatised. Indeed, the memory of this humiliation was so burnt on the recollection of all those involved that even thirty years later, Jephcott, in an otherwise pardonably satisfied circular, sent on his retirement as managing director in 1956 to all Glaxo employees, went out of his way, when praising his staff for their loyalty and industry, to pay tribute to 'the forbearance' of those investors who 'provided us with capital . . . whose money, by 1926, we had largely lost'.[8]

These capital reconstructions took place against a background of quarrels and tension between the Nathan brothers which stretched over many years. The worst and most prolonged rifts were between the Wellington and London offices of the firm, or more specifically, between David Nathan and his brothers in England. David was unable to forget the early days when he had been his father's chief lieutenant and his touchy yet critical nature prevented harmonious working. The difficulties of communication between London and Wellington and the varying business perspectives of the two offices, both exacerbated by the war conditions of 1914–1918, led to ready misunderstanding. Over the same period David's ill-health made him more nervous and irascible and, shortly before his death in 1920, there was a major explosion between him and Alec. It was of considerable bitterness even reaching outside the family circle. Alec complained to a Glaxo manager of David's 'stupidity [and] viciousness',[9] and told another correspondent in August 1919:

you will not and cannot alter the convictions of a man over 60 who has been convinced all these years that he is the only member of the firm and family that has brains, that all the rest are fools – some he reckons so foolish that he flatters them to keep them, others also fools but they have the impudence not only to differ with him but to let him and others know – for these he has nought but defamation of character – but in David's treatment to Phill one has a demonstration of the iron hand of old age and habit – the pernicious habit of the bully always having had his own way getting into an uncontrollable rage when one of lesser importance reports his actions to his superiors . . . the London Board Policy of ever taking the yielding, persuasive bordering on apologetic attitude towards [Wellington] and D. J. Nathan is and has been a large contributing force to the present position and has developed, increased and encouraged David to take up the domineering, egotistical and stupid attitude.[10]

David's disagreements and criticisms of London policy were comprehensive. During the last few years of his life, he found fault with, or made unpopular interventions in, London's appointment of overseas agents, their marketing and advertising arrangements, and their general expenses.[11] Even after David's death, the next surviving brother in Wellington, Fred, consistently complained of 'a lack of understanding and sympathy by the London office'. As examples, he cited London's opposition, in the period from 1917, to the Antipodean proposal to develop a Glaxo Malted Food which was only terminated by London producing its own Glaxo Malted Food in 1922, as well as mistakes on the invoices sent by London to Australia. 'It is no exaggeration', Fred wrote, 'to say that the Export Department connected with Osnaburgh Street [the Glaxo Department] is appallingly or shockingly ignorant of ordinary trade conditions.' Not one [invoice] is made out correctly, and we are in continued trouble with the Customs Department and are put to all sorts of inconvenience and very great expense – so much so now that we are sorely afraid that the Customs will absolutely refuse to accept our invoices in the future'.[12]

Alec was equally critical of David and Wellington. He instanced the latter's attitude to supplying tinned Glaxo for the British market. In August 1919 he wrote:

Nothing we can place before Wellington Office appears to convey to them how essentially vital it is in dealing with a proprietary article that one should hand to their public the same uniform article in every tin at every purchase. Standardisation of physical appearance, get-up and style is as necessary as standardisation of quality and quantity. This is one of the many obstacles we have to overcome in having our factories so far from the seat of our operations ... if [Wellington] would look upon themselves as suppliers to valued clients ... and it was necessary for them to comply with instructions to retain the business one would have more confidence in their compliance and adaptability. Instead they take the view that they do & we do not know our business and it is their function to teach us on matters, the details of which they are ignorant ... till they have more respect and value for [London], give to them more liberal and just credit for the ability they have displayed and are constantly displaying, it appears somewhat hopeless to get the two houses to work with cooperation and in coordination.

Alec was particularly exercised at David's 'foolish' refusal to tell London the cost price of the Glaxo powder which he supplied to the British market. This refusal, Alec considered, was due to Wellington's

total lack of expert knowledge of running a proprietary article trade. They have never awakened to the fact that this form of trading is different to the ordinary merchant's business ... their six or seven years trading with Glaxo in New Zealand and Australia has taught them nothing ... they think they know everything [and] set themselves up as destructive critics of all constructive work.[13]

He wrote to them in August 1919:

In secluded little NZ you people have got out of touch with conditions caused by the wars, you have had no conception of the obstacles and difficulties that have presented themselves, you have lived in a place where you had only to have goods to sell them with a profit, and the world had been a market for what you produce. Had you a deeper knowledge, had you been more familiar with real war conditions, you would at least be more just in passing out captious criticism.[14]

In reply the Antipodean partners 'pointed out many times that it is a matter of extreme difficulty to run a proprietary business with one article alone that has to bear the whole cost of the organisation, and that it would

be a matter of comparative simplicity to get this agency kindred lines so that
the overhead would be spread'. Dinneford's Magnesia and Kruschen's Salts
were products that 'could have been obtained had ordinary tact and business
knowledge been brought to bear upon the subject'.[15] There is, however,
nothing to indicate whether Wellington was right or wrong about this.

The differences between London and Wellington over policy exacerbated
the tensions inherent in the system of dual control and led to recurrent
discussion of the constitution of the Nathan main board, on which both
London and Wellington offices were represented, but with the New Zealand
directors in a minority. In 1923 Fred Nathan suggested that the New
Zealand local board (which then comprised himself, his brother Philip and
H. E. Pacey who, formerly Chairman and Managing Director of the Dairy
Association, had joined Nathans in 1919) should recruit either Holmes, late
Inspector of the Union Bank of Australia and director of the New Zealand
Loan & Mercantile Agency, or Sir James Coates of the National Bank of
New Zealand. They also suggested that the London directorate be aug-
mented by the appointment of Sir Alexander Prince. Prince had formerly
been chairman and managing director of the Dover firm of Sir Richard
Dickeson, Army victuallers and contractors with branches at London,
Dublin, Aldershot, Gibraltar and other military stations, and had headed the
Navy and Army Canteen Board in 1917–1918. As Fred Nathan wrote, 'such
an addition to the Board – one who is not connected with the business at all
and can look at things dispassionately and from an outside point of view –
would be of very great value'.[16] Nothing, however, came of these proposals.

In 1924 the London board was briefly joined by the Glaswegian Sir
Charles Davidson, then a London stockbroker, who had risen to promi-
nence during the war as chairman of the Statistical Committee in the War
Office's Supply Department (1917–1918) and as deputy chairman of Establishments at the Ministry of Munitions (1918–1921). But Davidson fell ill
soon after his election, and attended only one board meeting before his
resignation in 1925. The New Zealand directors then revived the question of
the main board's directorate. In 1926 after a London attempt to dislodge or
demote Fred Nathan and H. E. Pacey from their board, the two New
Zealanders urged:

that the Main Board should be strengthened by the appointment thereto of suitable
persons who are resident in Britain but who are not members of the Staff. In the
absence of adjustment on these lines we inclined to the view that our presence on the
Main Board had more elements of advantage than of disadvantage to the Company.
We are not aware of any occasion when the present arrangement has really been an
hindrance . . . Distance and want of local colour sometimes detracts from our service
to the Company when London problems are concerned, but on the other hand, when
New Zealand and Australasian problems are concerned, we believe our responsibility as Members of the Main Board has materially aided co-operation.

Despite 'the apparent unwillingness of the London Members of the Main Board to agree to outside appointments', Wellington continued to urge that at least half of the Board should be non-executive Directors. They wrote: 'The Company is now an International Institution which requires different organisation as compared with the days when it was a New Zealand and largely a family Company.'[17]

By that time too, as Wellington told London in 1925, they had little patience left with 'the same old argument used by you that we must conserve our resources for "Glaxo" and "Glax-ovo". That has been the keynote of the business for some years, and tens of thousands of pounds have been and are being consistently spent with this object and the rest of the business starved.' To the New Zealand partners it seemed that 'the English Glaxo business has practically disappeared', and that the firm needed 'every effort used to increase the merchant side of the business'. They were anxious to extend their premises in Wellington, but were unable to do so when the debt of Glaxo Manufacturing Co (NZ) Ltd was increasing at a minimum annual rate of £10,000. Louis remonstrated while on a visit to London in August in 1925:

This Dominion is going ahead and will continue to go ahead. Prices that are being realized for produce will ensure this, but it is impossible to cater for business and enlarge the scope of our operations here unless we have accommodation . . . a halt in this excessive expenditure in the one department to the detriment of the other portion of the business should be made, and more attention should be given to the merchant side . . . If you look at the matter dispassionately in the very poor success of Glax-ovo, it is most unwise for Nathan and Co to permit this debt to go on increasing. It may prove a source of great danger.[18]

The New Zealanders wanted the debt to be kept to its present figure, and for Glaxo Manufacturing (NZ) to invest in securities outside the Nathan firm. The difficulties were not resolved in 1925 and re-emerged a few years later.

The end of the Nathan family struggles

Between 1928 and 1931, the last battle in the struggle for supremacy between Wellington and London was fought. The main protagonists were, in London, Alec Nathan who had become Chairman of the company in 1927, and in New Zealand his brother, Fred. Also involved were some of the non-family directors who had joined the Board in recent years, particularly F. C. Randall (secretary of the company from 1916 and a director from 1926), H. E. Pacey and Harry Jephcott, whose obvious business ability and commitment to the company had led to his appointment in 1925 as General Manager of the Glaxo Department and, in 1929 to his joining the Board. In January 1929 Alec Nathan complained about the New Zealand accounts for

1928, which showed the family directors in Wellington, Phil Nathan and Fred Nathan, having borrowed respectively £848 and £1,250 from the company, in the latter case interest-free by 'special authorisation'. Alec pressed for these debts to be expunged, and threatened trouble with the auditors in passing the group accounts.[19] At the same time, F. C. Randall launched some wider criticisms of the finance and liquid resources of the group. He alleged that the Wellington directors were ignorant of their own finances, and consequently failed to control expenditure, instancing their bank overdraft of £53,646 in 1930 and their debt of £12,559 to London. The Wellington office had not made any returns on their local trade for years, and the only information available was the annual balance made at the end of each August. They claimed to need an annual minimum of £100,000 to run the business, but were unable or reluctant to itemise this figure for their London colleagues; moreover in 1930, £43,947 of capital was tied up in stocks and the company had debtors worth £11,352. Their position was further complicated by their practice of discounting drafts against export shipments of Glaxo powder some time before they paid the Glaxo Manufacturing Company (New Zealand) for the powder they had supplied. In this way they partly lived off the monies of their subsidiary manufacturing company.

Randall urged the necessity for central control of all the group's finances and demanded the acceptance by the overseas branches of this principle, together with the reorganisation of the latter's financial departments so as to provide full data on which centralised controls could be based. In particular, he recommended specific financial limits for Wellington's trading business, and the allocation to Wellington of a margin of accommodation for peak payments and for financing, handling and shipping both dairy produce and Glaxo powder to the London market. He also aired the possibility of transferring the accumulating surplus cash not required for ordinary current trading by Glaxo Manufacturing in New Zealand to the parent company of Joseph Nathan either in Wellington or London. Generally, Randall wanted to increase the liquidity of Joseph Nathan & Company, and of Glaxo Manufacturing, either by cash, credit or banking accommodation.

In June 1929 Alec Nathan wrote again to his New Zealand colleagues saying that, since becoming Chairman, it had been his constant care 'to establish in the business mutual respect, confidence and assurance'. He felt that he had succeeded everywhere except in his dealings with Wellington Office. The 'methods and procedures' of his brothers, Fred and Phil, as he told them bluntly, lowered 'the prestige and reputation of Wellington House' which was 'hurtful both to Wellington House Directors, and to the business of the Company as a whole'. Elsewhere each branch was managed by a committee of managers of equal authority. In London, the committee

(a)

(b)

15 (a) The New Zealand factory, Te Araho and (b) a Glaxo advertising postcard of the interwar years.

for the company's business as a whole comprised Alec Nathan, Sydney Jacobs and Randall, while the London Glaxo committee was composed of Jephcott, Hugo Wolff the sales manager, Colonel E. A. Rose and Alec Nathan. But in Wellington, so Alec remonstrated, 'whilst you certainly have a committee that sits at regular intervals, you nevertheless do not have that teamwork and the precautionary deliberation' necessary before any decisions were taken. 'Had you been so equipped, you would not in the last twelve months have invested something like £25,000 into outside business', Alec wrote. 'You would have realised that Wellington House already has many thousands of pounds invested of the Company's money, and that they are showing no proper return for the money.' Alec specifically blamed his elder brother, Fred, for refusing to accept formal procedures suggested previously by London which would have prevented incoherent external investment, and warned that the 'London directors are not prepared to allow the existing procedure to be continued': they insisted upon the engagement of 'a really first class Manager . . . to work in close association with and under Mr Fred', and the operation of the New Zealand branch by 'a Committee of people of equal authority and prestige and influence as the General Manager'.[20]

Only days after this letter was sent, and before it was received, Fred Nathan in Wellington conceded that financial control there should be assumed by H. E. Pacey, who had recently returned to New Zealand after his discussions with the London directors in March. It is clear that, in a discreet way, Pacey had made common cause with London office against the unpredictable autocracy of Fred Nathan; and that Alec Nathan was appealing outside the family circle to Pacey as a force to curb his elder brother and to impose some consistency and order on the policies of Wellington office. In the comparative backwater of New Zealand, Fred had continued to run his office as if it was still a minor nineteenth-century trading firm which would make money so long as it followed one man's hunch. It now fell to Pacey to impose both the systems and the strategy that were essential to an international distributive company in the twentieth century. Within a matter of months 'there was a complete understanding between Wellington and London finance departments . . . based on the personal contact that Mr Pacey had established by coming to London'.[21] The budgeting idiosyncrasies became a matter of the past but the old tensions between London and the Antipodes did not, however, immediately dissolve. In November 1929 Alec Nathan refuted Wellington's belief that the London directors interfered in the New Zealand business in 'an unjustifiable, or even unwarrantable, way'. He argued that 'the fraternal and anxious interest that we take in your progress' reflected the great importance of Wellington's performance to the parent company; they could not extend to the New

Zealanders the 'latitude' allowed to lesser associated companies, whether Trengrouse & Nathan or the subsidiaries in India and Australia.[22]

Clashes of personality, however, and organisational difficulties between London and Wellington continued to bedevil the company. The Wellington business had six trading departments: iron and wire, case binding, dairying, pharmaceutical, cheese and tobacco. It also held various agencies, for electric heaters, motors and cables and in May 1928, on an impulse of Fred Nathan, had opened a Sports Department, specialising in tennis equipment. This promised to be a 'wonderful' proposition, but collapsed in 1929 after massive rows between its two executive heads.[23] It was evident to all the Wellington directors that in New Zealand wholesalers were increasingly taking a financial interest in retail or multiple shops and that, unless their firm followed suit, trade in most of its profitable merchandise lines would soon be captured by competitors. Fred Nathan and Pacey were keen to confront the competition and in 1930 wanted to buy an interest in the grocery retailing business of Oswald M. Smith of Dunedin, with forty-eight shops throughout New Zealand; but the London directors insisted that Wellington should not dissipate their energies in new developments or extensions. In taking this decision, which seemed astonishing from Wellington's perspective, they recognised that it would lead to reduced sales in the tobacco department, and would probably harm the trade in town and country butter, hard cheese, tea and sundry groceries; but their adherence to the overall principle of consolidation and non-diversification in New Zealand was absolute. Alec Nathan, Randall, Jephcott and even Rose and Wolff in London grew convinced that the old Wellington trading business was a sideshow that belonged to the past and would never justify the capital needed to run it properly. The money could be better used in London.

As it was, and in a classic illustration of the difficulties of communication and dual control between the two offices, in February 1930, before London's refusal to agree to the Smith investment had reached Wellington, Pacey seized what seemed to him a golden opportunity which might easily elude their grasp. He contracted to invest £6,000 in Oswald M. Smith Ltd, in return for an assurance of the store's orders for butter, cheese (processed and hard), tobacco and other goods. The London directors accepted this defeat of their views with handsome magnanimity: indeed, with a forbearance and tolerance that would have been unthinkable between the offices even a few years before. The deal, however, provided ample justification for all of London's worst fears. By December 1930 Pacey was writing that their expectations were disappointed, and that some of their trade actually 'had shrunken in volume'. Smith, in fact, was engaged with another company in respect of some of the lines which he contracted to Pacey, who wrote 'Mr Oswald Smith does not know what a contract means ... His view is that I am rather inflexible, if not indeed a little truculent ... [so] I have not obtruded myself and Mr F. J. Nathan has latterly conducted the negotiations as he did in the early stage.' Smith seemed unwilling to meet the situation adequately, Pacey found. 'In a general way I work to the proposition that a business house should avoid legal proceedings whenever it is possible but Smith's attitude has been so unreasonable and unjust that I personally feel we should ... institute legal proceedings.'[24]

In the event, Pacey served notice of termination of the agreement and recovered the investment of £6,000 although the final instalment of this was not received until March 1932. These reverses, caused by inadequate consideration of the original deal and incompatible personalities in management, and marked by difficulties in recovering Wellington's investment, resembled the exasperation met in 1928–1929, over their abortive Sports Department. In September 1930 even Fred Nathan conceded 'that London cannot go on indefinitely permitting losses to be made at the New Zealand end'. He and Pacey took a 20 per cent reduction of salary, imposed a 10 per cent reduction on other salaries and wages and reduced the number of staff employed. The total saving was about £3,300.[25]

The Smith affair, although unaccompanied by recriminations from London, clearly vindicated the latter's policy, and undermined any surviving capacity of Fred Nathan and Pacey to resist it. In financial and strategic matters, London was thereafter dominant, although not always supreme. In 1931, London wrote to 'insist' that Wellington did not invest any money in new ventures (and specifically in a device that physically supported fruit trees), only to learn later that Wellington had done so all the same. With Bank Rate at 7 per cent, the Nathan group as a whole was desperate to reduce New Zealand's loss and to free its capital at a time of 'exceptionally unfavourable' business conditions. 'Throughout the world', Alec Nathan wrote in October 1931, 'our activities are restricted by the need of capital: some of these prospects are more than usually bright, so much so, that there is no doubt that had we the means of exploitation they would yield extra profits distributable as dividends.'[26]

Alec Nathan remained dissatisfied with the Wellington board. In 1936, writing to Pacey opposing the proposed election to the board of Joseph Nathan in New Zealand of a long-serving employee, he deplored the principle of making a man a director solely on length of service, adding that in this particular case the candidate 'has neither the ability, judgment or independent courage' required. Alec Nathan told Pacey bluntly that he believed the New Zealand board's 'weakness is due to its personnel ... it lacks independent criticism ... which would be a helpful strength for you as Managing Director'. Without mentioning names he made it clear that it was with his elderly brothers that he found fault, writing that 'under the present unavoidable circumstances' (that is, while they remained alive) it was hard to bring a more 'broad vision of business' to the New Zealand board.[27]

In London F. C. Randall was exasperated by the timid attitude of the Nathan board to finance. Since the collapse of the share price of their publicly issued stock, the London board had consistently discouraged any references to their shares in newspapers like the *Economist* or *The Financial Times*. In 1929 he wrote that that policy had been slightly modified, 'and while we take no steps to obtain newspaper references to our shares, we have made arrangements with a financial advertising agency – a branch of the London Press Exchange who handle our Glaxo advertising – whereby any news of interest, such as dividends, net profits, etc., are passed to them and by their influence and activities obtain a wider press publicity than we have obtained previously'. Randall surpassed the Nathan family directors in London in his enthusiasm for financial public relations work, and regarded it as 'a duty of the directors to take legitimate and proper steps to make the shares of the company marketable and at proper prices'. He took even more active steps to raise the market price of their shares. 'In the past the market has been more or less left to itself', he wrote in March 1929, 'and as a result today our shares stand at prices quite unjustified by their real intrinsic values.'

He considered that it was an adverse reflection on the company's credit for its first Preference capital to be valued on an 8 per cent or 9 per cent basis, and in the late 1920s began buying the shares on his own account when they were offered at low prices and selling when there was an unsatisfied demand in the market. On these transactions he made about 10 per cent on his capital in a year, but his real hope was to maintain a more stable market in the shares. In mid March 1929 the 7 per cent Preference shares stood at between 17s-3d; 8 per cent Preferred Ordinary at between 8s-6d and 8s-9d; and the Ordinary shares at between 2s-3d and 2s-9d. 'It is hoped', Randall averred, 'that the intrinsic merits of the shares will be better recognised in the future and that by the public buying, prices will be raised to reflect the true value of the company's credit as a dividend payer.'[28]

Randall argued that the expiry, due in 1936, of the New Zealand dairy manufacturing agreement would transform conditions within Joseph Nathan & Company. He believed that the company's capital was unbalanced with only £31,854 in ordinary shares after 1926. The distribution of capital, in his view, should have been equal between cumulative preference and ordinary shares, with greater liquidity the eventual object. He discounted the possibility of successfully approaching the shareholders for a further reorganisation of capital, and propounded an elaborate scheme dependent on paying a dividend of at least 50 per cent on the ordinary capital for at least 5 years in succession, costing about £15,500 a year (50 per cent of £31,854) to service. On that basis he hoped to issue the company's shilling ordinary shares at five shillings, thus receiving £155,000 in cash for an extra £31,000 nominal capital. Randall accepted that his scheme was 'in the nature of a dream in figures', and in the conditions of 1930 pure 'phantasy'.[29] But his proposal prompted his colleague Jephcott, always pragmatic and fertile of ideas, to formulate an alternative scheme.

Jephcott's idea, which was eventually adopted, was to accumulate a reserve of £155,000 by paying modest dividends and thus conserving cash resources. He aimed to give as many benefits as possible to the original ordinary shareholders: by declaring a 10 per cent dividend on a net profit of £75,000 the reserve would be annually augmented by £25,000 which he felt would be the best way of helping the original shareholders to recover their lost capital. Jephcott opposed any scheme that would increase the capital or the charge on the profits for dividend payments. From the outset Alec Nathan, and colleagues like Hugo Wolff, supported Jephcott's counter-proposals and rejected Randall's more complex ideas. Alec Nathan thought the company had always suffered from unsound finance and overtrading. He refused to collude in selling his birthright as an original ordinary share-holder (who were all family members or close friends) to the general public through any new issue of capital. Recalling 'the sacrifices' of the share-holders, 'he was immovably opposed' to Randall's policy and 'infinitely preferred Mr Jephcott's method and ideas'.[30]

Fred Nathan in New Zealand shared his brother's cautious view about company finance. 'A dividend on the ordinary shares should not be paid until we were as certain as it was humanly possible to be that we should continue to pay that dividend, whatever it might be, without any interrup-tion', he wrote in March 1930. He advised waiting to appraise the result of next year's trading in Australia and New Zealand before fixing a dividend rate, although he sympathised with Randall's view that the Nathan Com-pany's shares were undervalued. H. E. Pacey offered another shrewd consideration, which became a major issue later on, when he noted that a dividend of 10 per cent, as foreshadowed by Randall, 'might suggest profiteering which might cause milk suppliers and others to exert greater pressure in the hope of getting their share of affluence'.[31] As it was, the cautious assumptions and policies which characterised the discussions of the 1920s and of Randall's proposals in 1930 were handed down as a legacy even to Glaxo Laboratories which, until the 1960s, remained wary of all but the most conservative policies on equity and capital structure.

In 1932 profits (net and before tax) of J. E. Nathan & Co reached their nadir of the decade, £21,825, but recovery started in the following year. Even so, dividend payments were a recurring problem, as London wrote to Wellington in July 1934:

the thinnest of the ice on which our Profit and Loss has travelled during the past few years and will travel in the coming two years if we visualise a Profit and Loss Account as needing sufficient balance to meet at any rate 'some of our dividends', may cause many sleepless nights.[32]

Much of the improvement was due to the activities of the Glaxo department, both in dried milk and its new diversification, pharmaceuticals, as the next chapter explores.

4

Diversification into pharmaceuticals: Glaxo Laboratories Ltd

In the interwar years the scope of the work of the Glaxo department expanded. While dried milk sales were badly affected by the depression – though they recovered in the later 1930s – the department became increasingly aware of and interested in the significant aspects of nutritional research. The identification of accessory food factors – vitamins – attracted the interest of Harry Jephcott, who saw their potential. Mothers, nurses and doctors frequently quizzed Nurse Kennedy and the Glaxo advisory service on the nutritional adequacy of their dried milk in feeding infants. Producing and marketing vitamin products as well as a new, vitamin-enriched proprietary food, Farex, turned Jephcott's and thus the Glaxo department's attention to the developments of the period in the pharmaceutical industry.

Nutritional research and accessory food factors

A series of experiments in nutrition research, comparing vitamin-enriched with vitamin-depleted diets, was conducted in the period between 1873 and 1906. The term 'vitamine' was coined in 1912 by Casimir Funk of the Lister Institute for Preventive Medicine in London: his paper in the *Journal of State Medicine* attributed beriberi, scurvy, pellagra (a disease characterised by diarrhoea and dermatitis leading to mental disorder and death), and tentatively rickets to dietary deficiency, and proposed that the substances whose absence caused these illnesses should be called vitamines (because they were vital to life and, so he believed, contained amine). In 1920 Jack Drummond advocated deleting the surplus 'e' from vitamines as the Chemical Society's standard nomenclature reserved 'amine' for compounds containing nitrogen; he also recommended using alphabetical letters to distinguish different vitamins.

As a Glaxo researcher wrote in 1938, 'To talk, as is often done, of the discovery of vitamins – whether the credit thereof be given to Hopkins, Funk, McCollum, Babcock, Ragnar, Berg, Eijkman, Grijvis, or any other of the distinguished scientists who first made experiments with "accessory food factors" – is to sacrifice historical accuracy to sub-conscious hero-worship.' Research into nutrition reflected an increasing interest in the scientific bases of nutrition, accompanied by a growing awareness that diet and health were connected, and was perhaps partly a reaction against the predominatingly bacteriological view of disease. 'People were beginning to wonder, moreover, not only at the prevalence of disease despite great advances in social hygiene, and the prevalence of poverty despite the economic triumphs of the Victorian age, but also at the patent correlation between disease and poverty.'[1]

The study by Sir John Bland-Sutton in 1889 of lion cubs at the London Zoological Gardens, together with a long experience of treating rachitic children with cod liver oil and other fats, confirmed the medical view that rickets was due to a fat-deficient diet.[2] In 1897 Dr Christiaan Eijkman, serving the Dutch colonial service in Java, where the wards of the prison hospital were full of patients suffering from beriberi, noticed that the hens in the yard were, like his patients, suffering from paralysis of the legs and had high mortality. The supposition that the hens had been infected from the wards was discounted by Eijkman when the hens recovered after an accidental change in their food. Both patients and hens were fed on a diet of milled rice and, after a number of experiments, Eijkman found that he could induce paralysis in hens by restricting their diet to polished rice. He next demonstrated that hens fed on whole unmilled rice, with germ and bran, remained healthy and that rice polishings, fed apart from highly milled rice, prevented and cured the paralysis. Eijkman was the first researcher to produce experimentally a food deficiency disease and to conduct vitamin experiments in a laboratory; he showed considerable originality of mind, and was belatedly rewarded with a Nobel prize a few months before his death in 1930. Grijvis, a colleague of Eijkman, later showed that beans were as effective as milled rice in preventing leg paralysis in birds, and began curing human beriberi patients with an extract of beans.[3]

The next great additions to knowledge of accessory food factors were made in experiments at the University of Wisconsin from 1906 conducted by Stephen Moulton Babcock. He fed three groups of heifers on different cereals, maize, wheat and oats, with the ration of each group containing standard amounts of protein, carbohydrates and fat. Babcock found that after a year the corn-fed heifers produced fit, vigorous offspring after a healthy pregnancy. However, all the calves of the wheat-fed heifers were either still-born or died within hours of birth, while the young of the oats-fed group, although almost full-weight at birth, survived only a few months. These results were followed up by agricultural research scientists in the USA, inspiring further work by Elmer McCollum and Harry Steenbock. In the early twentieth century it was discovered that rickets was curable not only by sunlight, but also by the rays of a quartz mercury vapour lamp, without any dietary or medicinal treatment whatever. Hess and Unger demonstrated in 1919 that the diet of New York negresses, whose breast-fed children were usually rachitic, was often deficient in fat, and noted that the amount of milk drunk by the mothers was small. It had also long been observed that rickets developed most commonly in winter, when cows were fed on more artificial foods. Work on nutrition was given added urgency, and became a major concern, during the First World War. Dehydrated and canned food became the staple wartime diet and intensified research on 'accessory food factors'.

The experience of the besieged British forces commanded by Major-General Sir Charles Townshend at Kut-el Amara, of Russian civil prisoners at Archangel, and of the privation suffered in Vienna at the end of the war, increased understanding of the subject. Sir Frederick Gowland Hopkins, Professor of Biochemistry at Cambridge University and a pioneer of vitamin theory, in a series of lectures in early 1919 on 'Physiology and National Needs', spoke of vitamins as 'Unknown but Essential Accessory Factors', of diet. 'The absolute absence of vitamins meant disease, their relative absence malnutrition', he declared, and identified vitamins as accumulating in the tissues of herbivorous animals.[4] Parallel work on dietetic problems was conducted at the Lister Institute in London, and the *Biochemical Journal* for December 1918 contained a series of papers by Lister Institute research staff (Sir Arthur Harden, S. S. Zilva, Ellen M. Def, Frances M. Tozer, Ruth F. Skelton) on accessory food factors and the relative antiscorbutic (preventing or curing scurvy) value of raw, heated and dry cabbage. One of Dr Delf's most significant findings was that the antiscorbutic vitamin in cabbage was rapidly destroyed by heat or prolonged cooking. In a research paper published in 1921 Jephcott suggested a cognate hypothesis that in the process of making dried milk, where 'milk is held at high temperatures for a very considerable time', its antiscorbutic factor was 'very considerably affected, even if not entirely destroyed'.[5] It is a tribute to the Nathans' developing respect for scientific enquiry that Jephcott was allowed to publish such a commercially inconvenient hypothesis.

Sir Edward Mellanby and his wife, May, were respectively engaged on research into rickets and the effects of accessory food factors on dental health. Mellanby demonstrated that rickets could be produced or prevented in puppy dogs by varying the intake of fat in an otherwise balanced diet;[6] and later in 1919 the Medical Research Committee published its first comprehensive 'Report on the Present State of Knowledge Concerning Accessory Food Factors (Vitamines)'. Hopkins had urged in his lecture on vitamins that 'the backing of the public was needed to stimulate the administrator and the politician' to apply appropriate lessons for national nutrition, and public knowledge was soon aroused. In December 1919, in the House of Commons, a Labour Member of Parliament asked the Prime Minister for legislation compelling margarine manufacturers to ensure that their product contained vitamins equal to natural butter, and to which much of butter's food value was due; Monmouthshire County Council indeed sent Lloyd George a resolution to similar effect.[7] Though the government resisted these remonstrances as premature, they showed the advances in public knowledge that were occurring. In 1920, Harriette Chick and Elsie Dalyell, sponsored by the British Research Council and the Lister Institute, demonstrated the value of applying detailed quantitative chemistry to child diet. Clearly interest in the subject was intensifying.

The implications for the Glaxo department

Jephcott was determined to conduct experiments to try to clarify the conflicting evidence as to the presence or absence in dried milk of the antiscorbutic accessory food factor, or vitamin, commonly called 'water-soluble C'. In January 1920 he recruited Alfred Louis Bacharach (1891–1966) to join the small scientific group at the Glaxo department. Bacharach, who described himself throughout his life as a food chemist, and retired as Glaxo's chief executive scientific officer in 1956, was a quirky but pervasive influence throughout the organisation. Reared in Hampstead, a scholar of St Paul's School in Kensington and Clare College, Cambridge, Bacharach was on the staff of the Wellcome Chemical Research Laboratory from 1915 to 1918 and then spent a year at the Wellcome Chemical Works, before joining the nascent scientific department of Nathans because he disliked the tedious daily journey from Hampstead to the Wellcome works at Dartford. Bacharach was a man of emphatic and extraordinary character. In some respects he had a close resemblance to Jephcott. He was inquisitive, zealous, infectiously enthusiastic about laboratory discoveries, but whereas Jephcott was taciturn and discreet, Bacharach was flamboyant and loquacious. In the inter-war period he was immersed in the affairs of the intellectual Left. A former Cambridge Fabian, he contributed to socialist periodicals, intrigued behind the scenes in the Independent Labour Party, and for nearly forty years was associated with the Working Men's College at Camden Town in north London. He was immersed in music and the life of musicians. His first book, *The Musical Companion*, was published in 1934, and was followed by *Lives of the Great Composers* (1935), *British Music of our Time* (1946), and *The Music Masters* (1948–1954). An accomplished pianist, as Programme Secretary of the Working Men's College, he compèred with inimitable liveliness the Chamber Music concerts each Sunday

evening for twenty years. This remarkable polymath was equally devoted to
Alpine rock-climbing and French gastronomy, and in later life was a
convivial member of the Savage Club. His other talents were literary and
syntactical. He listed 'punctuation' as one of his recreations in *Who's Who*,
and was passionately concerned about English grammar. Editors of learned
journals in chemistry, biochemistry or nutrition received a constant stream
of typed postcards with his violet-inked signature commenting with whimsi-
cal humour on slipshod writing that had appeared in their journal. 'The rule
within the Glaxo organisation that he should edit all papers for submission
to scientific and technical journals at first almost led to riot, but on his
retirement those who had caused so much green ink to flow made him a
special presentation in appreciation of his work for them.'[8]

Bacharach tried to reduce the barriers which existed between scientists
working in industrial, governmental and academic milieux. Always emphasising the unity of scientific endeavour, he sat on many committees which
bounded scientific disciplines. He joined the Society of Analytical Chemists
in 1919, served continuously on its Publications Committee for thirty-four
years, sat on its Council for ten years, and was its Vice-President in 1936–
1937 and 1961–1962. Together with Lord Boyd-Orr and Dame Harriette
Chick, he was one of the founders of the Nutrition Society in 1941, serving
as its Treasurer for ten years and becoming President in 1959. He was Vice-
President of both the Royal Institute of Chemistry and the Society of
Chemical Industry. He was also active in the Biochemical Society, and
altogether for these five scientific societies put in a total of about 140
committee years, arranging meetings, assisting publications and developing
vigorous working groups. 'Nutritional science, especially on its experimental side . . . is a borderland subject, where chemistry and physiology meet,
often along with physical chemistry, and even physics to say nothing of
contacts with zoology and botany (including bacteriology) and the potent
weapon of statistics', wrote Bacharach in 1938, adding that it was also 'a
branch of biology, for it is concerned with what happens when certain living
organisms kill, eat and inwardly digest (or try to) certain other living
organisms'.[9] This diversity in nutritional science appealed to Bacharach's
special talents and eclecticism.

When he and Jephcott began work little was known of the chemical
nature of vitamins, and the only possible experiments, with animals under
Home Office licence, in Jephcott's own words, 'were not only troublesome
and time-consuming, but lacked . . . precision'.[10] Their conclusions on the
'Antiscorbutic Value of Dried Milk', based on a long series of experiments
on guinea-pigs, were published in the *Biochemical Journal* of 1921. Bacharach and Jephcott judged that the antiscorbutic values of summer and winter
milks were about equal to one another, and to those of the original raw

milks; but neutralised milk had slightly less antiscorbutic value than raw milk; and spray process dried milk was markedly deficient in antiscorbutic value.[11] They followed contemporary clinical opinion held by those with experience of using dried milk for infant feeding that fresh milk dried by the roller process and stored in air-tight vessels contained sufficient antiscorbutic accessory food factor to prevent scurvy in infants fed solely on a milk diet. Such dried milk equalled raw milk in antiscorbutic value, although neither was rich in antiscorbutic vitamin. For infants only taking small quantities of milk or sustained by a mainly farinaceous diet, the addition of fruit juice was essential.

This conclusion was some comfort to the Nathans and indeed the company had Jephcott's learned paper translated into French as 'La Valeur Antiscorbutique du Lait Sec' and published in 1924 by their representative in Brussels. The work was followed up both by Bacharach,[12] and by Jephcott; a paper read to the Society of Analysts in May 1923 on 'Estimation of Fat, Lactose and Moisture in Dried Milks' was based on examination and analysis of over 25,000 samples.[13] Generally the findings confirmed the contemporary view that dried milk contained relatively little antiscorbutic vitamin, and that doses of fresh orange juice should be taken to compensate for this deficiency. The recent research of Mellanby, the Lister Institute team and others, clearly suggested that fat-soluble vitamins were essential both for growth in young children and as an anti-rachitic factor. In consequence, Jephcott began casting around for a possible refinement of Glaxo powder.

Other exciting work on accessory food factors was being conducted in the United States by researchers such as Professor Elmer V. McCollum of Johns Hopkins University in Baltimore, Dr Theodore Zucker of Columbia University and Dr Harry Steenbock of the University of Wisconsin. With his usual zealous curiosity, Jephcott was anxious to meet them and study their latest results, and in 1923 seized the opportunity to do so while visiting the USA under the pretext of attending the International Dairy Congress held in Washington. There he delivered a paper on 'The Attainment of Bacterial Purity in the Manufacture of Dried Milk' which was the fruit of his work since 1919 in both London and New Zealand, and a subsequent paper on 'Fat in Commercial Casein'.[14] For some years both Hopkins and American researchers had tried to induce animals to grow on synthetic mixtures of proteins, fats and carbohydrates, with pure and ascertainable ingredients. In 1909, McCollum announced that he had identified a 'purified' diet, including butter-fat and milk sugar, on which rats could grow provided that it was palatable and not too monotonous. Subsequently, Osborne and Lafayette B. Mendel of Yale, using fat and sugar of other origin, could not replicate the trials, and in further research, McCollum discovered that the survival and growth of his rats depended on the fat used: butter-fat and egg-yolk induced growth, but olive oil and lard did not. Thus, in 1913 McCollum and his collaborator, Davis, concluded that certain fats contained an essential nutrient, 'Fat Soluble A', although almost a decade passed before McCollum discovered that the substance in fat contained two factors. By 1923, however, he had distinguished between the growth-inducing Factor A and the anti-rachitic factors in vitamin science; these he designated respectively vitamins A and D. Jephcott telephoned McCollum while on his visit to the USA in 1923, and to his surprise was invited to McCollum's laboratory, where the experiments were demonstrated and the evidence produced.

Shortly afterwards, while in New York, Jephcott heard a further report of Theodore Zucker's recent perfection of a process for extracting Vitamin D from fish-liver oil, which he also investigated. A Frenchman, Armand Trousseau had shown as early as 1861, that vegetable oils were useless in curing human rickets, but that other fats (chiefly cod liver oil) had high efficacy. Trousseau's results, however, had been largely neglected. It was only after the First World War that two years' trials on young Viennese children conducted by the Lister Institute in collaboration with Austrian doctors, gave 'a dramatic and easily comprehensible demonstration that rickets can be prevented or cured equally by cod liver oil or by ultra-violet light'.[15] Before visiting America, Jephcott had felt that vitamin-fortified Glaxo would hold an enormous market advantage. It would appease mothers and the medical profession who were concerned that Glaxo lacked fat-soluble and antiscorbutic vitamins, and quieten those Labour MPs and municipal councils who distrusted processed food. He now seized the opportunity afforded by his meetings with McCollum and Zucker. At his prompting, the Nathan company within a few months had secured the British licence under Zucker's extraction process, and in 1924 the company began making and marketing vitamin D extract in phials for drop dosage.

This product, Ostelin vitamin D, was the earliest *standardised* vitamin concentrate marketed in Britain from a preparation of cod liver oil. The first phial, sold in August 1924, was described as 'unsaponifiable fraction of cod liver oil'. Its manufacturing process resulted in the isolation of an anti-rachitic fraction with an activity 2,000 times that of the usual cod liver oil. The Glaxo department's preparation was the equivalent in vitamin D to fifty times its own volume in high-grade cod liver oil. The vitamin content was suspended in glycerine for convenient administration to the patient: Ostelin provided the first means by which vitamin D could be therapeutically administered in drop doses, and soon replaced cod liver oil in common medical practice. Although Ostelin had a pronounced fish taste and aroma, it was less nauseating than ordinary cod liver oil. At this time, in 1924, vitamin D was normally referred to as the anti-rachitic factor, indicating the limited conception of its potential then current. It was considered beneficial in treating rickets, poor bone development, poorly formed teeth, eczema, tetanus, wasting diseases such as tuberculosis, nervous disorders or spasmophilia (nervous childhood disturbances often in conjunction with rickets). However, vitamin D prophylaxis and therapy was soon extended to all conditions of defective calcium and phosphorous metabolism. The product was immediately well-received. By January 1925, the *Lancet* was recommending use of Ostelin 'where the ordinary administration of cod liver oil is attended with difficulty'; two years later, it praised Ostelin as 'a reliable and concentrated preparation'.[16]

Clearly Jephcott's visit to the USA in 1923, and the subsequent and rapid diversification by the Glaxo department into marketing vitamin extracts in 1924, were critical to the development of the company. Relying on what Sir Frank Hartley (Director of Research at British Drug Houses, 1946–1962, and later Dean of the School of Pharmacy at London University), called 'his fantastic intuitive sense',[17] and showing exemplary judgement and timing, Jephcott's acquisition of the British commercial rights to a major scientific advance, transformed the Glaxo department's business and benefitted British public health enormously.

The development of Glaxo's vitamin products

The discoveries of the early 1920s were followed by other important advances in vitamin science and nutrition theory, which affected the Nathans' Glaxo business. The Accessory Food Factors Committee was established in 1918 jointly by the British Medical Research Committee and the Lister Institute; originally chaired by Sir Frederick Gowland Hopkins, it comprised Dame Harriette Chick, Sir Jack Drummond, Sir Arthur Harden and Sir Edward Mellanby. The Committee published, between 1919 and 1932, a series of monographs 'of increasing size to correspond with the rapid increase of knowledge, each one supplanting its predecessor as the current textbook on the subject'.[18]

In 1924, the American Harry Steenbock had discovered (as did other researchers independently around the same time) that the anti-rachitic properties of substances like cotton seed oil, olive oil or rolled oats, were increased by irradiation. Steenbock demonstrated that the anti-rachitic action derived from the properties of ultra-violet light. The University of Wisconsin proved dilatory in patenting the processes he had discovered and he therefore assigned his patent rights to the Wisconsin Alumni Research Foundation (WARF), a trust company specially formed by friends of the University. The patents proved highly lucrative, and WARF soon became one of the richest self-supporting research institutions in the United States. Steenbock's action in taking out the patent was, however, criticised. The

16 The pilot plant for making the Glaxo Department's first pharmaceutical product, vitamin D.

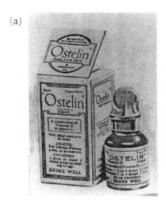

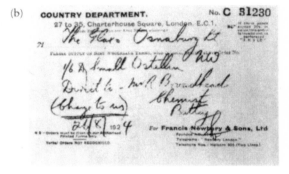

17 (a) Ostelin Liquid and (b) the first order for it.

patent was drawn in wide general terms to cover various possible developments in vitamin D research, and as the British Medical Research Council,
under the chairmanship of Lord D'Abernon, objected in 1931, Steenbock
had 'in effect patented a law of nature' concerning ultra-violet light.
Consequently, no one could use a mercury vapour lamp to make vitamin D
commercially without paying royalties to WARF, and, when British
researchers later discovered the parent substance of vitamin D, Ergosterol,
from which – by the action of ultra-violet light – far more potent preparations could be obtained than by Steenbock's process, they nevertheless
found that Steenbock's patent covered the manufacture of irradiated
Ergosterol. He could not have made his discovery of 1924 without the
benefit of earlier researchers' unpatented work and it seemed therefore
wholly unreasonable that he should acquire the power to control the result
of so much previous and so much subsequent work.

The cereal manufacturer, Quaker Oats, was the first food producer to market irradiated food under Steenbock's patent, but within a short time many other companies followed suit. Vitamins proved a relatively inexpensive additive with which advertisers could stimulate the nutritional awareness of consumers. The original licences under the WARF patents for Ergosterol (the standard solution of cod liver oil under Steenbock's process) went to Abbott Laboratories, Mead Johnson, Parke Davis, E. R. Squibb and to the Winthrop Medical Company, but as soon as it could be arranged by Jephcott, the Glaxo department abandoned the Zucker process it had been using (see page 74) and acquired a licence to use the Steenbock process. Ostelin was first prepared from Ergosterol by irradiation in 1929. Between June 1930 and October 1932, Nathans paid $60,038 in royalties on Steenbock's patent, and $120,813 in the following twenty-six months to the end of December 1934. The Nathan payment of $67,207 for 1934 placed the company as fourth largest royalty payer (out of a total of thirty-one, paying a total of $816,986), after Parke Davis ($145,617), Squibb ($79,128) and the Irradiated Fluid Milk Company ($77,268).[19]

When irradiated by ultra-violet light, Ergosterol was an anti-rachitic agent of great power: a rat with experimental rickets was curable by a daily dose of one ten-thousandth of a milligram. Its rapidity and efficacy did not render the traditional cod liver oil obsolete as an anti-rachitic agent, because the latter also contained vitamin A and iodine; but it was, nevertheless, a major scientific and marketing advance for the Glaxo department. For the consumer, the most immediate advantage of preparing Ostelin by irradiating Ergosterol was that it rid the product of its fish taste.

Nutrition research at this time was vast in output. McCollum and Simmonds, in the 1929 edition of their *Newer Knowledge of Nutrition*, noted that whereas the 1926 edition contained 1,870 references, the citation of some 8,000 references would now be needed to cover all recent nutrition research.[20] Characteristically Jephcott himself was not idle in research during this period of spectacular advance. Despite his other business responsibilities, he published, in collaboration with colleagues, several scientific papers on vitamin research, which were the first of what was soon to become a flood of research papers initially sub-titled 'From the Glaxo Research Laboratory'. Throughout there was no question of restraining these publications: they were seen as bringing distinction to the Nathan company and as extending its traditional policy of establishing a reputation for unblemished respectability in professional and medical circles.

Increasing amounts of this work were delegated by Jephcott to Bacharach who explored the problem of vitamin analysis at a time when it presented a major problem. It was essential for the Glaxo department to have accurate estimation of vitamin D, but the uncertain and contradictory results from the classical assay with rats led him to systematic study of the albino rat in

biochemical investigation. Bacharach imported a breeding stock of geneti-
cally identical rats from the Wistar Institute in Philadelphia and personally
supervised strict brother–sister mating according to the Wistar pattern; by
this procedure, begun in 1924, he developed the WAG (Wistar Albina
Glaxo) rat, of which large colonies were bred in many European universities, descended from Bacharach's original Glaxo colony.[21] Bacharach
abominated imprecision and, well before 1935, had pioneered the use of
statistical analysis in biochemical evaluation. He did much to publicise the
aid that simple mathematics could render in evaluating biological results and
in the planning of assays so as to save time, materials and equipment. The
statistical term 'metameter' was coined by him when working on bioassay
problems, (biochemical analysis) and his interest in assay variations drew
him into many collaborative planned trials in which the activities of
different laboratories were coordinated. He also pioneered other new
methods, such as colorimetry (the determination of concentration by
intensity of colour) in the 1920s, ultraviolet spectrophotometry and statistics
in the 1930s, and microbiological assay and chromatography (an analytical
technique) in the 1940s. He wrote with effortless fluency, contributing *inter
alia* a series of popular books on nutrition and pharmacology.

In the late 1920s researchers at Gottingen and another team at the
National Institute of Medical Research in Hampstead succeeded, almost
simultaneously, although by different methods, in isolating from irradiated
Ergosterol a substance which the English dubbed 'Calciferol' (vitamin D2).
Pure Calciferol, free from contaminants, had an effect on the experimental
rickets of Bacharach's albino rats exactly 40,000 times that of the previous
International Standard Preparation. In the years that followed Glaxo
researchers replaced the early and crude vitamin D preparations by pure
crystalline Calciferol, which yielded great advantages in improving the
purity and precision of the dosage. Pure crysalline Calciferol was isolated in
1932, and thereafter the separation of pure Calciferol from crude irradiated
Ergosterol became the basis of Ostelin production. Calciferol had about
four times the anti-rachitic power of irradiated Ergosterol. 'Calciferol GL'
was the name of the pure crystalline vitamin D from which the Glaxo
department made Ostelin from 1932. This refined method eliminated
impurities and made the final product more stable chemically, especially as
Calciferol as a pure substance could be standardised much more accurately.
Ostelin was marketed by 1931 in both liquid and tablet form and in a
number of package sizes.

During the First World War dangerous shortages of vitamin A had been
experienced in places where dairy produce and green vegetables or carrots
had become unobtainable. The most important source of vitamin A in the
Western diet was milk-fat. Vitamin A, as was later discovered, is necessary

to form one of the sensitive pigments of the retina, and deficiency of the vitamin manifests itself in extreme form by night blindness (functional hemeralopia). Milder deficiency of vitamin A (or carotene) may impair sight in dim light, raise the dark adaptation threshold or prolong the period of adaptation to low light intensities. Deficiency of vitamin A can also produce degenerative changes in the mucus membranes of the respiratory and alimentary tracts, and of the urinogenitary system. These tracts normally possess a marked resistance to bacterial invasion but, with a deficiency of vitamin A, this can vanish and the victim is consequently more vulnerable to secondary infections. One authority, writing in 1936, concluded 'that, in such countries as England and USA, the diet of average families, even of the poorer classes, contains sufficient vitamin A', mainly derived from milk fat. Although 'the effects of vitamin A deficiency *have* been observed, though with comparative rarity, among the children of the poor in England . . . as far as the countries of Western civilisation are concerned, the giving of "extra" vitamin A does not seem to assist greatly in the prevention and cure of certain diseases'.[22] The most that could be said was that an increased intake of vitamin A helped develop a strong and healthy body liable to reduced damage from the attacks of micro-organisms. With the market defined in these terms, the Glaxo department therefore developed a range of products containing vitamin A: Adexolin capsules, Adexolin Liquid, Adexolin emulsion, Ostomalt and Maltoline.

In countries where there was no shortage of sunlight and ultra-violet light, the question of anti-rachitic factors was less pressing. Typically, in Antipodean medical circles, there was little interest in vitamin D. 'It will take some time before it becomes a burning question', Fred Nathan wrote to London in 1929, 'and never . . . will become the same burning question in this country as it is with you'.[23] By 1931 the Nathans were selling Glaxo vitamin products in India, China, the Dutch East Indies, Greece, Italy, Turkey, Argentina, Brazil and Cuba as well as in Britain, New Zealand and Australia (see chapter 5).

Farex

In 1932 the Nathans marketed a new proprietary infant food, Farex, launched in May of that year and followed two years later with a soluble version. Its handling in the introductory phase showed that for all their experience, even in the 1930s the Nathans had not perfected their techniques for developing or selling proprietary products. Farex was a farinaceous vitamin-fortified food intended to provide children and infants with a healthy balanced diet. Like other products from the Glaxo department at this time, it represented a mixture of advances made in North America adapted for the growing British therapeutic market. However, in the development and marketing details, the Nathans and Jephcott were not unerring.

The idea of a vitamin-fortified cereal food had arisen from research undertaken at Toronto by Dr F. F. Tisdall. Eager to divert dwindling research grants towards his work for the Hospital for Sick Children, Tisdall sought business sponsors to finance the Paediatric Research Foundation through its business front – National Foods Ltd. His first success was in obtaining the support of General Baking Inc, which introduced vitamin D into their bread, and shortly afterwards Tisdall was approached to conduct further research for Mead Johnson and Co, manufacturers of infant diet materials at Evansville, Indiana. Tisdall undertook considerable work on recipes for Mead Johnson before discovering that he was forced, by US patent law, to omit vitamin D from the constituents. This was because the first vitamin D licence issued by the WARF trustees had been an exclusive licence to Quaker Oats (see page 78).

Jephcott monitored these developments, as he did other germane scientific advances in the United States. In October 1930 the Glaxo department was sent a sample of cereal food by Mead Johnson, while the *American Journal of Diseases of Children* of that year carried an article by Tisdall. Jephcott wrote to Tisdall, who forwarded his letter to Mead Johnson, and an invitation followed for Jephcott to visit their Indiana plant. On that trip, in April 1931, Jephcott also met Tisdall to discuss the possibility of production for markets outside the United States. Jephcott was not the only person in Britain to have followed Tisdall's work, and before long several doctors wrote to Tisdall enquiring about his research. He referred these enquiries to the Nathans and, as a result, pressure built up on the company to produce a vitamin-fortified farinaceous food. The company adapted Tisdall's formula to meet British tastes, but made no attempt to publicise the change of recipe.[24] In fact the adjustment of blending was covert, and it was decided that should questions be raised about the new flavour, it would be attributed to improvements in manufacture, possibly with reference to Tisdall himself. Another difference was that whereas Mead Johnson's cereal food was coarse-ground, Farex was fine-ground. The Glaxo department saw this distinction as important, and was at pains to ensure that its product could be fed to infants. As Bacharach repeatedly emphasised, they were committed to the fine ground form precisely because they could not simultaneously combat the popular predilection for finely powdered cereals and the general prejudice against cereal food for infants. The latter task alone was formidable.

The Glaxo department anticipated a demand for soluble cereal not only in the home market, but also in Europe (see chapter 5). To render the cereals soluble the starches had to be converted into sugars such as dextrins. Glaxo researchers had been experimenting with baking dough for some time before Mead Johnson produced a new soluble cereal food 'Pablum', which suggested to Bacharach that if a coarse form of Farex in which the cereal constituents were largely soluble could be produced, it could be sold in an unground form for adults and in a fine-ground version for infants. This insight resulted in the launching of a soluble New Farex in October 1934.

Sales of Farex increased considerably after the launch of the new, soluble variety. In the first six months after the initial product launch in March 1932, 1,318 lbs of Farex worth only £84 were sold. In the following year to September 1933, 4,031 lbs worth £254 were sold, rising to 5,396 lbs (£338) for the period from October 1933 until September 1934. But in the following six months covering from October 1934 to March 1935, sales of Glaxo's New Farex rose to 21,734 lbs worth £1,534.

Jephcott had never considered the original Farex recipe of 1932 as being the most desirable one. He confirmed this view in a letter to Tisdall:

Farex is slowly beginning to get on its feet. If only we had a more receptive crowd of doctors life would be easier. In addition, there is quite a little complaint that the cereal is flavourless. As a breakfast cereal I doubt whether it will ever go here to a large extent, certainly not in its present form. For one thing, the doctor will not advise any breakfast cereal, and if the medical support were removed, unless as far as English customers were concerned the flavour, texture, etc., heartily appealed to them, which it does not, they would never buy it. In that respect history is merely repeating itself. It is characteristic of this country that no one eats anything because it is good for him but solely because it gives him pleasure. He will only eat something because it is good for him if he is actually ill and the doctor has advised it. As you can well appreciate, this puts a nasty limitation on the market. However, we are not despondent.[25]

There were two factors behind Jephcott's fatalism. The first was that although sales of the 'New Farex' had increased they were still inadequate and the second was the problems experienced in launching the new product onto the market. In some respects the British retail trade of the early 1930s had not kept abreast of recent advances in the pharmaceutical industry, and the Glaxo department had difficulty in pitching their sales to overcome this market resistance. Bacharach and Jephcott saw the need to educate 'ignorant' doctors and their public, yet the hurried marketing of Farex was matched by inadequate consumer research and incompletely prepared propaganda. A common-sense product such as Farex should have enjoyed more and earlier success than it managed. By today's criteria Farex was a 'high street' product, whose slow 'take-off' was in part due to being marketed and distributed through 'ethical' channels. The days when 'health' and 'enjoyment' could be marketed simultaneously rather than exclusively were yet to come. There was, however, little effort to generate public

interest in the product, as indicated by the low initial sales and the
reluctance to publicise improvements in flavour from 1933.

Despite the launch of new soluble Farex in 1934, the company remained
curiously equivocal and indecisive in its approach to its farinaceous vitamin-
fortified food products. Thus, in 1935 a board memorandum surveying the
sales performance of new and old Farex, declared that 'the sooner we are
quite clear in our own minds on the two foods and the propaganda for them
the less trouble they will be later when it really will matter a lot'. It
complained that 'Old Farex' was hardly pushed at all, and that the image of
'New Farex' was barely defined:

The reason why there is confusion and why the sales of the old product have not
fallen off to nothing is chiefly, as I see it, that the start of the new product marked the
first time that we really did intensive propaganda for the name Farex. This
propaganda may have had faults in not making completely clear the fact that there
were two products, one 'soluble' and one not, but the prime fact is that it advertised
a name and a certain number of people have gone to chemists' and asked for that
product by name.[26]

Unfortunately, few figures survive for sales between 1934 and 1939, but the
rate of increase in that period was apparently even, and this success was
partly due to more rationalised marketing. In particular, it was decided to
re-name 'Old Farex' as 'Farex Cereal Food', retaining Farex exclusively for
the new product. In doing this the company imitated Mead Johnson's two
differentiated products, 'Mead's Cereal' and 'Pablum'. The rivalry with
these products became increasingly pronounced in 1935, especially as the
launch of New Farex provoked a dispute with Mead Johnson about patent
rights. One of the factors behind the Glaxo department's (and later the
company's) success has been its ability to adapt other people's ideas; in his
time, this was often facilitated by Jephcott's business mind and legal
training (he read for the Bar in his spare time and was called to the Middle
Temple in 1925), which together enabled him to assess the legal and
commercial vulnerability of his rivals. Control of patents was crucial in
identifying and developing new markets.

Mead Johnson's attempt to assert their patent rights over refinements of
Farex made by the Glaxo Department was less an attempt to block a market
rival than to extract a share of the increased profits. With Mead Johnson's
original mix, the Glaxo department had elected to pay royalties to Tisdall
via National Foods, but with the new process adapted from Pablum it
ceased to pay royalties to National Foods, but instead took out (unknown to
National Foods) its own patent on the process. A previous agreement had
been made with Tisdall that in those parts of the world where Mead
Johnson were unable to handle marketing, and the Nathan Company was
more appropriate, sole rights would be reserved to the latter. Mead Johnson

agreed to this. Later, when Pablum was launched, the Glaxo department was informed in general terms of the new procedure of manufacture, but no details were furnished to aid the British in carrying out the process, and Bacharach's staff devised their own process to manufacture Farex. When in September 1934 Mead Johnson obtained a British patent for a process of preparing a cereal food in soluble form, Bacharach's team had already undertaken considerable experimental work and had devised means of producing New Farex, somewhat differently – so they claimed – from the procedure described by Mead Johnson.

Nathans suspected that Mead Johnson were looking for a 5 per cent royalty, but their belief that the Mead Johnson patent was 'the weakest thing that ever crawled past a patent examiner' was confirmed when Sir Stafford Cripps, KC, then a leading patent lawyer, concluded that the Mead Johnson patent, although superior would not withstand a challenge. The problem for Nathans was not whether to challenge it, but how to do so without jeopardising the cordial relations between the two companies (National Foods had effectively withdrawn from contention). Rather than issue a direct challenge, the Nathans proposed a quid pro quo, each side being left to their own devices in Britain and North America respectively. Initially this suggestion angered Mead Johnson's patent attorney, who was, however, confounded when his client effectively conceded that the two manufacturing processes were, to all intents and purposes, different. The threat of litigation thereafter receded although the newly formed Glaxo Laboratories sent $1,000 to Tisdall's Paediatric Research shortly afterwards. Nevertheless a spirit of keen rivalry persisted between the research staff of Glaxo and those of Mead Johnson about the relative merits of Farex and Pablum for some years.

Despite Farex's faltering launch, it had been established as a leading infant food by the late 1930s and, after the outbreak of war, demand for it further increased. With its complicated international patent position it typified the new line of pharmaceutical products to which the Glaxo department became increasingly committed in the 1930s. However, in the handling of Mead Johnson, as much in the product's ill-defined marketing strategy, the Glaxo department betrayed its inexperience. The lessons learnt from the Farex episode of 1930–1935 were, however, applied to the company's handling of new pharmaceuticals.

Glaxo Laboratories Ltd

In 1935 it was decided that the growth of the Glaxo department was sufficient to justify a greater separation from the Nathan parent company. Glaxo Laboratories Ltd was incorporated as a private limited company, and

wholly owned subsidiary, with a capital of £400,000. Alec Nathan was the
company's Chairman and Harry Jephcott General Manager; it was agreed
that the company's policy should be to market proprietary pharmaceutical
products having reasonable claims to novelty.[27] Throughout the 1930s
Jephcott urged on his colleagues the need to concentrate their efforts on the
pharmaceutical business which in his view offered the best and most exciting
prospects for the future.

The pharmaceutical industry in Britain consisted mainly of small firms in
the interwar period, many of whom had developed from the manufacturing
chemist of the nineteenth century and whose business largely involved the
reprocessing of commodity drugs. The largest ethical proprietary business
had sales of up to £1m with profits in the region of £100,000. Firms such as
Beechams, specialising in advertised proprietaries, grew fast in the 1930s and
their profits increased. Beechams reported an increase of some 40 per cent in
1936, to just over £500,000.[28] Elsewhere larger firms, particularly in Germany and the USA, were devoting much greater research resources to the
development of synthetic drugs and the industry was standing on the brink
of discoveries which would revolutionise it. (See chapter 6.) In Glaxo
progress was slow and the company's 1938 Review concluded that 'our total
expenditure on research for the future, in contradiction to investigation of
present problems, is still probably too small in relation to our business and
possibly even too small to secure the best results from the expenditures
which we do incur. The present total annual cost of our long-dated research
does not exceed £5,000.'[29] But few British pharmaceutical companies then
spent more than that (see chapter 6).

Glaxo's long-term research was in the main undertaken in conjunction
with outside bodies such as the Lister Institute and the National Institute for
Medical Research. A consultative committee of external scientific advisers
was appointed and from them Glaxo Laboratories received not only 'the
benefit of specific advice directed towards problems upon which we are
working' but also 'substantial and useful co-operation from the chemical
departments of the principal universities in the country'.[30]

By 1938 small-scale research was being carried out on a number of
projects including the synthesis of vitamin A and of iodine compounds, the
development of a new acridine compound and the isolation of bacterial
antigens and the pituitary hormones.[31] Glaxo's researchers were also
working on the liver extraction process which produced Examen and the use
of residues from that process. After the discovery in the 1920s that fresh
liver, taken orally, was effective against pernicious anaemia, there were
intensive attempts to isolate and extract the effective substance from liver.
In the early 1930s Per Laland and Aage Klem of the Norwegian pharmaceutical company Nyegaard & Co were successful in developing a process

for the preparation of liver extract which could be administered by injection; the product was Examen and by agreement in 1936 Nyegaard gave Glaxo Laboratories an exclusive licence to manufacture and sell Examen not only in the British Empire but also in North and South America and in parts of Europe and Asia. The agreement provided that Nyegaard would supply Glaxo with all the technical information necessary on the process and manufacturing methods and in return Glaxo would pay the Norwegian company a royalty on the sales it made of Examen (with an advance payment of $7,500) during the life of the patent. The companies agreed to inform each other of improvements in the process that either developed. Further experiments, halted by the outbreak of the Second World War, carried out by Laland and Klem to purify the liver fractions took them to the verge of the isolation of the antianaemic principle – vitamin B_{12} – the post-war discovery of Merck and Lester Smith of Glaxo (see page 178).[32]

It is clear that Jephcott and most of his colleagues found the pharmaceutical business more stimulating and challenging than the non-scientific side and, quite apart from any question of financial rewards or profit-earning capacity, they were drawn by the pioneering nature of pharmaceutical production. Jephcott had a keen sense of adventure and even, in his restrained way, of fun: and there can be no doubt which side of the business, in Britain and abroad, gave more fun. As well as the scientific challenge, there was a strong commercial incentive for Glaxo to diversify into vitamins and pharmaceuticals. As the figures in the table below show, from 1935 to 1939 pharmaceuticals consistently showed a larger profit on a smaller turnover, when compared with Glaxo's food products. Potentially, pharmaceuticals could yield more profit than processed dairy products or food generally and, as this became increasingly apparent after 1929, Glaxo's policy reflected it.

Certainly the Nathans' attempts to diversify into food products were disappointing. Trengouse & Nathan (see page 55), after six years of losses, at last made a small profit in 1935 and 1936. George Bowles Nicholls, acquired in 1930, stayed in the red throughout the decade.[33]

In 1934 Jephcott summarised to Glaxo's Greek partner (see chapter 5) the irrefutable commercial reasons for developing the fine chemicals as opposed to the food business. Jephcott wrote:

With regard to the sale of foods, the position in Greece appears to me to bear a very strong resemblance to that existing in quite a number of countries at the present time. The real dead cost of the food plus the ordinary selling costs i.e. discounts etc., necessitates a selling price exceeding that which a large proportion of the consuming public could afford even in better times. It may be . . . that if it were possible to spend a considerable sum on advertising, the volume of sales could be lifted, but since the

Table 1. *Glaxo Laboratories Ltd turnover and net income 1935–1939*

		Turnover	Percentage	Net income	Percentage
1935/6	Food	251,978	53	54,719	36
	Pharmaceuticals	221,054	47	95,588	64
1936/7	Food	295,267	51	74,092	37
	Pharmaceuticals	280,302	49	126,969	63
1937/8	Food	382,490	53	100,777	38
	Pharmaceuticals	344,819	47	166,822	62
1938/9	Food	495,609	54	137,268	41
	Pharmaceuticals	417,322	46	195,704	59

Source: Glaxo archives: authors' calculations

margin on the food is so small, it is obvious that were the money spent on advertising it would be impossible to recoup oneself for this expenditure.

In such circumstances, the only possibility of trading in foods without loss is to take such business as can be obtained easily and inexpensively as a result of the prestige and reputation of the food and adopt such proceedings as you have done with regard to the additional discount to the chemists, etc., so as to secure the maximum amount of goodwill from the retail distributor.

It is not that we are not anxious to preserve the food turnover – we are most anxious to do so – but we cannot afford to do it at a loss and we must hold the trade as best we can at some small profit, awaiting the return of more favourable times, which we hope will expand the market.

With regard to the pharmaceuticals the picture is fortunately a more attractive one.[34]

Jephcott, who more than anyone else was responsible both for the details and the broad strategy of the company's innovations, wrote with satisfaction in 1934 that 'our business is tending more and more into pharmaceutical channels'.[35] He argued that greater profits and – what counted at least equally with Alec Nathan – greater benefits to society would accrue by orientating the business increasingly towards developing its pharmaceutical specialities. As the pharmaceutical business began to flourish, the question of accommodation became more pressing. The growth of the Glaxo department during the First World War had necessitated the occupation of premises in various parts of London. Considerable inefficiency resulted, and after 1918 all Glaxo's activities were consolidated at 56 Osnaburgh Street, where it was anticipated that the routine and stereotyped packing of large quantities of Glaxo powder could be accommodated for many years. However, the basis of these predictions was upset by the marketing of the first vitamin D concentrate, Ostelin, in 1924, and by 1929 there was again considerable accommodation pressure, with enforced dispersal to premises at Regent House, Southampton Street (1929) and at Hayes (1930).

A board meeting in 1933 resolved to segregate the food from the pharmaceutical business, and a sub-committee of Alec Nathan, Jephcott and Randall was appointed to prepare a scheme. It was later decided that such segregation was impracticable, but instead it was agreed to unite all sections of Glaxo's business in premises outside central London. For that purpose a site was bought at Greenford in Middlesex. Linking the Midlands and London, the Grand Union Canal traversed Greenford and it had attracted William Perkin to set up his factory there in 1857, to manufacture his new discovery, aniline dye. Other business had moved into Greenford in the twentieth century, including, in 1921, the Nathans' associates, J. Lyons & Co.[36]

The plans for Greenford envisaged facilities not only for the immediate requirements of the business, including pharmaceutical and fine chemical production, but also included a substantial area, which was not immediately required, available for future extensions. Although the original Greenford building provided what was estimated to be comfortable room for expansion in all departments, growth proved to be so rapid with some products that extensions were needed before the contractor's twelve-months maintenance period had expired, and from 1935 to 1947 builders were continuously present at Greenford, although the amount of work in hand varied. Within twelve years the floor area at Greenford doubled.

The first plans for new buildings were set in hand in March 1934. Glaxo employed as architects Messrs Wallis, Gilbert & Partners, who had designed a number of factories in the west London suburbs, including the famous Firestone factory on the Great West Road and the Hoover building on Western Avenue. At the same time, Herbert Palmer, then aged twenty-seven, who had joined the Glaxo department after graduating in Commerce at London University, was made responsible for the Greenford project. Palmer had been sales representative for Glaxo products in Brussels for a time before returning to England as Jephcott's personal assistant. Jephcott had ensured that Palmer gained wide experience of the business, such as standing in for the factory manager during the latter's visit to India, and he insisted that Palmer be put in charge of works on the Greenford site, albeit under the nominal control of the production director, Colonel Rose. Palmer successfully liaised between the builders, architects, local authorities and the company, and for the rest of his career with Glaxo (until 1971) had a crucial role in the construction of the company's factories, at home and overseas.

Sketch plans for the first stage of the Greenford site were ready by September 1934, and the provisional plans at an estimated cost of £114,000 were approved by the board in December of that year. Existing office space of 10,000 square feet was to be increased to 22,700 square feet (16,000 previously), while space for pharmaceutical manufacturing and packing was

18 Glaxo's new factory at Greenford.

raised from 9,500 to 19,000 square feet, and bulk storage space from 5,000 to 14,0000 square feet. The laboratories of the newly formed Glaxo company were the first to move into the new premises at Greenford. The factory departments followed and then the office and administrative staff, so that Greenford was fully operational in January 1936.

With the space and incentive to expand its pharmaceutical activities, other new products were developed in the immediate pre-war years, including vaccines, tablets, X-ray media and medicaments. By 1939 the original 250 staff at Greenford had expanded to nearly 600.[37] In line with Alec Nathan's benevolent paternalistic views, staff amenities were provided at Greenford on a generous scale although 'economy was practised keenly and vigilantly in all [other] operations'. There was a large canteen and recreation centre; sports were encouraged and in the pleasant grounds, tennis courts were made.[38]

Dried milk supplies

With the onset of the slump in 1930–1931 the whole group was seriously affected by the onerous terms of its agreement of 1919 with the New Zealand Cooperative Dairy Suppliers. Pacey warned in June 1931 that butter, cheese and casein were yielding low prices, and that the powder-drying programme at Matangi would have to be curtailed. He wanted to terminate the contract with Te Aroha, an objective supported in London, where it was felt that Bunnythorpe (the Nathans' original milk-drying factory) could meet any shortfall in supply. Sydney Jacobs, (who had joined the company in 1898 and was now a director in London), wrote that it was increasingly difficult 'to take a sufficient quantity of powder at a price which would make a profit possible' and warned that 'a very serious menace to the operations of our Glaxo Department' was looming in the near future. London told Wellington, 'Our chief fear is engaging to take an annual quantity which we could not use in what we are certain are declining markets for our New Zealand manufacture'.[39] In speaking to the New Zealand Cooperative Dairy Co in July 1931 about adjusting the Glaxo factory contracts, Pacey:

represented that the contracts were made in a period of inflation; that inflated arrangements were being adjusted in all walks of life in all parts of the world: that the rental payment clause is, under present deflated conditions, an intolerable burden and that owing to civil military and economic influences in India, Argentina, Spain and other parts of the World our business had been interfered with: our output could not be maintained at the capacity of the Factory as provided in the Agreements and that reduction of contract capacity is desired: that the reduced values of Butter, Cheese and Casein which at one time were a way out had ceased to provide a means of meeting the difficulty and that an all round revision is urgently called for ... I asked [them] to give play to the Hoover doctrine and to be influenced by the spirit which animated the British people and not the French, the significance of which was appreciated. I also urged the folly 'of killing the goose which lays the golden egg'.[40]

The original contract of 1919 had assumed an unrealistic level of demand for Glaxo powder, and had assured the New Zealand Dairy Cooperative of a high level of orders. In order to minimise its losses, the surplus milk which could not be disposed of as dried powder was processed into butter and casein, but in 1930–1931 the demand for these also receded greatly, and the company could no longer pay its suppliers even the minimum prices stipulated in the contract of 1919 without loss. Ordinary, full-cream milk powder was in over-supply throughout the world and this put extra pressure on the Nathans diversification into processed cheese.

There was an additional threat. In 1931 the company heard that Britain's Labour Government might implement legislation forcing the pasteurisation of milk for human consumption, which would knock the bottom out of the traditional Glaxo powder market.

In the nature of the present Government in England, it is a natural development, and a very justifiable one, as an approach to assisting the agriculturist. The effect of this procedure on us may not be immediate, but will be as 'a rolling stone', and if carried vigorously along will seriously affect us, and other sellers of Dried Milk to Welfare Centres, more severely as the years go by.[41]

In the event, however, the Government fell before it had introduced the necessary legislation. By 1933 deteriorating political and economic conditions imposed themselves even more forcibly on the Glaxo department. The sale of commercial dried milk in Britain, as Alec Nathan wrote in January of that year, had been materially affected by 'the development of Nationalistic feeling in England'. Some manufacturers (for example Cadbury, Fry and Rowntree) insisted on using only dried milk made by English manufacturers. Others, while preferring to purchase only British milk, were willing to buy Empire dried milk of equal quality and freshness so long as its price was lower than that of English milk. Those who would still buy foreign dried milk did so on criteria of price and quality.

The Glaxo department had often considered acquiring an English source of supply, but there were still adequate reasons for not doing so in the early 1930s. The prices of New Zealand dried milk were always fixed by the world price of butter, and consequently the cost price of New Zealand milk was always less than that of milk used for English manufacturing. The cost price of dried milk was always less in a butter producing country than in an area where the sales and prices of wet milk determined the cost price of dried milk. Though in the past there might have been fears of Britain imposing an import duty on foreign dried milk, the Nathans had been reassured by the resolutions of the Imperial Economic Conference at Ottawa in 1932 on dominion trade preference that no such duty could be imposed before 1936. In the meantime, Empire dried milk (such as theirs from New Zealand) could still compete favourably with indigenous dried milk in Britain.

On the other hand, the fact that New Zealand was the source of Glaxo's supplies did hold great disadvantages for British marketing. The London office required regularity of manufacture coupled with uniform supplies month by month, but instead was faced with fluctuating deliveries, so that it was sometimes overwhelmingly overstocked with powder and at another period hopelessly short. Matangi's output peaked between October and January of each year, petered out in February and March, and fell to almost nothing from April to August. As Glaxo powder consumption in Britain remained almost uniform throughout the year, London was obliged to have money locked up for months in the storage of powder which, when sold, was stale and hence uncompetitive with fresh powder.

It seems extraordinary in retrospect that no attempt was ever made by the London office, after twenty years of the business, to reduce such discrepancies between supply and demand. Wellington's failure to appreciate the problem, or to devise a solution, is a measure of their distance from appreciating the work of the London office or the British market; but it is also a poor reflection on Alec Nathan and his team that they waited until the world slump, and corresponding troubles for the company, in the early

1930s, before making concerted efforts to balance supply and demand of dried powder in Britain. In 1933 Alec proposed an adjustment of output between New Zealand and Australia. He wanted the Port Fairy factory in Southern Australia to produce a quantity equal to Matangi's capacity during the months when Matangi was not producing (May to August or September); and for the Commercial Dried Milk Department in London to create a new demand for its product so that Matangi could always manufacture up to capacity. Up to 1933 the Commercial Milk Department had made, on average, a minimum net profit of £7,000, but Alec Nathan was keen that it should do better. As he summarised the position to Wellington, the latter's main object should be uniform monthly output with regularity and freshness in supplies, rather than giving, as they did, priority to economy in cost of production.

Pacey accepted that uniform monthly supplies were 'increasingly important', and reported that New Zealanders were trying to replicate Danish dairy methods to obtain a minimum variation between summer and winter output. The whole political question of imports continued to worry the company. By April 1933 there were 'many doubts in the air as to the future trend of events' in Britain. While the Ministry of Agriculture under Walter Elliot had been given fuller powers to support British agriculture, and the Dutch, as the chief source of Britain's dried milk imported from the Continent, were apprehensive of quota restrictions, a trade agreement with Denmark was concluded which seemed to cut across any preferential or protective tariff policy. The Glaxo department had just won a contract for New Zealand milk powder from the catering chain, J. Lyons & Co., in competition with English supplies offered at £48 per ton delivered. Dutch supplies however could be obtained at £35 delivered into store, duty paid, with delivery spread until November and Glaxo considered that 'the English manufacturers must be losing money' at £48 per ton, cautioning that without 'immediate and drastic action' on foreign dried milk, 'the Dutch prices will set the pace and the present strong competition will continue'.[42]

In the mid 1930s, sales of Glaxo powder started to improve. In Britain the reformulated products, Ostermilk I (1929) and Ostermilk II (1932) did particularly well. Although far from the boom years of 1919 and 1920, (see page 46) 1,443 tons of dried milk were sold in 1936–1937: the total value of sales was £226,888 and nearly half of that went to municipal authorities.[43]

In 1937 Glaxo opened its first milk-drying factory in Britain, at Driffield in Yorkshire; the factory was, like Greenford, designed by Wallis, Gilbert & Partners and was built in three months by Richard Costain & Co Ltd. Its first manager was Ted Farmer, who started his career in Glaxo as Jephcott's first assistant in 1919. During its first season of operation (1937–1938) the factory produced 1,348,000 lbs of milk powder, but it needed to produce

19 The first milk-drying factory in Britain opened at Driffield in 1937. This
photograph, taken just after the war, shows milk churns arriving.

more than that in order to reduce the operating cost per lb of powder to be
comparable with imports from Australia and New Zealand. In 1938 Glaxo
noted:

> it will of course be recognised that the cost of milk for drying at Driffield is out of all
> proportion to similar costs in the Dominions and it will require all the special
> advantages of lower packing and transport costs and modern equipment to be able to
> produce at figures comparable with Dominion imports.
>
> On the other hand, the factory has already fully justified itself by the invaluable
> services rendered in respect of small quantities of export powder required and in the
> difficult circumstances of the recent crisis which occurred when Dominion powder
> was necessarily in short supply.[44]

In Britain Glaxo continued its traditional policy of directing promotional
activity at the general medical profession, and at para-medical staff.
Circularisation and advertising continued, as did the work of the Glaxo
Baby Department and the publication of the Baby Book, both of which
became known to mothers throughout the country. But increasingly after
1930 travelling representatives were appointed to call upon doctors, hospitals, charitable institutions, chemists, matrons of nursing homes (especially

20 Tablet manufacture at Greenford, 1938.

those taking maternity cases) and maternity and child welfare departments and centres. On these professional audiences the merits of Glaxo products were pressed discreetly and respectfully. The Working Instructions issued to Glaxo representatives in 1936 convey the flavour of their approach. 'Members of our representative staff must always bear in mind when making calls that to the customer they will reflect the policy and character of the House. For this reason great care must be taken never to promise more than the House has authorised, nor to make any statement which the House cannot support.' Deferential moderation was the keynote: 'There is no more important part of a representative's mental make-up than the ability to exercise tact, and a representative should never place himself in such a position that it is difficult, embarrassing or impossible for the House to support his attitude to any particular customer.'[45]

Representatives were enjoined to be constructive and restrained in their sales pitch: 'The policy of the House is never to run down competitors; many have organisations which are worthy of every admiration, and a representative does not lose anything by acknowledging this on suitable occasions. While no opportunity must be missed of selling our own organisation and services to customers, it is in no circumstances necessary to

21 Glaxo Laboratories' exhibition stand, 1938.

disparage a competitive House.'[46] An interesting sidelight on the mobility
and methods of Glaxo's travelling representatives is provided by Alec
Nathan's explanation in 1929 of why in Britain he had stopped equipping his
men with motor cars:

One would naturally think that, in supplying a representative with a car, it would
enable him to contact people who are off the railway track with greater convenience
and less expense. Actual experience proves that this is not the case. A man does not
contact those out of the way people; he simply leaves them alone.

In England a man driving a car has his mind so concentrated upon his driving that
he is ill-fitted to carry out an important interview with either a trader or a Doctor. It
affects both his nerves and his mentality ... by either walking or going by tram or
train, and the responsibility for its guidance and direction not being his, [a man] is
able during his journey to adopt a line of talk and conversation, and is therefore
much better equipped to carry out his interview than the man who drives a motor
car.

This average representative is not a mechanic; nor has he any real love for a motor
car. Our experience in this respect has been both bad and expensive, expense being
incurred even for a car not being oiled.[47]

Conclusion

Of the major British pharmaceutical manufacturers existing at the outbreak of the Second World War, Allen & Hanburys and May & Baker had interests in pharmacy and fine chemicals stretching back over a century, while Boots derived from the diversification into research and production of a multiple retail pharmacist. Control of Boots was in American hands between 1920 and 1933 and ownership of May & Baker had been French since 1927.[48] In the British pharmaceutical sector, Glaxo Laboratories was a hybrid. It sprang from a family of New Zealand traders who strayed into proprietary trading from an international import/export business. However, although it repeatedly betrayed its inexperience at this diversification, after fifteen years it had established itself as an eager and innovative newcomer among its older and staider competitors. After another fifteen years it could show a modern factory at Greenford, an expanding range of products and a growing scientific reputation. Much of the responsibility for this lay in the energy and instinct of Harry Jephcott and his increasingly devoted managers, working under the shrewd, benevolent but cautious chairmanship of Alec Nathan in London. Such growth, however, would have been impossible given the limited British markets for Glaxo products; and the company was always international in its basis and attitudes. The course of this early internationalisation is explained in the next chapter.

5

Early internationalisation and the growth of overseas markets 1909–1939

From an early date the Nathan family, with their international merchandising expertise, saw the possibilities of selling Glaxo powder in markets outside Britain and New Zealand. Agents were appointed in some countries before the outbreak of the First World War and by 1914 exports represented more than a third of the turnover of Glaxo powder. The shortage of Glaxo supplies (and sometimes their poor quality) almost destroyed the trade during the war and prevented further development in the immediate post-war years. The export business started to revive in 1922 and by 1925 had grown to represent nearly a half of the value of the Glaxo department's total turnover.

There was in the earlier years a division of international marketing responsibility between the London and Wellington offices. Its exact details are unclear, but Alec Nathan wrote in 1919 'that if the strict word of the arrangement was kept, [London] should not be able to do any Export Business except with South America and Spain'.[1] In both those countries London had appointed agents before 1914.

As the business developed the Nathans were forced to begin limited local production when protective tariffs or other discriminatory regulations, intended by governments to develop local productive expertise, were introduced. The diversification into pharmaceuticals also stimulated the establishment of manufacturing capacity overseas; vitamin products were highly suitable for local production, since they could be produced on a small scale for a modest cost in capital equipment and staff. The mixing of vitamins and dried milk to produce Ostelin was viable in small laboratories attached to the local offices overseas.[2] A pattern of development – the early stages of multi-nationalism – can then be discerned in Glaxo's overseas operations, before 1939, as the table below shows.

Within the overall pattern, each operation varied according to the market, the country and the individuals concerned. There was little uniformity in the appointment of agents. In line with the Nathan practice, some were cousins

Table 2. *Total turnover and value of export sales of the Nathans' Glaxo department, 1911–1925*

Year	Total turnover £	Value of export sales £	Export sales as a proportion of total turnover Percentage
1911	20,000	5,214	26.0
1912	30,000	11,409	38.0
1913	50,000	19,442	38.8
1914	70,000	25,448	36.4
1915	120,000	31,757	26.5
1916	200,000	28,550	14.3
1917	390,000	24,745	6.3
1918	550,000	18,269	3.3
1919	890,000	49,259	5.5
1920	1,350,000	104,439	7.7
1921	1,540,000	123,153	8.0
1922	1,090,000	170,045	15.6
1923	780,000	233,487	29.9
1924	725,000	287,226	39.6
1925	652,500	314,982	48.3

Source: Glaxo archives

and connections by marriage – a 'kissing kin' network – appointed to loosely defined agencies carrying generous commission or expenses. Others were found through the trade papers or recommended by fellow, often Jewish, businessmen. In 1910, for example, the Nathans in London appointed a Glaxo agency in Indo-Burma, with the agent undertaking to purchase £150,000 worth of Glaxo powder over three years. Between 1910 and the closing of the agency on the outbreak of war in 1914, it had, in fact, bought £8,840 worth of Glaxo powder, but as Alec Nathan later wrote, 'they did *everything* to create the sales ... and there had been no semblance of friction'.[3]

South America

By comparison, there was considerable friction with Frederick Harrison, appointed agent in South America (see page 35) in 1909. The continent was to prove a difficult, if sometimes rewarding market for the Nathans. The South American subcontinent was one in which British business was pre-eminent before 1914. Although foreign competition began to increase after

22 The Bunnythorpe factory receiving milk in the 1920s.

1890, the great network of British banks, merchant houses and agencies was deeply entrenched before the First World War: indeed by 1913 British investment in the subcontinent has been estimated to be £1,000 million, far ahead of the nearest rival, the French, with about £350 million.[4] Harrison's original agreement excluded Argentina, Brazil, Paraguay and Patagonian Chile, but was subsequently extended to embrace the whole of the South American continent. Despite this, his was the least profitable of the Glaxo department's overseas agencies, and was characterised by recurrent threats of litigation and bad debts. Harrison himself complained that the milk powder supplied to him was often impure and rancid, with the consignments sent to Chile from June 1914 being particularly unsatisfactory. Glaxo Half Cream and Glaxo Full Cream were introduced from 1912 through selling agents, with promotional work done through chemists directed at the public. Harrison's profits (by agreement defined as the difference between the wholesale price and the dealer's price which he was able to obtain – a type of arrangement later abandoned as the Nathans gained experience), fell in Chile from £5,860 in 1913 to £3,222 in 1914 and to a mere £964 in 1915. However, these figures were also affected by the wartime dislocation of freight shipping and by the difficulty of obtaining tin supplies in Britain. The

Table 3. *The growth of Glaxo Laboratories'*
foreign manufacturing subsidiaries pre-1945

Country	Date of earliest secondary manufacture	Date of earliest primary manufacture
New Zealand		before 1905; 1920
Australia	1920	1921
India	1924	
Argentina		1933
Greece	1932–42	
Italy	1935	

Source: Glaxo archives

Note: With the exceptions of the joint venture in Greece, and of
the Italian company where minority shareholders existed
in 1932–1946, all these subsidiaries were wholly owned by
Joseph Nathan & Company. By secondary manufacture is
meant chemical manipulation of products already developed from raw materials. By primary manufacture is
meant processing of raw materials.

number of cases of Glaxo powder shipped to South America fell from 2,212
in 1914 to 1,664 in 1915, recovering to 2,538 in 1916. These interruptions
meant that stocks dwindled and by 1916–1917 the market in Argentina was
characterised by irregularly distributed stocks in a number of isolated
chemists.

Alec Nathan had little patience with Harrison, and clashed with him in
February 1917 when the formation of a South American subsidiary was
under discussion. Harrison contended that he must have the decisive voice in
the policy of any new South American company, whereas Alec Nathan
insisted that as South America contributed only a small part of the
worldwide Glaxo powder business, supreme control must rest with the
Nathans. On this difference of principle the proposal foundered, and
probably thereafter neither party to the agreement of 1909 was keen that it
should run its full term (to December 1930). Despite protests from the
London office in 1918 David Nathan arranged for the New Zealand
company to supply 300 cases of Glaxo powder to South American customers
not connected with Harrison. The sale breached the Nathans' contract with
their agent and, as Louis Nathan predicted in an irritated telegram to David,
it persuaded Harrison to resign. He proceeded to sue the Nathans in
London. Before the dispute reached the courts, Harrison died and the case
was settled out-of-court with a payment to his widow, but not before his
solicitors had alleged that 'very considerable quantities of defective "Glaxo"

have been supplied with such disastrous consequences to the health of the children of the countries affected that the governing authorities have ordered large quantities of "Glaxo" to be destroyed'.[5]

In Harrison's place, the Nathans appointed Charles C. Richardson, who had been working for the company since 1910, most recently in Belgium, seeking to establish a market for Glaxo powder there. Richardson spoke fluent Spanish but, despite his suitability and the relatively large amount of money which the Nathans were willing to commit to South America (£10,000 was authorised in 1921 and it was later doubled to £20,000), it was an inauspicious time. The disruption caused to British trade by the First World War had severe repercussions in South America, and the decades after 1918 saw a steady decline in British influence and activity there. The Glaxo department's marketing efforts after 1918 occurred in a worrying political and historical context. Both the company's long-term success, and its recurrent short-term setbacks, must be seen in the perspective of British commercial stagnation and retreat in the subcontinent. It is only then that its overall achievement, and the local nature of some of its difficulties, can be properly appreciated. As the British representative in Bolivia reported in 1929:

American influence over this country is developing by leaps and bounds, and this is only to be expected as a result of the loans contracted in the States. In a few years everything will be American ... and we will find ourselves pushed out ... A British commercial traveller is a *rara avis* in this country, and when they come they limit themselves to a cursory visit to the capital and a still more cursory visit to Oruro.

We, as a nation, have during the course of centuries built up a reputation in this continent for enterprise, industry and good workmanship. Why should we surrender the fruits of all this and these valuable markets without a struggle to the Americans who come in at the eleventh hour with their reputation for crooked dealing and inferior goods? We should change our methods.[6]

Similarly the British representative in Peru also lamented in 1929:

Great Britain used to occupy first place in this country. She has now surrendered this place to the United States of America and ... is now in danger of losing even the second place to German, Belgian and Italian competition. Complaints reach one on all sides of apathy at home, the incomprehensible unwillingness of British firms to do business with this country, where there is a market, and of the frequent bad management on the part of local representatives of British firms. It is scarcely for us to blame the war when, after the United States of America, Germany and Belgium are our principal rivals.[7]

In addition to this increasingly pressing international competition, by the 1930s there were also strong indigenous forces developing which added to the local complexities. Nationalism, tariffs and other restrictions were becoming widespread.

In pharmaceuticals the Germans were well-placed in Latin American markets. This was partly because the vast majority of pharmacists and chemists in the subcontinent were German, or German-trained, and considered the nationality and source of pharmaceutical products as more important than small price differentials. Before 1914 British consular reports from South America had constantly drawn attention to the hard-sell methods of American travellers in patent medicines and to the leading position of Germany in drugs, contrasting both with the fact that in these markets Britain seemed to be making no effort to build up trade. British pharmaceutical export performances reflected that; in 1913 Britain held only 5 per cent of the market for patent medicines and drugs in Venezuela and only 8 per cent in Guatemala although it supplied 25 per cent of the market in Peru.[8]

In Argentina, the Glaxo products (full cream and half cream) were reintroduced between 1919 and 1921 by Richardson. He opened an office in Buenos Aires in 1922, cleared the market of outdated stocks and replaced them with fresh supplies, imported from Britain ready packed for sale. Intensive promotional work followed in the next few years, and a small laboratory was opened in 1924, for the preparation of Ostelin. Around 1930 Colloidal Calcium with Ostelin (CC and O) was imported from London in finished form and added to the products on sale, becoming one of the Glaxo department's best known products in the export market. It was followed in 1931 by Ostomalt and Adexolin capsules and drops, with local manufacture being undertaken wherever possible. The company was obliged to begin local manufacture by both the practice of competitors and Argentinian industrial trends. Alec Nathan visited Argentina in 1931, and during his visit the decision was taken to manufacture baby foods locally. An experimental dairy farm was leased in Quequen, 350 miles south of Buenos Aires, where a milk drying plant was set up with second-hand equipment from New Zealand. Glaxo baby foods manufactured and packed at Quequen were first marketed in Argentina in 1932.

Richardson, however, found the political climate in the Argentine an increasingly unsympathetic environment for foreign (and particularly British) businessmen. From 1932 until 1943 Argentina was controlled by a right-wing coalition (or *Concordancia*) under General Agustin Justo. The support for this regime came from an oligarchy of the great landowners, who were pro-British, as they sold most of their products to the United Kingdom. Thus, under an agreement reached in 1933 by Walter Runciman, President of the Board of Trade, British purchases of Argentine beef were assured in return for preferential treatment of British exports to Argentina. Despite the apparently encouraging tone of the agreement, by 1935 Richardson was warning the company in London 'of many indications', including recent attacks on the beef interests of Lord Vestey, that Argentina would soon:

> have no time for foreigners and still less for ourselves, because they owe to Britain's brains, capital and efforts, all that they are. We see so many indications of this spirit . . . that do not get the publicity that Vestey's affair has received, and which Vestey very timely . . . gave it . . . Mind you . . . we are ourselves to blame to a certain extent in that the B[uenos] A[ires] British Empire Exhibition was somewhat of a tactless display of the 'here we are' spirit, which these people will resent, their resentment being fanned by US commercial interests and by the Italian racial interests and animosity.[9]

These nationalistic tendencies, which culminated in a pro-German military *coup* in June 1943, overshadowed some aspects of Glaxo's business in Argentina. Richardson wrote in 1936:

> The necessity of having a qualified chemist with an Argentine title permanently on our premises has not yet arrived but it might do so at any moment. Brazil has already established this regulation and it will not be long before Argentina acts likewise, since these countries copy one another in all such respects. A further danger is that competitive firms – and the methods that some of these people adopt in order to have a 'dig' at competitive firms are not always of the cleanest – might get the Ministry of Health to act arbitrarily against us . . . we can however guard against this danger by having an Argentine assistant chemist with an Argentine degree to affix the signatures. This chemist we have in our staff, a woman, of not much capacity, but quite good enough . . . for routine work: it would be advisable, should we have such a signature, to have it from an Argentine woman chemist rather than from a man. Women have generally a higher sense of loyalty than men have and this is particularly the case with this race of which such a large percentage of men seem to be innately disloyal.[10]

Jephcott visited Argentina for the first time in 1933, when the Richardson agency was taken over by a joint stock company entitled Ch. C. Richardson S.A.C. e.I, a subsidiary of the Nathan parent company. Jephcott lavished his customary attention on both the formation of the new company and the discussions regarding its future policy. Many new products were added to the range during 1934, with local manufacture undertaken under the supervision of a qualified chemist from London. Baberlac Simple (Babeurre-Acid-Milk) was introduced as a baby food in 1935 and other pharmaceutical products in the Glaxo range were introduced between 1936 and 1941.

Although Richardson introduced Glaxo products into Uruguay, Chile and Paraguay, none of the three republics could approach the Argentine's sales potential because they were by comparison sparsely inhabited and poorer in all respects. Sales therefore remained small. Glaxo products were also imported into Brazil where, despite the difficulties, Richardson urged the parent company to establish local packing or manufacture. In support he

NEWS FROM OVERSEAS

23 Directors (including Charles Richardson) and staff of the Argentinian company in 1941.

alleged that economic nationalism was more 'rabid' in Brazil than elsewhere. But Jephcott deferred the decision: he was, he said, wary of the 'repercussions ... of local packing in countries rife with regulations of all sorts',[11] which might make the company vulnerable to an arbitrary or vindictive prosecution which would damage its reputation.

Cuba presents an extreme example of the kind of political difficulties which the company faced in the subcontinent. Edward L. R. McGough, who had previously been one of Glaxo's medical representatives in Argentina, went to Cuba in 1927 and under his direction the Havana office became fully independent of Richardson's supervision in 1933. McGough subsequently took over not only the Caribbean, but also all of northern Latin America, which was not covered from Argentina. By the time that he eventually retired in 1963, McGough had come to enjoy a legendary reputation among Glaxo's overseas representatives. Riots in Cuba against the autocracy of General Gerardo Machado y Morales came to a climax in August 1933 with a general strike which forced Machado to flee abroad. In the unsettled political conditions which followed, the new president, C. M. de Cespedes y Quesada, was overthrown after a few months, and thereafter there was a succession of presidents manipulated by Fulgencio Batista y Zaldivar, a former sergeant who had emerged as the military leader on Machado's downfall. During these disturbances in Havana, the central wholesaler's premises were attacked; the strikers destroyed the records and an accumulation of orders, and despoiled stocks in the warehouse. When Jephcott met McGough in 1934 in New York he noted that 'although McGough is a cheerful and almost phlegmatic person, his experiences in Havana during

24 The Cuban company's exhibition stand.

the last twelve months have certainly shaken him and . . . the change of scene will have done him good'. McGough was paid a salary plus commission upon turnover exceeding a certain volume, the volume calculated to provide sufficient gross profit to pay all estimated market expenses. On this arrangement Jephcott commented:

McGough exhibits characteristics which we have observed in other Scotchmen. He is hardworking, enthusiastic and loyal to the core, but withal has a keen sense of his own personal financial welfare . . . the commission arrangement has acted as a very great incentive and has probably been almost a determining factor in McGough's putting up with the personal discomforts and at times considerable risk of remaining in Havana throughout the riots . . .[12]

Notwithstanding the political and business problems in Cuba, at the meeting in New York, McGough and Jephcott planned to expand efforts to market Glaxo's products in the country. Jephcott wrote:

In future he [McGough] is to be provided with more complete information regarding the true trading position in the Cuban market so that he may fully appreciate not only the turnover, which at present is what he mainly sees, but also the profits and the true cost of the market. He has really quite good business acumen . . . the more he knows of the true state of affairs, the better and more intelligent service we are likely to get from him.[13]

The outbreak of the Second World War in 1939 exacerbated many of the problems and the trends that Glaxo had faced in the preceding years in

South America. As Richardson wrote in 1941, pointing to the future as well as reviewing the past:

These countries are bent upon creating their own industries, and this war is the additional stimulus born out of necessity. This process started during [the] last war and is not requiring much impetus. Universal free trade is ... utopical [sic], since all these countries are creating a manufacturing working-class which cannot well be dismissed, and the governments need the revenue from industry for development of their resources and for armaments. Only very highly specialised industries will stand much chance to export from Europe, those depending on highly technical services. On the other hand, Latin-American labour lacks the ground sense of Northern races; they are apt to run amok in their aspirations for reaching the moon. This spirit breeds, in its turn, a sort of totalitarian mind in the governing and directing classes. The seed is there ... for serious social clashes in time to come, owing to lack of fairness and self control in both camps.[14]

North America

Under the Nathans' arrangements for dividing overseas marketing between London and New Zealand (see page 98), Canada – normally regarded as the preserve of UK companies – seems at first to have come under Wellington's aegis. An agent was appointed in 1910 and then late in 1914 David Nathan visited Canada and organised a Glaxo advertising campaign, despite Alec's warning that under war conditions a substantial loss would be made.[15] In 1916 a new agent was appointed but the business did not flourish and it was not until the 1930s that a new venture in Canada, aimed also at the US market, was launched for Glaxo's pharmaceutical products. This early venture by Glaxo Laboratories into the United States was little known even among the higher echelons of management at Greenford, and its origins and performance remain wreathed in obscurity. At a later stage of Glaxo's international development, after the period covered by this book, senior executives often lamented that the group had not tried to penetrate the huge USA market, or to establish a presence there, without realising that for seven years after 1934 Glaxo Laboratories had provided most of the finance for a joint venture in North America.

In 1934 Jephcott arranged for Joseph Nathan & Company and the Montreal pharmaceutical and biological chemists, Ayerst, McKenna & Harrison (AMH) to form a joint company in the United States to sell initially Glaxo's hormonal product, Emmenin, for which AMH held the Canadian licence. Under an agreement made in October that year, AMH incorporated a new company in New York State, called Ayerst, McKenna, Harrison (United States) on the understanding that this subsidiary would be run jointly with the Nathan interests. The latter originally subscribed $25,000 in cash for 250 non-cumulative 6 per cent shares, while AMH were allotted an identical issue of shares as payment for the transfer of their US business to the New York company. The spirit of the agreement is conveyed in the contract of October 1934, which stated, *inter alia*, 'whilst it is recognised that this clause has no legal effect, it is desired to record that the spirit of this undertaking is mutual helpfulness and if it is found in practice to be unfair in any respect either party shall feel free to suggest to the other party that changes shall be made'. Nathans had an option to subscribe for further cumulative preferred shares up to a total of $100,000 in instalments as required. Other shares were issued to both parties in consideration for their giving the American company their trademarks, secret formulae, and research knowledge, giving the Canadians a majority holding. Of the eight directors, the Canadians nominated five, and Nathans three. Once the English company had subscribed its shares in full, it would be entitled to increase the number of its nominee directors to five if, for example, it was dissatisfied with the conduct of the Canadian company. By an agreement of November 1936, Nathans' rights and liabilities under the earlier agreement were transferred to Glaxo Laboratories.

In the USA, only proprietary lines were sold, particularly Emmenin. This was an oestrogene, prescribed for patients requiring oestrogenic therapy but not suffering from a gross deficiency of the hormone. Medical practitioners who prescribed Emmenin as a hormonal treatment for fertility problems were almost invariably those with wealthier practices and the product supported a generous mark-up with a high profit margin in the mid 1930s. Glaxo and AMH continued research on it, and by 1941 the product being sold was six times more potent than that of 1934.

Although Glaxo Laboratories provided most of the finance for AMH's managers to develop the American company jointly, they did so with occasional shows of reluctance or adjurations of economy and caution. When in 1937, for example, the Canadians resolved to extend their factory at Rouses Point, Jephcott wrote that Glaxo Laboratories 'accept the decisions you have reached', but forcefully urged that 'one of you at least looks upon himself as personally and particularly responsible for being devil's advocate in so far as this building expenditure is concerned, and watches every dollar's worth of expenditure'. Glaxo's experiences proved 'very conclusively the absolute necessity of this', so Jephcott wrote, citing the case of one foreign subsidiary which had recently been authorised to spend £10,000 on renovating a building, but finally presented a bill for £18,000 'with the comment that it had not been realised until the bills were presented how the additional expenditure had crept in'. Jephcott noted, 'the comments which were passed at a Board meeting held on receipt of this information, I should intensely dislike repeating to yourselves'.[16]

Jephcott visited Montreal in 1935, and was satisfied with progress made in both Canada and the USA. There were representatives working New England, New York, Chicago and Detroit, while AMH was personally responsible for the principal men in Boston. Joe Hutchinson, who had been a Glaxo medical representative in England from 1920 to 1934 and then went to Canada for the company, also covered Philadelphia. Sales in the USA from October 1934 to May 1935 totalled $23,633, but gross profit margins suffered from import duties on capsules, the high cost of packing at Rouses Point owing to the small output and the high primary production cost of Emmenin. As Jephcott reported, 'these difficulties are mainly the outcome of the immaturity of the American company and should be susceptible of self-elimination with growth'. Postal propaganda was organised along traditional British lines, but no effort was made to reach all American doctors, or even all doctors in the target areas. It was fortunate that in the USA doctors were more specialised than in Britain, because Emmenin and Glaxo's other American lines mainly interested gynaecologists, which enabled a sales effort without excessive cost. All correspondence between the two companies was directed personally through Jephcott and Joe Hutchinson.[17]

As early as 1936 Jephcott was finding fault with the management of the American company. He felt that the Canadian company had got 'on its feet so rapidly' because its directors:

were almost wholly dependent on it for their personal incomes and that the American subsidiary's relative failure was attributable to the fact that no-one's pockets would suffer severely if it failed. I gravely doubt whether the American company will be successful until, although the policy be decided by the Board, the carrying out of that policy be in the hands of one person and be conducted elsewhere than in your office in Montreal . . . I have never known any subsidiary or associated company successfully operated (in contra-distinction to directed) as a part-time occupation, the more so when the principal executives are surrounded by all the current demands upon their attention of their primary responsibilities. I was conscious of this acutely when last in Montreal and you will recall . . . discussions as to the desirable location of the American company's office. On grounds of believed economy – false economy in my opinion – it was agreed to let matters rest . . . Are we not trying to work a foreign company as a department? It can't be done. You have already found this to be so in the manufacturing sense. From experience I can assure you it is equally fallacious in every other sense.[18]

In any case the business was precarious as over three-quarters of it was in one line, Emmenin.

Exact figures on the New York company's finances are obscure, but it was stated in 1941 that the British 'put in the lion's share of the cash', while AMH's cash contribution was 'negligible'. By 1940 Glaxo Laboratories' North American representative, Joe Hutchinson, began to suspect that AMH wanted to squeeze their British partners out of the American subsidiary, and in the following year, difficulties over trans-Atlantic supply of a solvent used in manufacturing Emmenin, and over royalty payments, led to a mutual breakdown of trust, and indeed to some bitterness between London and Montreal. In October 1941 an independent arbitrator from Price Waterhouse started work in New York to dissolve the partnership and apportion the assets of the local subsidiary. Jephcott's last-minute proposal of a joint holding company to adjust the difficulties was ignored, as the Canadians contended that dual control had proved a failure; the British disputed this contention, and felt that some of AMH's directors were hoping to take advantage of Glaxo Laboratories' temporary difficulties, and get control of the American assets on the cheap. Glaxo's lowest valuation of the subsidiary was $275,000, of which their share on an asset basis in September 1941 was $170,000, excluding goodwill.[19] In the event the Price Waterhouse arbitrator valued the shares in the American subsidiary which Glaxo was selling to Canadian AMH at $224,350 comprising 1,070 preferred stock at $105 per share worth $112,350 and 1,600 common stock at $70 per share worth $112,000.

The dissolution of Glaxo Laboratories' North American interests provoked some analysis. 'Doubtless', Hutchinson wrote to the arbitrator, 'you have wondered why a company which has become so virile in the United States in a relatively short space of time with a proud earning capacity over several years should, in a year when the spending power of the American public was unprecedented and when industry was reviving at a tremendously high tempo, suffer, unlike other pharmaceutical firms, such a serious reverse in earnings'. He attributed this to the fact that since the company began operations in 1934, it had been run by an executive committee of only three directors, of whom only Hutchinson had been fully employed in the USA. It was not until November 1939 that he had been allowed a full-time sales assistant, and he felt that his colleagues had lived 'in a fool's paradise'.[20]

Unfortunately, the reactions of Glaxo Laboratories' directors to their withdrawal from the US market were not recorded in detail under the pressure of war conditions. The venture seems to have been profitable and potentially more so. Jephcott cannot possibly have found the New York subsidiary a discouraging precedent for North American enterprise, but in the event Glaxo did not attempt to re-establish itself in the USA market until the 1970s. Few British companies did establish themselves in the USA in the interwar years. Most of them looked rather to the countries of the Empire for their main overseas markets. Not only did Australia, New Zealand and South Africa appear as 'natural' markets, but also the belief voiced by Sir Alfred Mond was widely held: 'Our future stability rests upon promoting the economic prosperity of the Empire.'[21]

Australia

Since its earliest days in New Zealand, the Nathan company looked to Australia to extend its business. At the beginning, dried milk powder was sent in bulk from New Zealand to Melbourne, where it was packed in one-pound tins before marketing. By 1912 Ted Nathan (son of David Nathan) was working in Sydney, calling upon doctors and chemists with samples and literature, and shortly afterwards a firm with offices in Little Collins Street, Melbourne, called the Bacchus Marsh Condensed Milk Company, was licensed by the Wellington office to manufacture powder under the Nathans' process. At the same time, a Glaxo agent was appointed for New South Wales, and Ted Nathan was transferred to cover sales in the state of Victoria. These re-arrangements signalled Glaxo's first concerted attempt to enter the Australian market, for which the stimulus seems to have been largely fiscal. Originally there had been no import duty on New Zealand dried powder packaged at Melbourne, but subsequently a tariff was imposed as part of the 'new protectionism' of the Labour government of 1908–1913. This robbed Glaxo of any competitive edge, and it was to circumvent this difficulty that Bacchus Marsh, as a native Australian firm, was appointed to manufacture Glaxo powder.

The agreement had an early expiry date and in 1914, probably because of the insecurity of his company's future relations with the Nathans, the managing director of Bacchus Marsh instructed his staff to use their equipment operated under the licence from Wellington to devise a new product analogous to Glaxo. This was hardly fair dealing, and was done with celerity before the expiry of the licensing agreement. The Nathans may already have suspected his intentions, for it was reported in 1914 that on one occasion they made an unheralded inspection of the Bacchus Marsh plant, and the new prototype machinery had to be hurriedly concealed.[22] In the event, when the manufacturing agreement was not renewed, Bacchus Marsh marketed a new product called Lactogen, which was a homogenised version of Glaxo. For some time the Nathans had been reproducing in Australia the classic advertising campaign for the original Glaxo powder in Britain; this too was copied by Bacchus Marsh, who also employed nurses to call on mothers extolling the product. Lactogen soon became a keen competitor of Glaxo in Australia, and was bought by Nestlé, who made a great success of it. Nestlé distributed a much wider range of foodstuffs to wholesalers and retailers than Glaxo, and therefore exercised much greater influence with shopkeepers: the company also could afford larger advertising and promotion budgets.

The Australian Fisher government's protectionism provided the Nathans with their first experience of what was to become an increasingly common obstacle to the spread of their overseas business: tariff duties on imported Glaxo products. The obvious response was to begin local manufacturing in the protected market, which in later years Glaxo almost invariably did. In 1912–1913, however, the Nathans had little experience either of circumventing protectionism or of organising subsidiaries manufacturing abroad. It is not clear how they were introduced to Bacchus Marsh, or what sort of reputation the latter enjoyed, but the general judgement of the Nathans of potential business partners (as the cases of Hatmaker and Harrison showed) was not always sound. In this instance, the Wellington office itself does not seem to have felt confidence in Bacchus Marsh, since the licensing agreement was for little more than a trial period. Events proved that Wellington's policy was the worst possible one for the circumstances. The licensee realised that he lacked the licensor's confidence, and had little incentive to make their relations a success. The Nathans' almost ungracious distrust reaped a sour harvest: short-dated licences led to long-term competitors educated in Glaxo's techniques. The Bacchus Marsh *mésalliance* was a mistake from which both London and Wellington learned, and it was not repeated.

David Nathan was much involved in Australian policy at this time, and following the lapse of the Bacchus Marsh contract, he reverted to bulk imports of Glaxo which were subject to duty and packed in Melbourne. He visited Australia to investigate trade conditions and the possibility of building an Australian factory. In 1914 Victor Hyams was appointed Glaxo's purchasing agent in Australia, and he opened the head office of Glaxo Manufacturing Co (Australia) Ltd, at Castlereagh Street in Sydney. Hyams had merchandising experience, but no background in proprietary article trading: he received no salary, and had to pay his own office expenses out of his commission. The Nathans paid all advertising costs.

The contribution of Hyams to Glaxo's development in Australia was debatable. The war years of 1914–1918 were 'highly prosperous' for Glaxo in Australia, but Alec Nathan wrote in 1935 'that during the war period trade simply drifted into Glaxo', without much effort or thought by Hyams. His real business interest was merchandising and brokerage, in which he involved Glaxo, but he was no:

expert or capable proprietary article trader. When trading conditions and competition became more normal [in peacetime], he could not hold the trade . . . during the first year [1921–1922] of the Australian company's existence a loss of £30,000 (more or less) was made . . . largely due to the ignorance and superficial knowledge of the Glaxo method of building trade. Instead of the Glaxo method being intelligently adapted to Australian conditions, it was foolishly and unintelligently adopted . . . In 1922 Mr Victor Hyams visited London to get a more intimate knowledge of Joseph Nathan & Co's business and the Glaxo business, but his time was mainly occupied with what we term merchandising.[23]

Between 1920 and 1924, Hyams indulged in a certain amount of merchandise brokerage business, but after he and the Glaxo office moved from Sydney to Melbourne in 1924, he developed the merchandise business on an ambitious scale. In London there was much dissatisfaction with Ted Nathan's handling of sales and Hyams' diversion of capital into his merchandising speculations to the detriment of Glaxo's advertising budget. London's interventions to remedy matters were not well-received, and consequently were not invariably successful.

In 1921, Louis Nathan, a London managing director, visited Australia together with Archibald Sandercock (see page 46). Their activities enraged Fred Nathan in Wellington, who felt that both men lacked the requisite knowledge and sympathy for advising on Australian strategy. Fred complained: 'when these two gentlemen passed through Australia (and it was just a passing through) they were so dissatisfied with the way the business was being handled that they determined to reorganise that business, and to give control of it to the General Manager of Glaxo in London'. As a result of the visit, Hyams was sent to London, ostensibly to learn the trade in proprietary articles, including advertising and selling methods, while Sandercock directed the Australian business from London. Sandercock launched an ambitious advertising campaign, and determined to promote Glaxo in new size tins at new prices. This change entailed 'a good deal of upsetting of the trade, and the market was kept as short of stock as possible so that the old stock tin would be absorbed before the new size tin was put on the market'. These manoeuvres immediately brought discriminatory action from the Australian government under legislation dealing with the sale of foodstuffs, 'and the result was that for two months the trade fell away very grievously'. As Fred lamented to Louis Nathan, 'instead of meeting the position calmly, reviewing the whole position, and consulting with those in charge in Australia, London immediately took steps to control the expenditure in Australia, and they did it in such a drastic manner that it had so seriously affected their turnover that, in spite of anything they may do, it will be utterly impossible to run that branch of the business at a profit'.[24] A decade later, Alec Nathan noted:

There has never been a properly staffed and equipped organisation for the promotion and development of the Glaxo trade – at the best there has been a couple of men at intermittent periods calling upon the doctors with the addition of some small and totally insufficient trade contact and, finally, no persistent and consistent policy, supported by continuous propaganda and advertising suitable for the physical conditions of the country and the competition ... Victor Hyams still has and will always have a feeling that he made an ill-rewarded, ill-recognised personal sacrifice for the Company. Until recently he held the view that he had built a highly successful and profitable merchandise business from the ruins of the Glaxo business having deceived himself by not realising that he himself was a large contributory factor towards this ruin.[25]

As soon as conditions stabilised after the First World War, the Nathans reverted to their idea of starting milk drying in Australia, which David Nathan had been examining just before the outbreak of hostilities in 1914. During 1919 Fred Nathan investigated the milk producing areas of Victoria, and eventually secured a twenty-seven-acre factory site at Port Fairy, on the south western coast of the state. The factory's potential milk area extended inland for some twenty miles roughly in a semi-circle behind the factory. Although Port Fairy was 180 miles (then at least six-hours train journey) from Melbourne, there were attractively low freight charges on coastal shipping between the two places.

Fred Nathan remained in overall charge of the Port Fairy project and recruited Harold Revell to negotiate with milk suppliers in Illowa and adjacent districts. These suppliers had previously sold to Nestlé's factory at Dennington, ten miles from Port Fairy, outside Warnambool, and when the Nathans' intention to start milk drying in Victoria was discovered by Nestlé, the latter unsuccessfully resorted to legal action. In August 1919 Revell reached agreement with the milk producers, and became the first Secretary of the newly formed South Western Co-operative Milk & Trading Company which entered contractual relations with Glaxo similar to those being agreed with local milk producers in New Zealand at the same time (see pages 50–1). Building began in 1920 of a milk-drying factory with ten dual roller drying machines, largely on the lines of the Matangi factory in New Zealand. The factory opened for drying on 21 October, in the middle of a visit of some months' duration by Harry and Doris Jephcott who established the chemical and bacteriological testing routines.

In April 1921 Glaxo Manufacturing (Australia) Ltd was incorporated at Sydney with capital of £500,000, with the Port Fairy facilities standing in its books at a value of £73,782. At the same time another local subsidiary, Joseph Nathan & Co (Australia) Ltd, was also registered; the companies were merged in 1928 to become Joseph Nathan & Co (Australia) Pty Ltd. As Hyams was clearly preoccupied with merchandising and brokerage, E. W. Doutch, who was recruited as Secretary of Glaxo Manufacturing in 1921, largely took responsibility for operating Port Fairy. Ted Doutch was a large man of intimidating appearance who suffered recurrent nervous troubles as a result of his experiences during the First World War: on several occasions during the interwar period he vanished from the office on rest cures. Hyams was appointed in 1920 as Director and General Manager at a salary of £1,250 without commission, while Ted Nathan was put in charge of Glaxo sales. It is noticeable that, as in both New Zealand and London, most of the senior positions were held by the Nathans' co-religionists (men like Rose, Wolff, Hyams or Doutch), although in the 1920s gentiles like Jephcott and Randall were rising in the organisation.

The manager at Port Fairy throughout almost all the interwar period was an Irishman, Paddy Walsh, who was recruited by the Nathans from New Zealand, where he had experience of milk processing. At an early stage in Port Fairy's history, the Nathans told Walsh that they were thinking of closing the factory and dismissing him, as an economy, but that if he could keep the place in profit, without bothering head office in Melbourne or Sydney, they would let it survive. As a result, Walsh ran the place in a rough and autocratic manner unusual even by Australian standards. He was known to stand over workers loading railway wagons, brandishing his shillelagh, and in an area with high seasonal unemployment, would pay his workers for only five hours work daily, even though the men mostly worked another eight hours daily: he made it clear that if they objected, they could leave. His exploits, not only at the factory, but among the bars and women at Port Fairy, were legendary in the town some forty years after his retirement, and were in striking contrast to the methods of some of the managers sent from England in the 1950s (see page 307). Walsh is remembered by his former workers as a 'terribly hard' employer, 'a tyrant' with 'no scruples', and 'no sympathies with anyone' who was 'stingy'. His favourite *obiter dictum* was 'Always sack the best men: by Jesu it makes the other bastards work'; in local parlance, he was a 'hard doer'. By the late 1930s, the Nathans were anxious to limit Walsh's power, and they sent some younger managers to join him at Port Fairy. This led to some years of strife before Glaxo finally dislodged him from the factory after the Second World War.[26]

However, operations at Port Fairy had scarcely begun before Glaxo was hit by the severe worldwide slump in demand. Australian production of Glaxo powder, having risen from 94.75 tons in the first half of 1921 to 110.75 tons in the second half, fell to 105.5 tons and 96 tons for the comparable periods in 1922. London's requirements were far exceeded by the output of the four New Zealand drying factories now supplemented by Port Fairy: indeed in 1922 Wellington told the Australians that London only needed sufficient new milk powder to freshen up stock. Orders allotted to Port Fairy were drastically reduced. It became imperative to find alternative uses for the milk which the Nathans had contracted to take but which exceeded requirements. A decision was taken therefore to diversify into cheese and butter manufacture. In 1922 a large cheese factory with small curing room and a butter-making section was opened, with the products marketed under the Bonnieport brand (derived from the conjunction of Port Fairy with the slogan 'Glaxo makes *bonnie* babies'). Bonnieport cheese won top-grade awards in export cheese in both 1931–1932 and 1932–1933, and

was a considerable success. In 1926 Port Fairy began supplying cheese to the
Kraft Company, whose annual orders had risen to 700 tons by 1933; the
virtual cessation of milk powder export orders between 1927 and 1933 led to
a proposal in 1931 that the Port Fairy factory should be sold to the Kraft
Company for £75,000. But in the event no sale resulted from the proposal.

By the mid 1930s, when London's demand for milk powder revived,
Paddy Walsh wished to give precedence to cheese production. After
discussions in 1935–1936, the London office enforced the decision that
priority be given to milk drying, but manufacturing milk powder for export
did not become Port Fairy's primary work until after the formation of Glaxo
Laboratories (Australia) Ltd in 1938. During the depression years, especially
after 1929, a bare minimum was spent on maintaining the milk powder
plant, and when exports to Britain were resumed, various latent defects
materialised. Both London and Wellington sent men to Port Fairy in 1936 to
reorganise the plant and instil current milk-drying practices into the
Australia management. After 1931, when Glaxo began the limited manufacture in Australia of some of its vitamin products, installing its equipment in
a section of the South Yarra factory of White, Tomkins & Courage, the
Nathans also become involved in marketing the latter firm's Jelly Crystals
and Essences, and developed its own range of grocers' sundries such as
cordials, imitation essences and creamy shaped objects.

The pharmaceutical business made a modest beginning with unspectacu-
lar growth until 1934. Its inauguration occurred at a time when the overall
Australian business, including Hyams' brokerage activities, was hit by the
depression. In July 1931 it was estimated that the following year's turnover
would fall by 10 per cent to £327,000. In 1932 the unproductive office in
Adelaide was shut and there were other retrenchments of sales staff in
Sydney. The Melbourne management urged in 1933 that Glaxo should begin
wireless advertising of babyfoods in Australia, but London vetoed this
proposal, and insisted that the advertising effort should be concentrated on
medical representation. The babyfoods business continued to deteriorate
until it reached a critical position in 1934 when Hyams, reviewing the
position, argued that, unless another £500 was allocated to babyfood
advertising, sales would soon vanish entirely. London office, whose hold on
the Australian Glaxo department was steadily strengthening, rejected
Hyams' idea, and Alec Nathan left for Australia with the avowed aim of
establishing a separate organisation for the Glaxo department there. This
news was badly received in Melbourne: Doutch complained that London
were 'treating us like boys', and his colleagues agreed bitterly that London
had not grasped that grown men were in charge in Australia.[27]

Alec Nathan reached Melbourne in October 1934, and enforced a wide-
ranging reconstruction of the business. Alec had little personal patience with

Hyams and gave his regime short shrift. So far as the Glaxo side of the Nathan business was concerned, he made several reforms: the existing Glaxo division was expanded to cover sales as well as manufacturing; Glaxo Laboratories in London in future directed sales policy and advised on personnel matters, as well as supplying technical advice as hitherto. Separate books and accounts were kept, so that the operation of the Glaxo business could be seen separately from the general business. The senior management of Joseph Nathan & Co. (Australia) Pty Ltd, was purged by Alec in the months that followed. Crucially, in January 1935 Hyams was replaced as chairman by Edwin Nixon (a distinguished Melbourne accountant, with high-level civil service connections, who was later knighted for his wartime munitions work) and Doutch was succeeded as Secretary, by Rupert Pearce. It was also agreed that all pharmaceuticals which could be imported from London at a lower cost, with the exception of Glaxo, Ostomalt and Glucose-D, would not be packed in Australia. When economic recovery stimulated a rise in the demand for dried milk, Jephcott visited Australia in 1938. He made an agreement with the Hyams, father and son, who bought the merchandising business and resigned from the Glaxo company. Thereafter the two pursued their separate paths.

India

In India, traditionally there was a large overseas market for British manufactured goods and it proved no exception to the rule for Glaxo. In the interwar years it was, according to Alec Nathan, the most profitable overseas Glaxo business.[28] The London office had appointed H. J. Foster as agent there in 1914. Officially part of the New Zealand office's territory at that date, India was supplied during the First World War with Glaxo powder from New Zealand. There were problems of quality and continuity of supply but it was not until 1919 that it was decided that it was possible to supply India from London. In 1924 H. J. Foster incorporated his business as a private company. The Nathans took an interest in the company and when Foster died in 1925 they acquired the rest of the shares from his estate.[29] Edward Foster (no relation of H. J. Foster) then went to India to take over the business on Glaxo's behalf. Before the First World War he had been attached to the Glaxo office in London with the remit 'to visit, investigate and open up trade connections in China'. Although he made some progress the war prevented further active propaganda or action. In 1919 there was a row between David Nathan in Wellington and Alec Nathan over the former's obstinate determination to appoint his son, Ted, as representative in China. 'David must be a man without a well-defined moral sense', Alec wrote.[30] It was a storm in a teacup; there cannot have been any great

25 Glaxo's Indian factory – showing the H J Foster name.

expectations of China as a market for it was dominated by the Japanese whose infringement of patent rights amounted, as early as 1908, to what was generally regarded as piracy.[31]

Alec Nathan had great confidence in Edward Foster's ability and, from 1925, Foster had a free hand in India to develop the business. In the summer of 1930 the relationships between the London office and all the overseas branches, and especially New Zealand, were urgently scrutinised in the light of the world economic crisis. The Glaxo committee in London decided that a reconstruction of the export organisation was overdue and they offered the management of the Export Department to Foster.

This, however, posed the problem of what to do about India. Jephcott, Wolff, Rose and Alec Nathan were all anxious about the future of Indian sales if Foster returned to London. As Alec Nathan wrote to Wellington in June 1930, 'you can realise that it would not do for us to reorganise the English internal export organisation at a cost that would mean a loss of efficiency and of the profit earning capacity of the Indian organisation'.[32] They therefore hoped, somewhat unrealistically, that although living in London and directing the Glaxo export department, Foster would remain 'super-in-charge' of the Indian company, and would make 'short, spasmodic and intermittent visits to India' to oversee the work there. In order to arm him with the necessary authority throughout the Glaxo organisation, the

London directors of Joseph Nathan unanimously proposed electing Foster to their board. Indeed, he made this a condition of acceptance, arguing that for him to resign as managing director of the firm in India to become merely general manager of a London export department, would hurt both his own and his firm's prestige, and might even injure the latter's financial standing.[33]

Here a major snag was met. According to the Articles of Association of Joseph Nathan & Company, it could have a maximum of nine directors. As there were then only eight, Foster could be elected without altering the Articles and without difficulty, but certain of the London directors then insisted that Hugo Wolff, 'by reason of his work and the length of his service', and 'especially in consideration of the later growth and development of the Glaxo business . . . has a "right" . . . to the vacant position as a director in priority to Mr E. W. Foster'. They tried to solve this puzzle by asking Pacey and Fred Nathan in New Zealand if they would 'voluntarily and spontaneously decide to resign' their directorships in the parent company because 'they are so far separated from . . . the seat of Government'.[34] Unsurprisingly both Wellington directors rejected this proposal. They urged that it was wrong to appoint Wolff to the board merely on the basis of his length of service, and that the appointment should go to whoever was best suited by personality and experience. The request for their retirement, however delicately phrased, so Fred wrote, 'is exploiting rather unfairly the position in which you find yourselves'.[35] As a result of this impasse, Foster remained in India, and did not join the London office, which was perhaps as well since his abilities were exaggerated by his supporters and the plan for him to remain 'super-in-charge' of India was unlikely to work in practice. This was probably the last occasion on which the passionate personal emotions of the Nathans, with their heightened resentments and somewhat exaggerated loyalties to Hugo Wolff, seriously disrupted the strategy of Glaxo.

Foster died in 1933 and, partly as a result, Jephcott made a long-planned visit to India in the following year. Foster's death left the Indian business in disarray. He had taken none of his subordinates into his confidence, so that it proved impossible to fathom much of what he had been doing. Consultations with his European staff were unknown, and the first such consultation meeting which his successor E. L. C. Gwilt (see page 273) held after Foster's death caused something of a sensation in the office. Foster had neglected personal contact with his own sub-offices, and had paid little attention to his staff's reports from Calcutta or Madras. He had also failed to recognise or encourage his best assistants. As Jephcott wrote in 1934:

Whatever was the reason for getting rid of our old agent Katarah in Karachi it has been a great mistake. We picked up a dud with no organisation. K[atarah] is a power in that area. He took up C[ow] & G[ate] and has just wiped us out of the North West

District. In Colombo for many months C[ow] & G[ate] have been underselling us. We have now only the shreds of the trade.[36]

Foster had regarded the firm as doing agency business, with the Glaxo department in London merely his principals. In 1930–1931, after the failure of the attempt to recruit him to London as export manager, he anxiously sought additional non-Glaxo business to increase his firm's gross income. In doing so, he diverted much of his personal time and attention, together with that of his staff, from Glaxo agency work to pushing soap produced locally by the Tata Oil Mills and other products such as Maclean's toothpaste and Aspro brand aspirin: indeed, he did this to an extent which would not have been acceptable to London office had it been known to them.

Subsequently the increase in pharmaceutical business, with its higher margin of gross profit, drew his flagging attention back to Glaxo. Even so Jephcott believed that Foster was 'at sea with the pharmaceutical business', which was conducted on unorthodox lines. After Foster's death, Jephcott reported that the Bombay staff were doing useful work, but clearly had 'lacked the leadership of someone who was thoroughly *au fait* with the pharmaceutical business'. One senior European employee of Foster's in Bombay told Jephcott in 1934, 'we have always looked upon this as purely an Indian agency business'. Jephcott thought this attitude was disastrous, and that the blame for it lay in London and not in India. He was convinced that, had the total gross profit which arose on Glaxo proprietary articles appeared in the Foster firm's books, this incentive would have stimulated sales considerably.[37]

During Jephcott's Indian tour he and Gwilt personally interviewed every European member of the staff in Bombay, Calcutta and Madras, every Indian medical representative and every Indian broker. They contacted many wholesale and retail dealers in the bazaars of Bombay, Delhi, Calcutta and Madras. Jephcott put much effort and thought into these interviews. In dealing with the Indian brokers and representatives, for example, he decided that it was essential to see them individually, as he found that otherwise the most fluent English speaker so dominated the proceedings that little or no information was obtained from the others. Moreover, it was only by individual interviews that he could overcome the Indian tendency to give polite and palatable answers: it required all of Jephcott's skill and patience to conduct cross-examinations without posing leading questions. But by the end of this exhaustive and exhausting process, Jephcott believed himself expert in the Indian market. His findings were intriguing.

Without exception, every representative, broker and dealer identified economic circumstances as the chief cause of the fall in Glaxo business in the last years of Foster's life. They subsequently admitted that the poor quality of Glaxo's stocks in India had influenced this decline, but none of them placed much emphasis on that. All agreed that more than half of their existing trade was with the native population: estimates varied from 50 per cent to 90 per cent, and Jephcott concluded that 75 or 80 per cent was the correct aggregate figure.

Jephcott discovered (what had apparently not been realised by London during Foster's lifetime) that few Europeans, or Europeanised Indians, bought Glaxo products and that Glaxo's competitors had almost entirely captured the European trade. A large proportion of the Anglo-Indian markets, and that of Indians in lesser official jobs, had also been gained by competitors. For the vast majority of Glaxo consumers, price was the primary consideration, mainly because Glaxo tins were not dated, and were therefore distrusted by educated customers. Glaxo's medical representatives in particular reported that doctors repeatedly asked why their tins were undated.

Representatives and brokers unanimously condemned Foster's business methods which had led to marked overstocking. Until shortly before Foster's death, stock was only replaced when actual complaints were received. This meant that considerable amounts of deteriorated stocks existed in the market, especially after sales declined in the early 1930s. In 1933 a system of stock examination and replacement was adopted, the stocks of dealers being inspected and all bearing codemarks of twelve months or more being replaced or credited. This helped to clear the market, but was insufficient, partly because twelve months after packing date was too long, and partly because brokers were unable to visit all stockists. While Jephcott was in India in 1934, various improvements in packing and dating were agreed.

Jephcott also found Glaxo's advertising in decline. Much of the Indian advertising was conceived and designed in London, and although talented in its way, scarcely met the needs of the market. The chief preoccupation of the Bombay office had been to avoid paying an advertising agent's commission, an objective achieved only to the wider detriment of the business. Jephcott was disappointed to find that there was no native advertising agency, but as educated Indians considered such work carried lower social prestige than other professions, there were in Bombay only three advertising agencies, of which one was manifestly incompetent. Another, J. Walter Thompson, had to decline Jephcott's overtures because Horlicks, whose account they were already handling, objected. In the event, the third agency, Stronachs, proved suitable, and campaigns better attuned to local conditions were launched.

The appointment of a trained pharmacist, Reg Haryott, marked a change of emphasis, with Glaxo proprietary pharmaceuticals taking an increasing amount of business. To support Gwilt's attempts to build a solid organisation to replace Edward Foster's autocracy, the Indian company was given an increased commission of 14 per cent on Glaxo sales. In expanding the administration of the Indian company, Gwilt encountered some problems in recruiting European staff of sufficient calibre, while resident suspicion of Indian labour persisted. Telegrams were sent between Greenford and Bombay in code: Jephcott felt uneasy about dictating letters in India. Gwilt noted that Glaxo's auditors considered that the chances of fraud in India were ten times as great as in England. Fosters gradually relinquished the other agency businesses so that, by 1937, Gwilt reported that, with turnover up to £200,000, 54 per cent of the profit of £38,000 was contributed by Glaxo pharmaceuticals, 44 per cent by Glaxo proprietaries including Ostermilk and only 2 per cent from business for other than the parent company. The capital of H. J. Foster was increased from £11,250 to £71,250 (Rs 9.5 lakhs) in 1938, so as to reflect better the earning power of the company and to increase the manufacturing side of the business.

From the time of the boycott of British goods organised by Gandhi, members of the Foster agency had been aware of the need to begin local manufacture, but Jephcott was largely responsible for the London office approaching this proposition with reserve. Packing of Glaxo powder from imported bulk milk powder began in 1933 at Sewri, Bombay and these operations were expanded with the construction of a new packing factory and offices at Worli, involving an investment of £36,600, which was completed in 1939. In the early 1930s milk powder supplied to the Indian company from New Zealand, via Britain, often arrived with slight rancidity. Although a specialist from Greenford was sent out to address this problem, the quality of the milk powder was only stabilised when the better facilities of the '1939 Building' at Worli became operative. Demand for Glaxo products improved correspondingly and India retained its position as Glaxo's largest overseas business at the end of the 1930s.

Glaxo in Italy

British businessmen did not, on the whole, look to compete in European markets in the interwar years. In 1919 Alec Nathan wrote: 'business will have to be done with Germany but no chances or risk can be taken – we know in spite of written agreements that they are only scraps of paper to them'.[38] Germany, however, had traditionally a low consumption of dried milk powder for infant feeding, and mothers there normally used – under medical advice – boiled cows' milk. By 1918, Britain aside, the only European countries in which dried milk was widely used, were France and Belgium. But the most dynamic, if not the most stable, of the European countries was Italy, described as early as 1890 by the Marquess of Dufferin and Ava as 'a little too enterprising' for British comfort.[39] The Italians were not a nation who generally attracted British business, although some multinationals such as Courtaulds and Vickers made a considerable effort there. However, for the Nathans in the 1920s, Italy seemed the most promising European opportunity and, several generations later, the Italian subsidiary proved a centre of enterprise and strategy.

In March 1923 Glaxo appointed a Verona firm of merchants and distributors, Carattoni & Monti, as its exclusive distribution agents for Italy and the Italian colonies, an agreement renewed in July 1926 and again in June 1929. In October of the latter year, the London director, Frederick Randall, and Ernest Samuel (a Nathan family connection; see page 128), while *en route* to Greece, discussed with Count Bompiani, the director of Carattoni & Monti responsible for the Glaxo agency, the possibility of forming a company owned jointly by Carattoni & Monti and the Nathans to conduct the Glaxo and possibly other agency business. In recommending this idea, Randall wrote from Verona:

the basis of this company should be the purchase of Ostelin from London and the packing of the product here . . . The idea behind this new company would be to build slowly and as required an organisation capable of giving the complete service of marketing, advertising, selling and – if desirable – distributing proprietary articles. This could be done on the back of the savings which . . . can be effected by packing Ostelin here.[40]

Bompiani was the son-in-law of Monti, and Randall anticipated good work from him if he could be persuaded to abandon his sundry other interests.

But the proposal for Nathans to form a joint company with Carattoni & Monti was declined by the London directors as unsound and uneconomic. Following the rejection of his suggestion, Randall advised that 'the best way to provide for the undoubted need of our own established organisation in Italy is to have a young and active London-trained man living in the territory, gradually over a period of two or three years becoming acquainted with every agent and sub-agent who handles our goods, and the duty of such local representatives should include not only learning the language but becoming acquainted with all the various districts'.[41]

The purely Glaxo section of Carattoni & Monti's business (covering propaganda and circularising by fifteen clerks, mostly young girls) cost £1,800 in 1929, excluding pension contributions. Randall wrote:

The handling of labour in Italy is a delicate process and employers have to work very carefully as otherwise disgruntled staffs are apt to go to leading Fascisti officials or to their unions . . . [who] enforce often unfair terms on employers. The Government policy is to foster advances to gigantic organisations, such as Fiat, Snia Viscosa, etc., to give the country a good appearance in the eyes of other nations, but small traders find it difficult to obtain sufficient credit.[42]

He also advised:

from observations made and discussions overheard it does seem that it is always better, even if a little more costly to separate our propaganda and advertising from distribution. In effect, in Italy the method adopted has been to not only build an organisation for someone else, which could be a most effective instrument in the hands of a competitor like the Italian milk firm, Polengi, if we removed our agency and left the organisation unemployed, but we have also educated Count Bompiani and staffs in our method and mentality. We have given him for nothing the great skill accumulated in the Glaxo organisation over a long period of years, and in effect we are now asked to pay him for the ability which we have conferred upon him at our expense.[43]

This distrust of Bompiani must have revived memories of the Australian debacle of 1913–1914 when Bacchus Marsh learnt the Glaxo techniques before marketing their own Lactogen, which under Nestlé's direction later became such an uncomfortable competitor. Partly as a result of Randall's apprehensions, discussions were resumed in 1930, and in the following year it was agreed that the Nathans would form an Italian company, which would appoint Carattoni & Monti as their distributors.

Earlier in 1930, H. A. (Peter) Gent (a Cambridge graduate in law and modern languages) had become the Nathans' resident representative in Italy. He and Bompiani were appointed managing directors of the new company S.A. Italiana Nathan Bompiani, which was formed in March 1932: the other directors were Commendatore Monti, Alec Nathan and Randall. Gent from the outset showed himself to be intelligent, sage and diplomatic in handling both staff and outsiders. As a young man he regarded Jephcott as his mentor. Fluent on paper and persuasive in discussion, Gent was charming and humorous; by the standards of most Glaxo managing directors overseas, he was stylish, dashing and distinctive for his finely honed financial sense. He remained responsible for the Italian company throughout the period covered by this book and repeatedly proved his ability in all aspects of the business (see chapter 16).

The Nathans subscribed 80 per cent (about £4,000) of the total capital of 500,000 lire of the new company, with 20 per cent held by Monti, Bompiani and Dr Carattoni. This £4,000 constituted the only money directly invested in the Italian subsidiary for almost half a century: thereafter, all developments and expansion were funded from internal resources. Monti and Bompiani were to receive 10 per cent of the new company's net profits by way of remuneration.

In its first full year of operations, sales totalling 1.2 million lire (£13,333) yielded profits of 35,899.5 lire (£400) representing only a 3 per cent return. From the outset in 1931 the possibility of local manufacture of Glaxo powder was considered, and increases in import duties in 1933 brought this under urgent consideration, but low annual sales of about 70 tons led to its rejection then. There were further difficulties following the imposition of new import quotas in 1935, although Gent and Bompiani made official representations that the value of the primary products which Glaxo imported was minimal against the value of Italian materials employed in the industry. By 1937 Bompiani had developed his own perfumery business, and spent so little time on Glaxo matters that Gent sought his resignation. After painfully protracted negotiations over the valuation of Bompiani's shareholding, he finally resigned as a director in November 1938.

London was cautious about the development of the Italian business. Randall wrote after his tour of Italy, Greece and Turkey in 1929:

Generally in all countries, before attempting to formulate either a scheme for a company or a basis for amalgamation with other interests, I made careful investigations as to business customs, accountancy methods, the conduct of limited companies, and other forms of business organisation, cost of living, supply of and demand for suitable personnel, the basis of credit in the country and the average risk involved, the cost of capital and whether capital was available to small or large traders, the conditions governing . . . the marketing of shares in companies, etc.

Such systematic examination of overseas markets before embarking upon investments was by no means the hallmark of all British companies in the inter-war period, although a more typical mixture of canniness and insularity was revealed by Randall's observations of 1929

that in negotiating with businessmen of other nationalities it is difficult always to get them to give you hard facts on which you can rely without very long and arduous discussions . . . It is a trait of the foreigner that when approached by an English firm, his ideas of remuneration are magnified many times more than if he were negotiating with one of his own countrymen.[44]

Premises had been rented in 1931 in Via Filopanti in Verona for the local packing of Glaxo powder and of Ostelin and Adexolin. Colloidal Calcium with Ostelin was also packed locally from imported filled ampoules. Operations were difficult because of the Mussolini regime's policy of autarchy, which prevented the registration of new products; following the imposition of severe import restrictions in 1935–1936, a small laboratory (under an English chemist) was installed for the local manufacture of Colloidal Calcium and Ostelin, for which the trade name Calci-Ostelin was registered in 1938. In 1936, when the company's name was changed to S.A. Italiana Laboratori Glaxo, Jephcott succeeded Alec Nathan as its president.

In the late 1930s there was considerable demand in Italy for vitamin B1 ampoules and tablets, but their introduction by Glaxo Laboratories was delayed because they could not achieve a competitive price. Gent had hoped to introduce a range of new Glaxo products, but new registrations were rendered impossible by the political situation. Ostelin, Calci-Ostelin, Adexolin and Erbolin therefore remained the only products marketed before the war. By 1939 Glaxo had an established base in Italy but sales remained sluggish and profits low.

Glaxo in Greece

During the 1920s the Glaxo department acquired as its agent in Greece Stamatis Harvalias (1889–1949), although in the early days no formal written agreement existed. Both sides were free to terminate the arrangement at any time, and the relationship was only sustained by mutual satisfaction and goodwill. At the time of his appointment Harvalias was not a man of substantial means, and for some years the Nathans' Glaxo department carried the risk of his trade. By the end of the 1920s thought was being given in London to the possibility of strengthening the links with Harvalias and developing business in Greece, possibly by means of a joint venture sales company. Frederick Randall was sent to Greece in 1929 to explore this possibility. Reporting on his return, he paid tribute to the enthusiastic enterprise of Harvalias, but betrayed an English horror at Balkan business methods, reflecting both the commercial inexperience of the Glaxo department in the 1920s and the exacting standards of probity which Alec Nathan had inculcated into his staff. 'From his ability, we have derived substantial service and today in Greece Glaxo appears to be a household word . . . so that . . . a change of agent might . . . possibly reduce results', so Randall wrote of Harvalias:

The agent himself has been built up from a business point of view and from a knowledge of proprietary trading . . . by his contact with . . . the Glaxo department. This is again an example of the results obtained by educating a man in how to conduct a business and leaving him the whole complete organisation within his . . . direction. He has now obtained a position of some substance and has an independent point of view, but like most foreigners commences by asking the impossible when negotiating with an Englishman.

In obtaining figures from him he was perfectly frank . . . although we were not in a position to say that such information was correct or otherwise. When the figures given by him were analysed and assessed, obviously to his detriment, he then produced several more books, which according to him proved quite a new set of circumstances. Never at any time during the negotiations was he prepared to discuss facts as they really existed . . . One should visualise the fluidity of Harvalias's mind pitted against the determination of the English mind to get down to facts, and when, after days of debating, the English mind says that he cannot recommend his principal to enter upon the quicksand of Greek business conditions . . . It is a common phase of business life out there to keep two complete sets of books. In addition, it is quite customary for agents . . . to go to the manufacturers' offices and receive payment in money which never goes into any books . . . we should be merely inviting complete dissatisfaction to attempt to keep alongside a man schooled in such methods which are common to the whole business community . . . I emphatically recommend the board not to embark upon a local company in association with a man established in business in Greece ... A study of Greek conditions on the spot is an ample illustration of the danger of sitting down in a London office and hearing about recounted everyday events and customs in business circles in Athens. Unless one has lived, even for a few days, amongst such circumstances one is apt to overemphasise their importance.[45]

Despite Randall's views, in 1932 Glaxo bought a 50 per cent holding (7,500 shares) in the Stam Harvalias Commercial and Manufacturing Company of Athens.

Originally the company was conceived purely as an agency company, handling medical foods and vitamin preparations on a commission basis, but this was revised in 1933 when the preparation and packing of Ostelin and Adexolin, and the packing of ampoules, was undertaken locally. The company continued to be supplied with Calciferol and vitamin A concentrates from Britain, and originally was similarly supplied with ampoules in bulk; but under later Greek legislation, any product (such as filled ampoules) which only required to be packed and underwent no preparation or manufacture, was deemed a pharmaceutical speciality, and its import from Britain was forbidden.

From the outset Harvalias considered that the future growth of Glaxo's range of products would lie in pharmaceuticals, and he concentrated even his attempts to market their food products on Greek chemists' shops. Greek grocers were selling dried milk to the public at a profit varying between 5 and 7.5 per cent: for the chemists this was an insufficient margin, and Harvalias stirred their interest by allowing them an extra discount of 5 per cent on their invoices. Moreover, he confined the chemists to sales of Glaxo half-cream powder, Babeurre Glaxo, and Defiance products bought and sold on medical advice.

When Glaxo first entered the Greek market they had to compete with the established Nutricia range of products which cost up to 25 per cent less than Glaxo's equivalent items. There was a sizeable demand for dried milk for infants as fresh milk was unsafe for feeding babies, although in 1933 a pioneer factory, arranged on an American system, was opened in Athens to bottle pasteurised milk. Doctors' advice and prescriptions were the main forces in the market, and it was impossible for Harvalias to run a major advertising campaign aimed at either the medical profession or the public, both because his company could not afford it and because of fears that it would provoke a chauvinist political or fiscal response against the British connection. In 1934, Nestlé began systematic preliminary work on entering the Greek market as rivals to Nutricia and Glaxo, and when Harvalias visited Corinth in October that year he found Nestlé's representative calling on chemists and doctors of the city introducing a half-cream powder called

Nestogen and distributing samples, thermometers and other little presents. Despite these obstacles, Harvalias claimed by November 1934 that 'the majority of Chemists in the great towns sell Glaxo foods'.[46]

The German firm of Bayer held a high reputation in Greece, and their Vigantol brand was well-established when Glaxo began marketing Ostelin liquid in competition. Indeed, in 1937 the British representative in Athens, Sir Sydney Waterlow, in describing Nazi Germany's calculated penetration of the vulnerable Greek economy, listed pharmaceutical products as among the German exports which held predominance in Greece.[47] Ostelin liquid of 5,000 units was sold for 40 drachmas, whereas Vigantol, with 10,000 units, cost 75 drachmas: and generally, doctors regarded the German vitamin product as better value and more effective. Harvalias had much more success with Ostelin ampoules, free samples of which were unsparingly sent to doctors, often with a favourable response.

Until 1935 Harvalias did not market Adexolin aggressively. But, as he told Jephcott in November 1934, 'my increased knowledge in connection with Vitamin A encourages me to extend my activities, but the means at my disposal do not permit to carry out a scheme with the object of fully persuading doctors and Mothers of the importance of Vitamin A to the Embryo, Baby & Child . . . During the current year I shall present Adexolin as substitute of Cod Liver oil, the consumption of which is important in Greece. I shall watch the product and according to how it moves along, I shall develop my activities.'[48]

Other minor problems also arose. Ernest L. Samuel, a businessman living in Jerusalem who seems to have been a family friend of the Nathans, was an active (but not always effective) director of the Harvalias company in the early days. He also, amid his other commitments, represented the Nathans' commercial interests in Turkey and the Middle East. At the insistence of his wife, he maintained homes in both England and Palestine, between which he and she travelled frequently. He expected the Nathan companies to shoulder the consequent expense, 'and the total cost of Mr Samuel and his wife', as Jephcott noted drily in 1934, was borne by the Glaxo department. As Samuel had little understanding of the pharmaceutical business, Jephcott insisted to Alec Nathan that it was 'an uneconomic and unbusinesslike procedure to extend the sphere of Mr Samuel's activities', and indeed that 'the indefinite continuance' of Samuel's arrangement with Glaxo 'cannot be justified on business grounds'.[49] As part of his campaign in the 1930s to be rid of the Nathans' 'kissing kin' from the company's overseas representation, he proposed that Samuel be paid £300 for visiting Turkey twice a year for a total of a month or six weeks, and eventually got his way, as was his wont.

Glaxo's activities in Greece were closely conditioned by the political and economic environment there. With a rebellion in March 1935, and the restoration of the monarchy in November of that year, there was considerable political unrest, and by August 1936, as the British Envoy in Athens reported, 'the abuse of party politics had brought the country to a state of disintegration'.[50] Political disorder was mirrored by a desperately improvised economic policy. With a rapidly dwindling gold reserve and a dangerous expansion of credit, financial collapse seemed imminent. On 4 August, to resolve this crisis, a Greek 'strong man', General Joannes Metaxas, seized power, and imposed a dictatorship (or 'concentration of powers', as it was euphemistically described. The Constitution was suspended, and an economic programme swiftly announced which embodied budgetary retrenchment, stabilisation of domestic and foreign credit, and coordination of all national productive resources by State planning. The Metaxas regime worked with surprising success for several years; as with other European dictators of the period, the spread of communism was 'parried by boons showered on the underdog' in conjunction with a public works programme characterised by 'patriotic ambition combined with excessive self-confidence'.[51]

Of even more importance to Glaxo, Metaxas increased the Bank of Greece's gold cover by drastic exchange and import restrictions, maintained the previous legislation of 1934–1935 that prohibited certain classes of trained mechanical and scientific work to be done by foreigners, and imposed a change on foreign work permits that amounted to a swingeing tax.[52] These developments immediately affected Glaxo Laboratories' Greek business, and were carefully monitored by Jephcott. He visited Athens in November 1936, during the early months of Metaxas' rule, and on his return submitted a comprehensive report on the prospects for business there. Greece, he wrote:

is a country of limited population, roughly 6 million or one seventh that of Italy, and the vast proportion of that population is poor. As a market in point of potential business it is to be compared with, say, the million and a quarter of New Zealand.

Greece is now under an absolute dictatorship and the nationalistic tendency is marked. The opinion locally is that this state of affairs will last and may create more settled conditions. In the meantime foreign trade and business relations are under severe restrictions ... Exchange and foreign trade, whether import or export, are strictly controlled. Importations are by permit only. As far as England is concerned, there is no trade agreement and a heavy adverse trade balance in the Greek sense. A trade agreement ... has just been concluded with Italy.

As to the head of the business, Jephcott wrote that:

Mr Harvalias is desirous, almost to the point of obsession, of having the financial position of the company of outstanding strength and above any possible reproach. This is, I believe, a reflection of the esteem in which he holds his association with a substantial English company; nor has he been lacking in personal sacrifice in order to live up to his ideals.[53]

Although Harvalias was entitled as managing director, under the articles of association, to a monthly salary of 23,500 drachmas plus 10 per cent of profits, between 1931 and 1933 when the company was making a loss, he voluntarily reduced his salary to 18,000 drachmas, nor did he restore it to its old level in the profitable years, 1934–1936. He preferred to restrict himself to an annual salary equivalent to £400, and to forego his percentage of profits and share dividend, in order to place the company in a stronger position. As a result of this self-sacrifice, and of the conservative financial policy pursued by Harvalias, the balance sheet, so Jephcott wrote in 1936:

is probably steadier than that of any of our subsidiary companies. There is no goodwill, all the assets are tangible and conservatively valued, and cash in hand exceeds two-thirds of the total capital. In other words, at a break-up valuation our shares are probably covered, whilst as a going concern they are worth probably twice their par value.[54]

In other ways, too, Harvalias seemed an ideal partner. Around 1934, as his own responsibility, he built a new factory in Athens for the expanding pharmaceutical business. Jephcott reported to Alec Nathan that:

The whole factory was spotlessly clean and will probably be kept so even when there are manufacturing operations in progress, for Mr Harvalias has a real sense of tidiness and labour is cheap. Whilst taken as a whole it is too cut up and too full of amateurish mechanical contrivances to appeal to the English eye, that should not detract from the credit due to the courage and care which have gone to its building. Mr Harvalias was warmly congratulated on it. It is unquestionably the apple of his eye.[55]

The Greek company bore all propaganda costs, consisting principally of circulars and samples. The cost of producing and distributing Baby Books was also carried by the company, but Harvalias judged (and Jephcott agreed) that further advertising in the public press would be impolitic and provocative, and might result in prohibition of Glaxo Laboratories' imports. They did, however, insert advertising in three Greek medical journals and two trade papers costing a total of about £50 in 1936–1937. There was only limited representation and, until the range of products was widened, additional costs incurred by broadening the sales representation seemed unremunerative. Jephcott judged Harvalias' promotional activities were both efficient and sufficient.

As to the company's general administrative methods, with an office staff of four, Jephcott opined:

All records appeared to be meticulously kept and filed in a manner with which Greenford compares unfavourably. Both here and in the factory the cost of labour –

about one-third that in England – probably has a bearing upon this and without excessive expense it is possible to carry an abundance of staff . . .

Of Mr Harvalias himself I formed better impressions than on any previous occasion. Judged from the standpoint of Greece, I should say that he is exceptionally keen, reliable and energetic. He is undoubtedly most anxious to foster the growth of the pharmaceutical business . . . [and] has become ambitious to build a substantial company. It may be that with increasing prosperity his keenness will diminish, but of that there is no present sign.[56]

In all these comments, Jephcott unwittingly was as eloquent about his own standards and outlook as about those of Harvalias. His acute human judgement, his intense care over the human element in business and his supreme capacity to motivate his subordinates were all manifest in his approach to the Harvalias organisation. Throughout his business life he consulted his staff, encouraged individual initiative, drew on special talents and treated everyone with unadorned but automatic courtesy. To treat employees in any other way smacked to Jephcott of inefficient use of human resources. Turning to future prospects in 1936, Jephcott concluded:

so far as the Greek company is concerned, the outlook is good and would be very good but for import restrictions. At present pharmaceutically it is strictly limited in its products unless substantial expansion of manufacturing facilities were provided and a competent English technologist employed. Whether such policy of expansion for local production could be justified is a matter of gravest doubt; nor is it possible to try out the market by importation and only to take up manufacture when sales have justified it. Import restrictions prevent this except . . . [under] the trade agreement with Italy [of 1937] . . . In any event it is probably impossible for a permit for residence to be obtained for an English chemist; this is definitely so if paid by the Greek company.[57]

Peter Gent accompanied Jephcott to Athens, and established a *rapport* with Harvalias. He replaced Randall as a director of the Greek company in December 1936. A reliable nominee was needed on the Athens board, and Gent was the obvious candidate not only because as an Italian resident he could reach Greece over a weekend, but also because of the trade and diplomatic *detente* between the two countries in the late 1930s. Indeed, owing to currency and foreign exchange controls, no Greek profits whatever reached London by direct transfer; but import duties and remittances could be adjusted more satisfactorily if Greece's Italian ally was used as an intermediary. By the late 1930s Glaxo Laboratories was receiving annual net profits from Greece of up to £2,000. Glaxo's policy, largely framed by Jephcott, showed considerable political sophistication and discretion in running the Italian and Greek subsidiaries in increasingly well-coordinated tandem. 'The relation between Italy and Greece is essentially that of wolf and lamb', a British diplomat wrote in 1937, but it was one which was turned by Jephcott and Gent to Glaxo's advantage.[58]

Conclusion

The growth of Glaxo's overseas businesses up to 1939 was sufficient for the parent company to view itself as an international operation. The constraints to its further development were imposed both by a shortage of resources in finance and personnel, and the parent company's reluctance to commit itself to overseas investment. Political, economic and social difficulties, as well as the problems of communication with and management of businesses a long way away from the parent, all contributed to the varying performances of the overseas subsidiaries in this period.

II

Pharmaceuticals in Britain

6

Glaxo Laboratories and the hinge of fortune: the Second World War

Food manufacturing and trading activities

Even before the declaration of war in September 1939, it was recognised that food supplies would have to be as carefully organised by the State as the supply of munitions and petroleum oil or the distribution of civilian manpower. Much of Britain's food was imported, and it was realised that supplies would be disrupted not only by enemy action but by the allocation of merchant shipping for other strategic purposes. Elaborate contingency planning was undertaken in the period from 1937, based partly on an analysis of the experience of the Ministry of Food of 1916–1918. Ration books were printed well in advance of the outbreak of hostilities and the second Ministry of Food was established in September 1939 to put into action the plans decided upon in the preceding two years. 'The outbreak of war found this country better fitted than ever before to apply the findings of nutritional science to the task of feeding the population.'[1] To assist in this task the Ministry recruited advisers with experience of nutrition and the food industry. From 1941 to 1943 Harry Jephcott was Adviser on Manufactured Foods to the Ministry. In his absence from Glaxo, Colonel Rose acted as Managing Director.

Despite (or because of) food rationing, which for bacon, butter and sugar was imposed in 1940, Nathan's food subsidiaries performed better during the war. Both Stewarts with their chain of shops along the South Coast and Trengrouse & Nathan showed improved profits. The Glaxo subsidiary was particularly busy. Farex sales increased, as did those of Ostermilk; the latter tripled between 1939 and 1943.[2] The firm also took Government contracts to test (and pack into family-size cartons) dried egg, which arrived at Greenford in bulk containers from the USA. Dried skim milk, to be known as National Household Milk, was also tested and packaged.[3] Rationing and shortages of packaging materials such as glass, paper and cardboard made this more difficult. Bombing also affected the company's food operations although only to a limited extent until 1944 when a V1 flying bomb demolished the food-blending floor at Greenford.[4] The offices at Osnaburgh Street also sustained considerable damage. Although the company's involvement in food production was vital, its pharmaceutical activities were of even greater importance not only to the national war effort but also the long-term development of Glaxo Laboratories.

Pharmaceuticals

In 1939 Glaxo's home pharmaceutical sales were larger than food sales and made a greater contribution to profitability. However, more than half (54 per cent) of what the company termed 'pharmaceutical turnover' was derived from the sale of Glucodin (Glucose D) not considered by later standards to be a pharmaceutical. This anomaly or imbalance changed dramatically during the war. By 1943 Glucodin represented only 28 per cent of pharmaceutical sales. Vitamin output was increased to meet war demands; vitamin D was supplied in continuous bulk to manufacturers of margarine and feedstuffs; vitamins A and D in the shape of Adexolin capsules were supplied in quantity to clinics who distributed them free to expectant and nursing mothers; tablets of vitamin B_1 (Berin), vitamin C (Celin) and capsules of wheat-germ oil to provide vitamin E, were also produced to meet the need for the nutritional supplements recommended to the Ministry of Food by its scientific advisers and the Medical Research Council. The sale of vaccines also doubled between 1939 and 1943.

Glaxo's research and technical department was led during the war by Frank A. Robinson (1908–1988), who had joined the company as a chemist in 1933 (see chapter 8). Most of the scientifically qualified staff were exempted from call-up and the department was therefore well placed to respond to the exigencies of war. In July 1939 the bacteriological department of Glaxo was joined by Dr Joseph Ungar, a refugee from Czechoslovakia who left his country shortly before the outbreak of hostilities there. Ungar, who had completed his medical studies at Charles University, Prague, in 1927, specialised in research in immunology, both in Prague and Paris, and for the last three years had directed his own bacteriological and serological laboratory at Prague.[5] His knowledge and experience were to prove a valuable acquisition.

In 1939 the British pharmaceutical industry consisted of a large number of small firms, some long established as manufacturers of galenicals and proprietary medicines. The systematic application of chemistry to the treatment of disease – termed chemotherapy at the time though the word has since come to have a more specialised use – started late in the nineteenth

26 The production of National Dried Milk was an important part of Glaxo's war work.

century. The large, successful and prosperous German dyestuffs manufacturers – particularly Bayer and Hoechst – were first to apply their related research on dyestuffs to pharmaceuticals. The introduction of the pain-killer, phenacetin in 1888 was followed by those of Sulfonal, a sedative, and Veronal, a barbiturate; aspirin (acetyl-salicylic acid) was marketed from 1897.[6] The work of Paul Erhlich led to the discovery of the arsenical drugs, effective in treating venereal disease and the need to produce arsenicals in Britain during the First World War had taken Burroughs Wellcome and May

& Baker into the research and manufacture of chemical drugs in the interwar years. May & Baker's discovery of the first sulphonamide drug – M&B 693 – meant that from 1938 there was for the first time a cure available for bacterial pneumonia.[7] Although research in the industry had expanded in the interwar years, the pharmaceutical firms were limited by their size as to the amount of research they could afford to finance. Britain's largest chemical company, ICI, had only just started to take an interest in pharmaceuticals.[8]

German chemical superiority in the inter-war years meant that many patented pharmaceutical products were imported into Britain. Supplies terminated abruptly at the start of the war and, at the Government's request, British pharmaceutical manufacturers analysed, researched, developed and produced substitutes. At Greenford radiographic media and anaesthetic preparations were investigated and manufactured. The research department also worked on the synthesis of vitamin B_1, required in the early years of the war on a commercial scale to enrich white flour which was deficient in the vitamin but occupied less shipping space than brown flour.

It is a platitude worth repeating as far as both the British pharmaceutical industry and Glaxo are concerned, that war provided a 'technological forcing house'.[9] Memories of the First World War, when Britain and allied countries found themselves hobbled in research and production facilities for medicine because of their previous dependence on German and Swiss supplies, were instrumental in framing the industry's decision to form a cooperative research and production organisation during the Second World War.[10] This body in turn drew Glaxo Laboratories into the centre of the British pharmaceutical industry.

The Therapeutic Research Corporation

The Therapeutic Research Corporation (hereafter TRC) was formed in 1941 (capitalised at £500,000, shared equally by the five partners) and originally comprised representatives of Boots, May & Baker, British Drug Houses, Glaxo Laboratories and Burroughs Wellcome. They were joined by representatives of ICI Pharmaceutical Division after the latter's formation in 1942. The idea of TRC, as a body to coordinate and extend research, came from T. R. G. Bennett, chairman and managing director of the Wellcome Foundation.[11] He then enlisted the support of May & Baker, which since its introduction of sulphapyridine (M&B 693), in 1938, had held the best reputation for commercial research in Britain. Bennett and the other businessmen were mindful of the disastrous effects felt in the First World War of the retarded research and production facilities for medicines in

Table 4. *Research output of British drug companies 1936–1941*[12]

Company	Patents	Articles	Ph.D.
British Drug Houses	7	32	5
Boots	12	10	24
Glaxo	13	34	8
May & Baker	40	11	15
Burroughs Wellcome	6	220	24

Britain, and realised that German science and industry were still better coordinated and more advanced in chemotherapy.

A survey into the research capability of its members was carried out by the TRC at the start, giving some indication of the relative strengths of the partners. Glaxo took second place in terms of the number of patents and the number of articles but dropped to fourth place in ranking by the number of doctorates.

Its members conceived the TRC as having three main functions. First, they expected it to pool and coordinate research in selected fields of common interest so as to ascertain the most promising new drugs and devise satisfactory manufacturing processes. TRC was also intended to provide research subsidies on a far larger scale than hitherto in the pharmaceutical industry. This was increasingly required as academic laboratories, unsubsidised by industry, were able to cover only a diminishing area of chemical research applied to drugs. Secondly, the promoters of TRC desired to arrange the pooling of manufacturing facilities of new products among member companies best qualified to undertake production. In such cases, the product would be sold to other TRC members at a reasonable, but nominal, profit. The third and final aim of the new body was to present the views of the pharmaceutical industry on important policy matters (such as the industry's relations with a future National Health Service, or therapeutic research) to the Government, the medical profession or other interested parties. Bennett and his colleagues anticipated that it would fall 'within the power of the pharmaceutical industry to make or mar the progress of therapeutics'. As Sir Frank Hartley, Secretary of the TRC, later wrote:

It was thought that as long as important members of the industry remained uncooperative, the stress of competition would result in undue haste in the marketing of new drugs, in the marketing of inferior substitutes for some successful drug made by another firm and in the marketing of the same drug under different names ... In addition, it was considered that wasteful duplication of research should be eliminated and the ... constant interchange of ideas between the various units would be expected to have a fertilising effect ... It was considered that if the Group constantly bore in mind its high calling in the development of therapeutics, its influence with the medical profession would grow and it would be able to speak in matters of health ... with an authority greater than that of a concern interested solely in making profits. It was acknowleged that the proposed Corporation should be able effectively to protect the interests of the members of the group against the development of monopolies, foreign or British, particularly in connection with the provision of intermediates essential in the manufacture of pharmaceuticals.[13]

The advances in drug therapies in the late 1930s had excited Jephcott and some of his Glaxo colleagues with their scientific and commercial potential. There had been, however, little opportunity for Glaxo Laboratories to diversify into these new lines of research and production before the outbreak of war in 1939. Nevertheless, its activities in fine chemicals, since the marketing of Ostelin in 1924, justified Bennett and his colleagues in approaching Glaxo Laboratories to join TRC on its formation. Jephcott accepted with alacrity, and though he must have realised that he would be representing a junior member of the Corporation, he also recognised that it would be a central clearing-house for pharmaceutical information and policy so long as the war continued. Glaxo's contacts with the Wisconsin Alumni Research Foundation (WARF – see page 75) soon proved useful to TRC, as for example when WARF invited Glaxo Laboratories to act as their agents, and as a trading company under licence on similar terms to sublicensees, in respect of various patented anticoagulants (drugs which acted to prevent the clotting of blood). Glaxo Laboratories was transformed into an intermediary between WARF and TRC to the benefit of all three.

From the outset, however, there was tension within TRC, caused at least in part by the competitive traditions of the past. Boots distrusted May & Baker who, in turn, doubted the good intentions of British Drug Houses. The member companies seemed unable to discard their old habits, although they were all surprisingly ignorant of their respective research potential and often misunderstood each other's business. As TRC research work advanced, other problems arose. Dual loyalties were created which seemed to cause the immediate interests of member companies to suffer: senior workers suffered physical and mental strain from the extra burden of work, responsibility and 'anxiety to uphold prestige'; scientific doubts about particular research projects prevented the unreserved collaboration that had been anticipated.[14] Altogether there was a plenitude of 'inter-related factors creating unintended sacrifices and imposing unintended burdens which [would] not disappear under any machinery of collaboration which stopped short of the seemingly impractical assumption of complete rationalisation'.[15] This was certainly the conclusion of Glaxo Laboratories, based on its wartime experience of the TRC.

The admission of Glaxo Laboratories to TRC in 1941 was an acknowledgement of the reputation it had already secured in the pharmaceutical industry under Jephcott's guidance. Dr Lester Smith and F. A. Robinson were the members nominated by Glaxo Laboratories to TRC's Research Panel in October 1941, while Colonel E. A. Rose was chosen in November as Jephcott's understudy for Glaxo Laboratories at TRC. (The other original board members were T. R. G. Bennett (Chairman) of Wellcome, Dr T. B. Maxwell of May & Baker, C. A. Hill of B.D.H. and Lord Trent of Boots.) Jephcott was involved in all TRC's early deliberations on such subjects as medical patents, the nomenclature of products and research programmes in sulphonamide and other chemo-therapeutic substances. In 1943 he served as Chairman of the Corporation. But as far as the development of Glaxo Laboratories was concerned, the crucial aspect of TRC was its involvement with penicillin.

Penicillin

The early study of penicillin is well known, and documented.[16] The first penicillin mould was discovered fortuitously by Alexander Fleming in 1928, and described by him in an article in the *British Journal of Experimental Pathology* in 1929. This article is more cited than read, for the fact is that Fleming misinterpreted and misunderstood his observations in 1928 and never demonstrated the therapeutic effects of penicillin. These were only discovered over a decade later by a research team at Oxford University, headed by Howard Florey and Ernst Chain. They were investigating bacterial antagonism when Chain disinterred Fleming's forgotten paper of 1928 from its scientific *obliette*, and began the research which led to the discovery of penicillin's therapeutic properties.

In Britain during most of the Second World War, penicillin mould was grown by surface culture on a very small scale in vessels such as milk churns or glass flasks, known in Glaxo as bedpans. United States manufacturers did not perfect deep fermentation production methods until later in the war, in 1943–1944. Fine chemicals manufacturers on both sides of the Atlantic were reluctant to commit large investment, especially during wartime when both research and production facilities were so stretched, to pioneer a substance which had not undergone complete clinical testing and which continued to present so many production problems. It was hard to extract or purify, and highly unstable; the purification method was ill-adapted to large-scale production; and the likelihood that chemists would succeed in developing a synthetic product heightened the reluctance of industry to invest in production facilities using surface cultures that were, it seemed, bound to be rendered obsolete within a few years. It was not only in Britain that there

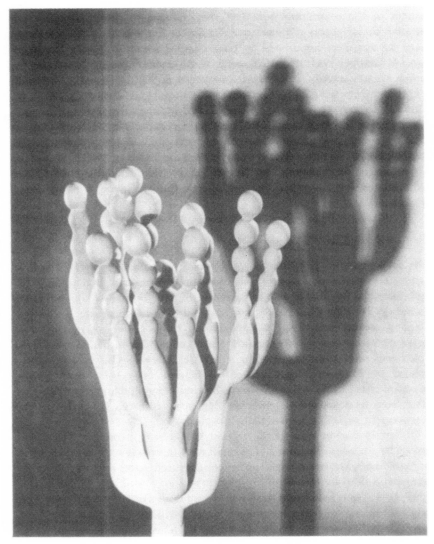

27 A model of penicillin, showing its structure.

was this hesitancy. When Florey and an Oxford associate toured the USA in
1941, the research directors of major American pharmaceutical companies
all reiterated the view that penicillin was too experimental to justify priority
in research and development. Eventually the Merck and Squibb companies
yielded, and began penicillin production.

TRC did little to interest British officialdom in coordinating or financing penicillin work, at least in comparison with American wartime agencies such as the Office of Scientific Research and Development and the War Production Board. Though it collaborated with the Ministry of Supply and other bodies, its achievements in penicillin work were much more limited than those of the War Production Board, which by 1943–1944 had twenty-five American companies exchanging information and setting standards for the mass production of penicillin. Research was initiated by companies like Squibb, Merck, Parke Davis, Sharp & Dohme, Pfizer, and Lederle, together with Abbot Laboratories, Lilly, Upjohn and Wyeth. By late 1943 limited quantities of penicillin were available for American civilian use as the requirements of the armed forces had been met. In the first half of 1943, total US penicillin production was about 800 million units, but in the following six months over 20 billion units were produced, sufficient to cope with 20,000 seriously ill patients. Production during 1944 rose to 1,633 billion units. The US Office for Scientific Research and Development's price fell from $200 per million units of penicillin in 1943 to $6 per million units in 1945.

All this American activity seemed to contemporaries to be in sharp contrast to the aloof attitude of the Medical Research Council, the Ministry of Supply and TRC. One of TRC's main tasks was perceived as reporting to the British government on progress towards the target of supplying the full penicillin needs of the armed services, a target which in any case involved production of penicillin on a more modest scale than that of the USA. There has been much unfair criticism of British industry for its tardy and tentative work on wartime antibiotics, but critics under-estimate the desperate pressure for other drugs to be produced with the limited available facilities, and also neglect the difficulties of the war economy haunted by bombs, manpower shortages, lack of materials and accommodation. In 1942 TRC approached Lord McGowan, the Chairman of ICI, enquiring if his company would collaborate in penicillin research. Until this time ICI's pharmaceutical activities had been only a small part of their Dyestuffs Group, but their recent inventions had included Paludrine (the anti-malarial drug which replaced the German drug Mepacrine) and Sulphamezathine (a very commonly used and successful sulphonamide). Imperial Chemicals (Pharmaceuticals) Ltd was set up as a selling company for tax reasons in 1942, but a proper Pharmaceuticals Division was not formed until 1944, and for many years after that it remained a demoralised and neglected dependency of the Dyestuffs Division.[17] The approach to McGowan was followed by discussions with A. J. Quig of IC Pharmaceuticals (ICP), and in August 1942, TRC and ICP agreed a defined area of cooperation in penicillin production. By this stage ICP had been producing small quantities of penicillin for some months and had supplied Florey with penicillin for his clinical tests. ICP's activities at this time have become reasonably well-known: less publicity, however, has attended Glaxo Laboratories' decision early in 1942 to open a small penicillin-producing plant in a disused cheese factory at Aylesbury in Buckinghamshire.

For Glaxo Laboratories the production possibilities of penicillin were alluring. As one of the smaller and more flexible members of TRC they were not burdened with extensive plants already committed to producing drugs of proven efficacy for the war effort. In many respects, penicillin production by surface cultures in milk churns and horizontal milk bottles, the British method before the Americans perfected fermentation techniques, was cognate to Glaxo's processed cheese and dairy food business. The technological divide between antibiotics and processing cheese was immense, but in the primitive early days, some of the materials were related. Glaxo's Aylesbury factory was launched with the support of the Ministry of Supply to reproduce, on a larger scale, the methods of Florey's Oxford laboratory, a few miles away. Predictably, within the Glaxo hierarchy, Jephcott was 'the man who urged this move most strongly'[18] although Herbert Palmer (see page 89) was put in charge of its organisation.

The first cultures of penicillin *notatum* used at Glaxo in 1942 were obtained from Professor Harold Raistrick, a biochemist who had left ICI in 1929 for the London School of Hygiene and Tropical Medicine, and who had obtained his cultures from his colleague, Alexander Fleming. Dr R. D. Andrews of Glaxo then began the company's own scientific investigations of penicillin's morphology, the production potency of various cultures, the production of spore suspensions and methods of inoculation. By August 1942 the company was able to notify TRC that it had filed provisional application for a patent entitled 'Isolation of an anti-bacterial substance produced by a mould', although it was not the first TRC member to file a penicillin patent (Boots by this time had already filed a completed specification of a Penicillin A patent).

Glaxo Laboratories' first penicillin patent was assigned to TRC in September 1942, but Jephcott counselled TRC against 'taking out an immoderate number of patents, the value of which to the Corporation would vary in different countries'. He appreciated that US products' patents were valuable, but suggested that in foreign countries where there was no immediate prospect of manufacture, TRC 'might not want to make a large capital investment [in patents] which would be of a depreciating nature'.[19]

In December 1942 Glaxo Laboratories accepted an offer from Burroughs Wellcome to share half the cost of setting up the Aylesbury plant. Glaxo's plant was built with financial support from the Ministry of Supply at about

(a)

(b)

28 Penicillin production using (a) the flat pan surface culture and (b) racks of pans being checked for growth.

the same time as Burroughs Wellcome were also establishing their capacity to manufacture penicillin. At Jephcott's instigation, Glaxo soon opened two further penicillin factories, one at Watford on the upper storey of a rubber vulcanising plant, and the third in a converted cattle-food factory at Stratford in east London. In all three operations the company acted as direct agents for the Ministry of Supply, but throughout the war years the plants retained a rather improvised appearance. Despite its *ad hoc* nature, for a time before it was closed in 1946, the Watford factory was producing 90 per cent of Britain's penicillin. To the outside observer the principal feature of the factories 'was their conveyor systems, carrying glass flasks and bottles to the sterilizer, to the seeding department where large numbers of women injected mould spores into the flasks, to the incubator rooms, out of these rooms to the processing, and extraction plant, and back to the sterilizer'.[20]

Despite the hurry with which the British penicillin plants were erected, by the time of the Sicilian invasion of 1943, Glaxo Laboratories together with other British companies such as Boots, Distillers and Burroughs Wellcome, were producing enough penicillin to meet the needs of British military forces. These were particularly important in Italy where, as well as other infections, the venereal disease, gonorrhoea, was widespread.

Jephcott represented the TRC on the General Penicillin Committee, and his advice on the strategy of increasing national penicillin output was crucial. He urged that if sufficient (mostly unskilled) labour was available, non-mechanical methods would lead to a far greater increase in penicillin output than mechanised factory work. The urgency of increasing immediate supplies meant that it might prove dangerous to experiment with mechanical mass production techniques, and Glaxo Laboratories in common with other British pharmaceutical manufacturers merely scaled-up the laboratory production techniques of Chain and Florey. Jephcott himself was sceptical about the economic production possibilities of penicillin synthesis.[21]

By 1944 British penicillin output had reached an adequate figure for wartime needs, and the General Penicillin Committee began work on estimating postwar civilian requirements, and the best means of satisfying them. It was decided to build two large modern factories to establish production on a secure long-term basis, and by mid 1944 plans were afoot for Glaxo Laboratories and the Distillers Company to build and operate plants at Barnard Castle in County Durham and at Speke, near Liverpool, respectively. The trans-Atlantic traffic in scientific research information on antibiotics was by then well-established, and at this stage in 1944 it became known that the American company, Pfizer, had made a breakthrough in penicillin production. Pfizer was not then a pharmaceutical company, but as a supplier of chemicals and ingredients to the food and drink industry, had pioneered deep fermentation techniques as part of its ordinary business.

With some boldness, they had built a pilot plant for the deep fermentation of penicillin in 1943, and by 1944 their risk had been vindicated triumphantly. As soon as it was evident that large-scale production of penicillin was possible by the deep fermentation technique, Jephcott and an ICI representative were sent by the Ministry of Supply to the USA early in 1944.

Jephcott was primed before his departure for the United States with a series of detailed questions which his scientific staff wanted him to ask the Americans about penicillin production. The information they required included everything possible on construction materials, on the relative amounts used of mild steel, cast iron, alloys, stoneware, enamel or rubber, on the possibilities of contamination by copper, zinc or other metals, on the design of pumps, pipes and equipment, and the methods of deep culture and tray culture processes.[22] Jephcott made an extensive tour of the various American penicillin plants, and returned convinced of the inevitability of Britain having to adopt the Americans' deep fermentation techniques. The Ministry of Supply's responses to this enthusiasm was, it seemed to Glaxo Laboratories, tardy and luke-warm. Any British use of Pfizer's expertise would have to be under licence, and in Glaxo's discussion of the terms of such licences, difficulties arose over the access of government officials to the plants, the exchange of information, the level of royalties and the extent to which they would be payable on supplies to the British government. Meanwhile Glaxo, in conjunction with Boots, opened negotiations with Pfizer for a British licensing arrangement. Although Jephcott was careful not to undermine Glaxo's negotiating position, there was no mistaking his keenness to reach agreement quickly and effectively. While this bargaining between Boots, Glaxo Laboratories, the Ministry of Supply and the American manufacturers pursued its laborious course, even more conclusive evidence of the superiority of the deep fermentation methods was crossing the Atlantic to Britain.

In October 1944 Jephcott revisited New York, and under the auspices of the British Supply Mission there headed by Sir Walter Venning, had lengthy discussions with representatives of Merck, Pfizer and Squibb about a penicillin agreement. The Americans were unstintingly helpful, and a provisional agreement on these highly technical matters was reached by the end of the month. Under its terms, Glaxo Laboratories and Boots were to act for the Ministry of Supply in taking deep-fermentation processes licences from Pfizer in return for royalties. But in February 1945 Boots withdrew leaving Glaxo Laboratories to continue the discussions alone and the following month the talks collapsed while Jephcott was in India. The difficulty was that Pfizer were insisting, in order to get a guaranteed minimum royalty, that Glaxo Laboratories should have a plant of double Barnard Castle's proposed capacity, and to this the Ministry of Supply would not consent. It was impossible for Glaxo Laboratories to bridge the gap between British bureaucrats and American manufacturers. Jephcott assured John Smith of Pfizer that he was willing to embark for New York to revive discussions. 'Regret Developments During My Absence in India Whence I have Just Returned', he cabled, 'Personally Believe Having Regard [to] Progress [of] War And on Basics We Undertake All Capital Cost Without Any Government Assistance Ministry Might Not Object to Purely Commercial Agreement Between Pfizer [and] Glaxo As Individual Companies Subject [to] Treasury Approval [of] Any Royalty Or Other Remittances.'[23]

Jephcott was determined that his company should remain in postwar penicillin production. 'It was well known in the trade that we were the first to establish in this country a productive unit which produced penicillin in sensible quantity', he noted. In February 1945 Glaxo Laboratories was producing 70 per cent of total UK supply. Although the latest penicillin works at Stratford had been covered by a Capital Assistance Scheme and had not required any outlay of the company's resources, the company had invested considerable sums of its own money, £14,000 at Aylesbury and £68,900 at Watford.

Previously, in January 1945, the Ministry of Supply had warned the company that surface-culture methods at Barnard Castle might have to be abandoned. Glaxo had responded by sending Herbert Palmer to the USA to discuss with Merck and Squibb the possibility of licences to use their penicillin production processes. In addition, during Jephcott's absence in India, and following the collapse of the provisional arrangements with Boots and Pfizer, his co-directors had approached Distillers (who had charge of the proposed Speke penicillin plant) about a possible penicillin working arrangement. The board, however, acknowledged that there was some doubt 'how far under the new circumstances we can continue in penicillin if we come in late, the Americans in the meanwhile having got it, in both our home and export markets'.[24] After a long board meeting at the end of March, the directors unanimously agreed that Glaxo Laboratories should try to stay a penicillin producer, and within weeks Jephcott had returned to America with renewed zeal for a licensing agreement. On 26 April he signed contracts with Merck and Squibb for their information on penicillin fermentation by the deep culture method, in return for a royalty of 5 per cent payable for five years on Glaxo's penicillin sales under the Merck/Squibb processes. When Jephcott signed the American agreement of April 1945, the TRC's other members, still negotiating through the Ministry of Supply, 'regarded this as rather fast footwork'.[25]

As Jephcott reported to his directors in May, Merck were also interested in an extended working agreement with Glaxo Laboratories covering other pharmaceutical developments, such as liver extract, casein and vitamin D_3. In addition, Squibb had indicated that they would renounce the British market if Glaxo Laboratories kept out of Canada, Mexico and the USA. In a decision which was to have the most far-reaching effects on the development of Glaxo Laboratories for over forty years, Jephcott advised that such extended working agreements with Merck and Squibb would be most advantageous, 'on the assumption that it is not our intention to develop the Canadian and USA markets'.[26] In the same month, Jephcott also saw Sir Graham Hayman of Distillers, who was sympathetic but non-committal about penicillin collaboration. Distillers' policy, according to Hayman, was to produce penicillin or other medical products for which they had knowledge or facilities, but not to distribute or market them directly. Distillers wished to conserve the goodwill of their existing pharmaceutical customers with whom they did big business in solvents and for that reason they favoured an arrangement whereby Glaxo undertook their distribution of penicillin.[27]

As soon as possible after the signature of the Merck and Squibb agreements in April, Herbert Palmer and three colleagues went to the USA to study the American companies' techniques. Palmer returned in late July, having been given every facility, and began supervising the building at Barnard Castle of Britain's first deep-fermentation facilities. It was a highly significant move for Glaxo's future in the pharmaceutical industry.

Glaxo's overseas business in wartime

Glaxo's overseas subsidiaries, whose growth in the inter-war years has been chronicled in chapter 5, met with varying fortunes during the war. There were difficulties common to them all, particularly in communication and in obtaining supplies. For all of them the war brought six years of greater isolation, for there was neither time nor opportunity for Greenford managers to globe-trot.

In India the Second World War created both major difficulties and significant opportunities for the company's largest overseas subsidiary, the Foster firm. Two immediate problems were the departure of many European sales representatives to join the armed forces and the difficulty of obtaining supplies from Britain. The former was resolved by training Indian medical representatives, so that the sales force fell only from twenty-seven to twenty-three. The latter was more problematic with alternative sources having to be found in Australia or the United States. The company also felt the repercussions of the Japanese advances through South East Asia, with the loss of a significant consignment from Foster's agent in Rangoon. A recurrent problem was the re-routing of cargoes as a result of enemy action, and the high cost of freight charges. A countervailing advantage, on the other hand, was the reduction or removal of foreign, particularly German, competition. Consequently Fosters were able to develop small but rewarding markets for new products as well as obtaining the vitamin C business formerly held by Bayer.

Local manufacture of Minadex began during 1943–1944, with the company obtaining raw materials and intermediates such as vitamins A and E, from the United States. Even from this source some wartime disruption of supply was experienced. In the case of Glucodin, Fosters were frustrated by a shortage which developed as a result of farmers preferring to feed pigs on their corn rather than selling it to Corn Products for conversion into starch for glucose. Shortages helped to create a situation in India where 'the black market in drugs flourished more prolifically than in any other commodity'; drugs were mere 'shuttles of speculation', until legislation was extended to cover them from November 1943, with the Drug Control Order.[28] As the demand for Indian independence grew, war problems were superseded by the political upheaval within India itself. Although Bombay was not as badly affected as Calcutta, Foster's managers were disturbed by the unrest and tension prevalent in most large towns in India.

The war also had a profound effect on Glaxo in Australia. From 1941 the Ministry of Food in Britain required maximum production of milk powder, and in consequence the role of processed cheese in the business steadily diminished. One of Glaxo's main suppliers was a firm called Hoadley, who supplied them with the glucose (45 tons in 1941) and dextrose.[29] To finance expansion arising out of the Hoadley deal, in 1943 the Glaxo subsidiary, with Australian government permission, issued 30,000 ordinary shares of £1, with ten shillings payable on allotment. Through the war all the requirements of intravenous dextrose for both Australian and American forces in the south-west Pacific were met, together with dextrose needed for Glucodin. The former Hoadley factory undertook the first commercial scale production of crystalline dextrose from wheat flour. Subsequently Glaxo signed a contract for supplies with a specialist plant which opened in the New South Wales wheat belt.

War conditions made it difficult for Greenford to supply many of its agents and subsidiaries, particularly those further away, as in South America. Charles Richardson, managing director in Argentina, died suddenly in November 1941 whilst visiting the milk drying plant in Quequen. As its founder, Richardson had run 'a one-man show' which was as autocratic as it was successful. Without him the business floundered. Although supplies continued to be made, both from Argentina and through agents in the USA, to some South American markets, such as Brazil and Chile, in others such as Paraguay, the Glaxo presence virtually disappeared.

Nearer home in Europe, when Italy entered the war in 1940, Gent and the other English staff of Glaxo's subsidiary, had to leave the country and the company was placed, in October, under a sequestrator, Baron Mario Ostini, managing director of the Instituto Nazionale Opoterapico of Pisa. The company's assets were valued in an inventory prepared for the sequestrator in January 1941, at 5.658 million lire, and an auditor's report later in the year concluded, 'it is a very sound business, excellently directed, and one which, under the prudent administration of the sequestrator, is continuing in production with complete self-sufficiency'. Around the same time the company bought the premises in Via Filopanti which it had occupied since 1931: operations continued throughout the war, although handicapped by lack of raw materials. Ostini showed fairness and judgement in his activities as sequestrator, and the company was free of undue interference until February 1943, when two officials of the Montecatini organisation's pharmaceutical subsidiary, S.A. Farmaceutici Italia of Milan, arrived in Verona with authority from the Minister of Corporations to take immediate possession of Laboratori Glaxo, and to buy the enemy-held shares of the company. Ostini, however, resisted these manoeuvres, and was able to delay the decrees from becoming operative. Indeed he was so equitable in his treatment of British interests that, although the 10 per cent royalty on sales accruing to Glaxo Laboratories was initially cancelled after Gent's departure, Ostini, after his confirmation as sequestrator, annulled this decision and back-dated the credits, so that by 31 August 1945, royalties of 4.16 million lire stood to the credit of the British parent company. In July 1944 manufacturing was transferred to the Aschiri caves at Quinzano, outside Verona, to escape Allied bombing. When Baron Ostini was cut off from Verona by the Allied advance in 1944, a new sequestrator, Dr Ugo Noceti of Genoa, was appointed by the Ente di Gestione e Liquidazione Immobiliare (Agency of Management and Liquidation of Real Property) of Mussolini's short-lived northern republic of Salo. This transfer was supervised by the company accountant, Azzino Azzini, who was responsible more than anyone else for the survival and commercial continuity of the company during the war.

During this period, control of the Italian-owned shares became dispersed among several individuals, but in December 1945, all the shares were bought back by Glaxo Laboratories for about 6 million lire, met out of the accumulated profits in Italy. The transaction was supervised by Peter Gent who was at that time on the staff of the Allied Commission in Rome, and was able to exert considerable influence with the Allied Property Controller leading to the release of the company from control as early as November 1945. Gent returned as managing director in February 1946.

The Anglo-Iranian Pharmaceutical Company

There was one new overseas venture in which Glaxo became involved during the war. In November 1942, Glaxo Laboratories signed an agreement with Boots Pure Drug Company, British Drug Houses, The Wellcome Foundation and Evans Sons Lescher & Webb, to incorporate a company called the Anglo-Iranian Pharmaceutical Company Ltd (AIPC). By the end of 1948 the company had entered into voluntary liquidation, its short and troubled history mirroring not only the decline of British enterprise in Iran but also the perils of subordinating commercial criteria to political consider-ations at the behest of governments (as also occurred at the Port Fairy factory in the 1950s).[30] While Glaxo Laboratories did not play an exclusive part in its chequered history, which was only a side-show in the group's development, the reasons for the failure of leading British manufacturers to establish themselves in a country that was to enjoy unprecedented post-war growth remain salutary.

The turmoil of 1942 was an inauspicious time for the formation of the Anglo-Iranian Pharmaceutical Company, although British business con-cessions were viewed as crucial to maintaining British influence in the country in the wake of the abdication of the pro-German Shah, Reza Shah Pahlavi.[31] Black market hoarding of medical products concerned the Foreign Office in London, and became urgent after requests from the Persian Government for further stocks of quinine. A week before the five companies signed the agreement, Dr Millspaugh, an American subject, was appointed as financial advisor to the Iranian government. Although Millspaugh's influence waned in 1944, in 1943 many senior administrative posts were filled by Americans and the British Foreign Office desired a British joint pharmaceutical venture as a counter-balance to US influence. The Ameri-cans declined to complicate their position in Iran by joining a joint Anglo-US concern. Ostensibly, however, their reluctance to co-operate was due to apprehension about the consequences of the Iranian government's mono-poly on the procurement of medical supplies. In 1943–1944 the AIPC made some solid progress, even though a personal emissary of President Roosevelt commented that the British were so unpopular by 1943 that if the Iranians had to choose between them and the Russians they would choose the latter.[32]

By 1944 the mood in Iran amongst British diplomatic and commercial circles was optimistic. Confident of a military victory the AIPC looked forward to establishing trade on less complicated terms. The Board of Trade saw British exports to Iran as playing a vital part in protecting and

29 Inspecting the bomb damage to the Greenford factory.

consolidating British interests in the Middle East.[33] These sanguine attitudes were not justified by events. With the cessation of hostilities in 1945, Iranian politics became increasingly xenophobic, and financial strains in the local economy during the late 1940s led to discrimination against British banking and commercial consortia, which foreshadowed the full-scale attack on the Anglo-Iranian Oil Company in the 1950s. Despite steady, if modest, sales in 1946 and 1947 which, in other conditions would have shown a profit, difficulties over foreign exchange and import restrictions forced the company to decide, in 1948, to liquidate their stocks of pharmaceuticals in Iran and withdraw.

The AIPC proved to be an unfortunate venture. For Glaxo's management and Jephcott, it enhanced the conviction that was to dominate the company's post-war overseas activities: that they should concentrate on the countries of the Commonwealth.

Conclusion

For Glaxo Laboratories the Second World War was the hinge of its fortunes. Throughout the 1930s, Jephcott had, as his influence in the company increased, urged upon it the greater benefit to be derived from a commitment to pharmaceuticals. Although his arguments were partially accepted, progress was slow, so slow that Jephcott seriously considered resignation in 1938, and a retreat to farming in New Zealand. But the expertise in food as well as pharmaceuticals stood the company in good stead when it became involved in the development of penicillin. By the end of the war it was an indisputable fact that Glaxo was predominantly a pharmaceutical company and in British terms, a major one. To sustain and develop its position, both at home and abroad, in the post-war world would require reconstruction and resources.

7

Pharmaceuticals triumphant 1946–1962

The aftermath of war

The war years and the commitment to penicillin had made it clear, both within and without the company, that Glaxo Laboratories had become a pharmaceutical house. It was therefore logical for the parent company to rid itself of its merchandising and ancillary businesses. In the two years after the war the food interests of Nathans – Trengrouse & Nathan, Bowles Nicholls and Stewarts – were sold, as too were the trading interests in New Zealand. This left the parent Nathan company with its one subsidiary, Glaxo Laboratories. In January 1947, by a share for share transfer, Glaxo Laboratories acquired the assets of its parent and, at the same time, became a public company. J. E. Nathan & Co went into voluntary liquidation. Sir Harry Jephcott who had been knighted in 1946 was already Chairman and Managing Director of Glaxo, for in June 1946 Alec Nathan had retired from business life. At the Glaxo Board meeting:

individual tributes were paid to him by all present for the excellent building up of the old Glaxo Department but for which solid foundation the existing Glaxo Laboratories business could not so readily have been erected. He had endeared himself to all the staff under his control and had won a reputation for justice and fair dealing which none would forget.[1]

When Glaxo Laboratories Ltd was established, Archibald Sandercock became, by seniority, Deputy Chairman and Deputy Managing Director, but he retired in 1948 (he died in October that year) and was succeeded by Herbert Palmer, long groomed by Jephcott for the position.

With the restructuring of the Glaxo group in 1947, the board was joined by several knights with civil service backgrounds, intended to make executive contributions to an increasingly large and bureaucratised company. Jephcott's many wartime visits to India, and the dissolution of the Indian Civil Service after Independence, were responsible for his recruitment

30 Newspaper headlines on the post-war restructuring.

of two directors, Sir Robert Hutchings (1897–1976) and Sir Jeremy Raisman (1892–1978). Hutchings, who had been a senior official of the Indian Government's wartime Food Department (when Jephcott was its adviser on milk powder) and afterwards Member for Food and Agriculture on Lord

Mountbatten's Executive Council for India, was given responsibility for personnel and training. A committed Christian and a man of conscientious outlook, he was, according to Field Marshall Wavell, 'a good man, sensible and resolute', although some of the proconsular habits which he retained seemed incongruous at Greenford: 'Uncle Robert' combined benevolence with discipline in a good manner, and his ingrained ministerial habit of assuming all within his 'superior charge' (his own phase) led to many long-remembered stories.[2] Raisman, who was a non-executive director at Glaxo, was Finance Member of the Indian Government in 1939–1945, and Indian delegate to the Bretton Woods Conference and later Vice-chairman of Lloyds Bank in the 1950s. In India he was 'good and sound', according to the Viceroy, Wavell, 'patient and tactful in meeting opposition'. As a director of Glaxo, too, he was a source of equable and solid advice.[3] The third knight to join the reconstructed board, Sir Maurice Hutton (1904–1970), was given overall responsibility for sales. A stockbroker who had joined the Ministry of Food on the outbreak of war, Hutton headed the British Food Mission in North America in 1944–1948, and the British Supply Office in the USA (1947–1948). An active and convivial man, with considerable business experience and instinct, he nevertheless failed to carry weight within the company. In 1955 he emigrated to Australia, where he collected a panoply of directorships from local subsidiaries of British multinationals. Finally there was Sir Cyril Entwistle (1887–1974), a barrister and company director who had been Conservative MP for Bolton until the Labour landslide of 1945.

In the 'new' Glaxo company, with senior managers mainly chosen by himself, Jephcott's ideas and objectives dominated. He enjoyed his responsibilities and to him business was a constant intellectual challenge, replete with creative satisfaction. He would have agreed with A. N. Whitehead that 'desire for money will produce hard-fistedness but not enterprise'.[4] As he wrote in 1938 to the Managing Director of the Australian subsidiary, 'although one cannot ignore the financial aspects of living, I do not feel . . . they are the most important . . . The greatest thing I know is to be able to go to the office in the morning with a sense of pleasurable anticipation.'[5] He constantly tried to imbue Glaxo managers at home and abroad with this zest for business life, and became a life-long inspiration to some of his employees. The attempts of some American or Japanese companies to impose a narrow monomaniacal commitment on their staff were repellent to him: a man of catholic taste and broad outlook, he admired those characteristics in others. 'An inbred wholly absorbed businessman is not only a bore to his home and friends, but in time becomes insular, maybe highly expert and intelligent, but nevertheless an insulated business machine.'[6] He himself was an ardent photographer, who for years developed, printed and enlarged his own negatives; he maintained an interest in carpentry and cabinet-making until the Second World War; built his own radio receiver in 1927 and a reinforced concrete air-raid shelter in his garden in 1939. In all of these recreations he showed his self-sufficiency and pleasure in personal achievement. 'Committees can never take action successfully and effectively', he had told Herbert Palmer in 1939. 'In the finality individuals have got to do whatever is to be done.'[7]

Reconstruction and expansion

Many of the difficulties faced by Glaxo in the immediate post-war period were general to industry. Shortages of building materials meant that a government licensing scheme operated, leading to considerable delays: for example, it was not until June 1946 that Glaxo was granted licences to reconstruct at Greenford the buildings destroyed by enemy action in August 1944.[8] The company was not short of funds either for reconstruction or expansion. As Jephcott later recalled, 'at the conclusion of the war, mainly in consequence of restraints imposed by Government upon capital expenditures, the Company's financial position was good and it was able to undertake the capital expenditures necessary'.[9] Government restraints on capital expenditure remained, for the Labour Government which took office in 1945 was faced with an economy distorted and disrupted by war. The Government's need to control inflation (which had risen sharply), reduce the national debt, contain the balance of payments deficit, export as much as possible, and limit expenditure overseas, meant that industrial expansion was still subject to central controls.

In the early summer of 1946, difficulties arose with Glaxo's penicillin contracts. It became clear that the comparatively low domestic prices which the British Government intended to pay Glaxo Laboratories for their penicillin supplies 'were likely to have severe repercussions in the United States and might well seriously affect the relationship between Merck and Squibb and ourselves'. Jephcott visited America in May to keep abreast of the latest penicillin developments, and immediately on arrival cautioned Merck and Squibb of the prices which had been determined for domestic sale in Britain. Merck had been forewarned by May & Baker, but Squibb had no previous information and the UK prices were a 'severe shock' to them. Jephcott immediately assured both American manufacturers that he 'appreciated that there were no obligations under the agreement for any continued exchange of information and if, having regard to the adverse effect, as they saw it, of the UK price structure they felt they would prefer to withdraw ... I wished them to feel completely free to do so'. Squibb forthwith contacted Roland Robinson (later Lord Martonmere), then Conservative MP for Blackpool and a director of their British subsidiary

Lenthéric, to try to exert political pressure for an adjustment of prices: Jephcott also saw Robinson, who was visiting America. Jephcott was especially keen to learn about a potent new penicillin strain, Q.176, which had been isolated partly as a result of a research grant made by the Wisconsin Alumni Research Foundation. In deference to the views of the scientific workers, no endeavour had been made to obtain patent or other protection for Q.176, and when Jephcott met WARF's trustees, they were very critical of the way in which US manufacturers had used the new strain thereby enhancing their own profits.

There were difficulties, too, at Barnard Castle. The location of the factory had not been entirely the company's choice, and in any case was not intended for the penicillin fermentation process as it developed. Antibiotic production by fermentation was more expensive at Barnard Castle because of the problem of effluent disposal; in the event, however, the company contrived to manufacture antibiotics at Barnard Castle until the late 1960s, transporting the effluent by road tanker to the coast for disposal. Further development to extend the group's production and other facilities at Greenford was, it seemed, unlikely to be permitted. In the years since 1935 the immediate vicinity of the Greenford factory had become a built-up area within which larger-scale and more noxious chemical manufacture was unacceptable to the local authority, quite apart from the difficulties of effluent disposal. Additionally, there was a labour shortage in the London area and it was feared that the Board of Trade might oppose substantial further re-development by Glaxo Laboratories at Greenford as likely to accentuate housing and labour problems during the period of post-war reconstruction. For these reasons, therefore, a site of 100 acres at Ulverston in North Lancashire was bought, on which building work began in January 1947.

The board was clear that it was necessary to centralise the company's activities, not only to minimise the loss of time and energy in travel for staff, but also to improve control, maximise economies in production and technical services and secure distribution and economies by avoiding split transactions. It therefore proposed to transfer penicillin production from Barnard Castle to Ulverston as soon as practicable and to carry on manufacturing at Barnard Castle only streptomycin (see p. 179) and other experimental fermentations, while the major penicillin fermentation work, including research and development, was to be moved to Ulverston. Farex production was to be gradually transferred to Barnard Castle from Greenford leaving the latter to concentrate on pharmaceutical operations which required volume rather than diversity. Greenford was to provide general research facilities, other than fermentation, and to produce vaccines and fine

31 At Glaxo's new Barnard Castle factory penicillin was produced by the fermentation process. Ensuring the necessary sterility of the 10,000 gallons of liquid food in each vat where the penicillium mould was to grow as well as keeping the 'brew' at the right temperature presented considerable chemical engineering problems.

32 Penicillin and later streptomycin were made at the new Ulverston factory on the east side of the Furness Peninsula, where production started in April 1948.

chemicals of small volume. A policy was also initiated and implemented in 1949–1950 'to eliminate trivial products and consolidated packs'. Reviewing it in 1953, Jephcott thought it had been a success, although he felt the company had not 'allowed adequately for the sellers' market in which we then operated, nor did we anticipate the manner in which the policy would be interpreted in the Greenford factory.'[10]

In the immediate post-war years, Glaxo's penicillin production was dictated both by the shortage of the drug and what the company saw as 'an obligation to produce only those forms of penicillin or penicillin preparations which we believed were best for the patient'.[11] At the same time increased production and improving production efficiency led to a sharp and prolonged fall in the price of penicillin. Glaxo Laboratories, with effect from February 1950, reduced all its prices of penicillin products (crystalline and procaine) by amounts varying from 10 per cent to 25 per cent, and this process continued throughout the 1950s. As Jephcott pointed out to the shareholders in 1951, if the volume of sales and the money value of them were taken as 100 per cent in 1947, the volume in 1951 was 506 per cent but the value in that year was 237 per cent. Glaxo's own figures show a fall in the production cost of procaine penicillin between 1949 and 1953 of 79 per cent and for crystalline penicillin of 8 per cent. Over the same period wage rates rose between 8 and 17 per cent and packaging and other overhead costs rose correspondingly.[12] In 1952 American competition and other circumstances obliged Glaxo Laboratories to reduce its price for penicillin and its preparations, streptomycin and dihydrostreptomycin by an average of 15 per cent, which, if the volume of turnover had remained constant, would have resulted in a net reduction of profit of £950,000: in the event a reduction in production costs led to a smaller loss of profit.

All this had repercussions both at home and abroad. Although British exports of penicillin rose steadily in volume over this period, the financial projections on which Glaxo Laboratories launched its antibiotic developments were knocked away. In turn, this meant that Jephcott placed an increasing emphasis on improved production techniques to reduce costs. Justified though this emphasis was, it was sometimes a distraction to research and development, and created a commercial environment in which fundamental work to develop major new products was less likely.

Research policy

Reconstruction and expansion together would have been problematical at any time; for Glaxo in the immediate post-war years, undertaken against a background of restrictions and shortages, they were the more so. In the pharmaceutical industry it was an exciting time, with the marketing of many innovations. As Glaxo became committed to antibiotic production and research, the company learned the importance of patenting new products. In 1949 this was acknowledged with the establishment of the Patent Committee, whose members included the Patent Officer, Austin Bide, who had joined the company as a research chemist in 1940. New products, the results of research, had to be protected both at home and overseas, where Glaxo was also reconstructing and developing its activities (see chapters 11–15). Patent specification, litigation and licensing became highly important in the 1950s as the therapeutic revolution gained speed. Even more important in the early 1950s was the need for a 'realistic' research programme, with 'clearly defined objectives'.[13]

In July 1952 Sir Henry Tizard who, on his recent retirement as chairman of the Government's Advisory Council on Scientific Policy and Defence Research Policy had been recruited by his friend Jephcott to the board of Glaxo Laboratories, delivered the Messel Memorial Lecture entitled 'The Strategy of Science'.[14] It is a revealing expression of the attitudes and assumptions which governed the research efforts and development programmes of Glaxo in the two decades after the end of the Second World War, representing not only the accumulated wisdom of Tizard himself, but also the beliefs which made him such a congenial colleague to Jephcott.

'The word strategy was not part of the English language before the nineteenth century', Tizard observed; 'it finds no place in Dr Johnson's dictionary'. In science, as in warfare, he distinguished between strategy and tactics.

When I speak of the strategy of science I mean the art of so directing the application or advance of science as to make the most rapid progress of society, or of knowledge. When I speak of the tactics of science I mean the procedure or skilful devices calculated to gain the strategic end; in other words 'research'. And just as the strategy of war may be profoundly modified by some new advance of tactics, so must strategy of the application of science to industry depend not only on technical skill and knowledge but on the economic circumstances of different countries.[15]

Tizard confessed to 'perplexity and frustration' at Britain's condition in 1952,

and the small probability that we shall recover real economic stability in my lifetime ... In this year 1952, seven years after the Second World War ended, we still depend on charity from overseas to avoid bankruptcy. Shortage of raw materials, high taxation, controls and restrictions hamper enterprise and adventure ... the serious state of the country is ... hidden by a false facade of full employment and of record output and of profits of the manufacturing industries ... For many years before the last war we were in a state of unstable equilibrium, exposed to the storms of any adverse world event outside our control. There has been a longstanding weakness in the British economy, which becomes more difficult to eradicate the more the population expands.[16]

Jephcott was similarly preoccupied with the vulnerability of the national economy and its consequent constrictions on the company's research options. As part of government policy, he noted in 1952, companies' total expenditure on capital account was limited in order to provide for the national armaments programme; the total sum available to industry – some £500 million annually – was, he considered, 'of doubtful adequacy to maintain industrial plants in fully effective production'.[17] For this reason Jephcott in the early 1950s suspected that 'it may indeed be in the national interest that the present proportion of expenditure upon long-term research should not be maintained', as the effect of reducing it would be 'to focus research activities upon improvements that will not involve heavy capital expenditure, but can be brought to fruition by modifying current techniques'.

Accordingly, Jephcott urged that research should be orientated towards the goal of 'enhanced productivity', and deplored the 'false values' which meant that there were 'no academic medals attaching to most applied research'. Indeed, according to Greenford's postwar director of research, Jephcott often posed as 'an old devil' who believed that research was 'just a parasite on the organisation': of course, no-one in his heart knew better that this was not the case, but the pose suited his purpose on the research and development committee (see chapter 8), particularly given his conviction that it was only 'by increased efficiency gained with little or no capital expenditure that industry can best aid the national economic problem and ward off inflationary pressure'.[18] Tizard too believed that Britain had

33 Industrial relations at Greenford had been paternalistic in the days of
Alec Nathan. A Joint Advisory Committee, seen here at a meeting late in
1946, was set up just after the war.

paid far too much attention until recently to the need for fundamental research in
industry, and far too little to the need for development and skilled application of
what is already known. It is useless to increase scientific capital . . . if it bears no
interest . . . When money resources are limited it becomes all the more necessary to
concentrate the scientific resources. Strategy is all important.[19]

There were other inhibitions on the company's research tactics in the early
1950s. Building licences were required before any major new development
could be put into practice, and the granting of such licences was a slow and
sometimes uncertain business. 'Against this background industry may
hesitate to invest in research that, if successful, cannot be brought to
production so that, in consequence, the cost of research cannot be recovered
until some uncertain future date, by which time the process may have lost its
novelty and possibly even have been outmoded', Jephcott wrote. With the
government limiting capital expenditure by industry, responsibility for
allocating licences and resources rested with the central bureaucracy. 'In
these circumstances', Jephcott considered, 'it is almost inevitable that
permanent officials, seeking precedents for guidance, will look to past
performance rather than future hopes. In short, established industry that can
point to output in the "datum period", will almost inevitably get preference.' These attitudes, so Jephcott warned in 1952, had 'most seriously
prejudice[d]' Britain's industrial future.[20]

The course of business 1951–1957

Although Glaxo continued to expand its product range and its volume of sales at home and overseas in these years, its profits fell in 1953–54 and then remained static (at around £2.5m) until the late 1950s (see table A4). The main reason, as the company pointed out in its evidence submitted in 1953 to the Guillebaud Committee (which reported on the cost of the National Health Service in 1956) was the falling prices of both antibiotics and other pharmaceutical products. The company noted:

In money value the most important single drug we produce is penicillin; second to that is streptomycin . . . the price of penicillin to a hospital in 1948 was 6/4d for a 1 mega vial and of streptomycin 16/ for a 1 gram vial. Today those prices have been reduced to 2/ and 3/3 respectively, which are 31 per cent and 20 per cent of the 1948 levels. Even though this is an extreme example, it demonstrates a general truth. We market approximately 50 pharmaceutical products, of which about 20 were sold before the war. Of that 20, four only are now supplied at prices above, but 11 are at prices below those ruling in 1939.[21]

Succinctly the Glaxo memorandum pointed out the company's priorities: 'the interests of a business such as ours demand the devotion of at least as much attention to overseas as to domestic circumstances, to the more distant future as to the present and to the marketing of new as to the sale of existing products'.

Much of Glaxo's resources were devoted to the search for and introduction of new products in these years, a quest which bore fruit at the end of the decade. In British terms Glaxo's commitment to research and development put it in the front rank. In its evidence to Guillebaud, the company put its annual spending on research at between £450,000 and £500,000; by comparison, ICI told Guillebaud that in 1952 it spent £520,000 on medicinal research, while Wellcome also gave a figure of £500,000, although only £300,000 of that was spent in the UK.[22] These amounts, however, were small when compared with the resources put into research by the American pharmaceutical corporations (see page 168). The ratio was reflected in drug discoveries: of the total new drugs patented between 1941 and 1963, British companies accounted for less than 5 per cent, the Swiss for nearly 8 per cent, German and French companies for some 9 per cent, while those attributable to American sources numbered 61 per cent.[23]

In 1952 Glaxo acquired a new product through the purchase of Dextran Ltd. The company had been established in 1942 as the East Anglian Chemical Company to exploit *dextran* as a substitute plasma – the fluid portion of blood in which cells and corpuscles are suspended. Dextran had been further developed at Birmingham University before the company went into commercial production in 1949 at a factory at Aycliffe in Yorkshire.

34 Lord Woolton visited Greenford in July 1952 and here is seen looking
at penicillin packing with Sir Robert Hutchings (right) and Sir Maurice
Hutton (left).

With a small production and administrative staff (less than thirty) the
company had arranged to market its product through Crookes Laboratories, but hoped that its major customer would be the Ministry of Health.
Dextran urged on the Ministry the 'strategic value' of its product as 'the only
suitable plasma substitute ... that will preserve life in the event of atomic
warfare with its high percentage of death from shock and burns'; but the
Ministry rejected suggestions that it should stockpile dextran for a national
emergency. By 1952, when attempts to get the approval of the US Food and
Drug Administration for Intradex (an improved product) failed, the company was in financial straits with no funds to develop its new anticoagulant,
dextran sulphate, which it considered to be as effective and cheaper than
existing products in that market. In July 1952 Glaxo paid £56,000 for the
issued capital and 'B' debentures of Dextran and made a loan of £16,000 for
the purchase of Dextran's 'A' Debentures.[24] A year later the manufacture of
Intradex was transferred to Barnard Castle. In Britain Intradex sales were
never large (in 1962 their value was only £8,000) but the manufacture, by
fermentation, fitted with Glaxo's own interests and skills at Barnard Castle
and Ulverston.

35 A cartoon published in the *Glaxo Bulletin* in 1953 showing stalwarts of the home sales force, including the Chairman's brother, Charles.

The pharmaceutical industry

The pharmaceutical industry and the environment within which it operated changed rapidly in the 1950s. The establishment of the National Health Service stimulated the industry's development but also led to increasing public scrutiny of the industry and its pricing structure, first through the Guillebaud Committee, then in 1959 the Hinchliffe Committee and ultimately the investigations of the Sainsbury Committee in 1967. Concern with the need to monitor pharmaceutical profits led to the establishment of the Voluntary Price Regulation Scheme in 1957. At the same time British pharmaceutical companies found themselves increasingly threatened on their home ground by their competitors from abroad, particularly the USA. In the two decades after the war over thirty foreign-owned subsidiaries of pharmaceutical companies established themselves in Britain either directly, or through the purchase of one of the smaller UK pharmaceutical firms.[25] This situation gave cause for serious concern to Glaxo's management and to that of other, smaller pharmaceutical manufacturers in Great Britain.

In April 1957 the directors of Glaxo were presented with a paper showing a comparative analysis of Glaxo's financial results in the preceding year with those of three US drug companies. In 1958 the study was extended to cover eight US companies, Eli Lilly, Merck, Pfizer, Parke Davis, Abbot, Smith Kline & French, Schering and Searle. Outside this group there were only four ethical (prescription) drug companies of major importance in the United States – Squibb, Lederle, Wyeth and Bristol Laboratories. Data for these four companies was not available since each was a subsidiary of an organisation with substantial interests outside pharmaceuticals. Whether capital employed or turnover was taken as the yardstick, the size of the Glaxo group was far below the US average. In 1957 only one (Searle) of the eight US companies employed smaller resources and had a lower total turnover than Glaxo. Eli Lilly's employed capital was almost four times that of the Glaxo group. Pfizer, with rather less than three times Glaxo's capital, achieved a turnover in pharmaceuticals between four and five times as great. The size afforded by the North American market was important to the scale of the US companies' operations. While in 1956–1957 two-thirds of Glaxo's consolidated turnover arose in overseas markets, of the US companies only Pfizer derived more than one-third of its sales revenue from overseas operations: the proportion for the rest varied from 14 to 30 per cent.

Comparatively high profit margins were characteristic of North American trading. While gross trading profit as a return on capital employed for the US companies ranged from 2 to 40 per cent more than Glaxo's ratio, net profit before tax showed smaller differentials in most cases, varying from 3 to 26 per cent. The US companies all spent more on selling and administrative expenses, paid out a higher proportion of net profit in dividends and allocated a larger proportion of profit to research.[26]

The comparative exercise revealed in more detail what was already known to Glaxo's directors; that the strength and size of the US companies gave them greater technical resources with which to compete in British and world markets. In these circumstances, smaller British pharmaceutical houses felt vulnerable to American predators, particularly at a time when the pace of general merger activity, leading to greater concentration in manufacturing industry, was quickening.[27]

There has been as yet little historical analysis as to why most of the many small enterprises in the British pharmaceutical industry remained independent and increasingly vulnerable in the period after the Second World War. Dr Michael Robson has recently suggested that not only are commercial strategies rarely made explicit at the time, but even in retrospect their direction is almost impossible to extricate from the detail which surrounds key decisions. There were joint ventures and agreements between pharmaceutical manufacturers – for example between Allen & Hanburys and British Drug Houses to market insulin in the 1920s and later the Therapeutic Research Corporation – but they were generally short-lived and appear to

Table 5. *Glaxo's performance compared with that of eight US companies, 1957*

	Glaxo Group	Glaxo Group (excl. Foods)	Eli Lilly	Merck	Pfizer	Parke Davis	Abbott	SKF	Schering	Searle
1 Capital employed (£000)	15,800	...	61,110	52,940	45,390	41,760	29,060	15,870	17,660	9,630
Proportion of capital employed represented by:										
Capital employed overseas	42.4%	...	5.4%	19.6%	39.5%	26.7%	21.4%	...	...	...
Total turnover	134.0%	...	116.7%	126.2%	163.0%	138.9%	137.0%	236.0%	163.2%	113.0%
Net profit before tax	36.4%	...	38.7%	31.0%	33.8%	46.7%	30.2%	90.0%	62.4%	52.8%
2 Turnover (£000)	21,180	16,360	71,360	66,760	73,980	57,960	39,740	41,250	28,820	10,920
Proportion of total turnover represented by:										
Turnover overseas	65.2%	...	...	26.5%	37.0%	30.2%	24.0%	...	19.5%	14.0%
Gross trading profit	39.9%	...	...	55.3%	51.2%	66.2%	61.5%	68.8%	79.5%	72.3%
Selling, adm., etc. expenses	17.6%	...	...	26.7%	26.6%	30.7%	32.9%	23.2%	38.1%	} 25.3%
Research expenses	2.5%	3.3%	6.6%	7.0%	9.4%	4.1%	4.5%	6.6%	6.5%	
Net profit before tax	19.7%	...	33.1%	24.6%	20.7%	33.6%	22.1%	38.2%	38.2%	46.2%
3 Net profit before tax (£000)	4,170	—	23,650	16,390	15,340	19,510	8,790	15,750	11,010	5,080
Proportion represented by:										
Tax	55.9%	—	51.2%	49.7%	46.7%	49.0%	48.5%	53.4%	50.2%	51.4%
Dividends paid	9.2%	—	24.0%	29.7%	26.7%	26.2%	30.3%	} 46.6%	15.4%	32.4%
Retained profits	34.9%	—	24.8%	20.6%	26.6%	24.9%	21.2%		34.6%	16.2%

Note: Glaxo Group, 1956/57; SKF, 1956 and 1957; all other US companies, 1957.

Table 6. *Capital employed and profit ratios: Glaxo and Allen & Hanburys 1953–1957*

Year	Capital employed £	Profit before tax £	Ratio Percentage
1953:			
Glaxo	10,355,914	2,065,635	30
A & H	3,106,921	234,766	7.6
1954:			
Glaxo	11,499,167	2,933,263	26
A & H	3,165,100	299,035	7.2
1955:			
Glaxo	12,651,012	2,909,108	23
A & H	3,301,830	325,734	9.9
1956:			
Glaxo	13,895,992	3,106,055	22
A & H	3,335,116	296,922	8.9
1957:			
Glaxo	15,799,133	4,169,882	26
A & H	3,820,077	382,538	10

Source: Memo 25 April 1958, H. J. Papers, Packet 43, Glaxo Archives.

have foundered on personal differences between the individuals concerned, often dissolving into acrimony. Dr Robson attributes the failure to merge to the lack of 'a major charismatic visionary figure around whom any merger scheme could crystallize'.[28]

The Glaxo – Allen & Hanburys' merger

Allen & Hanburys, whose origins dated back to Quaker enterprise in the eighteenth century, had developed from making proprietary products into an ethical drug manufacturer.[29] Despite an enviable reputation in the industry, considerable overseas interests and extensive research facilities at Ware, in Hertfordshire, Allen & Hanburys stagnated in the early 1950s. By 1957, as the table above shows, its capital employed was only a fifth of Glaxo's, showing only a small increase over the previous five years; Allen & Hanburys' profit record was similarly stagnant, giving a low return on capital.

As Jephcott later recorded, at a Pharmaceutical Society luncheon in July 1957, he found himself sitting next to Cyril Maplethorpe of A & H:

Conversation ... turned on the future of the pharmaceutical industry in the UK. I informed him of my enquiries regarding the magnitude of the US companies' interest in the UK market, and their apparent policy to secure the major part of it at any cost. I said that, having regard to the weight of certain US companies in men and money, it was, in my opinion only a matter of time before the British concerns were swamped out of existence, the smaller going to the wall first. A & H consequently before Glaxo.

To my surprise, Maplethorpe's reply was one of prompt and emphatic agreement, and an expression of desire to talk over the situation with me.[30]

The discussions that followed were leisurely and punctuated by Jephcott's absences on visits abroad. Palmer and Wilkins visited A & H's factory and Wilkins also went to the research establishment at Ware. There, he informed Jephcott, 'he was well impressed by what he had seen, and by those whom he met, particularly some of the younger executives but, in respect of buildings and equipment, there was an obvious evidence of shortage of cash for capital expenditures, but of this we were well aware'.[31]

In March 1958 the two parties began to discuss the detail of the offer to be made by Glaxo: the A & H directors, particularly the Hanbury family, proud of their traditions and antiquity, insisted it should be called a 'marriage' and not a merger, least of all an acquisition. According to Jephcott:

The problem which was obvious arose from the fact that the Stock Exchange valued our shares on the basis of a 4 per cent return, whilst Allenbury's [sic] were on a 6 per cent basis, but, in addition, the asset value behind Allenbury's shares was 50 per cent more than the then ruling market price of 60/ for a £1 Ordinary. On the other hand, our own asset value was less than the market price, so that we could not argue that there was any offset. We had to accept that the asset value of Allenbury's stock was approximately 91/ and we suggested either a combination of our 7 per cent Preference shares plus a proportion of Ordinary or, in the alternative, 14 Glaxo Ordinary for 5 A & H.

Allen & Hanburys' response was swift; the mixed Preference and Ordinary proposal 'did not appeal to them ... they felt, on grounds of value apart from convenience, three GL Ordinary Shares for one A & H would be more acceptable'. To that the Glaxo Board agreed on 31 March and, after further meetings, the offer and its acceptance were made public on 8 April.

Business history affords many illustrations of the difficulty of carrying into effect the rationalisation policies necessary to achieve the benefits projected from such a merger. One frequent obstacle for members of old family firms was the loss of 'personal autonomy and direct command relationships in their own firms'.[32] Jephcott was aware of the problem: his record of the meeting immediately before the merger was agreed with J.C. (afterwards Sir John) Hanbury, noted that the latter, 'approached the whole matter in a very statesmanlike manner, and said that the proposal had at first come as something of a shock to him, which was very understandable having regard to the long family history of the company but, nevertheless, having given it mature thought, he was convinced that it was the right thing to do and was very happy to think of an association with us'.[33]

At the end of the first full year of A & H's membership of the Glaxo Group, Jephcott recorded that he saw no reason to regret the original decision to merge, but admitted to some disappointment at the slowness of amalgamation at the operational level. In that year A & H represented 19 per cent of the Group's capital employed and contributed 12 per cent of Group profits. In a speech to the directors of A & H, Jephcott warned of the dangers of parochialism and urged the necessity of 'group thinking' at all levels. He was, he intimated, disappointed with the progress that there had been in both organisations' recognising the activities best conducted jointly while, for the sake of goodwill, preserving individual corporate identity. They were moving in the right direction, Jephcott concluded, in achieving the objective of the merger, technical strength to face competition at home and overseas but time was not on their side.[34]

Although Jephcott realised the necessity for Glaxo to become larger, both by merger and by self-generated growth, he regretted that the size of the Group made it impossible for him to maintain the personal knowledge of and contracts with all the staff which had characterised his period of office as Managing Director. In 1956, when he was sixty-four, Jephcott felt it was time for a younger man to take on the more onerous duties and Herbert Palmer succeeded him as Managing Director although Jephcott continued as Chairman. At the same time Fred Wilkins became Deputy Managing Director; more ambitious and extrovert than Palmer, Wilkins hoped, intended and manoeuvred to succeed Jephcott as Chairman and there was, until 1963 when Jephcott finally retired, considerable rivalry between the two men which reverberated through the Group. In the event neither succeeded him, but that is outside the scope of this history. In the meantime the reins remained in Jephcott's hands and it was he who orchestrated Glaxo's next major acquisition.

The merger with Evans Medical

Like Allen & Hanburys, Evans Medical Ltd was a long-established family business, founded originally in 1809 in Worcester. John Evans and his brother were chemists and druggists but in 1818 John left Worcester for London where in 1821 he started his own business and later developed it in partnership with J. S. Lescher. A branch was opened in Liverpool in the 1830s where later laboratories and manufacturing facilities were established. At its separate Biological Institute in Runcorn the company developed a specialism in vaccines which was expanded after 1945. Evans' factory was destroyed during the Second World War and the company built a new factory at Speke, near Liverpool. In the post-war years Evans Medical expanded considerably as the company had, like Glaxo developed considerable overseas interests.[35] With net assets of £3m (the Glaxo figure was £24m), a reputation for growth and success and a strong cash position, Evans Medical was, as it found to its cost in 1960, in a vulnerable position. Through the merchant bank, Warburgs, approaches were made in June 1960 to Ian Fergusson, Chairman and Managing Director of Evans (and a descendant of John Evans) by Fisons, who had recently failed in a bid to acquire British Drug Houses.

Fergusson, by his own account, did not look favourably upon the suggestion that Fisons might make a formal offer for Evans Medical. He felt they had little to offer his company, which in any case was 'confident [of] our own destiny'. But at the same time Jephcott wrote to Fergusson in June 1960, suggesting a meeting, which took place in September. Early in January 1961 Fisons made an offer to purchase Evans Medical. A meeting swiftly followed on 5 January between Fergusson, Jephcott and his fellow director, Sir Jeremy Raisman. With assurances from Jephcott that 'he would like to deal with this in precisely the same way as they had dealt with Allen & Hanburys'[36] the idea of combination with Glaxo was, it was ascertained, appealing to Fergusson. It only remained to settle the financial terms. While Evans wanted a cash offer Jephcott's advisers emphasised to him 'that he was in no position to make a big cash offer'. After private consultations 'Jephcott said that whereas personally he would greatly welcome and be very anxious for an association, cash was the stumbling block. The best he could suggest was one Glaxo 10/ share for two Evans Medical 5/ stock units'.[37] Fergusson indicated that he thought this would be acceptable and on those terms the formal offer was made. Whereas the Fisons offer valued Evans at £6.75m, the Glaxo offer was worth £8.33m and it was recommended to and accepted by the shareholders of Evans Medical. As Fergusson minuted in a note to Evans managerial staff:

It is appreciated that many members of the staff may feel some regret that we cannot continue alone to progress as satisfactorily as the group has done in recent years. The winds of change are, however, blowing over industry throughout the world and the trend towards larger and ever larger units is something which cannot be avoided and must, therefore, be accepted.[38]

As Jephcott had promised, Evans Medical retained its separate identity within the Glaxo Group and was treated in the same way as Allen & Hanburys.

The Glaxo Group, 1962

Following the acquisition of Evans Medical, the Glaxo Group Ltd was formally constituted as the new parent company in January 1962 with Jephcott as Chairman and Palmer as Managing Director. A new subsidiary company – Glaxo Laboratories Ltd – was to carry on manufacturing and trading activities and another new subsidiary, Glaxo Research Ltd was to be responsible for R and D. Significant of the growing recognition of Glaxo of its place in the pharmaceutical world was the presentation to the directors in August 1962 of the first 'appreciation of the total UK pharmaceutical market'.[39] A series of tables showed Glaxo's position in relation to other pharmaceutical manufacturers. Although Glaxo had only two entries (Crystapen – an antibiotic – and Efcortelan – a corticosteroid) in the list of twenty leading ethical products, in the table of twenty leading manufacturers, Glaxo's percentage share of total ethicals gave it third place (4.7 per cent) after Pfizer with 9 per cent and Lederle with 9.1 per cent. With Allen & Hanburys and Evans added, Glaxo's share increased to 7.7 per cent. In most of the ten therapeutic classes of ethical products in which Glaxo was involved, the company secured a reasonable market share, but in antibiotics, corticosteroids and dermatological preparations it was particularly successful. The success with Grisovin (a dermatological product – see chapter 9) was particularly marked: Glaxo had nearly 79 per cent of the market (admittedly a small one) and ICI, with Fulcin only 21 per cent.

The success of Glaxo's research and development programme (see chapter 8) was reflected in the results for the year ending in June 1962. Corticosteroids represented more than a quarter of the total value of pharmaceutical sales, almost the same amount as the sales of antibiotics (mainly penicillin). The results also reflected the constraints within which the company had to operate: vaccines produced slightly less than budgeted, because less polivirin vaccine had been taken up and that requirement was governed by the Ministry of Health. Half of Glaxo's home turnover came from foods, and most of that from one product, Ostermilk 2, with which Glaxo dominated the market for infant milks.[40] In 1962 the company opened its second milk-drying factory in Great Britain, at Kendal. Although Glaxo regarded itself and it was publicly seen as primarily a pharmaceutical company, the business of dried milk, in which it had established itself in the first decade of the century and which in turn had been the stimulus for the involvement with pharmaceuticals, was still, sixty years on, an important part of the business.

8

Research and development: a strategy of science?

The immediate post-war years

In 1945 Frank Robinson, Glaxo's director of research, left the company (he became successively research director for Distillers (1945–1948), Allen & Hanburys (1948–1960) and Twyford Laboratories). He was replaced by T. F. Macrae (b. 1906). Educated at Glasgow and Munich Universities (where he did biochemical work on enzymes), Macrae had worked on pituitary hormones for the Lister Institute (1931–1933) and on cancer research at the London Hospital (1933–1935), before appointment to the nutrition department of the Lister Institute. After war service with the RAF as a nutrition expert, he was recruited by Jephcott after demobilisation, and remained research director for almost twenty years.

When, early in 1946, it was decided to overhaul Glaxo's research, the company found its capacity for change circumscribed by various factors. Foremost among these was the cramped accommodation for research activities; but there was little hope of immediate improvement, given post-war shortages of building materials and the stringency of centralised building controls. 'Not only is it impossible to obtain additional accommodation for research, it is impossible to obtain buildings within which to manufacture and pack the products that may result from such research', a memorandum noted in February 1946, adding that as Glaxo Laboratories was generally 'experienced in, and equipped for, the production of materials in relatively small quantities – in kilos rather than tons ... [a] product having a high activity and a small dosage fits in most readily with our present organisation'.[1]

Research functions within a company like Glaxo Laboratories fell into four main categories: first, research to improve existing manufacturing processes; second, research to devise new methods of producing known substances; third, research to produce new substances with a structure related to that of substances known to have useful physiological properties,

175

for example analogues; fourth, research into compounds with novel structures and physiologically unknown properties. Work in the first category was less attractive to a research chemist, but was also less speculative and offered the best prospect of quickly paying its way. As a Glaxo policy paper on research declared in 1946: 'only by working at the highest efficiency can we do our duty at home by making our products available at the lowest cost, contribute our quota to postwar reconstruction by keeping ourselves in a competitive position in export markets, and at the same time continue to pay high wages and salaries'.[2] A typical example of the utility of this sort of research occurred in Calciferol production, where two modifications made in 1945 increased overall yields by some 9 per cent.

Process research therefore enjoyed the highest priority at Greenford in the immediate post-war period, followed by research to devise new methods of producing known substances in which the company was already commercially interested. The third category of research, for new substances such as analogues, had the attraction of requiring minimal pharmacological work, as the nature of the physiological activity involved was known in advance. However, in 1946 Glaxo Laboratories anticipated that the introduction of a National Health Service, as promised by the new Labour Government, would lower the demand for proprietary products and hence reduce the scope for this kind of research. 'It will undoubtedly be much more difficult than hitherto to market a product having similar uses to one already available unless its superiority is beyond question', the company predicted.[3] On the other hand, research in related spheres, such as developing a water-soluble derivative with vitamin K activity, had some attractions because of their wide applications.

Research on compounds with novel structures, while attractive to research chemists, represented 'the highest degree of speculation on the part of the Company', and over-stretched existing pharmacological facilities. In 1946, at least, Glaxo felt that such work should be conducted in future on a far smaller scale than hitherto with researchers engaged on it being of high calibre but few in number.[4] For the reasons outlined above, Glaxo determined to concentrate its research effort in three main areas, penicillin and streptomycin (see below) and vitamin B_{12}.

Vitamin B_{12}

In 1926 two US scientists had discovered that pernicious anaemia, which hitherto had been a fatal and incurable disease, could be treated with an intensive diet of raw liver. In early pernicious anaemia therapy, it was impracticable to administer large amounts of liver, and it was instead necessary to prepare extracts whose strength was specified by their equiva-

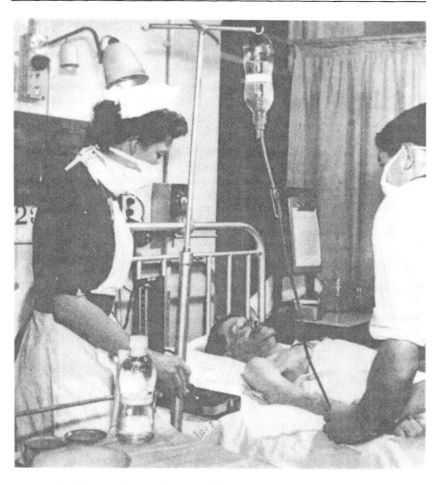

36 Dextran being administered to a patient in hospital.

lence to raw liver. During the 1930s, the quest for an active principle involved an immense amount of biochemical research, resulting in an improvement of manufacturing techniques but the active factor remained elusive, chiefly because highly purified liver extracts, despite their potency, contained only an infinitesimal quantity of the factor. Its nature was unknown and there was no test available other than actual clinical trials on cases of pernicious anaemia in relapse. As such tests, of their nature, could not be standardised, each step in this long train of work towards isolation had to await the result of tedious confirmatory chemical trials.

Glaxo's research laboratories began work to isolate the anti-anaemia factor from liver extracts during the 1930s, and in 1936 the company was able to acquire a licence to use the process, developed by two Norwegian doctors, Laland and Klem, to make a highly purified liver extract (see chapter 4). This was successfully marketed by Glaxo Laboratories as Examen; it was, however, a cumbersome process for, according to Jephcott, from a ton of liver only 'a few grains' of the anti-anaemia factor could be produced. When wartime shortages of ox liver arose, a short-lived attempt to make the product alternatively based on pig liver failed; but it was in 1946 that the head of Glaxo's Biological Unit, Dr E. Lester Smith, made a breakthrough in identifying the factor using chromagraphic techniques.

In chromatography a plant extract is dissolved in petrol, poured on to a column of alumina, and washed through with more petrol. In the course of half an hour at least six different pigments appear in narrow rings down the column: green at the top, then yellow, orange-brown, red and orange. The various pigments are the natural colouring matters present in most plants, the chlorophylls, xanthophylls and carotenes. Chromatography was thus invaluable in dividing up an otherwise intractable mixture, either for analytical purposes, or to prepare a specimen of one of the compounds. Although chromatography was developed in 1906, by Tswett, a Russian botanist, it proved invaluable in medical and nutritional research. In the late 1930s and 1940s adaptations of Tswett's technique assisted in the isolation of nearly every new biological factor (except proteins). Thus, before molecular distillation was perfected, vitamin A was purified by chromatography on columns of alumina or calcium.

Vitamin D_3 was isolated from fish liver oils, and pro-vitamin D_2 (7-dehydrocholesterol) was concentrated chromatographically from several natural sources, such as mussels and earthworms. The technique was also indispensable in isolating, characterising and synthesising vitamins E and K. Equally significantly for Glaxo's researchers, both penicillin and streptomycin needed chromatographic assistance. Such was the company's interest in the techniques that Bacharach in 1941 produced an English translation of the standard reference book on the technique.[5]

Using these methods, Lester Smith made the startling and useful discovery that the anti-anaemic activity followed a deep pink band between the dark brown and yellow zones on a partition chromatogram from refined liver extract. By repeated chromatography and other purification methods he produced a series of fractions of increasing activity. A dose of only 0.3 milligram (300 micrograms) of the best fraction gave a full response in regeneration of red cells, haemoglobin and reticulocytes, while clinical trials at the Royal Victoria Infirmary, Newcastle-upon-Tyne, indicated that the material was also effective in treating the neurological complications of pernicious anaemia and in relieving the lingual symptoms. The material was purer than any previously available, but was amorphous. Smith's success was first reported in a letter published in *Nature* on 24 April 1948, but had been preceded by an announcement from Merck whose researchers in the USA had also progressed to the stage of isolating a red crystalline substance which they dubbed vitamin B_{12} (see page 244). A month later, in a paper read on 29 May to a meeting in Oxford of the Biochemical Society, Smith reported that, after further extensive purification, the material which he had isolated had also been crystallized.

The new substance had remarkable potency. The single dose for producing optimal haemopoietic response in pernicious anaemia was about 15 micrograms, equivalent to one microgram daily, in comparison with a dosage level of folic acid over 10,000 times as great. While Merck isolated the substance by microbiological assay, Smith's team 'used the more cumbersome though therapeutically more specific method of testing on cases of pernicious anaemia in relapse'.[6] Following this significant research work, Glaxo began to market 'Cytamen' in the autumn of 1949 with a range of strengths of vitamin B_{12} and production started at Ulverston in the following year. Development work in 1950–1951 simplified the process and produced improved yields of crystalline vitamin B_{12}. Glaxo's research resulted in important additions to the product range in the 1950s in the various formulations of vitamin B_{12}.

The development of Streptomycin

In 1939 Selman Waksman (who was to be the 1952 Nobel Laureate in Medicine) and his collaborators began a detailed study of the production by soil organisms of antibiotics with therapeutic value. They isolated and examined several thousand actinomycetes, a group of unicellular plants standing in structure and organisation somewhere between moulds and bacteria. Waksman's team paid particular attention to species inhibiting the growth of gram-negative organisms, and had their first success in isolating a substance which they called streptothricin, which was, however, too toxic for general therapeutic use. In 1944 Waksman and others reported the discovery of a relatively non-toxic metabolite of *Streptomyces griseus* which they named streptomycin, but for two years they had difficulty in producing streptomycin in quantities and under conditions that made concentration, extraction and purification possible. Only in 1946 was it found that the addition of streptomycin itself to the culture medium favoured the growth of streptomycin producers while inhibiting the non-producers; but this discovery proved a breakthrough in isolating new and more active strains.

Streptomycin afforded new hope for certain tuberculous conditions which had previously shown 100 per cent mortality, notably meningal and miliary tuberculosis, in which it proved a real life-saver. In the early tests, results were obtained by giving both intra-muscular and intra-thecal injections, as use of the dual route secured effective levels of streptomycin in the cerebro-spinal fluid. Streptomycin therapy, so it was reported as early as 1946, was most useful in patients with progressive tuberculosis, the suppressive treatment for a few months often resulting in permanent control of their infection. Treatment of bone tuberculosis was less promising. Dihydrostrep-tomycin (discovered by Merck in 1946) was as effective as streptomycin in all tuberculous conditions in which it was tried, and showed lower toxicity under prolonged administration.

The drug was effective in other infections, including septicaemia, pneumonia and uninary tract infections, but careful monitoring was necessary to guard against developing drug resistance, especially with urinary tract infections. Short courses of treatment with fairly large doses proved to be preferable. A single dose of 0.5 gram of streptomycin usually cured gonor-rhoea, but had no effect upon any accompanying syphilitic infection: the masking of the latter infection, as occurred with penicillin therapy, was therefore absent. The drug was also suitable for treating cases of bowel infection or operations, undulant fever, megingitis, shingella dysentery, bacterial endocarditis and bubonic plague.

Initially, streptomycin was produced by surface culture of *Streptomycin griseus* or yeast or malt extract media, but production was soon attained by means of deep fermentation in tanks, with continuous agitation and aeration. As such it held considerable attraction for Glaxo, with its expertise in deep fermentation techniques. Glaxo first became involved with strepto-mycin during 1945, and in January of the following year the company's medical director, Hector Walker, submitted a report to the board recom-mending that the company undertake large-scale streptomycin production at a new factory, similar to Barnard Castle, with an initial outlay of £250,000 rising to a total of £400,000. 'The Board were of the unanimous opinion that it opened up a field of such medical importance in the treatment of Tuberculosis, Whooping Cough and Typhoid that we could not afford to keep out', and adopted Walker's suggestions.[7]

On a visit to the USA some months later, Jephcott reached an understand-ing with Merck about streptomycin licensing, but negotiations on royalties continued until 1947, with Jephcott reporting in September of that year that Merck's proposals for collaboration upon streptomycin production resem-bled the existing penicillin agreement except that there would be no minimum royalty, that the liability for royalty payment would continue for fifteen years and that there would be continuous interchange of information throughout the agreement. Streptomycin was manufactured at Barnard

Castle in 1948 and 1949, until the new plant at Ulverston (see page 159) was ready to go into production late in 1949.

The organisation of Glaxo's research and development

Research and development work for Glaxo was carried on after 1950 at two establishments, Greenford and Sefton Park in Buckinghamshire, the latter opening in that year for antibiotics research. At Greenford, Dr T. F. Macrae was director of research and at Sefton Park, Dr Sandy Campbell. Both establishments were governed by the company's Research and Development Committee, which for most of the 1950s was chaired by Jephcott and included Herbert Palmer, Sir Henry Tizard, Sir Robert Hutchings, Sir Maurice Hutton, Dr A. H. (Sandy) Campbell, Dr Fred Wilkins, Dr Hector Walker, Dr Tom Macrae and Austin Bide. As chairman both of the committee and of the company, Jephcott was prominent in shaping and directing research policy, particularly where it was affected by the company's financial position (see chapter 7). He also acted as the committee's principal conduit of information to Glaxo's board of directors. Tizard's personality and experience made him an important influence, until his death in 1959, on both the strategy and the tactics of the committee.[8] According to his biographers:

He was master of the searching question. He had the patience to listen, the power to think, the ability to decide, the courage to change his mind. He had little interest and less belief in size for its own sake ... He was constantly looking ahead ... Tizard had the great gift of being able to talk on seemingly equal terms to people of all kinds of ages, and to find out what they thought about things ... He regarded each as an individual worthy of his attention, and he had a happy knack of throwing out the challenging remark that would stimulate response ... Tizard had a flair for inspiring people with some of his own enthusiasm for getting things done ... He was always throwing off ideas about all sorts of things, and producing in those who picked them up an urge to put them into effect ... his choice was sometimes influenced by a 'hunch', but the workings of his mind were so well integrated that his hunches were often as well based as the carefully thought out conclusions of other men. At any rate most of them worked.[9]

In Tizard's view:

Great men of science are good strategists, though they may now know it. Of the countless experiments they might make, they seem to choose the right ones with unerring instinct. Strategy, in this sense, is more important for the advance of science than good tactics.

He cited the physicist, Sir Joseph Thomson, as one not labelled among the world's great experimenters, but who 'was certainly one of the world's greatest scientists':

The ideal director of research in industry is a strategist, first and foremost. He must spend laborious days and nights studying the industry he serves – and what is just as important, studying the men who run it. He must inspire his own staff with the joy of practical achievement. He must deal gently but firmly with accountants who do not like doing what has never been done before. He must be a welcome visitor to the factories, always ready to help and slow to criticise. It is not at all necessary that he should be a distinguished scientist, though he must be or have been an experimenter.[10]

The other committee members represented Glaxo's internal laboratory, scientific, medical and patent interests and personnel. The laboratory directors, Macrae and Campbell, submitted regular progress reports, research proposals and budget projections to the committee from Greenford and Sefton Park. Wilkins performed similar duties on behalf of the northern factories, Ulverston and Barnard Castle, and their research facilities, which grew after the transfer of penicillin and streptomycin process research there in 1954 (a northern group research and development committee, to liaise with Greenford and Sefton Park was established in 1953).

Sir Robert Hutchings also addressed research policy and projects and their impact on Glaxo's patent protection especially in the period when he chaired the patent Committee. Sir Maurice Hutton took part in Research and Development Committee discussions about future research and expenditures, although his actual contribution to committee decisions was minimal. Walker evaluated Glaxo's research programme's medical potential in the context of contemporary medical opinion.

Research and Development Committee members initially met four times a year to discuss the individual laboratory research reports and supplementary technical documents circulated to them before the meeting and decide what action to take. As the volume of technical material issued from the research laboratories increased, from late 1953, interim meetings were also arranged to preview progress reports and to make preliminary recommendations. Jephcott, Tizard, Campbell and Macrae presided over these sessions and summarised major laboratory research issues at general Research and Development Committee meetings.

Although considerable power resided with the committee, its deliberations and conclusions were not sacrosanct. Tom Macrae, the research director, was an independent-minded and iconoclastic Scot who suspected that Jephcott 'never read the minutes' of the committee, and he therefore discreetly ignored at least minor decisions which he disliked. 'The Old Man knew we paid no attention', according to Macrae, who after each meeting used to say to his deputy, Arthur Hems, 'my neck is out again as usual'. Macrae was helped in his habit of spending his research budget regardless of the allotments made in the committee by a ruling which Tizard extracted from the committee that 10 per cent of the research department's total income could be spent on whatever it liked, without mandate from the committee or anyone else. It was always difficult to keep accurate accounts in the research department, and Macrae made no effort to ease the difficulties. 'My God was that 10 per cent stretched!', Macrae later recollected; and he felt profound gratitude for this and other examples of sympathetic understanding to Tizard, whom he called 'the greatest man I have encountered in life'.[11]

Other personal influences could be detected in the workings of the committee, and indeed of the group's research and development. Jephcott and Walker were longstanding personal friends from the 1920s (when Walker's medical treatment saved the life of Jephcott's elder son), and there was an enduring bond between the two men. But Walker and Macrae were both fearlessly outspoken men, and clashed at an early stage in their relations. Thereafter, a tendency arose for any proposal by one man to be opposed or rebutted by the other. This antipathy had pervasive results, for example, the insistence by Walker, in contradiction of Macrae's view, that penicillin research should concentrate on the injectable rather than the oral formulation in the 1950s, was a decision which in retrospect seems mistaken. Macrae always felt that the pharmacology section of Allen & Hanburys research laboratories excelled that at Greenford, because of the insistence of Jephcott and Walker (himself a doctor by training) that medical men should undertake pharmacological research to ensure proper toxic control.

Against this background, the company sought to coordinate its internal research. Several conditions limited the type of organised research which the company was prepared to undertake, including the size of existing facilities, previous product experience, and the need for a material part of this expenditure to be remunerative in the short-term rather than the long.

The short-term versus long-term debate

In 1952 Jephcott stressed to the committee the importance of high yield research projects which capitalized on existing facilities, represented short-term investment, and would sustain or enhance the firm's revenue and trading position. His explicit priorities for research and development were to maintain existing production at the highest level of economy, to discover products within the company's general expertise which appeared to have value and the possibility of a rapid return of the money invested in them, and to carry out long-term speculative works.[12] He told the committee that he:

could see nothing emerging from present research that would add to the Company's gross income within the next two years or more. The Company had to face increasing competition abroad; though it had some proprietary protection for its sales of pharmaceuticals and foods, no such cover existed for antibiotics upon which it was mainly dependent for its income. In order to maintain its position in the competitive existing market conditions, the Company must improve production techniques and reduce costs ... these factors should be borne in mind by the members of the Committee when considering the research programme.[13]

Tizard, responding to Jephcott's remarks, considered that Glaxo had two possible areas of research, fermentation or synthetic organic chemistry. He regarded the second of these as far more competitive, with success dependent on the skill and good fortune of particular individuals. He believed that prospects of new sources of revenue from this area of research were uncertain and hazardous. Fermentation, on the other hand, was not yet properly understood by anyone, and he considered it important for Glaxo to elucidate problems attached to fermentation, and especially the fermentation processes to which it was committed, in order to remain competitive. He considered that the company should be content to watch developments in the organic synthetic field and when particular inventions or discoveries looked promising, to intervene and develop them.

While Tizard's remarks addressed the future direction and long-term objectives of Glaxo's research and development programme, the majority of research reports and committee discussions at the opening of 1953 continued to revolve around short-term projects. Jephcott's decision to 'consider research expenditure more critically than in the past' further reinforced a policy emphasising production- and process-related research.[14] However, this pragmatic approach, issued at the executive level, did not represent the outlook and opinion of Glaxo's senior scientific staff. Although ostensibly deferring to Jephcott's directives, Macrae expressed his hope that 'some more long-term investigation will continue, for the biggest prizes in the form of novel products are most likely to come from long-term work'.[15]

The relationship between short- and long-term research policy was linked with questions about actual returns on research expenditures. Tizard first adumbrated the principle that 'costs involved in doing work to improve current production processes should be divorced from expenditure on new projects', as it was 'misleading to consider a figure of total "research" expenditure which in fact covered both these aspects'.[16] In fact the Glaxo Research and Development budget for 1952/53 included the costs incurred in setting up the cortisone production facility at the new factory at Montrose. In October 1953 Tizard issued a memorandum reassessing the Research and Development Committee's functions and primary concerns and reviewing Committee policy. In his view, the research work which the Committee reviewed fell into three categories:

(1) Production investigation aimed at improving productivity and lowering commercial costs.

(2) Pharmaceutical formulation and presentation, intended to improve products for consumer use; for which the initiative may arise from the Sales Department (e.g. complaints), directly from the Research Division, or in other ways, and

(5) Research and Development, the introduction of new processes and products.[17]

He suggested that process or production investigation (PID) should properly be related to manufacturing costs, and doubted if the committee was qualified to decide on the relative importance of such projects, or indeed could afford time to do so. Instead he recommended that the committee should collect production information showing real relative increases in efficiency resulting from such expenditures. Tizard stressed the necessity of distinguishing between PID work and research, a distinction which had in the past been blurred. He maintained that the committee's principal priority should be focused on shaping policies for new and future research, observing:

Though the Company enjoys a high reputation, and has a fair commercial record, it has not succeeded in introducing anything new of any importance. Its future stability will depend on its success in this respect. At present we pay large royalties to America, [see page 246] while the royalties we receive from foreign countries do not entirely cover expenditures on patents.[18]

Glaxo's failure to excel in this regard, Tizard suggested, was not the result of scientific incapacity, shortage of money or shortage of staff. But he believed that poor decisions on prospective research projects had been made at the outset. As a remedial measure, he called for comprehensively written research proposals which investigated the expenditure, staff allotments, facilities and marketing provisions involved in new and prospective research ventures. Tizard's recommendations were accepted by the committee, which also agreed to meet at six-monthly intervals.

Tizard's remarks renewed the debate about the future direction of Glaxo's research policy and long-term expenditure. Several members, including Wilkins, Campbell and Tizard himself, argued that Glaxo was spending too high a proportion of its research budget on chemical research as opposed to the fermentation field in which, they agreed, Glaxo Laboratories had by far the greater experience. Wilkins and Hutton advocated extending the company's research activities in the fermentation field, but felt that attention should not be diverted from seeking new chemical processes. Campbell urged continued research into vitamin B_{12}, for which sales were rising rapidly but where there had been no appreciable improvement in yield

HECOGENIN FROM SISAL WASTE

HARVESTING SISAL LEAVES

In 1951, Drs.Callow Cornforth & Spensley of the National Institute for Medical Research showed that hecogenin could be obtained from the waste-liquors from sisal manufacture in East Africa.
This discovery provided a potential starting material in the Commonwealth for cortisone manufacture. Isolation involves partial hydrolysis of the soluble glycosides by fermentation and subsequent chemical hydrolysis. The solid concentrate is extracted at Glaxo's factory Ulverston and the sapogenin is purified by crystallisation.

HECOGENIN EXTRACTION PLANT, RUIRU, EAST AFRICA

HECOGENIN CONCENTRATE READY FOR SHIPPING TO BRITAIN

PLANT FOR PURIFICATION OF HECOGENIN AT ULVERSTON

37 The beginning of cortisone production.

over the previous five years. Macrae, however, argued the need for expenditure on research into cortisone-synthesis from hecogenin, which represented a long-term project, and in fact much of Glaxo's research and development budget went into cortisone research in the early 1950s.

Corticosteroid research

In the late 1930s biochemists isolated the hormones known to be present in extracts of the cortex of the adrenal gland. Two of the five compounds isolated by researchers at the Mayo Clinic, Minnesota, were new to the scientific world and named compound A and compound G. The latter, re-named cortisone in 1949, was synthesized (in a 36-stage chemical process) by Merck and in 1948 was undergoing clinical trials. When used with patients suffering from rheumatoid arthritis, cortisone supressed the symptoms and alleviated the crippling pain but without curing the disease. When the results of the cortisone trials became publicly known, there was an outburst of demand for the drug. By 1950 with world-wide shortage of the drug, many companies had embarked on the search for a commercial production process for cortisone and its analogue, hydrocortisone – the latter first synthesized by G. D. Searle & Company, but expensively.

The problem in moving to large-scale production was the raw material. All existing laboratory processes were based on bile acids, which had to be purchased with dollars, then in short supply in Britain. Glaxo decided to use ergosterol, familiar to them for some years as the source of vitamin D. Although ergosterol was costly, it was anticipated that its production in large quantities by fermentation would reduce costs. For two years from 1950 between one-third and two-thirds of Glaxo's research budget went into the cortisone project. Success in solving the problem, however, did not give Glaxo the advantage that had been anticipated. Writing of cortisone in 1951, Jephcott lamented:

both in the academic and in the more technical field ... we are well behind the US – by 'well' I mean years. With all our virtues, which I do not under estimate, [we] are ... children in the Cortisone world ... and ... mere pigmies [sic] compared with Merck.[19]

In its concentration on ergosterol as the key to cortisone production, the Glaxo research department believed itself to be ahead of Merck, pre-occupied with bile, or Syntex and Yarms, companies that were trying other approaches. In the event the Americans proved not to be so pre-occupied with other routes as to overlook ergosterol. By November 1951, Jephcott was bracing his colleagues to face the fact:

that there is emerging from the Americans a prior-dated patent structure related to ergosterol which will mean that, in spite of all our efforts measured in time and money, we are subservient to the Americans and shall have the pleasure of paying twice – once directly for our research, within and without our own Research Department, and again to the Americans for having anticipated us ... This is no reflection upon UK research ability ... the Americans, and especially Merck, have a very real advantage arising from their success with bile. Their knowledge of reactions is an enormous asset.[20]

The ergosterol route, however, remained too expensive for the commercial production of cortisone products, particularly as world prices of the latter fell sharply in 1952. As the Research and Development Committee minuted: 'We now know that, even as a temporary measure, to make cortisone from ergosterol would cost the company twice as much as the Ministry of Health would be prepared to pay.'[21]

In these circumstances the committee suggested delaying further work on cortisone, a recommendation accepted by Macrae with reservations. Since 1950 Glaxo had led its researchers to believe that cortisone should take priority and Macrae feared demoralisation if the reversal was too abrupt. At Greenford nearly fifty of the seventy-four research staff had worked on the cortisone project, a large proportion for Glaxo (by contrast Upjohn in the

US had detailed 150 chemists to synthesize cortisone).[22] Meanwhile, plans went ahead to install production facilities for cortisone at Montrose based on using intermediates imported from Merck in the USA.

On that basis, however, any profit on cortisone for Glaxo would be small. The incentive for the company to find a cheaper intermediate was enhanced by the need to avoid dollar expenditure, an objective urged upon all of industry in the 1950s by successive British governments, as they wrestled with a balance of payments deficit. Therefore, when it became apparent that hecogenin, an extract of sisal juice, could be worked up into cortisone, Glaxo saw that it offered an escape from Merck's cortisone orbit, and moved briskly. By 1953 the development of hecogenin production in East Africa was under way with an experimental pilot plant on the Mitchell Cotts Estate in Kenya, and a larger 'first scale unit' on the Amboni estates in Tanganyika, both under the aegis of the National Research and Development Corporation. The NRDC sought to establish rather than to maintain the industry: the Amboni plant was intended to produce 'significant quantities' by July 1953 and reach large-scale production twelve–fifteen months later. During this latter stage, the NRDC were to relinquish control, with the African plants becoming owned and operated by the estate owners as NRDC licencees or sub-licencees. These latter were to prepare a crude hecogenin probably containing about 20–25 per cent of that material for supply to refiners in Britain, on a contract basis at the best price obtainable under prevailing market conditions. The refiners were to prepare the hecogenin and sell it. Although Glaxo Laboratories were cautious (and rightly so as events proved) about the NRDC's hopes of an early price of £15 per kilogram, the East African venture was seen as offering an opportunity for the company to become competitive with American and especially Merck expertise, and to obtain imported partly manufactured material whilst avoiding dollar expenditure.

By May 1954 Glaxo Laboratories had determined to secure direct control over its East African supplies of hecogenin, either by making a direct investment or by an arrangement with a sisal producer whereby the operation of getting the raw hecogenin would be conducted under Glaxo's control, with all subsequent stages in its hands. The company wanted no intermediaries, unless completely under its own thumb, an impossibility given the involvement of NRDC. Amboni were unwilling to be dictated to by Glaxo. When, in 1954, the latter indicated it was prepared to take over Amboni's investment in the hecogenin extraction plant, the company was told that Amboni had spare capital not employed, and was looking for remunerative investments.

As a major client Glaxo Laboratories could exercise considerable influence over Amboni, the refiners, and even the NRDC, but it clearly could not ensure adequate supplies to meet demand. By November 1954, the Glaxo order to the NRDC for 1000 kilograms of crude hecogenin was six months in arrears, while Amboni's plant, which had not yet touched 100 kilos per month, was being enlarged to 250 kilograms per month, although the greater capacity would not be installed and operating until February 1955. Glaxo, therefore, remained dependent for raw material supplies on Merck, who were aware that once Glaxo started producing from sterling raw materials it might well be the end, temporarily at least, of further imports from the States.

The dependence on Merck, however, proved an embarrassment. In 1955 the Ministry of Health, prompted by Boots, urged Jephcott to fix a release date for the British-made cortisone when it was clear that Glaxo had nothing like a sufficient quantity to meet demand:

The Ministry accepted that Glaxo had sought no more considerable import licences than were essential, and were not anxious to embarrass the company, which emphasised that ordinary retailers would profoundly dislike having to handle Boots material, and that there was a risk of handing the market over to the French manufacturer Roussell, if Glaxo were unable to extend their cortisone business. Under the circumstances the company pressed for further import licences for American supplies: the Ministry was hesitant, feeling that if the market could be supplied without dollars it ought not really to support an application for dollars.[23]

Jephcott, in negotiation with the Ministry of Health, 'made a good deal of play on the commercial sacrifices made by the company over polio vaccines' (see page 192).[24] To compound the problems, supplies of hydrocortisone alcohol and hydrocortisone acetate to Sharp & Dohme, produced by Glaxo's own synthesis, were of inadequate quality, although Sharp & Dohme were willing to receive non-Merck products. As a result even this order had to be met from Merck-type material also. An attempt to secure increased supplies of hecogenin from east Africa was therefore imperative. As a further precaution, finished hydrocortisone was added in small quantities from Roussell's fledgling operation in Britain, working from Australian ox-bile; additionally a cross-licensing agreement was signed with Syntex (the Mexican company which had pioneered the production of cortisone from sisal via hecogenin), to provide hecogenin for Glaxo's consumption.

Glaxo's cortisone and hydrocortisone products, Cortelan and Efcortelan, were successfully launched on the market in April 1955. By that time cortisone therapy was undergoing a reassessment. Because of the side-effects which had emerged and limitations found since their introduction, the use of cortisone and hydrocortisone had been restricted to cases of severe rheumatoid arthritis and specific skin complaints such as eczema. But there were those who envisaged other uses for cortisone: among them Hector Walker, who had been involved in adrenal research since 1924. He suggested in 1957 three other possible areas of use for cortisone: with antibiotics for the treatment of a first inflammation, in conjunction with streptomycin in cases of pulmonary tuberculosis, and in cases of severe shock where cortisone administered intravenously could keep the patient alive long enough for other measures to take effect.

The skills and expertise which had been developed at Greenford during the research on cortisone products were applied to allied steroid research and other cortisone-related products giving Glaxo a solid place among pharmaceutical companies in that therapeutic area. But cortisone research at Greenford taxed Glaxo both financially and psychologically in the early 1950s. The company's commitment to the project was sustained by a sense of public and moral obligation, as well as by company pride, through the failure to meet its original target of production in 1952 to successful and profitable production of a range of cortisone products by the late 1950s. But the development of cortisone also showed the risks in the pharmaceutical industry; as Jephcott wrote in 1962 'within ten years cortisone, whose production was a veritable *tour de force* in synthetic chemistry, accomplished only by great effort and at vast expense, has been almost completely replaced'.[25] While cortisone research was a new area for Glaxo in the 1950s, work on vaccines had started at Greenford during the war.

Vaccines

Despite the high commitment of staff and resources to cortisone research in the early 1950s, attention was also focused in these years on vaccines. It had been as a result of work done in the immunology department at Greenford that Glaxo was able to introduce in 1946 the first vaccine to combine protection against both whooping cough and diptheria simultaneously. Attention turned in the early 1950s to the BCG tuberculosis vaccine. Although the discovery of a safe and effective BCG vaccine had been announced by French researchers in 1923, it had been greeted with insularity and inertia by the Ministry of Health and discredited by a campaign of innuendo among British medical experts. Medical historians have since described in detail the lack of scientific rigour of the self-confessed experts who, to protect their own interests, denigrated the BCG vaccine because it devalued current therapeutic practices and discredited established institutional responses to the disease.[26] It was only after 1950, when the Medical Research Council launched a controlled trial of BCG, that its efficacy was grudingly accepted. General vaccination in schools began in 1953 and in response to this general programme, Glaxo, characteristically, addressed itself to the refining of production techniques. Several problems were

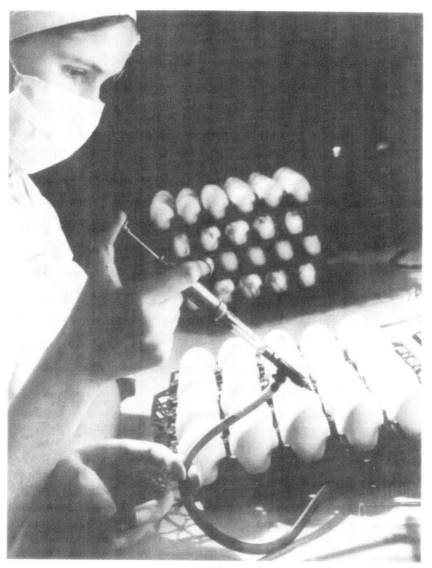

38 Whooping cough vaccine 1953.

associated with preparation of the vaccine, particularly contamination and the need to use the vaccine within two or three weeks of preparation. Research at Sefton Park led to the development of a commercial method for freeze-drying BCG tuberculosis vaccine, which was introduced in 1957.[27]

Between 1952 and 1955, Glaxo research was also directed to creating facilities for producing a poliomyelitis vaccine then being developed in the US. Unlike most Glaxo research proposals, introduced by internal laboratory directors or by academic scientists, the initiative for Glaxo's entry into poliomyelitis vaccine research and development originated at the Research Committee's executive level. In a memorandum in 1952, Hector Walker discussed current work in the poliomyelitis vaccine field by A. J. Rhodes, at the Connaught Medical Research Laboratory in Toronto and proposed it to the Committee as a possible research area. Rhodes was developing a technique for cultivating poliomyelitis virus which, if successful, would produce a vaccine from an attenuated strain. Walker recommended that Glaxo undertake production of an agent for active immunisation against poliomyelitis. In his view the project would not involve a large capital expenditure and, with the company's existing technical staff, it was expected that the project would take three years.

Jephcott was attracted by this proposal. Walker contacted Rhodes at Connaught, and Jephcott visited him during a business trip to North America. He also invited Rhodes to visit Glaxo, 'to discuss the problem generally in order that we might determine the merits of his work and discover whether the time was now ripe for his work to be developed on an industrial scale'.[28] Having talked with Rhodes, Jephcott reported to the Research and Development Committee in May 1953 that the anticipated annual cost of setting up a suitable laboratory was £22,000. He estimated that it would be a five-year venture. Tizard urged a more thorough study of the whole vaccine research area and its implications for Glaxo Laboratories and Jephcott suggested that outside authorities should be invited to prepare papers on virus work. By November 1953, however, Jephcott had received approval from Glaxo's Board of directors to begin virus research. He further announced that the agreement was reached 'with a particular and definite objective which will necessarily involve substantial expenditures over a period of years. The running cost of such a project is impossible to estimate accurately at this stage; whilst little expenditure will be incurred in this financial year, I expect the running cost to be about £50,000, perhaps more, a year.'[29] Walker's modest estimates had been left far behind. Accordingly, new laboratory facilities for virus research at Sefton Park were completed in July 1954, and by the end of the following year the project was ready to enter production. In April 1956 Britain's first supplies of poliomyelitis vaccine, known as polivirin, were issued by Glaxo Laboratories, on the instruction of the Ministry of Health, to public health departments throughout Britain to be used for immunising children aged between two and nine years. The interest in vaccines and immunological products at Glaxo persisted in the late 1950s. The expanded biological facilities at both Sefton Park and

Greenford allowed for investigations to begin into other virus fields, such as measles and mumps. The Research and Development Committee noted in 1955 that Glaxo was 'not alone in this sphere, but the number of firms engaged in it was few and we were at least as well, if not better, equipped than our competitors. To assist in financing this new and very promising venture economies would need to be made elsewhere in the research programme.'[30] Money, however, was not the only scarce resource in Glaxo's research programme in the 1950s.

Scientific staff

Although in 1962 Jephcott publicly said that for Glaxo 'recruitment of staff of appropriate background, training and calibre has not so far presented serious difficulty',[31] internal evidence suggests that recruitment of scientists of appropriate disciplines was a recurring problem for Glaxo Laboratories nor was it fully solved, in the period under consideration. There was, in the 1950s, a shortage of scientists in the country as a whole, a problem well recognised by Glaxo's management. Macrae wrote in 1952 of the national 'serious deficiency' of chemists, and went on to predict that:

we shall have to make do with a smaller proportion of graduates than has been our custom in the past, for the cost of graduate chemists has increased rapidly, particularly during the past year ... We are hoping to procure, from the local schools, boys and girls who have taken their general certificate of education at the advanced level, with a view to training them to make good the remainder of the deficiencies in the chemical laboratories.[32]

Jephcott was well aware of both the national problem and Glaxo's particular difficulties. In an influential essay, written in 1952 'How much research?', he described the contemporary national and economic climate which justified industrial research for greater productivity, and he advocated the immediate practical applications of chemical research. He appealed to academic institutions for scientific programmes to prepare research chemists at the highest level for the requirements of industry. At the same time, conscious of the large portion of the research budget consumed by salaries, Jephcott minuted 'that the percentage of graduates on the Greenford research staff was not unduly high notwithstanding that the main weight of research was on cortisone, a very highly specialised field; every effort should be made to ensure that graduates were employed to the best advantages'.[33]

Apart from the shortage of scientists, there were particular problems for Glaxo in recruiting professionals with specialised skills, such as pharmacology and bacteriology, to work on the antibiotic research programme leading to griseofulvin (see chapter 9). Tizard observed that the shortage of

39 Glaxo's work on vaccines included the development of vaccines effective against sheep and poultry diseases.

the type of person the company sought was due to the nature of university regulations governing higher research degrees. He suggested that it might be possible to overcome the difficulty by finding good graduates in, for example, chemistry, who could be financed by the company while they took an appropriate course in pharmacology and who would return to the company under contract.

In the mid 1950s the needs at Sefton Park for virus research and development were provided by training new staff in virological and tissue-culture techniques internally, as the majority had no previous experience in these fields. At Greenford there was difficulty in procuring an experienced experimental pathologist. The unit's senior level pharmacology needs were fulfilled by hiring a German scientist 'reputed to one of the best pharmacologists working in this country at present'.[34] Other senior level scientific research posts within Glaxo's biological unit required qualified and suitable personnel. At the end of 1955 Macrae reported that the microbiology, pharmacology and production units were staffed satisfactorily, but that in other units considerable difficulty was experienced in obtaining staff. The main problem was in procuring an experienced virologist to take charge of the Virus Unit, 'and as yet no success has resulted from the considerable effort made'. There were 'very few good virologists in this country, and we may have to engage a young man and send him for training to an MRC Laboratory, or elsewhere'. Other appointments remained unfilled, such as the biochemist to take charge of the Biochemistry section. This problem was easier to resolve, for there were already several good biochemists in the Glaxo organization.[35]

Glaxo's research laboratories principally depended on research within the company. The relative emphasis of the company's research expenditure on production or process-related research, undoubtedly reinforced this situation. Material documenting Glaxo's extramural research projects indicates that expenditure on outside research represented a small proportion – around 3 per cent – of Glaxo's total research and development budget. Some university contacts were used as outlets for identifying and investing in more speculative long-term research proposals and projects. Glaxo's contact with outside research associations most often related to development matters, as the testing of procaine penicillin and other antibiotic preparations, used as feed supplements, illustrated. Glaxo Laboratories worked with the Agricultural Research Council (ARC) and with the National Institute for Research in Dairying (NIRD) on similarly related experimental trials and tests. Greenford's vitamin B_{12} research also involved the NIRD and the Chester Beatty Institute. The company's cortisone project drew on outside support from several research organisations apart from university contacts and from one firm. Cortisone synthesis from hecogenin involved R and D individuals at the National Institute for Medical Research, at the National Research and Development Corporation and at the Medical Research Council.

The opportunities for collaborative activity, however, were not always seen as in the company's best interest. Campbell's proposal in 1952 to 're-open investigation with the MRC with a view to national collaboration on cortisone synthesis' was rejected by the R and D committee. The company's feeling, that 'to pursue such a course of action at the present time would result in an insupportable loss of reputation by the company' won the day although unsupported by direct evidence at the time and since.

One cooperative venture led to important developments in the next decade for Glaxo. In the mid 1950s Greenford's antibiotics researchers collaborated through the NRDC with scientists at Oxford University who were attempting to isolate and characterise the cephalosporin C component of the cephalosporium acremonium fermentation. Glaxo's fermentation unit was the first to produce sufficient yields of the compound to advance the work by the academic researchers, resulting in the confirmation of the structure of cephalosporin C in 1959. Subsequent chemical research at Greenford on the preparation of semi-synthetic cephalosporins resulted in the launch in 1964 of cephaloridine (Ceporin), Glaxo's first cephalosporin antibiotic. This was followed by the development of cephalexin (Ceporex), the first oral cephalosporin.

Allen & Hanburys' research and development

Allen & Hanburys, Britain's oldest pharmaceutical company, had pioneered the manufacture of cod liver oil and of malted and infant foods in the Victorian era and had enhanced the presentation of pastilles and tablets. As a result of post-war restructuring, pure and developmental research had been allocated a portion of the profits, thereby rewarding cost-effective projects. In 1947 the company had established a new Organic Chemistry Research Department, and by the end of the decade the annual research budget was running at around £40,000: half of it went on pharmaceutical research, a quarter on chemical research and the remainder on analytical, bacteriological and pharmacological research.

Much of this pharmaceutical expenditure was committed to penicillin production: lucrative though this business was, penicillin generated problems, mainly associated with its stability. The company developed and marketed a successful liver extract 'Hepalon' and did parallel work in the field of vitamin B_{12}. Like Glaxo, they investigated the production of cortisone, but limited their financial commitment, despite developing a product called 'Eucortone'. Allen & Hanburys' Board were guarded about its merits, although it was on this product that James Tait and Sylvia Simpson conducted research at the Middlesex Hospital resulting, in conjunction with Professor Tadeus Teichstein and his colleague Wettstein of Basel, in the development of Aldosterone.

Like Tait and Simpson, Allen & Hanburys used the newly developed technique of paper chromatography in their attempts to isolate vitamin B_{12}, and later established a biochemical laboratory to apply the technique in other fields. However, it was not in biochemistry but in the chemical department that their most successful product of this kind, Eulissin, was developed. Eulissin was crucial in anaesthesia: an anaesthetist needs to induce muscle flaccidity and insensibility to pain. Eulissin's function as a neuromuscular blocking agent meant that a lower and therefore safer dose of general anaesthetic could be administered to render patients unconscious. The anaesthetic qualities of 'curare' had been known in Europe since Laurence Keynes, serving with Sir Walter Raleigh in Venezuela, listed the herbs used on poisoned arrows. It was, however, only in the 1930s that the use of curare in anaesthesia was examined: in North America it was used both to reduce the frequency of vertebral facture during the newly developed technique of convulsive shock therapy, and to permit pelvic examinations of distressed female patients.

In Britain the Medical Research Council encouraged Allen & Hanburys' interest in anaesthesia. In 1935 Harold King had isolated tubocurarine, the active ingredients in curare, from a sample obtained from the British Museum. Under the auspices of the MRC, Allen & Hanburys prepared and tested various salts and derivatives from tubocurarine; but more significantly at the same time the company's organic chemical research department developed a process for manufacturing a new synthetic muscle relaxant known by the general title of Methonium compounds, sold under the name of Eulissin. By 1950 the company expected that, over the next few years the chemical laboratory would isolate several entirely new chemical compounds, the production of which would enhance its prosperity.

During the 1950s Allen & Hanburys made successive advances. Piriton, an antihistamine, was isolated and marketed, although, just as today, it was hard to ensure that its effect was specifically antihistianic; a water stable penicillin compound suitable for oral consumption was developed; in conjunction with Schering, Allen & Hanburys investigated and produced two drugs with psychotropic effect known as neuroleptics because of the emotional quietening, indifference and psychomotor-slowing induced by chlor-promazine on the central nervous system. They became subsequently known as Largactil (Chlorpromazine) and Fentazin (Perphenazine). The search for muscle relaxants led in 1956 to the discovery of the antibacterial and antifungal drug, Dequalinium chloride, which, in the form of Dequadin lozenges, was used to relieve mouth and throat infections.

Simultaneously Allen & Hanburys developed agricultural products, parallel to Glaxo's success with griseofulvin (see chapter 9). Medical antibiotics progressed alongside agricultural antibiotics in both companies' research programmes. Before the merger, Allen & Hanburys had also made considerable progress towards isolating a vaccine to treat lungworm in cattle; with a mortality rate of 30–40 per cent among infected animals, the vaccine promised to be of value both to the company and the agricultural community. Veterinary immunological work suggested possibilities in medicine where the chemotherapeutic approach had not always been successful.

After the merger

After the merger, Glaxo and Allen & Hanburys maintained their separate research establishments for almost two decades. The Board decided to divide research responsibilities broadly so that veterinary research was conducted by Allen & Hanburys at Ware and the medical implications of diseases such as bilharzia were studied by Glaxo Laboratories at Greenford. This was part of the deliberately gradual policy of change and rationalisation which was not completed until 1979.

In the early 1960s, with a research budget of nearly £1 million, five times as much as Allen & Hanburys, Glaxo was able to establish itself in the more substantial fields of blood cholesterol depressants, cephalosporin, antibiotics, griseofulvin, virus and poliomyelitis research. Equally the company's research staff had made advances in Brucella vaccine trials, swine fever projects, the examination of anaemia in piglets and even extended the veterinary application of Interferon to medicine. Apart from topical products such as Dequadin (lozenge) and Laurodin (antiseptic) the bulk of Allen & Hanburys' work had been involved in anti-microbiotic research. In an effort to comply with Ministry of Health costings the company's attempts to rationalise research affected this. Glaxo were unwilling to see Allen & Hanburys continue their research into the neuro-muscular blocking agent Toxiferene, and annexed it to Greenford, thus effectively also terminating Allen & Hanburys' related research into scholine. The drive to bring research under the Greenford umbrella in the name of rationalisation meant that Ware's research into parasitology was cut back. While in 1961 they were studying the effects of Dictyocaulus, Coccidiosis, Fasciola and Schistosoma, by 1962 research was confined solely to Dictyocaulus. The division and allocation of research was further complicated by the acquisition in 1961 of Evans Medical. In 1962, following re-organisation of the group, the research division of Glaxo Laboratories Ltd, based at Greenford, was incorporated as a separate company, Glaxo Research Ltd, a direct subsidiary of Glaxo Group Ltd.

Conclusion

In the post 1945 pharmaceutical industry 'advance was ... rapid and multifarious',[36] a circumstance reflected in Glaxo's research and development activities in this period. Glaxo's wartime and post-war product, penicillin, so important to the company's position in the industry, still required development work, as did vitamin B_{12}. The decision to go into cortisone taxed the company's research resources as did the search for new antibiotics. Recognition of the need for a fully disciplined research programme which balanced the requirements of short- and long-term research, was there at the outset, but proved far from easy to impose. In 1955 Jephcott could still say:

the objectives at which our research effort was aimed were too numerous and too diffuse. It was essential that projects should have clearly defined objectives, the succesful attainment of which would be of real value to the company.[37]

By 1962, with the additional research facilities brought in by merger, Glaxo's research and development began to approach the successful production of 'novel products of outstanding merit and widespread use', which the company needed to maintain and enhance its position in the world pharmaceutical industry.[38]

9

The development and commercial exploitation of griseofulvin

Throughout the 1940s and early 1950s, Glaxo's research and development activities did not result in the discovery or development of a major new marketable product. Developing fermentation techniques for penicillin production had absorbed the company's resources and interests during the war years, strongly supported by national demand and cooperative industrial support. The wartime research was focused on production or production-related demands and despite its successes created within Glaxo Laboratories an *ad hoc* research programme centred on short-term commercial prospects rather than long-term goals. Recognising the need for more long-term and more speculative projects, Glaxo directors began to undertake in the post-war period research programmes with potential commercial and scientific merit.

The commercial development of griseofulvin represented to Glaxo researchers and management a project vindicating the firm's investment in laboratory R and D. Developed initially as an agricultural product and later as a systemic fungistatic for human and veterinary application, griseofulvin proved a revolutionary agent in treating Dermatophytoses. Moreover, it was the first major commercial pharmaceutical product identified and developed by Glaxo, rather than licensed from the USA and manufactured by a process refined at Greenford. Its low toxicity and systemic activity created international medical interest and attracted wide attention in the professional press. Its commercial development at Sefton Park was also quick, drawing on scientific expertise and existing deep fermentation production facilities. Although previous ICI findings and extramural experimental work contributed to its development, griseofulvin project researchers and those involved with its promotion identified Glaxo with the antibiotic's success. As an organised laboratory research project of a speculative character, griseofulvin reaped a financial return on the investment within a short period. Both in that respect and as the first and most important 'novel' antibiotic develop-

40 Sefton Park in 1950.

ment in the period covered by this history, its story deserves detailed examination.

The research programme at Sefton Park

Established in 1950 for the purpose of antibiotics research, Sefton Park Laboratory's work centred almost entirely on process investigation and production-related research during its first two years of operation. Some 97 per cent of its research budget went towards improving streptomycin and penicillin production efficiency in this period. The remaining 3 per cent of resources supported other projects including vitamin B_{12} and new antibiotics research. By 1952, however, members of the R and D Committee began to feel that Sefton Park's research programme was too heavily occupied with problems arising from current production. Although process research augmented manufacturing efficiency, it detracted from clinical testing of new antibiotics and, at the laboratory level, cost valuable time. Yet it seemed unlikely that production research demands on Sefton Park's facilities would diminish or be transferred within the near future. The Committee therefore decided that, while maintaining existing research projects at Sefton Park, new research proposals would be considered for 1953.

Sefton Park's director, Dr Sandy Campbell, submitted several ideas to the R and D Committee, the most significant of which was a detailed project outline presented in July 1952. He recommended that Glaxo should increase its involvement in the new antibiotics field by expanding the current screening programme, designed to isolate new substances with potential pharmaceutical value, to deal with other new antibiotics of potential utility within alternative chemical fields. In particular he noted:

The interest currently being shown in systemic fungicides and insecticides creates an opportunity for the examination of the antibiotic substances in this connection. Clear demonstrations have already been given of the uptake of antibiotic substances by both the roots and foliage of the green plant with effective disease control resulting.[1]

Industrial laboratory research into new antibiotics was not a completely unventured field. Since penicillin's discovery, several large laboratories, particularly in the United States, had launched major research projects, but few new antibiotics of therapeutic importance had as yet resulted. The difficulty was not in locating substances demonstrating sufficient antibiosis, but in isolating new strains showing acceptable toxicity for clinical application. Toxicity was of paramount importance in researching new antibiotics for systemic administration and, Campbell argued, the investigation and development of industrial and agricultural antibiotics posed toxicity questions of a different, and less restrictive nature than those applying to pharmaceuticals.

It was recognised with concern, especially by Jephcott, that research in the antibiotics field was highly speculative and therefore expensive. Campbell, however, persevered in requesting approval of a substantial £20,000 increase in Sefton Park's budget for antibiotics research in 1952–1953. The additional funds were to be used to recruit additional laboratory staff and to expand, from one to seventeen, the number of research staff working on new antibiotics. While acknowledging the importance of this research for human and veterinary medicine, Campbell stressed again the importance of anti-fungal antibiotics in agriculture as a field which offered tremendous potential for future development. With no successful systemic antibiotic for treating plant diseases as yet on the market, Campbell predicted that the financial rewards to the company would be substantial were Glaxo Laboratories to succeed in this area.

Members of the R and D Committee accepted Campbell's research ideas in principle, but refused to increase Sefton Park's annual budget. On this point Jephcott was immovable, insisting that the laboratory's forthcoming research budget could not be raised above that of the previous year, a figure of £91,675. Rather than recruit new staff, Jephcott decided to divert Sefton

Park's financial resources and scientific personnel currently working on streptomycin research to the new antibiotics programme, once the earlier work was finished.

New agricultural and clinical antibiotics were explored at Sefton Park throughout 1952; by December laboratory workers had isolated several substances – A 228/A, A 228/B and A 432 – believed to be potentially useful in the control of fungal diseases in man and domestic animals, by injection or by surface treatment to the skin. Biological testing of the substances early the next year, however, was a disappointment, revealing that these strains harmed the central nervous system. Apparently discouraged by these results, and constrained by Jephcott's determination to contain costs (see pages 163 and 184), the R and D Committee initially rejected Campbell's request to conduct additional tests on the collection of new antibiotics accumulated at Sefton Park over the previous six months. However, after further discussions, in which Tizard supported Campbell, the Committee reluctantly allotted £3,000 for the purpose. Constrained by finance and by the fact that Glaxo's biological testing facilities were limited until laboratory extensions were completed in 1955, Campbell rationalised the selection of new antibiotics from his unit to be submitted for biological testing. He focused primarily on new materials of potential agricultural importance. Thus, by mid 1953 Sefton Park's antibiotics research programme was placing an increased emphasis on the identification of new substances potentially useful to combat plant diseases.

Opposition to further developments came from Jephcott (now in his fifties) whose approach to laboratory R and D became increasingly conservative in 1952–1953. He was fundamentally reluctant to accept new agricultural antibiotics research, favouring instead medical and veterinary applications. But a more important factor in his decision-making was Glaxo's economic performance. Sales and profits were poor in 1952 (see page 165) and late in the year Jephcott recommended a policy of retrenchment to R and D Committee members, suggesting that the company should concentrate on enhancing production efficiency rather than on new research development.

However, support for Campbell's research interests came from Tizard whose influential role in revising Glaxo R and D Committee policy was instrumental in expanding the firm's involvement in agricultural antibiotics. Tizard took issue with the company's organised research programme in late 1953, arguing that insufficient emphasis on new research in current R and D programmes would jeopardise prospects for competitive product development. Tizard believed that important advances *were* possible in biological work, but cautioned the company against further investments in organic chemistry, an area where Glaxo had less R and D experience than several of its competitors. He supported Campbell's advocacy of new antibiotic research involving biological fermentation techniques, as consistent with his long-term view of Glaxo's scientific development (see page 185).

In June 1954 two decisions were taken which altered Sefton Park's research programme. First, all fermentation research on existing production, quickly approaching the stage of marginal return on investment, was transferred to production laboratories at Ulverston and Barnard Castle. Tizard's wish for more exploratory and experimental work at the laboratory level played a large part in precipitating this relocation. Secondly, Glaxo's Executive Board decided to curtail all further work directed towards isolating new antibiotics, doubting the value of further efforts in this area as reflected in recent experimental work, both its own and that of other companies. But rather than abandon completely Sefton Park's expanded antibiotics programme, it was agreed that research on new antibiotics should continue, limited, however, to the purification of existing strains. Meomycin was considered worthy of investigation, and board members voted in favour of accepting Campbell's recommendation to investigate griseofulvin, an antifungal antibiotic originally identified before the war.

The origins of griseofulvin

In 1939 Harold Raistrick and his colleagues at the London School of Hygiene and Tropical Medicine discovered and isolated griseofulvin from the mycelium of *Penicillium Griseofulvum* Dierck, in the course of studying the chemical substances produced by the metabolism of numerous common moulds. They did not, however, screen it for antibiotic activity. Seven years later, Brain, Curtis, and Hemming of ICI obtained an antibiotic which they called 'Curling Factor', while investigating the mould flora of the soil at Wareham Heath in Dorset. One characteristic of this antibiotic was the unusual stunting and distortion which it caused to parts of *botrytis allii* and other fungi. A year later, in 1947, two other ICI workers demonstrated that the substances previously identified as 'curling factor' and 'griseofulvin' were identical. In 1949 Brain, Curtis and Hemming published a paper entitled 'Identity of Curling Factor with Griseofulvin'.[2] Based on *in-vitro* experiments conducted at ICI, Brain concluded that griseofulvin affected the morphogenesis of various fungal species, Basidiomycetes, Asocmycetes, Fungi Imperfecti and Sygomycetas (Mucorales), effectively curtailing fungal reproduction and growth. Griseofulvin had no evident effect on one group of fungi, Oomycetes, nor on certain yeasts. These observations led Brain to believe that griseofulvin was effective only against organisms with chitinous cell walls, thus defining the mode of antibiotic action on the particular chemistry and growth regulating systems of certain fungi.

Griseofulvin's utility for controlling pathogenic fungi in plants was demonstrated by Brain and others in 1951. Further experiments showed that the antibiotic acted as a systemic protectorant against fungal attack when added to the nutrient culture of lettuce seedlings and tomato plants. These findings were outlined in *Nature* in 1951.[3] By 1952 Brain also reported systemic control by griseofulvin of a variety of plant moulds, including grey mould of lettuce, early blight of tomato, chocolate spot of broad beans and a powdery mildew on barley growing in water treated cultures. At the same time, other ICI researchers established griseofulvin's chemical structure, and thus better defined its potential commercial value. But despite its interesting characteristics and biological properties, griseofulvin remained a scientific curiosity confined to small-scale laboratory or greenhouse experimentation until the mid 1950s. The antibiotic appeared too expensive to reproduce (by surface culture techniques) in quantities necessary for agricultural use and ICI abandoned commercial investigation of the substance.

Glaxo's development of griseofulvin as an agricultural chemical

Glaxo's interest in griseofulvin was awakened in 1952, when a laboratory researcher, Dr A. Rhodes, identified it as an antifungal agricultural antibiotic worthy of investigation, and indicated the potential for developing submerged culture fermentation techniques for the antibiotic's production. As a plant pathologist, Rhodes had acquired some research experience with griseofulvin at ICI before joining Glaxo Laboratories. A preliminary examination of griseofulvin's systemic action as a seed dressing, using material prepared from laboratory surface culture methods, was authorised, although there were no major advances for two years. However Rhodes' suggestion in 1952 reinforced, if not inspired, Campbell's ideas about developing antibiotic substances for potential agricultural use.

When Campbell obtained approval from Glaxo's executive committee to undertake a griseofulvin project in 1954, it was with a view to devising a submerged culture technique for commercial production. Glaxo's deep culture fermentation methods, already employed for penicillin and streptomycin production, suggested the most economical large-scale approach, and Glaxo researchers had acquired technical and scientific expertise in this kind of biological production technology. All aspects of manufacture, including variations of nutrients, fermentation conditions, and extraction techniques, had already been undertaken. The company had also found a way of increasing antibiotic yield by mutating the strain of penicillium mould in

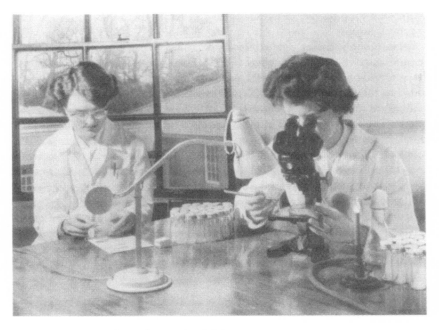

41 Research work on griseofulvin.

order to produce a new variant strain giving higher yields. These same developmental approaches were coordinated on a pilot scale at Sefton Park initially. As work proceeded, Campbell was able to report impressive laboratory progress to committee members by the spring of 1955.

The plan to carry out fermentation development of Griseofulvin with the view to having some ready for test this summer has been implemented with remarkable success. By December, we were able to start distributing the first of the six kilos of the pure crystalline antibiotic produced by the Pilot Plant. A review of a wide variety of practical trials should be possible within six months.[4]

Between 1955 and 1957 Sefton Park's researchers conducted trials on griseofulvin both at the laboratory site and at commercial nurseries in order to evaluate its performance under field conditions. In addition to Glaxo's sponsored trials, large quantities of griseofulvin were distributed to agricultural experiment stations both in Britain and abroad for evaluation. This arrangement enabled Glaxo to extend its field investigations and to gather a wide range of scientific observations at relatively little cost.

Investigation of griseofulvin's pharmacology undertaken at Greenford in 1955 revealed that it had no general toxic action on mammals. The company's most immediate interest in these test results was in connection with its application to the Ministry of Agriculture for permission to treat edible crops with the new antibiotic. In February 1956 the Ministry cleared griseofulvin from the risk of toxicity and allowed its use in field trials on all growing crops. Additional approval was obtained in the following year for the commercial use of griseofulvin in agriculture (after a review by the Ministry's Scientific Sub-Committee on poisonous substances used in agriculture and food storage). These early toxicity observations encouraged Glaxo researchers to consider griseofulvin's further potential as a veterinary and ultimately human antibiotic.

The development of griseofulvin within Glaxo was swift, drawing on previous preliminary scientific research and internal scientific expertise. However, marketing of any kind of agricultural antibiotic, such as griseofulvin (or 'Streptospray', also under way), required new strategies. Glaxo's marketing division was equipped to handle substances of *clinical* use only. Having reviewed the possibilities, Glaxo managers decided to seek an external marketing outlet that already dealt with a wide range of established synthetic products, maintained an agricultural sales force and had representatives in touch with commercial growers. To this end, in June 1955, Glaxo acquired control of the Murphy Chemical Company Ltd of Hertfordshire. The acquisition also meant that Glaxo could cultivate allied product fields without compromising its own identity as a pharmaceuticals manufacturer. Before griseofulvin's sales release, Murphy conducted commercial trials of the antibiotic, the most successful of which demonstrated its efficacy against Botrytis Rot. The antibiotic, however, remained expensive when compared with other available agricultural antifungals, and its commercial potential was, therefore, confined to valuable out-of-season crops, such as greenhouse lettuce. The Murphy Chemical Company began marketing griseofulvin as 'Grisovin 3 per cent Dust' in the autumn of 1957, the first commercial antibiotic available to growers in Britain. Its development may have been of greater significance in introducing antibiotics to the agricultural field than its actual use in plant disease control. To Glaxo Laboratories 'Grisovin 3 per cent Dust' represented the first stage in griseofulvin's commercial development.

Griseofulvin for medical and veterinary use

At the same time as the agricultural field trials began, griseofulvin's potential in clinical application started to generate interest. Previous observations had already determined the antibiotic's low systemic toxicity. By December 1954, toxicity test reports from Greenford on griseofulvin samples identified for Ministry of Agriculture clearance confirmed that it was 'innocuous' to those likely to be working with it; its sensitising properties were 'negligible' and when diluted it was 'non-irritating'.[5] These results led to the suggestion that, given the high fungistatic activity demonstrated, the possibility of employing griseofulvin in systemic treatment of some of the morbid systemic infections and diseases occuring in the tropics should be explored. More importantly, however, the low toxicity indications opened the way for further laboratory investigation. Within two months, Glaxo researchers issued an internal 'Griseofulvin Research Report' of high significance to Glaxo's interest in the antibiotic as a therapeutic chemical. The report announced that laboratory tests had shown griseofulvin active, *in vitro*, against dermatophytic fungi pathogenic to man.

Glaxo Laboratories' interest in griseofulvin's applications coincided with similar research endeavours elsewhere. Early in 1955 Campbell reported that research into curative treatment for human dermatophytes was currently being sponsored by the National Coal Board. The connection between Glaxo and the Coal Board was Dr J. C. Gentles, a medical mycologist working at Glasgow's Anderson College, Department of Bacteriology, who was also attached to Glasgow's Western Infirmary. Gentles served as advisor to the National Coal Board studying the incidence of athlete's foot in miners. Through this work, his interest in griseofulvin developed and Glaxo despatched some of the antibiotic to him for laboratory investigation in the early autumn of 1955.[6] Gentles' involvement in the griseofulvin project and his clinical trials at Glasgow were crucial to antibiotic development at Glaxo. However, the results of Gentles' first treatment of cases of human dermatophytes with griseofulvin by surface application were discouraging, and led Glaxo to defer additional clinical investigation for a time.

Meanwhile, work had been going on elsewhere. In 1956 ICI prepared two provisional patent applications for fungicidal compositions. The first related to compositions comprising griseofulvin for the treatment of fungal diseases of man and animals. The second applied to griseofulvin compositions suitable for oral administration, including tablets, pills and syrups for human treatment, and foodstuffs or mixtures of foodstuffs for animal treatment. Together, these two patents gave ICI provisional rights over the development and sale of griseofulvin as a systemic fungistatic for clinical or veterinary use. In March 1957, Glaxo researchers learned of the antibiotic's effectiveness against dermatophytic fungi when administered orally, when the abstract of ICI's provisional patent was made available to, and circulated within, the firm.

Within a month, Glaxo researchers proceeded with clinical trials investigating griseofulvin's systemic activity in coordination with Gentles at Glasgow. His first report indicated encouraging results: 'On the credit side there is the fact that the absorption rate is apparently very good, and also that treatment did apparently prevent infection.'[7]

Perceiving griseofulvin's possible future as a pharmaceutical product, Glaxo approached ICI in the spring of 1957 about reaching a griseofulvin agreement. Earlier discussions had confirmed that both companies held common interests in the investigation of griseofulvin's uses, since each of them maintained provisional patent rights which were necessary and complementary to the antibiotic's future commercial exploitation. Glaxo Laboratories held the rights to griseofulvin as a systemic agricultural antibiotic, and more importantly, maintained patent protection for the technological expertise necessary for griseofulvin's large-scale commercial production. ICI's claims to griseofulvin's use as an orally administered, systemic antifungal in the treatment of animal diseases, controlled the substance's possible clinical development.

The main features of the agreement reached between Glaxo and ICI, defining their relationship on griseofulvin were:

1.   To exchange royalty-free non-exclusive rights under all United Kingdom patents issuing from the Provisional Patent applications of both parties, and any corresponding patents issuing in countries foreign to the United Kingdom, to make, use and sell, for the prevention or treatment of animal (including human) diseases *only*, compositions containing griseofulvin embraced by the claims of the patents.

2.   That Glaxo will supply and ICI will purchase from Glaxo its total requirements of griseofulvin or material for the same for so long as Glaxo is able and willing to supply such requirements at a reasonable price.

3.   That the rights will be conveyed for the life of the patents or so long as Glaxo is able and willing to supply ICI with its total requirements, whichever is the shorter period.

4.   The rights are only sublicensable to subsidiaries and associated companies of both parties.[8]

The agreement established mutual control over rights to griseofulvin's future medical development, with rights to the product's use in horticulture and agriculture reserved to Glaxo.

After his preliminary observations in 1957, Gentles conducted additional experimental work on griseofulvin's systemic activity in laboratory animals. He also advised on trials extended to experimental ringworm in calves, subsequently conducted at the University of Glasgow's Veterinary Hospital, which reinforced his own work and aroused interest among professional colleagues. At a Medical Research Council meeting held in 1958 both Gentles and his Glaswegian veterinary colleague, Lauder, presented papers on their recent work. The impact was considerable: one Cambridge dermatologist described the work as 'epoch-making'.[9]

But even as Gentles' and Lauder's findings were circulated and experimental trials gave promise of griseofulvin's clinical success, toxicity reports shed doubt on the prospects of the antibiotic's commercial development. Initially in 1958 ICI research workers reported to Glaxo that they had found that griseofulvin induced abnormal effects on cell division in animals. This announcement led Glaxo to suspend their development programme, restricting the firm's extramural veterinary trials to a limited number of well-chosen cases. The latter were selected among people Glaxo officials considered 'competent' to make the necessary experimental observations.[10] Professional, clinical and veterinary competence also implied professional discretion, as possible misuse of the antibiotic without a complete understanding of its toxicity would jeopardise Glaxo's ethical reputation as well as the drug's commercial development. Glaxo's Medical Director, Hector Walker, was particularly fastidious in the matter, declining publicly to commit Glaxo to griseofulvin's clinical availability before checking ICI's findings. Reflecting on several successful experimental trials already conducted, Walker reported, in February 1958:

One can come to no conclusion at the present moment as to whether or not Griseofulvin is going to be a practicable systemic antifungal substance ... we must really wait until Ungar has repeated the ICI investigations, and there is rumour that ICI are going to make communication to *Nature* on the toxicity they have found. If they do this, it will be a serious problem to us, certainly in recommending any systemic or even agricultural use, and the fact that ICI found the toxic effects on very large doses will not just clear us for its use in very small doses until we understand more about it.[11]

In addition to these reservations, Walker also maintained that, although the Glasgow experiments demonstrated griseofulvin's systemic effectiveness *in vivo*, they did not show whether or not the antibiotic was an effective product for veterinary medicine: 'apart from everything else', Walker wrote to Palmer, 'the evidence of experimental ringworm could not necessarily be evidence of the value in the field'. Continuing to refuse to distribute the product freely for clinical veterinary use, Walker asserted, 'we are not yet in sight of a product that can be marketed'.[12]

The toxicity problem centred on apparently irreconcilable differences between Glaxo's evaluation and ICI's more recent laboratory findings. But a meeting of both parties convened in May 1958 led to an understanding of the way in which the widely differing results had been produced. The possibility of differences in the griseofulvin particle size causing variations between Glaxo and ICI results was discussed and it seemed likely that both higher doses injected intravenously and griseofulvin preparations of smaller particle size employed in the ICI examinations greatly affected absorption and thus the toxic effect. Glaxo scientists then pressed Dr Paget of ICI for a

I An early tin of Glaxo powder. Cover of the Glaxo baby book using the Glaxo medallion. Postcards were a popular medium for Glaxo advertising in the interwar years.

These plates are available for download in colour from www.cambridge.org/9780521425599

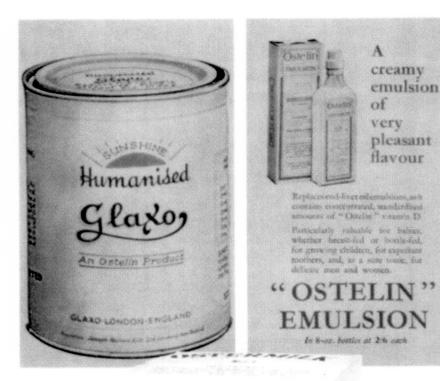

II Vitamin D was the Glaxo Department's first pharmaceutical product in 1924. It
was added to Glaxo powder, presented as Ostelin Emulsion and then as Ostermilk.

III Vitamin B$_{12}$, and the anti-pernicious anaemia factor was identified, isolated and crystallised at Greenford in 1948 after some years of work by a team led by Dr Lester Smith. The oil painting by Liam Breslin shows Dr Smith (on the left) with colleagues, Dr Parker and Dr Fantes in the laboratory. Below are crystals of vitamin B$_{12}$.

IV Portrait of Sir Harry Jephcott by Sir Gerald Kelly.

definitive statement as to whether he felt griseofulvin was dangerous to use. He replied cautiously that:

It was his considered opinion that the use of Griseofulvin in agriculture was perfectly safe. He said that ... he felt no harm could come from the ingestion of meat obtained from Griseofulvin-treated cattle ... agreed that the use of Griseofulvin in fungal diseases in cattle should be quite safe, with the rider that its use in milking cows should be avoided ... he would be very reluctant to sanction its use in man, particularly as fungal infections are not particularly serious. If the use of Griseofulvin should be suggested in fungal pneumonia, he would have no hesitation in using it since such a condition is invariably fatal. He could see no justification for its indiscriminate use for minor fungal infections in man, such as athlete's foot, since these infections were of no serious importance.[13]

The meeting ended with agreement to exchange both animals and griseofulvin preparations in order that each laboratory could resolve both preparation and strain differences.

Gentles' seminal research report piece appeared in *Nature* in August 1958.[14] ICI's announcement, 'Some Cytological Effects of Griseofulvin', was printed in the November journal.[15] Following these two pieces, Lauder and O'Sullivan submitted another report describing their more recent field trials using orally administered griseofulvin, which appeared in *Veterinary Record* at the end of November the same year.[16] Together these three papers formed the documentary triad of griseofulvin's clinical debut in the international scientific press.

ICI's willingness to cooperate with Glaxo Laboratories over griseofulvin-related publications involved more than a debate over the antibiotic's clinical toxicity. Also at issue were mutual company interests in the antibiotic's potential commercial profitability, dating back to the formal agreement of 1957. Clearly ICI would also reap the benefits of the drug's professional acceptance and product development should Glaxo be given a chance to establish its claims to griseofulvin's medical and veterinary value.

Although the companies had agreed to cooperate commercially, there is some evidence of scientific competition at the laboratory level. In June 1958, a year after the agreement, an ICI researcher named Martin contested the authenticity of Gentles' experimental trials and Glaxo's associated claims. He insisted that his own earlier experimental work on the oral use of griseofulvin against fungus disease in April 1956 had led ICI to make its provisional patent application for oral and intravenous griseofulvin formulations later the same year, although subsequent toxicity observations curtailed ICI's product development interests. Having since become aware of Gentles' work on experimental ringworm at Glasgow, Martin maintained that Gentles' observations confirmed earlier ICI evidence rather than representing new or original discoveries. Corresponding directly with

Lauder and Gentles, Martin pressed the scientists to acknowledge his previous experimental work at ICI in Lauder's forthcoming November publication about the antibiotic's systemic activity in cattle. Judging by correspondence surrounding the incident, Martin's letters challenged Glaxo's professional conduct and scientific integrity in introducing griseofulvin for experimental trial, and provoked a strong if localised furore.

As the author of the firm's two griseofulvin provisional patents, Martin alleged that Glaxo Laboratories had been aware of the 1956 unpublished experimental work conducted at ICI's laboratories. He also fostered the misconception that Glaxo approached Gentles and initiated the Glasgow experiments on the oral antibiotic when cognisant of Martin's work. Whether the ICI scientist believed Glaxo to be interlopers in his research territory, felt threatened by Gentles' published recognition, or considered Glaxo's experimental claims as an infringement of ICI's patent application, is unclear. Whatever Martin's suspicions, his letters insinuating misconduct by Glaxo put the latter's management on the defensive. Palmer supervised an extensive internal survey of the background to Glaxo's investigation of griseofulvin's systemic activity. The exercise revealed that at no time had the firm's scientific researchers received details of Martin's work on experimental fungal infections in guinea pigs, although most knew of ICI's provisional patents of 1956.

Writing to ICI about the allegations, in June 1958, Palmer stated, 'we have, in fact, only just now learned through this letter to Gentles, that such work has been done before'. He also denied the idea that Glaxo had inspired or instigated Gentles' work: 'He came to us with an inquiry whether we could provide him with material which might have certain characteristics for which he was looking, and we accordingly gave him supplies of Griseofulvin.'[17] With Palmer's assurance of Glaxo's integrity the matter ended and Glaxo and ICI continued to cooperate cordially.

In October 1958 the two companies refined their original agreement, with ICI agreeing to give Glaxo the right to sub-license independent third parties non-exclusively under its griseofulvin patent structure. This additional clause and prevailing patent holdings determined Glaxo's subsequent marketing strategy for the product. It was also agreed that 'any income derived by Glaxo from licensing or sub-licensing Glaxo and/or ICI Griseofulvin rights respectively will be shared fifty-fifty with ICI'.[18] Meanwhile, additional field trials sponsored by Glaxo and undertaken by Lauder at Glasgow's Veterinary School continued to be encouraging. The results enabled research workers to report: 'We are now presumably satisfied that any toxic effects likely to cause us embarrassment are unlikely to arise.'[19] Glaxo-sponsored griseofulvin trials on experimental animals had gone further than any other in demonstrating the antibiotic's systemic antifungal activity in animals and the work represented an important contribution to comparative pathology studies. In addition to veterinary application, experimental trials with griseofulvin suggested favourable possibilities in human treatment. In July 1958 Hector Walker despatched a supply of griseofulvin tablets to Professor Gustav Riehl in Vienna for clinical human trial. Riehl treated the first human cases of fungal infection with the antibiotic.

Griseofulvin in North America

The most extensively documented and publicised clinical experiences, however, were reported by Dr Harvey Blank, Professor of Dermatology at the University of Miami's School of Medicine, in 1958. Blank learned of griseofulvin's systemic fungistatic activity from Gentles' experimental work published in *Nature*, and wrote to Glaxo Laboratories requesting a supply of the antibiotic to treat a near fatal case of *T. rubrum*, an acute chronic fungal infection of the skin. Glaxo immediately sent both tablets and powder to the dermatologist; by the end of the month Blank reported that the griseofulvin medication had probably saved his patient's life. This result led Blank to extend clinical treatment to other similar cases, with equally satisfactory effect. Writing to Campbell in early November, Blank's report of his recent experience with the drug was nearly ecstatic:

If I said that we were excited and thrilled with the results with Griseofulvin I would be stating things in mild terms. We have a number of patients now with Trichophyton infections, some of them extremely widespread, including the palms and soles, some as long as fifteen years duration, who have shown clearing within one or two weeks. There has just never been anything like this before . . . there seems little doubt that in reasonable doses this drug will clear superficial fungus infections of the skin very promptly.[20]

Blank indicated that repeated blood, kidney function, liver function and other close observations had not revealed any signs of toxicity, nor were there any visible side-effects. Requesting an additional supply of griseofulvin, Blank told Glaxo that he expected his own successful experience with the antibiotic to generate considerable publicity:

With these truly remarkable clinical responses, it is impossible to keep the information about this from spreading out among the staff and others in the community. I have decided, therefore, that it would be wise to give an initial report at the meeting of the American Academy of Dermatology in Chicago in December, where I am scheduled to discuss superficial fungus infections on December 10th. This is a large meeting attended by over a thousand Dermatologists and the Daily Press covers it quite carefully, so that I am sure newspaper publicity will follow, as well as extreme professional interest.[21]

Blank understood the commercial implications of this kind of publicity, for he had already fielded inquiries from representatives of Johnson & Johnson, Lederle and Squibb, seeking details about the drug, and his clinical observations. Blank had been unforthcoming, but realised from these encounters that similar pressures would be placed upon him by other American pharmaceutical manufacturers once he made his own work public. He therefore suggested to Glaxo that the company complete its overseas licensing negotiations by the time he made his December presentation, stating, 'I will be most anxious to learn the status of your negotiations, for I fear the demands that will be made on us when this information becomes public'.[22]

Encouraged by Blank's report, Glaxo moved quickly to secure its position in the North American market. The company decided to apply the label 'Grisovin' to griseofulvin medical preparations, thus reinforcing the product's name recognition, and to assign 'Grisovin-H' to the firm's horticultural and agricultural products. (ICI adopted 'Fulcin' as its trademark name for corresponding clinical griseofulvin products.) Glaxo also moved quickly to identify the company with medical statements made about the new antifungal antibiotic. Anticipating a journal announcement on the subject, Glaxo's marketing department proposed informing readers of the drug's imminent availability and to ally the new product with Glaxo Laboratories' achievements:

Within a week or two of an expected letter in *Lancet* early next month about the clinical effectiveness of Griseofulvin in humans we would like to stake our claim and make known our name Grisovin by an advertisement announcement. This would say something to the effect that Griseofulvin, a development of Glaxo Research, will be made available as soon as possible for general prescription under the trade mark GRISOVIN.[23]

A similar announcement was considered for *Veterinary Record* to follow Lauder's recent article.

More importantly, Glaxo took immediate steps to arrange commercial outlets in the United States. Given the options available to the company through its prior agreements with ICI, permitting griseofulvin sales through subsidiaries or third-party sub-licensees, Glaxo decided to license firms overseas rather than establish its own subsidiary outlets. It was thought that licensing would maximise Glaxo's return on investment and place the company in a more favourable competitive position *vis-à-vis* ICI. By handling North American sales as it did, Glaxo received royalties, protected its manufacturing rights, and was able to supervise the control of bulk griseofulvin distribution: but it was a decision that was regretted by several of the managing directors of Glaxo's overseas subsidiaries, particularly in Canada.

In November 1958 Austin Bide visited the United States to settle sales

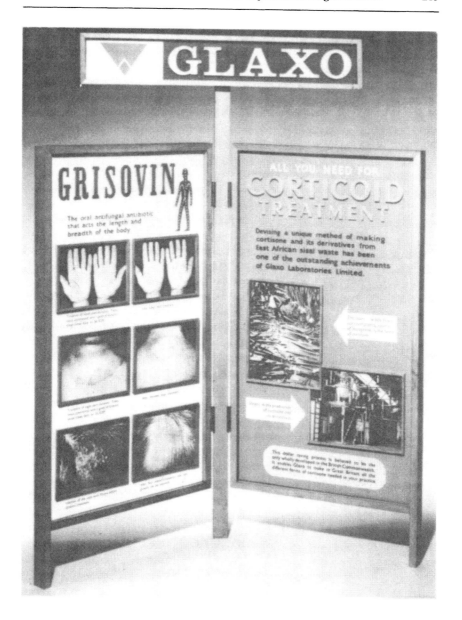

42 Publicity for Grisovin and cortisone products.

agreements with drug manufacturers there. His reception was mixed. Schering Corporation immediately indicated its desire to handle griseofulvin in the human field and in the veterinary field as well. Johnson & Johnson also expressed interest in purchasing the rights to market the antibiotic. Representatives of Du Pont, on the other hand, showed minimal enthusiasm for the product except, perhaps, in the veterinary field. Merck, Sharp & Dohme officials received Bide's US visit coolly, though by December they had become more eager to involve themselves with griseofulvin in the North American market. As the result of his meetings, Bide reached agreements with both Schering and Johnson & Johnson. Each agreed to handle griseofulvin material for 'Hand-outs' to clinicians and for conducting the necessary work leading to the Federal Government's Food and Drug Administration (FDA) approval. Each firm also agreed to pay Glaxo a royalty rate of 7.5 per cent on net sales, subject to a market survey, or 2.5 per cent on net sales if bulk material was purchased from Glaxo.

In assessing US demand, Bide pointed out both to Schering and Johnson & Johnson that Glaxo would be unable 'particularly in any long term, to satisfy the prospective needs to the US market for [griseofulvin] through bulk sales to US pharmaceutical formulators. It was clearly recognised that some arrangement with an American company having basic fermentation manufacturing capacity would have to be investigated without delay.'[24] In this connection, Merck, Sharp & Dohme's name was mentioned. Merck, as Bide knew, had manufacturing facilities capable of producing the material on a large scale. While both Schering and Johnson & Johnson were prepared to accept Merck's involvement if necessary, both were reluctant to do so. Schering, for instance, claimed that Merck would be partial in its supplies and liable to break restrictions from selling to independent third parties. Johnson & Johnson's reaction was less hostile, but both US companies adamantly believed that the domestic market was not large enough for three formulators, as Glaxo would also have to allow Merck to package and sell griseofulvin should it manufacture material in bulk supplies. In addition, ICI also retained the right to exercise its sales option in the US. Describing Johnson & Johnson's and Schering's opposition to Merck's inclusion in any US agreement, Bide explained, 'Their anxiety stems from a desire to keep the number of people marketing this product in the US to a minimum so that those engaged in it can foresee sufficient income to justify the heavy promotional expenditure which will be involved.'[25]

Taking these arguments into account, Glaxo proposed to expand its own production capacity for griseofulvin manufacture. Hoping to take advantage of improved economies of scale, Glaxo informed its North American outlets, 'By the end of March next we hope to have so developed our production procedures that we can then, if not before, reduce our price to you to 30 cents a gram (from current price of 50 cents a gram) . . . on present indications a price of 15 cents would ultimately be possible as we work up the process and secure the benefits of larger scale production.'[26]

Thus, a mixture of competition and cooperation characterised the development of griseofulvin marketing in the US. As the negotiations between Glaxo, Johnson & Johnson, Schering and ICI illustrated, the two licensees' opposition to additional licensees in North America prevented any commercial arrangement between Merck and Glaxo. Both Johnson & Johnson and Schering also reacted strongly to ICI's decision to undertake griseofulvin trials and marketing in the US. Although they recognised that ICI could legitimately exercise its rights to do so, Johnson & Johnson offered to raise its royalties to both Glaxo and ICI if the latter would reconsider its plans. The proposal was rejected by ICI and the company made arrangements to exploit the antibiotic in America through its US connection, American Home Products (AHP), and in Canada via AHP's pharmaceutical division, Ayerst McKenna (with which Glaxo had in the 1930s attempted to penetrate the North American market – see chapter 5).

Although Johnson & Johnson agreed to collaborate with Schering in submitting evidence to the Federal Food and Drug Administration (FDA), seeking approval for griseofulvin sales in the US, both firms refused to cooperate with ICI in this effort. In July 1959 the FDA approved the release of the antibiotic in the US market handled by Schering and Johnson & Johnson. ICI received similar FDA approval thereafter, but the delay gave competitive advantage to the two US companies. Despite the cooperation in the initial stages of American marketing, the two licensees were later highly competitive in promotional schemes and sales campaigns. In the course of these negotiations, Glaxo was able to exert little control over ICI's participation in the North American griseofulvin market.

Both Johnson & Johnson and Schering were well-known American pharmaceutical houses with experienced marketing personnel. Additionally, the former's acquisition of McNeil Laboratories of Philadelphia in January 1959 also brought 'one of the top medium-sized pharmaceutical houses in the US' into its sales project.[27] As the first to express keen interest in handling griseofulvin sales, the readiness of Johnson & Johnson and Schering to promote the product aggressively was essential to Glaxo's staking out its own territory in the American market-place; as early as January 1959, there were rumours that Squibb and possibly Pfizer were considering selling griseofulvin in the US, apparently without a licence and by manufacturing their own materials. Johnson & Johnson was also well placed to market in Australia, Mexico, Canada and Brazil, although the company did not immediately pursue claims to these locations. Schering expressed interest in handling Glaxo's export markets in Central and South American countries and possibly in Canada. Finally, Schering offered another type of outlet for griseofulvin development and sales. Having recently acquired White Laboratories, a business handling animal feed additives, the company was willing to engage in a cooperative testing programme with Glaxo exploring griseofulvin as an animal feed product.

Griseofulvin marketing elsewhere

Well before the antibiotic became commercially available and attracted widespread attention, Glaxo made arrangements for bulk griseofulvin sales over a range of foreign territories, involving Glaxo subsidiaries, commissioned agents, and independent second and third party licensees. Wherever possible, Glaxo established its own presence in the foreign country; Schering and Johnson & Johnson, for instance, both licensed to sell griseofulvin in America, were excluded by their agreement with Glaxo from selling the substance through their respective foreign subsidiaries (in Argentina, Brazil, Canada, Equador, Mexico, Peru, Uruguay or Venezuela) until ninety days after the date when Glaxo made their own first commercial sale in that country.

As well as setting up sales territories, Glaxo negotiated and bartered reciprocal sales terms with Lovens, the Danish pharmaceutical house, and in France with Clinbyla. Some arrangements involved more than griseofulvin. Lovens, for example, requested that a much larger export sales area be made available beyond the firm's Denmark home base to include several South American countries, France and Colonial France, Spain, the Near East, Ghana and many West African territories, among others. These were places where Glaxo itself had a strong interest or where Lovens' interests were competitive with other griseofulvin sub-licensees. After contemplating the Lovens terms, Palmer determined that Glaxo 'must go a long way to meet his request on a non-exclusive basis in view of his preparedness to admit us to many areas outside the UK in respect of preparations of his invention'.[28] Specifically, Glaxo wished to secure the rights to sell Estopen and Estomycin, both Lovens-produced items, in Colombia and Brazil. Glaxo officials, therefore, recommended withholding Ghana and Thailand from any immediate sales agreements with Lovens over griseofulvin, hoping to use these territories as bargaining chips in negotiating Estopen sales arrangements with the Danish firm.

Glaxo investigated the possibility of re-exporting bulk griseofulvin from its Italian subsidiary to despatch the material to an Israeli formulator: Israel represented a potential foreign market where commercial connections and political implications with respect to Arab countries were delicate. The firm also felt it was 'imperative to make arrangements for selling Griseofulvin in the Japanese market as quickly as possible', notwithstanding the presence of Schering and Johnson & Johnson's subsidiaries there, and hastened into a series of sub-licensing arrangements which caused some resentment to their local Japanese agent.[29] By March 1959 Glaxo had laid out the majority of its licensing arrangements covering export sales of griseofulvin.[30]

The launch of griseofulvin

Glaxo released 'Grisovin' on the British market on 6 April 1959, and, by arrangement, ICI also released its griseofulvin preparation 'Fulcin' on the same day. The extent of commercial and medical adoption of the antibiotic in Britain, the US and other foreign territories, varied according to levels of demand, professional receptivity and promotional schemes within the different areas. In Britain Glaxo dominated the griseofulvin market, holding exclusive rights to sell the agricultural preparation through Murphy and sharing non-exclusive rights for medical and veterinary formulations with ICI. In the veterinary field, there was no ordinary need for the product; ringworm in cattle, for instance, was not a serious problem unless it reached epidemic proportions. There were possible medical applications. But in most cases physicians operating within Britain's National Health Service were likely to prescribe more orthodox and less costly curatives for common fungal infections of the skin than griseofulvin. Only extreme cases of dermatophytes warranted supervised griseofulvin therapy. Hector Walker noted the idiosyncracies of Britain's medical community, observing their often reactionary behaviour and reluctance to accept new medications: 'Dermatologists – at least some of them – seem a little bit disturbed that a specific treatment is now available that represents a not unsizeable part of their total practice, and there are reactionary Dermatologists just as there are physicians when new treatments appear.'[31] Some venereologists had shown a similar response some forty years earlier to the anti-syphilis specific Salvarsan, when it was first marketed.[32]

Significant to the establishment of griseofulvin in the American and other foreign markets were the specific and specialised claims associated with the product. Glaxo expected veterinary demand would be small in the USA, but should enough interest be generated in the antibiotic's clinical qualities, the firm foresaw substantial commercial demand. As a Schering executive wrote, griseofulvin's American licensees needed to establish the product's unique claims before other competitors, and interlopers, offered the same or analogous formulations: 'If these firms enter (Squibb, Pfizer, Merck), in addition to Johnson & Johnson, ourselves and one of the American Home units, the product, to say the least, will lose its attractiveness as a speciality item.'[33]

Glaxo could do little to prevent outsiders from entering the US with sales of griseofulvin until it had fully secured patent protection. Even so, the product's presentation, upon which legitimate licensees intended to capitalise, affected their potential market shares:

When the patent is issued the question of what can be done will depend to a large extent upon the claims, and this will depend upon what is unique in the properties of the product. This focuses attention upon the great importance not only of expediting the patent proceedings as much as possible, but taking every possible action to strengthen the product claims or 'use' claims of the patent, for it is quite apparent that the process patent alone may prove to be of little value.[34]

Publicity and promotion played an important part in the antibiotic's adoption and sales in the US. Both Schering and Johnson & Johnson displayed the drug at the spring American Medical Association meeting of 1959, before receiving FDA approval. Following this exposure, Schering wrote to Glaxo:

The product has already made considerable history since ... it is the first product which has been actually promoted and detailed before it was actually put on the market. There is considerable interest here among not only Dermatologists but GP's [General Practitioners] in the development.[35]

Johnson & Johnson also planned an ambitious promotional campaign. In a Glaxo memo Palmer reported:

There is no doubt that they (J & J) continue to be excited by the prospects of this product and if the market is reserved to them they propose to spend a considerable sum of money, not merely on detailing the product to Dermatologists, but also on inducing the general public to go to the Dermatologists for treatment of troubles which hitherto have not been susceptible of effective medication. This line of advertising is acceptable to the American profession and he believes will be effective in boosting market demand.[36]

Launching griseofulvin preparations on the American and worldwide market involved professional promotions, as well as commercial ones, intended to strengthen the product's claims. In October 1959 McNeil Laboratories (Johnson & Johnson's subsidiary) funded an International Symposium on griseofulvin and dermatomycosis held at the University of Miami. Jointly sponsored by the University and convened by the mycologist, Dr Harvey Blank, the symposium attracted more than 200 physicians and investigators from eleven countries, generated global press coverage, and went a long way towards establishing griseofulvin's medical value and Glaxo's association with the drug's development.

The symposium featured some thirty-six professional papers, later published as a special edition of the American Medical Association's Archive of Dermatology. Campbell gave the first session's opening paper and reported on the early *in-vitro* laboratory work at Glaxo which led to subsequent important clinical and experimental work. Other presentations provided new information about the morphology of antifungal activity, griseofulvin's systemic distribution, and low toxicity. Nearly half the papers dealt with clinical studies, covering the experiences of more than 1,000 patients.[37]

Campbell and Gentles kept a high profile during the conference emphasising Glaxo's role in griseofulvin's development. According to one account: 'The scientific personality of Dr Campbell dominated all these sessions to the point where he dispelled any doubts existing, if indeed there were any doubts, to the satisfaction of everyone ... about the drug's therapeutic value.'[38]

Beyond these professional and promotional activities, Glaxo's research scientists and managers perceived the company as instrumental, if not indispensable, in griseofulvin's successful scientific development. Earlier in April 1959, shortly after the antibiotic's commercial introduction, Dermot Carey of ICI expressed dissatisfaction with the supposed sales impression left by Glaxo representatives working in the field. According to Carey's complaint: 'Some of [Glaxo's] people at home and overseas ... had begun broadcasting the thought that Griseofulvin was exclusively a Glaxo invention and that, if anything, ICI were the junior partners if not actual pirates of the discovery.'[39] Responding to this accusation, Palmer instructed his own staff to project a discreet yet positive impression of Glaxo's role in developing the new antibiotic:

I would ask that it be made clear to our representatives at home and overseas that it is no part of their business to decry whatever contribution ICI may have made to the Griseofulvin story. I see no particular need for them to even mention the company and if the matter is raised I can't see any particular discredit in our basing ourselves on the facts that this is a British invention in which we have played an important, if not major, part.[40]

Nevertheless, Glaxo executives, such as W. S. Hurran, perpetuated an image of griseofulvin as a Glaxo achievement and a successful product of Greenford's laboratory research. Writing to Campbell about the forthcoming Miami Symposium, Hurran stated:

I know you will agree with me that it is a very good thing indeed to keep our overseas people fed with the most up-to-date information just as quickly as possible so that they can maintain the impression, which for once is pretty well justified, that Glaxo are in the spearhead of a new development and not merely making the best of following behind others.[41]

In 1960 an overseas sales managers conference held at Greenford prompted the preparation of a 'statement of sales of Grisovin by Glaxo companies and of griseofulvin by licensees and agents', illustrating the extent of griseofulvin's initial acceptance in foreign territories and of Glaxo's presence overseas. Among the Glaxo subsidiaries distributing the drug were Argentina, Australia, Brazil, Canada, Ceylon, Colombia, Cuba, India, Italy, Malaya, New Zealand, Pakistan, South America and the Caribbean. Sales performances varied: Glaxo's subsidiary in Canada was especially poor, the result of the impact of competition from the American licensees (see page 259). In contrast Glaxo's normally demoralised and ineffective Brazilian subsidiary stood out exceptionally well; salesmen had worked enthusiastically and saw in *Grisovin* a chance to expand sales and to heighten the company's profile.

Starting in the summer of 1960, Glaxo began exploring fine particle griseofulvin in collaboration with American licensees. ICI also provided technical expertise in lending know-how on its superfine grinding process. This technical collaboration led to subsequent commercial agreement between the two companies applying to analogues and homologue griseofulvin.[42] By March 1962 'GRISOVIN FP' (Fine Particle) was being circulated for clinical trial.[43] Glaxo had discovered that griseofulvin blood levels varied inversely to particle size, meaning that the same blood levels could be obtained with the fine particle drug administered at about half the dose. In 1965 Glaxo completed fine particle griseofulvin for distribution and sale. The modified product was introduced on a 'phased withdrawal' programme executed over several months, enabling Glaxo gradually to substitute fine for coarse particle griseofulvin tablets on the market.[44]

Conclusion

When Glaxo turned its attention to griseofulvin its practical value as an agricultural chemical had yet to be demonstrated. As the first antifungal antibiotic ever studied under laboratory conditions, ICI had already made considerable advances by 1954 in identifying its chemical structure and biological action. This work revealed that the substance demonstrated effective biological activity, systemic action, stability and low phototoxicity. But no practicable method to synthesize the substance or to prepare it by means other than by surface culture had been developed. Glaxo Laboratories deserved much of the credit for that development.

III

Internationalisation of pharmaceuticals

10

Glaxo Laboratories and the international development of the pharmaceutical industry

The Multinational pharmaceutical industry

In the post-war period, as the therapeutic revolution gathered momentum, it became imperative for pharmaceutical companies to market their unique, novel and patented products abroad as well as at home. The vast increase in the number of ethical drugs introduced after 1944 revealed that no country had a monopoly of the innovation or the production of drugs. Even a country such as the USA, with its large and innovative pharmaceutical corporations and its own vast market, was obliged to import ethical drugs. The worldwide need for medicines and the pressure for swift amortisation of the high investment in research were also strong incentives to export pharmaceuticals.[1] Technological advantage often provided the first stimulus for pharmaceutical companies to internationalise. Import regulations and restrictions such as tariffs, quotas and bans imposed by governments for various economic and social reasons, spurred pharmaceutical companies on to establish foreign manufacturing establishments, as Glaxo's own overseas development before the Second World War (see chapter 5) illustrates.

Pharmaceutical companies differ from most other manufacturing businesses in their approach to multinational development. This is partly because of the unusual complexity and diversity of the local market conditions with which pharmaceutical companies are confronted. It is also partly inspired by the seniority of trained scientific personnel within the managerial hierarchies of pharmaceutical companies. Even when not directly or exclusively responsible for multinational strategy and organisation, the senior scientists nevertheless imbue the company culture with the need for clear, steady and coherent long-term views. One recent analysis of five US pharmaceutical multinationals (Baxter-Travenol, Merck Sharp & Dohme, Bristol-Myers, Warner-Lambert and Eli Lilly) found that they were distinguished by the time and care given to modifying the 'physiological' and even the 'psychological' characteristics of their organisations: in contrast to many other sectors, organisational development in pharmaceutical multi-nationals was normally, 'an adaptive, evolutionary process rather than a series of powerful, yet perhaps traumatic reorganisations'.[2] Instead of strategic structural reorganisations during liquidity or marketing crises, which characterised the multinational development and organisation of most British industrial sectors, Glaxo Laboratories 'developed, adjusted and integrated the required new skills, structure and processes gradually but continuously'.[3]

Pharmaceutical companies had to master the structure and operation of national health systems, the nature of government product registration processes, formal and informal demands for local self-sufficiency in specified products, and countless other national pressures. Yet simultaneously there had to be coordination, and even worldwide integration, of the research efforts, manufacturing capacity, product policy and other tasks of the pharmaceutical producer. The contribution from scientifically trained managers was enhanced by other special characteristics of the pharmaceutical business. The quality of the scientific research, the originality and efficacy of the product, or the ingenuity and pertinacity of production scientists in improving techniques or reducing unit costs, all rank together with the marketing campaign in determining success of a new product. Indeed, the success of the marketing depends on collaboration and liaison over details of the campaign with research and production specialists. These factors meant that the influence of scientists permeated the organisation of pharmaceutical companies, not least in their global development. Of its nature, such influence may have been imperceptible to those most affected by it; but in the context of multinational development, it contributed to both the clarity and steadiness of strategy, and to the relative freedom from traumatic policy changes precipitated by financial or marketing crises.

Other general characteristics of the world's pharmaceutical industry are identifiable. The low price elasticity of demand which typifies new pharmaceutical products encourages central control over international marketing strategy so that full advantage can be taken of commercial and pricing opportunities. Multiple organisational levels within companies are essential because of the special characteristics of the sector.

Centralised primary production is preferred, because of the economies of scale in transforming raw materials into crude products, and because of the stringent requirements of quality control: as a result, sub-contracting of foreign production has historically been rare. Nevertheless, economies have been possible or political advantages have accrued, where tabletting or filling of capsules has been undertaken nationally or regionally. Whereas basic research has normally been centralised to ensure coordination, local chemical trials are essential to meet the frequently exacting procedure for product registration: there are also theoretical opportunities for the regional-isation of product development. However, in the case of Glaxo Laboratories for several decades after 1945, there is evidence from New Zealand, Italy and other foreign subsidiaries that scientific staff and management at Greenford were unsympathetic to, and discouraging of, such efforts. The proliferation of multiple organisational levels in Glaxo as with other pharmaceutical companies, was further accentuated by variations in the maturity and volatility of the different markets in which they operated.

The analysis, previously mentioned, of the five US-based pharmaceutical multinationals found that they had undergone a 'gradual evolutionary process' with 'three distinct yet closely inter-related changes' which over-lapped but occurred sequentially: and similarities in Glaxo Laboratories' multinational development on a smaller scale can be found. Insufficient evidence, however, precludes the drawing of any conclusion that this evolutionary process was typical of UK pharmaceutical companies. In the British company's case, largely at Jephcott's instigation, new management skills were gradually developed during the 1930s to satisfy the increasing demands facing the company, as the Nathan family influence declined and new pharmaceutical lines flourished. Next, in the period immediately after 1945, the organisational structure was modified to allow better interaction between the new management hierarchies. There were changes not only in the organisational structure of subsidiary companies, but what often proved more important, in the individuals serving as managing director. Subse-quently, from the mid 1950s, there were attempts to institutionalise and depersonalise the systems for taking decisions in a volatile and dynamic operating environment.[4]

Glaxo's international development

Both in the period when the Glaxo department was simply a profitable part of Joseph Nathan & Company, and in the decade after the separate formation of Glaxo Laboratories Ltd, the foreign subsidiaries, which were of varying strength and independence, were simply charged with winning a strong market share. Overseas subsidiary managers with local expertise were largely autonomous: product and functional managers in London provided them with support and technical services but seldom intervened in subsidiaries' operations. The local managers' views were only occasionally challenged, mainly when new expenditure was proposed, or unexpected losses had been sustained.[5] Managers like C. C. Richardson in South America, Victor Hyams in Australia, or Edward Foster in India, can be more aptly compared with Chinese provincial warlords, not only beyond the influence of the central government, but apt to defy it, than with British colonial governors or Indian viceroys, controlled by the Colonial Office or India Office. During the 1930s, Jephcott, sometimes actively supported by Alec Nathan, worked to limit the warlords, but in the cases of Foster and Richardson, at least, it was death, rather than the London board, that curbed them.

After the Second World War, under Jephcott's guidance, Glaxo Laboratories' product and functional managers gradually asserted greater co-ordination and integration between the group's multinational activities, increased their influence on decisions and enhanced the company's world-wide reputation. The ease or difficulty of communications was important to this development. Hitherto the only means of swift communication had been telegraphy, with air mail both slow and embryonic.[6] This contributed significantly to the autonomy of industry's overseas subsidiaries, as few head office directors and executives had the time or energy to visit foreign factories regularly and effectively. Indeed, those directors who could be spared from London to travel for weeks or months notoriously tended to be the least dynamic or experienced.[7] Jephcott at Glaxo Laboratories in the 1930s was exceptional not only for his indefatigability in visiting Australia, Argentina, the Far East and elsewhere, but also in the timeliness and efficacy of his visits. Even so, they were no substitute for proper budgetary and marketing control by a central head office. After 1945 telephonic contact, and trans-continental air travel by senior executives, became more common and improved international coordination and integration, but only at the end of the period covered by this book, with the introduction of the Boeing 707 and Douglas DC8, and the advent of communication satellites, did technology bring centralised multinational control to its apotheosis.

From the 1950s overseas managers became acutely conscious of the increased power of product and functional managers in Britain, and tensions or open conflict developed between staff and line, particularly as the regime of Jephcott drew to its close, and his tradition of highly personalised loyalty was undermined. Glaxo Laboratories had to balance responsiveness to local overseas conditions with the need for a coherent and integrated world strategy: the attempts to mediate at senior management level led, not surprisingly, to occasional strains. Annual and subsequently more frequent conferences of the overseas managing directors were held in London from the early 1950s: these were the occasion for considerable interchange of strategic, commercial, scientific, financial, organisational and other infor-mation. In the same period Glaxo Laboratories set up a Subsidiary Companies Unit (SCU) at its London head office partly to serve as an intermediary between the parent company and its foreign subsidiaries, and this proved effective. A Central Technical Services Unit (CTSU) was formed at Greenford after the merger with Allen & Hanburys, charged with

43 Herbert Palmer on the left with Idris Lewis, arriving in Brazil in 1959.

assisting overseas companies on production, training of technical staff and exchange of technical information. The CTSU was also intended to work in collaboration with the Central Engineering Services Unit which was created to advise overseas companies on new manfuacturing facilites. By the late

1950s and early 1960s specific executives at London headquarters were selected to act for overseas subsidiary companies as 'friends at Court' although these executives did not have specific profit responsibility, and there were not separate national profit centres. The group's decision-taking on the strategy and operation of its subsidiaries' multinational activities became more integrated and sophisticated. Although this sometimes diminished Glaxo's flexibility, in the period before 1963 this gradual and evolutionary process worked with the minimum of trauma and a creditable level of success.

In the 1930s Jephcott had predicted that:

Our export business of the years gone by will take upon itself an entirely different aspect. The substantial markets will become separate entities, producing their own products as far as possible, or at least elaborating them on the spot, whilst the balance will diminish in volume ... of turnover, if they have not entirely disappeared. At present, excepting in Australia and New Zealand, the organisation in the local companies is young and relatively inexperienced, not so much in trading in their territories as in production and sales policy. As, however, they grow in experience, to a less and less extent will they be dependent on us in London and to a greater extent will they ... expect to work out their own salvation.[8]

The foreign direct investments of the Nathan firm, and later of Glaxo Laboratories, were import-substituting neither by intention nor by effect. Some of Glaxo's foreign outposts (in Argentina, Australia and New Zealand for example) partly served to procure cheap raw materials in the form of milk. Moreover, the divided control and ownership between Wellington and London, and the latter's buy-out of 1946, put Glaxo Laboratories in the rare category of a migrating multinational, along with British American Tobacco (dominated by US interests on its formation in 1902, but under majority British ownership from 1915 and under predominant British management from 1923) or the Gramophone Company, which from 1898 to 1931 (when it was reconstituted as Electrical and Musical Industries) had oscillating Anglo-American ownership.[9]

By the 1940s, the London headquarters had accumulated sufficiently comprehensive international knowledge to challenge overseas managers' appraisals of market needs or political pressure, and to subject the costs and efficiency of different operations to close and comparative analysis. Like its American competitors Glaxo found that one impediment to integrated global strategy was that British product and functional managers, charged with servicing the needs of overseas subsidiary companies and with maintaining information conduits to headquarters, lacked either expertise or organisational credibility to resist overseas managers' proposals authoritatively. 'The first challenge in building a more multi-dimensional organisation, therefore, was to develop managers who could represent these additional perspectives.'[10]

The Second World War, as Jephcott wrote in 1941, 'speeded up' the redefinition of the group's international priorities. 'Within our organisation a higher degree of self-sufficiency will need to be developed in a number of markets if we are to hold the position which we have gained during the past 15 to 20 years', he wrote. He had 'visualised this development' by the mid 1930s, and felt that, while the decision to begin primary production would depend on natural resources and size of population in local markets, different considerations would apply to secondary production, which did not require the same resources or the same degree of technical skill. 'The export of goods prepared ready for sale to the ultimate consumer will, I expect, disappear, never to return', he predicted of the post-war period, particularly in 'South American markets where American interests will do their best to gain a virtual monopoly'.[11] The pressure of a war economy always tends to make business people regard the future in stark terms, and Jephcott's predictions were unwontedly extreme. However, they nevertheless give an accurate picture of the Second World War as a catalyst in Glaxo's international development. As part of the post-1945 redefinition of business strategy, the overseas subsidiaries were restructured and extended. To give the international group more cohesion, and to reduce excessive individuality in some overseas subsidiaries, it was decided to foster the name of Glaxo Laboratories Ltd ubiquitously in the languages of the countries concerned, and nomenclature was changed accordingly. Firms such as Foster in India or Richardson in Argentina were not only re-named after Glaxo, but in other respects they were adapted to post-war conditions with new personnel, new targets and further emphasis on accommodating local social and political trends. New subsidiaries were established in Uruguay (1947), Pakistan (1948), South Africa (1948) and Canada (1950). Although other directors and managers made important contributions to these decisions, Jephcott (as both chairman and managing director from 1945) was decisive. A poor linguist, holding strong personal ties and sympathies with the Dominions, he concentrated on developing business mainly in the Commonwealth; in the immediate post-war years it could also be argued that the European mainland was too devastated and dislocated to offer stable or profitable business opportunities.

This focus on the Commonwealth was general to British multinational companies of the period: Reddaway estimated that 70 per cent of British foreign direct investment was placed in the Commonwealth during 1955–1963.[12] Jephcott himself was a director from 1950 to 1964 of the Metal Box Company, and a friend of its chairman, Sir Robert Barlow, whose father had supplied tins to the embryonic Glaxo department in Edwardian days.[13]

Interestingly, when planning Glaxo's overseas activities, Jephcott was wont to cite Metal Box's multinational experiences, which were similarly Commonwealth-orientated, and there was a strong if subliminal interchange between the strategies of the two companies. Jephcott's enthusiasm for doing business in Commonwealth countries was, however, tempered by his caution and perception of the situation. 'Nothing would give me more pleasure, and the Local Health Service more satisfaction, than that we should do general pharmaceutical manufacture in Rhodesia', he wrote in 1959, but he continued:

I cannot conceive a better method of turning a profitable market into a loss. If the Board is prepared to sacrifice its Rhodesian income it might at some distant date pay off, but it would be very distant. 300,000 Europeans don't constitute a manufacturing market . . . Metal Box have taken a gamble and put a first-class factory in Salisbury . . . the Manager is now scratching his head as to how . . . to keep it even ticking over. I have pulled Robert's leg . . . about it, and he replies that they had to go in. I don't understand the 'had to'.[14]

Glaxo Laboratories' wartime and post-war licensing arrangements with American manufacturers excluded them from the USA. It was not until the introduction in 1959 of the dermatological Grisovin (see chapter 9) that the company possessed a product of their own, sufficiently important to justify trying to break into the American market. Instead, they licensed it to Schering and to Johnson & Johnson, realising that the company lacked a sufficiently wide range of major products to contemplate trying to penetrate the huge US market, especially as the parent company's capitalisation was miniscule compared with its main American competitors. Moreover, the latter's technological and managerial maturity enabled Glaxo Laboratories to grant licences without anxiety about the quality of standards. In any case in the immediate post-war period the British Treasury imposed conditions upon developments requiring the use of non-sterling funds, especially US dollars, which made some new ventures impracticable.[15]

Manufacturing overseas

During Glaxo's early multi-nationalism, when the business was modest by any standard, the Nathans were usually driven to begin limited local overseas production by protective tariffs, or other discriminatory regulations designed by governments to develop local productive expertise in industrially backward economies. Customs and double taxation problems were also significant, but these in themselves were insufficient to persuade the Nathans to incorporate an overseas manufacturing subsidiary unless this was justified by the market attraction of the particular territory. Manufacturing usually began with secondary production, that is the formulation, filling and packaging of products already developed from raw materials. Glaxo was more inclined to enter upon primary production of milk and food products than of pharmaceuticals, since the manufacture of the raw materials or active ingredients for the latter required greater investment of both funds and technical personnel. This was particularly the case with penicillin and other antibiotics. Glaxo Laboratories' post-war multi-nationalism was closely associated with antibiotics and the company's pioneering work with penicillin and streptomycin. However, the world price of penicillin collapsed after 1950, throwing costings and market analysis awry. Within a comparatively short space of time penicillin was transformed from an expensive rarity into a common commodity. Of all overseas markets, the consequences of this transformation were most severe in Canada, but they disturbed Glaxo's multinational development widely during the 1950s.

Considerable thought was given in the early 1950s to the possibilities of manufacturing antibiotics overseas. Raw materials for penicillin and streptomycin production were 'overwhelmingly the biggest charge up to the crude state', so that the decision to manufacture crudes in Britain and finish production abroad turned on the local cost of fermentation of raw materials. 'If there were a location overseas at which suitable raw materials were available cheaply then a situation could very readily arise in which the project would have a substantial advantage over large scale manufacture in this country', Fred Wilkins wrote in 1952, echoing the opinion of Jephcott and other colleagues.[16] Hopes that Australia or South Africa might provide such a location were disappointed, although a small antibiotic plant was opened in Australia. Glaxo's primary production therefore remained concentrated in the north of England.

Primary production was often uneconomic on a small scale and London headquarters resisted any such proposal from a subsidiary whose local market was under-developed. This sometimes led to long intervals between the start of filling and packing operations, and the start of primary production: for example in Pakistan the former began in 1947, the latter not until 1963. Even with Glaxo's proprietary products, there could be a difficult period when sales were building up, but high prices invoiced at Greenford made it difficult to expand them further, nor were the sales large enough to justify the installation of manufacturing capacity: this was the case with Farex in Italy.

New foreign manufacturing subsidiaries were acquired in the 1950s by virtue of the parent company's amalgamations. The most important were those of Allen & Hanburys, including South Africa (established in 1912), Canada (c 1915) and Australia (1947). But Evans Medical, merged with Glaxo in 1961, had overseas interests too and, importantly for Glaxo's future, a foothold in France. All these operations had to be gradually merged together, a slow process which mostly took place after the period covered by this history.

The finance of Glaxo's international operations

The methods of financing the development of overseas subsidiaries in the late 1940s and 1950s varied according to local circumstances. The keynote was provided by Jephcott's injunction in 1955: 'it is profit, not turnover too expensively bought, that we look for, and . . . this can only be obtained by cooperation and economy – watching every [penny] spent, particularly on propaganda'.[17] Direct transfers of capital with Bank of England approval did occur; but many of the established overseas subsidiaries had been encouraged to pursue conservative financial policies which enabled some rebuilding programmes to be covered from reserves. This was just as well, for there were moments during 1945–1963 when Bank of England or Treasury policy seemed to some senior Glaxo managers to be at best myopic and at worst inimical to the interests of British industrial multinationals.

The matter was complicated. Whereas the authorities seldom objected to the parent company sub-licensing its foreign subsidiaries in new products or processes provided that royalties remitted to Britain were received in transferable sterling, which could be passed to the (usually North American) licensors, a different attitude arose when Glaxo wished to sub-license subsidiary companies where payment of a royalty from Britain in dollars was involved. In some important markets, such as Argentina, there were major problems arising from government regulations concerning the remittance of profits to the British parent company: accumulated funds were spent on extensions which in other circumstances would possibly not have been undertaken.

In 1949 capital employed overseas represented 40 per cent of Glaxo's total capital employed. By 1960 the ratio was 46 per cent, despite continued attempts to restrain overseas investment.[18] In May 1953, Jephcott cautioned the managing directors of the foreign subsidiaries that it was impossible

for the Company to maintain a continuation of the present rate of overseas investment much longer; indeed, a case could be made that we had gone too far already . . . the Board might well hesitate to raise new money in London for general overseas investment having regard to the uncertainty, in several countries, of exchange being available for securing such capital, and the possibility of arbitrary restrictions being placed upon dividends.

He advised them to explore 'the prospects of raising money locally'.[19] When the profits earned by each subsidiary, after local taxation, were taken together with the profits arising in London from sales to the subsidiary company (before tax, but after allowance for overheads), there was a great variation in the return on investment. There was also considerable variation between the overseas companies as to turnover from food production and that derived from pharmaceuticals (see appendix table 8). But in all countries, pharmaceutical products represented the lion's share of turnover.[20] In the mid 1950s food products represented over 30 per cent or more of total turnover only in Argentina and Australia, the latter at 44 per cent the largest of all.

Glaxo's direct foreign investment became more cautious as time proceeded. This was partly a result of the company's prudent financial policies which prevailed, as has already been discussed, both before and after Jephcott's heyday and partly because political and economic obstacles to the remittance of overseas profits, threats of expropriation and fierce price competition all made foreign investment less attractive. Jephcott's statement at an internal meeting of 1956 that 'he would be prepared to invest additional capital only if there was a reasonable certainty of an adequate return [because] ... recent capital investments abroad had not been particularly remunerative' is indicative of the hardening of approach.[21]

Overall, the increased multi-nationalism of the group, entailing more local production, was a response to political pressures, in the form of tariffs and other regulations, which became an ever-stronger feature of the business. Simultaneously, many overseas managing directors advocated the inauguration or extension of local manufacturing in their market. Their reasons were often irreproachable, although occasionally local managing directors failed to perceive their fiefs in an accurate international perspective or, more rarely, were indulging in empire-building. By 1957 Glaxo Laboratories were represented in nearly 70 countires, and had nine overseas subsidiary headquarters with manufacturing facilities at Verona, Wadeville (South Africa), Karachi, Bombay, Melbourne, Palmerston North (New Zealand), Niteroi (Brazil), Montevideo and Buenos Aires. In addition, there were territorial offices at Cairo, Singapore, Toronto, Havana and Santiago, and separate factories in Argentina, Australia and New Zealand.

Consultancy agreements were made with many of the overseas subsidiaries. Their purpose was to ensure a constant return to the parent company, which might not be obtainable by way of dividend. 'The fact that such agreements may reduce overall taxation payable by the Group is purely incidental', a confidential memorandum of 1953 claimed. 'The consultancy agreement is not a device for avoiding taxation. Nevertheless, such agreements are ... scrutinised by the Revenue Authorities in the countries concerned, who are anxious for their pound of flesh.'[22] There were three types of services rendered by the parent company to subsidiaries to justify a consultancy fee. London headquarters provided services in establishing and operating a distributing company, including the exclusive right to sell the company's products, as well as advice on organisation, office management and advertising. Secondly, a subsidiary undertaking the local filling, packing and labelling of products received in bulk paid fees in return for the right to use for locally packed goods the trademarks and goodwill of the parent company. Finally, services provided to subsidiaries engaged in local production, including research and production expertise, merited the payment of consultancy fees. In Glaxo's earlier consultancy agreements an attempt was made to cover the whole of the services by a single fee, payable as a percentage of turnover on all products sold; payments were made either in cash or by the issue of shares to the parent company. Events proved that a single percentage on total turnover was a handicap, as in India, where there was no provision in the original consultancy agreement for the introduction of new products. As a result the company was inhibited from considering new developments, as it was certain that questions concerning the consultancy agreement and the royalties payable, would be raised by the Indian authorities when official permission was sought to extend manufacturing facilities. A model agreement proved to be that drawn up for Pakistan which provided for differing percentages for the three types of services, applied in each case only to the turnover on the goods directly concerned. It proved far easier to secure the approval by taxation authorities of the payment of consultancy fees by the subsidiaries as tax-free expenses when the consultancy agreement followed the Pakistani example. Where a flat percentage on turnover was payable, as in India, the tax authorities held that the percentage was purely arbitrary, and only accepted as the subsidiary's tax free expenses the appropriate proportion, pro rata to sales, of the parent company's total expenditure on the services covered by the agreement.

Staffing the overseas companies and the relationship with Head Office

In the post-war period Glaxo Laboratories followed the practice of most pharmaceutical multinationals in maximising economies of scale by attempting to consolidate all research and development at the Greenford headquarters. Indeed, when a foreign subsidiary developed a new product, as occasionally happened by adaptation of existing drugs, Greenford's research and medical departments seemed unreceptive, justifying their not invariably affectionate soubriquet, 'the University of Greenford'. Similarly, as maintenance of volume was important in bulk production, the latter was confined to British factories where possible. International prices of drugs were also coordinated through the Subsidiary Companies Unit in London, thus avoiding reductions in one country creating pressure for price cuts

44 Portrait by Michael Noakes of Dr Fred Wilkins, who with Laurie Gullick was killed in October 1965 when the Vanguard aircraft in which they were travelling crashed in fog on landing at Heathrow.

elsewhere in the world. Marketing decisions, and relations with host governments, were usually left to the local managing director, who was nevertheless well aware of the views of Jephcott and other executive directors in Britain. The overseas subsidiary companies were outposts with relatively few staff, in which the personality of the local managing director was important to both strategy and performance. Until the 1960s several of these managing directors were trained pharmacists who had been recruited as Glaxo representatives in the 1930s. Although in the post-war period they displayed energy and enthusiasm, they lacked the management experience and aptitude that was required as the companies expanded in both turnover and personnel. 'He has dismally overworked himself in trying to make a good show, but the job has just been too much for him and he has not grown up', it was reported of the managing director in Brazil in 1954. 'Neither has he probably received the necessary supervision and sufficient backing that he should have had.'[23]

Jephcott's annual world tour (which enabled him to escape the English winter) gave him a chance to visit the overseas managing directors, many of whom were long-standing personal friends of his. These personal contacts were crucial to the group's multinational development until Jephcott's retirement in 1963, and overseas staff, down to factory workers, attest to the importance of his visits in clarifying their minds and remotivating employees. He was often accompanied by his wife ('the best honorary member the firm had ever had', as she was described as early as 1921),[24] who was suspected of keeping notebooks on the family circumstances of overseas staff. Jephcott's seemingly impromptu questions to employees whom he had not seen for several years about their children or their garden engendered feelings of both personal devotion and commitment to the company among staff at all levels.

This was for many years an effective, if subjective, way to direct multinational activities. But Jephcott himself often voiced the regret that after Glaxo Laboratories' merger with Allen & Hanburys in 1957–1958, the group became too large for him to maintain this quality of personal contact. Jephcott's foreign tours gave direction to Glaxo Laboratories' multinational business and illustrate the significance of personal entrepreneurship.[25] Managerial difficulties, sometimes in a personalised form, appeared in many of Glaxo's overseas subsidiaries. Jephcott always claimed that, although he always tried to avoid hurting other people's feelings, 'the first consideration must be the proper and effective conduct of the business', and that one could never allow managers to play 'whoopee with it', but in Australia and elsewhere, he proved in practice too tolerant and patient of individuals who 'played whoopee'.[26]

Policies on staffing varied among the overseas subsidiaries, but the 1950s saw worldwide efforts to reduce numbers of expatriate staff to the essential minimum, with local staff recruited and trained for top management. Care was taken to reduce any disparity between emoluments for expatriates and the salaries of locally recruited staff, so as to minimise ill-will. While local boards and managers were given unfettered discretion in appointments, London always preferred to have at least two British directors on each subsidiary board. Secondment of locally recruited staff to the British company, and as much interchange as possible, was practised. Staffing, nevertheless, presented considerable difficulties. As Sir Maurice Hutton wrote to Sir Robert Hutchings in 1952:

One of our most tricky recruiting problems lies in overseas posts. Ideally the type we want for these posts is a person of good character, a good administrator, good medical representative and with a good commercial nose. It is quite impossible that we should get anyone with these qualifications, ready made. The difficulties of recruiting pharmacists or filling posts by transfer from the medical representatives in the US are many . . . Our overseas people are going to find it increasingly difficult to recruit Europeans overseas. They will certainly have to recruit more natives, but they will probably wish to maintain a nucleus of British people.[27]

Ironically, the demands by local managing directors abroad for stronger support gave London's product and functional managers their chance to extend their controls, their access to privileged information and their coordination responsibilities. As exports and foreign direct investment grew, management required better information about and control over hitherto semi-autonomous subsidiaries. Product and functional managers, with their closer contact with operations, were appropriate sources of information and means of control, whose visits to subsidiaries were increasingly 'at the instruction of top management to report on a problem rather than at the request of the country managers to provide technical information or support'.[28]

The international development of Glaxo Laboratories shares some common features, but also shows some striking differences from existing accounts of British multinational growth. The role of tariff barriers in leading the company to form overseas manufacturing subsidiaries, the decision in the late 1940s to develop such subsidiaries within the Commonwealth and South America, and disappointing rates of return on direct investment in some subsidiaries occur in the histories of many other British companies. In this case, the inter-continental basis of control, with owner-managers divided between London and Wellington, resulted in policies being distinctively diffuse until the Second World War. But although the decision to begin limited local filling or production when taken by a pharmaceutical company before 1939 was much less momentous, involving less deliberation and less expense than a similar decision in another

45 The Steenbock process, which Glaxo was first licensed to use in 1929, produced ergosterol from yeast, purified it by crystallization and irradiated it to produce vitamin D. Output of calciferol continued to increase at Greenford in the post-war years, much of it for export.

manufacturing field, in the post-war world the contingent costs and risks spiralled, requiring adjustments of managerial attitudes.

Glaxo Laboratories' attempt to minimise its foreign investment and to encourage overseas subsidiaries to finance development themselves led to false economies and missed opportunities, although these failings can be exaggerated with the hindsight that over-simplifies. Glaxo's sensitivity to political pressures obliged the company to adapt to local circumstances and to accommodate social and other preferences of the market. 'Traditionally we are a UK organisation, largely concerned with export business, only shedding an export market under pressure of import duties or quotas and then only to the extent necessity dictates', Jephcott wrote in 1959. He went on to say, 'Political considerations may be even more important than present tariffs and quotas, although they will be reflected in the latter in due course.' He suspected that the time had already been reached when the group must be regarded 'as a worldwide organisation, operating in many markets of which the United Kingdom is but one'. Although Britain in 1959 represented 'the largest of these markets, it may not always be so'.[29] The chapters that follow give detailed accounts of the evolution and operation of Glaxo Laboratories in all the markets of its multinational operations from 1945 to 1963.

11

Across the Atlantic: North and South America

The United States has been a paramount influence on the history of Glaxo Laboratories. From the original diversification of 1923, into vitamins via the Zucker patents, which turned the then small Glaxo department towards pharmaceutical work, through to the antibiotic deep fermentation techniques in the 1940s and 1950s, the major technological and marketing stimuli to Glaxo's growth have come from the United States.

The company's relations with US pharmaceutical manufacturers were vital to its penicillin and streptomycin production during the war and in the period immediately afterwards. Glaxo's growth and particularly its strategic acquisitions in the late 1950s and early 1960s were a response to US competition. The technological superiority of the US pharmaceutical corporations not only ensured the continuation of licensing arrangements in the later 1950s and early 1960s, but also effectively inhibited Glaxo from attempting to establish a presence in the US itself. American success in overseas markets, particularly those most adjacent to itself, also limited Glaxo's operations. In both Canada, where British influence had for a long time predominated, and in the countries of South America, Glaxo's postwar operations were curtailed both by US competition and by the arrangements made by the parent company with some of the major US pharmaceutical houses. In some of the South American countries, particularly Argentina, Glaxo was well established before the war. In Canada, by contrast, Glaxo started almost from scratch in 1950 and paid the penalty of coming late into a market already dominated by the large US pharmaceutical corporations. For that and other reasons discussed below, the operation in Canada remained one of Glaxo's smallest overseas ventures.

Relations with US pharmaceutical manufacturers

Glaxo's commercial relations with major pharmaceutical companies in the USA were of the greatest importance to the group. Product development, marketing and finance were all profoundly affected by the arrangements concluded with companies such as Merck or Schering: these key areas of policy were not only crucial in themselves, but highly revealing of Glaxo Laboratories' self perception and appraisal of risks. The USA was recognised as the world's largest pharmaceutical market by all British manufacturers, but they regarded it as impenetrable, except through licensing agreements. Boots, for example, came to terms with Upjohn in 1952–1953, and ICI made arrangements with American Home Products.[1]

Between 1943 and 1948 Jephcott flew across the Atlantic several times each year. The visits were mainly made in connection with the negotiation of technical aid and licences in deep fermentation techniques for antibiotic production, but wider issues also arose. For example, in April 1947 Jephcott visited the United States to discuss a request made to Glaxo Laboratories by the Russian Trade Delegation in London that the company should help to establish a penicillin production plant in Soviet Russia. The original agreements with Merck and Squibb precluded the British company from establishing deep fermentation plants elsewhere. Jephcott reported thus to his London board: 'On arrival, I very quickly learnt that there was in the USA widespread feeling adverse to giving any kind of assistance to Russia.' Squibb's directors, he noted, took the view 'that communistic activities in the USA were directed from, and financially supported by, Russia', a view also advanced 'only in a somewhat less degree by Merck's'. Although Jephcott argued that the Russians would in any case acquire the information sooner or later, the American 'concession' that Glaxo could undertake the Russian proposal if they made a cash payment in New York of $1,000,000 prior to any information passing,[2] successfully prevented any British participation in the Soviet antibiotics programme.

During his American visit of April 1947, Jephcott noted that US manufacturers were marketing crystalline penicillin exclusively, and consequently there was sharp price competition as production exceeded demand even in export markets. New extraction plant was being used in American penicillin production which contributed to the fall in costs, but US manufacturers were reluctant to sanction its use in Britain, ostensibly because it required special engineering skill and because the size of the British domestic market supposedly precluded economic production. Jephcott, however, established that similar extraction equipment had been supplied to twelve penicillin manufacturers in the USA, one in Canada and six in Europe (including one in Britain), and estimated that appropriate extraction equipment for Ulverston would cost up to £150,000.

Under Glaxo's streptomycin agreement with Merck, effective from November 1947, the latter contracted to furnish the British company with all significant information both on the production process and on equipment, cultures, raw materials and intermediates used in the process, together with provisions for non-exclusive licensing. A second penicillin agreement of ten years' duration began in July 1951.

Jephcott was a wholehearted proponent of Anglo-American research cooperation, and sometimes his enthusiasm distressed members of the Glaxo research department, some of whom felt that he was over-generous in his treatment of the Americans. On one occasion he was disastrously indiscreet. When Lester Smith began research in 1946 on the anti-pernicious anaemia factor (see page 179), Jephcott remarked to him that it was essential for Glaxo to win the race to identify the factor: if the company came second, all their work would be wasted. At a crucial stage there was a breakthrough in the project when the use of modified partition chromatography by Smith's researchers produced columns with a bright pink zone. Jephcott, according to Tom Macrae, Greenford's research director, was always 'terribly friendly' with Merck, one of whose executives visited Greenford. Glaxo were unaware that Merck were also working on vitamin B_{12}, and in retrospect Macrae was suspicious about the motive for the visit; Jephcott, however, adjured, 'no secrets, tell them everything', and in Smith's laboratory he airily told the visiting American that Glaxo had discovered that the anti-pernicious anaemia factor was pinkish red. The researchers were astounded at Jephcott's indiscretion. Macrae afterwards said, 'I could have murdered him'. It gave immeasurable help to Merck, who in the event publicly announced their discovery of the factor a few weeks ahead of Greenford. This insouciance by Jephcott was traumatic for some of the scientists involved, although it was not wholly responsible for Merck's lead: deposits of the factor found in used fermentation liquor had already given the latter considerable advantage.[3]

Despite the information leakage over vitamin B_{12}, Jephcott retained an open attitude to scientific exchanges with potential competitors, an approach not always shared by the competitors. Typically he wrote in 1953 of collaboration with Merck:

It is an integral part of the scheme that we 'take our hair down' and are forthcoming in respect of all work which, if it should come to fruition, would ultimately be the subject of free exchange. In the long term I believe real advantage will accrue for both of us and I am anxious that Campbell should be frank and not by withholding information, give the visitors the wrong impression. Our good intentions are at stake.[4]

Other executives were more cautious, and on the occasion of this letter from Jephcott, Fred Wilkins (see page 172) privately warned the heads of departments at Ulverston and Barnard Castle that Estopen and Betapen were outside the Merck agreement. On the matter of production costs, Jephcott was less open, writing in 1954 that as he had always wished to avoid 'any kind of moral obligation to furnish Merck's with particulars of our production costs ... I have most carefully refrained from ever asking about theirs'.[5]

Perceptions of the American companies altered at Greenford and in Jephcott's mind in the 1950s. They gradually came to be seen as more of a threat, and intimacies which had been based on Jephcott's personal relations with key American executives cooled as the latter died or retired, or as younger colleagues like Wilkins began visiting the USA on Glaxo's behalf. Early in the decade, Jephcott was still able to write, after meeting Merck's president, James Kerrigan:

On the general question of Merck dollar investment in UK, although Kerrigan now has a much more liberal outlook, he still has to handle a Board which is pretty firmly against it ... Indeed if they were to adopt wholeheartedly a policy of investment in the UK, there really wouldn't be much, if any, room for us.[6]

A few years later however it was trepidation about American competition which partly prompted the merger with Allen & Hanbury. The relationship between Glaxo Laboratories and the US changed over the decade. In 1953 Merck's unusual position in the pharmaceutical industry led it to merge with Sharp & Dohme. Since Merck's effective entry into pharmaceuticals in 1936, when it introduced synthetic vitamin B, the company had shown more ability in discovering new products than in exploiting them. Merck were pioneers of synthetic vitamin B and B_1, streptomycin, vitamins B_6 and B_{12}, and cortisone, yet sales weakness undercut these triumphs. Most of Merck's products were sold not under its own label, but in bulk to other companies for distribution by them. With each major new product customers became ex-customers as soon as they could make it themselves. Thus Merck's sales fell from $120 million in 1951 to $106 million in 1952, largely because other companies had begun substantial cortisone production. The Sharp & Dohme merger was designed to remedy this situation.

To Merck's strengths in research and production, Sharp & Dohme added marketing expertise and a network of detail men. Sharp & Dohme was mainly of importance in distributing proprietary cortisone, a large and complicated operation, and had less importance in providing outlets for proprietary penicillin and streptomycin. Kerrigan liked to give Glaxo the impression that after the merger all emphasis was on cortisone, and that less attention was being paid to antibiotics. Initially there were differences of personality and approach. Some of Merck's executives regarded their Sharp & Dohme colleagues as hucksters; to Sharp & Dohme, Merck often seemed a mere collection of test-tube fiddlers; and each group kept to itself after the merger. Moreover, the top executives of both companies were nearing retirement age, and in 1955 a new president was selected, John Connor, who

Table 7. *Royalties paid by Glaxo Laboratories to Merck (gross) 1946–1956*

Year ended 30 June	Penicillin £	Streptomycin £	Vitamin B$_{12}$ £
1946	4,675[1]		
1947	28,012		
1948	33,057		
1949	57,191	19,040	
1950	77,723	43,188	
1951	100,572	73,627	
1951	9,720[2]		
1952	53,605	92,026	13,580
1953	48,403	84,619	12,765
1954	33,551	65,094	58,336
1955	28,740	63,095	81,075
1956	15,968[3]		
Totals	491,217	440,689	165,756

Notes: [1] Covering period from 1 February 1946 only
       [2] Covering period from 1 to 31 July 1951
       [3] Covering period from 1 July 1955 to 30 March 1956
Source: Glaxo Archives

had joined the company's legal staff eight years before. A graduate of Syracuse (1936) and Harvard Law School (1939), Connor in 1942 had become counsel to the Office of Scientific Research and Development. At OSRD, Connor was soon immersed in the wartime penicillin programme, which provided his introduction to scientific, and especially medical, research. Connor was responsible for the joint research and production effort in penicillin by ten US companies and dozens of US and British university, government and commercial laboratories. After the merger lower costs and better margins raised Merck, Sharp & Dohme's income, despite falling prices on such major products as antibiotics. In 1955 net profits after tax rose some 30 per cent to over $16 million, on a sales gain of less than 10 per cent (to about $160 million). Merck no longer needed to license all new products to competitors or sell them in bulk, but had the capacity to market them as company specialities if it wished. After 1956 the new company became 'more interested in acquiring products or any cooperation in certain products rather than in having royalties for licences for any discoveries that they have made' and hoped for 'a two-way traffic of products' with Glaxo Laboratories.[7] As table 7 shows the royalties Glaxo was paying Merck on penicillin and streptomycin peaked in 1951 and 1952 respectively, and thereafter started to decline.

Merck regarded vitamin B_{12} as being their equivalent, in terms of profitability, of Pfizer's Terramycin (the oxytetracycline which dominated the antibiotic market in the 1950s) and, whilst recognising that the margins were generous, were anxious to maintain them. Nevertheless, because of the difficulties of price maintenance in the USA, there were lapses, because Pfizer (to whom Merck supplied B_{12} in bulk) utilised the discount they had been given to cut the price. Merck did their utmost to retain their exclusive position with regard to vitamin B_{12} and would not, therefore, give Glaxo a licence to manufacture in Australia. Kerrigan, however, conceded that, in spite of their wishes, they might be forced to consider a wider licensing programme and, in that event, Glaxo's claims for Australia could not be disregarded. Similarly, although neither Merck nor Sharp & Dohme had any interest in Pakistan, an important market for Glaxo (see chapter 12), they were loath to contemplate extending Glaxo's licence to manufacture there. They preferred that Glaxo should try to hold the position by shipping out the crudest form of material and beginning a local chemical operation which would not involve them in extending the agreements between the two companies. Glaxo's subsidiary in Canada too found its activities constrained by the parent company's agreements with Merck (see page 256). Jephcott reported a conversation with Kerrigan in 1954: 'Throughout our talk, which was of the friendliest nature, it was obvious that the Sharp & Dohme end were averse to any extension, to other and new products in which Sharp & Dohme might have any interest, of the very cordial relations which have existed between Merck and ourselves.'[8] In the wide-ranging discussion of US competitors, Jephcott noted Kerrigan's view of Eli Lilly, 'tough and will drive a hard bargain, but are straight and would recognise a patent, whether you were able to detect infringement or not'. And, according to Jephcott, Kerrigan said that 'in their experience, almost without exception, the US manufacturers played the game'.[9]

For the historian at thirty years distance, there are some difficulties in reconstructing the detailed workings of Glaxo's arrangements with American manufacturers. Wilkins visited Merck, Sharp & Dohme during 1954 to try and determine whether Merck, since the merger, found technical collaboration with Glaxo embarrassing or difficult; and, if the drift was away from collaboration with Glaxo, to underline the advantages to Merck of collaboration, and to maintain good will at executive levels beneath Kerrigan. One particular tension had arisen. For the first time, Merck was going to receive an important process from a licensee, Glaxo Laboratories' screened broth (for streptomycin production), and there was anxiety in the American company about the effect on their other licensees. Since, if they kept it to themselves, they would have been unable to show licensees around their streptomycin plant, Merck decided to sidestep the question by pleading prior art and a slightly different process. In this they were helped by the reluctance of their technical staff to accept anything which they had not developed themselves. Certainly Merck had difficulty in getting one factory to accept some technical improvement from another even within their own organisation. Wilkins emphasised that technical collaboration meant reciprocity and that Glaxo wanted the long-term advantages of technical collaboration rather than the short term rake-off of licence fees. He added that, if Merck were producing streptomycin at Glaxo's outputs, they were annually losing $250,000 while they delayed in installing the screened broth process. 'They were very sensitive about this as Merck are undoubtedly having a very difficult time with penicillin and streptomycin just now', reported Wilkins. 'You could almost see them wince.'[10]

Wilkins anticipated that several years would elapse before competition in proprietary antibiotics between Glaxo Laboratories and Merck, Sharp & Dohme became an important or difficult problem, which left time to organise technical collaboration. Falling prices prevented Merck letting Glaxo have their processes for vitamin B_1 and C, but it was implied that the chief influence was German and Japanese competition. Prices quoted to Wilkins suggested that the Germans and Japanese were both selling in the USA at prices substantially less than those ruling in the respective home markets. According to Wilkins, Merck executives protested that they were 'very worried' about the level of expenditure on penicillin and streptomycin research and development:

where the margins are so small. They must maintain R & D to remain in the market, but the profits are so small that they don't justify their present expenditure. They would very willingly agree to collaborate on research programmes so as to reduce duplication and make our R & D budgets go further.

There are three difficulties

(1)   the impact of Anti-Trust Laws;
(2)   the cross-licensing of Merck's other licensees for discoveries of Glaxo;
(3)   Merck's lack of confidence in some of our R & D work.

Any collaborative arrangement to avoid duplication of research and development programmes would have infringed Anti Trust Laws, but there was a possibility of organising informal, non-mandatory collaboration to avoid this difficulty, which Merck examined. As to cross-licensing, Glaxo was 'most anxious to arrive at some compromise' as their 'main concern was the long term competitive advantages which we felt would come out of our collaboration'.[11]

Some Merck executives lacked confidence in Glaxo's research and development record. They warned that with an interlocking research and development programme, the Merck Research Department would transfer to Glaxo some of the responsibilities which it carried on behalf of Merck, to which they would not agree unless satisfied of the competence of Glaxo's researchers. 'They say that, so far, Glaxo has put very little in the kitty', wrote Wilkins. 'I could only accept this and say that we had recently made a start, so that there were a number of other things coming along which I thought might also be of value.' Wilkins proposed that 'in any event it would be unwise to attempt initially a comprehensive dove-tailing in our programmes; we should start in a small way and use a few examples to build up trust and confidence between us'. Merck, for example, wanted more effort on mutation.

If we add to this effort it is something additional, and no question of their shedding responsibilities to us arises. We have leads on agitation which Merck don't have. Whatever we do on this will be of value to them. By a judicious selection of topics we can get a start – and the rest will follow – The most important factors in Merck thinking just now is the selling price of penicillin, and the relation of profit margin, if any, to the R & D cost. If, by collaboration with us, they can reduce their R & D cost, they want to do it. It is therefore of particular importance that we should demonstrate our technical competence and effectiveness. The screened broth process has been most timely: if we could produce another winner it might well clinch things.[12]

Glaxo were also willing to help Merck in patent matters against other British manufacturers. Between 1954 and 1958 differences arose between Distillers and Merck over vitamin B_{12} patents and, at Jephcott's suggestion, Palmer wrote to the Americans advising:

that if you wish to bring some pressure on Distillers at this stage without instituting immediate legal proceedings, you could do worse than follow the old continental practice of drawing the attention of some of their agents overseas to the fact that by vending a Distillers product in the market served they are infringing your local patent rights.
There is one other feature in the total situation which I am sure you will not have overlooked, and that is that Distillers may well entertain the idea not merely of refusing to recognise your rights in this country, but also of breaking the price. I have no first hand information of their costs of production, but even six months ago Gross gave me the impression that he would be content, if necessary, with a bulk price about 25 per cent lower than the present level, and it is of course possible that his position has since improved. I think you should bear this in mind because we know that Distillers' plant is underemployed and he is undoubtedly looking for any opportunity for increased throughput.[13]

Glaxo were keen not to prejudice relations with Merck in other ways. In 1956 the American company complained about the tactics of Glaxo's representatives in talking about cortisone and hydrocortisone to doctors. Palmer immediately wrote to the sales department:

Whatever may be the rights and wrongs of the position, I think you should . . . lay off slamming Merck, Sharp & Dohme, either directly or by implication and I can't believe at this stage that any good can come of their basing their case on currency arguments. We have no need of such adventitious help; we know how much Merck,

Sharp & Dohme are using; we are supplying most of it ourselves and there would not, therefore, seem to be any point in making them in any sense a special target for verbal propaganda . . . we must assume that somebody has dropped a brick . . . and you ought to send a communication to all the representatives and tell them that whether it is in the cortisone field or not, our relationships with Merck, Sharp & Dohme here and elsewhere must not be damaged by incautious and somewhat silly references to the origin of their supplies or of their capital.[14]

Glaxo's commercial relationships were not restricted to Merck and the company had other licensing arrangements in the early 1950s in the United States, for example with Smith, Kline & French covering the manufacturing of L-thyroxine for the American market. The new antibiotics introduced in the United States were monitored with interest by Glaxo Laboratories; the company was 'sufficiently interested' in tetracycline, introduced in 1952, to enquire about the terms for a British licence but, perhaps fortunately, these proved too 'onerous' for by late 1954 the antibiotic had become the subject of acrimonious and damaging patent litigation.[15]

As the US pharmaceutical houses established themselves in Britain in the course of the 1950s, adjustments had to be made. When Merck, Sharp & Dohme were accepted on the Ministry of Health's tender list in 1955, Glaxo agreed to keep their sales manager in the United Kingdom, 'fully informed so that he does nothing to embarrass us or them in quoting the Ministry for Supplies'.[16] In early 1956 Palmer commented on Smith, Kline & French's purchase of the British firm of A. J. White, 'now . . . all our American friends have arrived and settled in the UK and we may expect even severer competition than we are now experiencing'.[17]

In the late 1950s falling profits, the absence of major new product introductions, the fragmentation of the market for corticosteroids, oral diuretics and certain antibiotics, combined to stimulate greater competition in the US pharmaceutical industry. At the same time the enquiry into drug prices and related matters, conducted by the US Senate Sub-committee on Anti Trust and Monopoly in 1961, under the chairmanship of Senator Estes Kefauver, put the industry under public scrutiny. By that time, too, there was increasing disagreement among Glaxo's senior executives about the licensing policy for new products in the United States. In practice Glaxo Laboratories licensed those American companies which were likely to achieve the greatest sales volume, so that in this way it could maximise its royalties: griseofulvin, for example, was licensed to Johnson & Johnson, because of their experience in selling dermatological products, and the technical exchange on corticosteroids with Schering was agreed for similar reasons. Palmer summarised the *rationale* for this policy in 1959:

If we have a first-class product of considerable potentiality that is capable of protection in the USA in a product as well as in a process sense, then . . . we could, with advantage, ... seek to trade when appropriate for compensating advantages in this market and others overseas in which we have a first-class selling organisation. Unfortunately we have not been in this position at any time that I could recall.

He denied that griseofulvin was a sufficiently big or novel product to provide 'this bargaining opportunity', and warned that Pfrizer, Merck, Sharp & Dohme and other US companies were 'becoming so powerful overseas that, except in rather special circumstances, it is unlikely that we shall find it possible to do a profitable trade with them'.[18] Palmer, like other managers in the Jephcott mould, was averse to risks or confrontational marketing.

The divergence between Glaxo Laboratories and its American counter-parts was highlighted by negotiations during the course of 1958 involving the delta-steroids, Prednisolone and Prednisone, which had been developed by Schering. Merck, Sharp & Dohme were developing Decadron, a stronger version of Prednisolone, but the British company disagreed with them over the patent position for this new product and, later in the year, concluded a research collaboration and licensing agreement with Schering both for the delta-steroids and another product for treating gastric ulcers, Dephenatil. Schering's breakthrough with delta-steroids, which owed something to the dynamism of its president, Francis Brown, had propelled the company into the first league of US pharmaceutical manufacturers, and it remained committed to developing new products to retain its lead in adrenocorticol steroids. Glaxo's expertise and preference, to the contrary, was in develop-ing economic manufacturing methods for established substances. These different approaches were implicit in some of the clauses of the 1958 agreement between Glaxo and Schering. It provided that, on Schering's disclosing to Glaxo a new substance, the latter would elect within thirty days whether to manufacture the new compound for testing with a view to exploring the possibilities of commercial synthesis.

In 1959 Palmer and Wilkins disagreed openly about most questions of strategy and management, and the licensing of new products was no exception. Countering Palmer's caution, Wilkins urged that Glaxo should imitate ICI's relationship with American Home Products, with its mutual obligation to offer one another new products.

If one follows this policy, it is clear that we might not maximise the royalty return from the sales of new products which we license, but we do get what is probably a much bigger advantage, the sales income coming from new products which are offered to us out of such an agreement. It is difficult to compare the two policies quantitatively because the gross return depends in the case of exchanging new products on the extent to which new products are actually offered, and their sales volume; ... we might expect to get more by way of return on a reciprocal product agreement than on direct licensing to Companies most experienced in a given market operation. I therefore suggest that we re-examine our attitude to this problem. It could be argued that the existing corticosteroid arrangements with Schering are of the reciprocal agreement type, although in this particular case the agreement is drawn in very narrow terms.[19]

Glaxo's problem was one which would recur until, well outside the period covered by this history, the company established itself in the USA; it also reflected the internal succession struggle then taking place within Glaxo (see page 172).

Canada

In the years immediately after 1945 Glaxo continued to make some pharmaceutical sales in the Canadian market, but did not develop the business to any extent. By 1950, however, the company began to consider entering the Canadian market on a determined and systematic basis. At that time Canada's population of over 13 million was largely served by pharmaceutical imports from the United States, but the market held attractions for British manufacturers because the Dominion was not only short of US dollars but also had a favourable annual balance of trade with Britain. A high proportion of Canadian pharmaceutical production derived from Canadian subsidiaries of American firms: total imports of medicinals in 1948 amounted to $13 million while exports were valued at $3 million; 90 per cent of Canadian imports of medicinals came from the USA. Medical practice in the USA influenced Canadian habits and methods, although the extent of surviving British influence was surprising. There was often a conscious desire to follow British medical practice, sometimes accompanied by definite pride in British medicine. Glaxo Laboratories felt that Canadian doctors were less critical or sceptical than those in Britain, not least in their attitude towards claims made by salesmen or manufacturers, 'a characteristic which for us is probably on the whole disadvantageous'.[20] Although hospital practice varied, there was a preponderance of private patients who bore the cost of all medicines, creating a preference for single-dose containers, or at least for a pack used for one patient only. Where health insurance schemes covered hospital expenses, as in British Columbia and Saskatchewan, the practice of taking multi-dose packs on grounds of economy was beginning to appear by 1950. Private practice was greatly affected by the American influence which had increased during the war; 'medical arts buildings' and 'clinics' were common. Doctors and pharmacists were courted on a luxurious scale, and Glaxo anticipated that to win business it would have to be competitive in every respect.[21]

In its initial soundings in Canada, Glaxo Laboratories found willingness and even anxiety to buy British at the top levels of society. The implications of the existing economic position were realised, and British efforts to sell to

Canada were welcome. But the goodwill towards Britain progressively diminished lower down the social scale, so that it was not by itself sufficient to induce government and hospital purchasing officials to buy British every time. For British goods to sell, they had to be of the right quality, at the right price, delivered at the right place at the right time. Unless these criteria were met it was futile to enter the Canadian market. British suppliers had a poor reputation in the matter of service, which had been unsatisfactory in several directions even among organisations formed since the dollar drive began.

In the highly competitive pharmaceutical market in Canada, Burroughs Wellcome was held in high esteem, but Glaxo Laboratories suspected that Wellcome's volume of sales did not match its reputation. British Drug Houses was by far the most successful British firm in Canada. Furthermore, Glaxo had intimations by July 1950 that German manufacturers were preparing to take an active interest in Canada: the German Schering Company and the British Schering Company were seeking the registration of certain names, the German Merck Company was also active and other companies showed interest in trade mark registration. Within Glaxo it was felt that, while the Canadians might buy British products in preference to American, they would prefer to buy Canadian rather than either of the other two. Supplies from a Canadian company would be regarded as Canadian, even if they had in fact been imported from Britain by a Canadian subsidiary of a British company. Most products in which Glaxo were interested were liable to import duty of either 15 per cent or 15.75 per cent, the corresponding rates on American products being 20 per cent or 22.5 per cent. An Anti-Dumping Duty made it impossible to invoice goods to Canada at less than home consumption value. Glaxo (Canada) Ltd, was established in the summer of 1950 with Joseph Hutchinson (see page 109) as managing director. Laurie Gullick, manager of Barnard Castle, was sent to give special assistance initially for a brief period although he stayed until 1965. Three representatives from the home sales department were seconded to the Canadian staff, but by February 1951 they had asked to be repatriated. As most of the staff were seconded to Canada while continuing on the Greenford payroll, the subsidiary did not bear its own operating costs until August 1951.

From the outset the Canadian subsidiary encountered difficulties. A senior official of the Food and Drugs Division of the Department of Health and Welfare at Ottawa visited Glaxo in 1950, and was given a detailed tour of its facilities. He made various minor criticisms of the aseptic precautions at Barnard Castle, which Glaxo hastened to adopt, fearing that he might advise Ottawa to cancel import licences. Unexpected obstacles were met from the Canadian authorities in obtaining release for sale of Glaxo's antibiotic products, which were meant to provide the major part of turnover. Because

46 Joseph Hutchinson and Laurie Gullick en route to Canada on board
the *Empress of Canada* in September 1950.

of the delay the antibiotics were not available for sale until three months
after the sales promotion staff had begun to work the market, which not
only thoroughly frustrated the staff, but also betrayed ample notice of Glaxo
Laboratories' intentions to its competitors.

Moreover, as Glaxo had no novel or distinctive product to offer, it proved hard for the representatives to get a hearing, and still more difficult to induce potential customers to substitute new and unknown brands in the place of well-known and long-established suppliers. It was soon abundantly clear that turnover in products without novelty would only be secured slowly by dint of long and persistent sales promotion, and that established competitors would make every effort to prevent Glaxo Laboratories from getting a footing. Finally, the British-controlled company found itself handicapped by the limits imposed by tariff regulations upon its profit margins, which were less than half those available to Canadian companies manufacturing within Canada. The permitted discount under anti-dumping laws on home whole-sale prices of 25 per cent was less than was commonly spent on sales promotion.

Antibiotics sales were made either to government organisations, to hospitals, or through the trade by prescription from private physicians. Of these, sales to government agencies were under sealed tender, and although Glaxo Laboratories expected to secure a reasonable proportion of the business, it was transacted at prices only marginally profitable to the Canadian subsidiary. Hospital sales were nominally at list prices, but in practice, secret discounts were given (usually in goods), and in some cases the goodwill of medical staff was essential. Penicillin was subject to particularly acute competition in the pharmaceutical market. In 1951 Merck complained about Glaxo's price-cutting of penicillin in the Canadian market, but shortly afterwards the whole price structure of penicillin in markets dominated by the US manufacturers fell sharply. Once world demand had ceased to exceed supply, Canadian antibiotic production focused upon the domestic market, to the virtual elimination of British or American imports. By December 1951 the price war had quickened, so that almost all companies cut the price of penicillin both to trade and hospitals. The decline in penicillin prices undermined completely the calculations on which the establishment of the Canadian subsidiary had been based.

Buyers were unwilling to commit themselves far ahead and gave numerous small orders rather than fewer large orders. For Glaxo to obtain these frequent small orders would have required intensive detailing by an increased number of representatives; with Hutchinson's small staff, turnover could not be improved under such conditions. In the six months to December 1952, the subsidiary company virtually broke even, but for all practical purposes, its profits were confined to one product, Estopen. The company was dependent on the sales of too narrow a range of proprietary products (although this later improved with the introduction of Intradex and Dionosil) and was further handicapped by its inadequate sales force, which could not even properly cover the area of Canada from Toronto to the West Coast to which its activities were restricted. In striking contrast to

Glaxo's small sales force, the Eli Lilly Corporation had employed fifty-five medical representatives to break into the Canadian market. Although Jephcott felt 'that the prospects in the Canadian market' were 'probably the best in any market in which we operate', he was reluctant to allocate funds for an adequate marketing campaign. 'In the absence of additional proprietary products of outstanding medical appeal', he told the London directors in 1953, 'additional expenditure is unlikely to be profit-earning within eighteen months, and I did not judge it wise to risk dissipating the whole of this limited capital of the Canadian Company by the immediate employment of sufficient medical representations to cover the whole Canadian market'.[22] This was a cautious approach, founded on twenty years' experience, and it is by no means sure that a bolder attitude would not have resulted in larger long-term losses; nevertheless, it prevented Glaxo (Canada) from making any dynamic impression on its market.

There were other tensions and considerations in North America. Merck regarded the prohibitions about Canada, included in its licensing agreements with Glaxo, as fundamental and Merck, Sharp & Dohme (Canada) insisted on the strict application of the exclusion clauses. One example of the difficulties for the Canadian company of Glaxo's patent agreements with Merck occurred over the cortisone product, Hemisuccinate. Hutchinson was distressed to have to refuse various enquiries about the supply of the product in 1958. Austin Bide examined all facets of Glaxo's hydrocortisone agreement for a loophole, but found that, as far as Canada was concerned, Glaxo was completely tied to Merck's coat-tails, with no room for manoeuvre. Earlier, in 1952 Hutchinson had begged for permission to begin vitamin B_{12} business in Canada. Doctors there regarded B_{12} as a Glaxo discovery, and the product appealed to vets. Jephcott replied that the Canadian subsidiary could buy bulk B_{12} from Merck and do what it liked with it in Canada, but Hutchinson doubted if Merck would fill and pack the material.

In May 1953 Hutchinson reported that his company had hitherto been selling streptomycin in Canada at the same prices as Merck, namely 28 cents for a one-gram vial and $1.28 for five grams, but that Merck's prices had now been cut to 24 cents and $1.1 respectively. If Hutchinson was to meet these prices, he would have had to sell streptomycin below the landed cost to him of the goods so long as home invoice prices remained at their present level. Hutchinson was told that Glaxo's invoice price to the Canadian company could not be reduced until the home price was brought down. It was anticipated that new landed costs to the Canadian company would be 23 cents and 97 cents approximately for the one- and five-gram packs respectively. Hutchinson was also introducing streptomycin combinations to the Canadian market – Seclomycin and Estomycin – and did not want any reproaches from Merck that the Canadian subsidiary was depressing prices.

On a visit to Toronto, Jephcott wrote, in January 1953, 'I'm very much happier about things here than I expected to be.' Hutchinson and Gullick were 'getting on pretty well, not agreeing on everything but not allowing any difference of opinion to get in the way of the job'.[23] They were enthusiastic about the sales prospects of Intradex blood plasma (see page 165), and although Jephcott was less optimistic, rightly as events were to prove, he characteristically said 'nothing to damp their enthusiasm'. According to Jephcott's analysis in 1953:

The Canadian company is operating in what is, in competitive fact, a US market and the competition which they have to meet is correspondingly fierce in all respects: products, packs and presentation, representation and postal propaganda. Their competitors work on short lines of communications with headquarters attuned to the Canadian conditions. Our fellows are very much further from their Head office and source of supply and neither of these understand in a sympathetic way their needs or their urgencies.

We have got to make up our mind whether we want the Canadian company to succeed or not. If we do want it to succeed, and I believe it can, we have got to give it much better support than we have done. In part, our failures have reflected a lack of precision and clarity upon their part and I have not failed to say so. But, in material respects . . . we have let them down because their requirements did not fit in with our production schedules or their orders were too trivial to be impressive.

If we are not prepared to give them the service from London, only two courses are open to us (a) to provide them with facilities for themselves (b) to close the show down.[24]

He found the number of representatives 'quite inadequate', especially if Intradex blood plasma was to be introduced and reported that the Canadians were working on their stocks, 'both for finance reasons and to avoid loss, since it is impossible to predict their future requirements with accuracy'. Small orders had been lost in Canada because of the London Export Department's long delays in giving delivery dates, and other departments in Britain were similarly inclined to give low priority to the Canadian subsidiary. Senior Glaxo research directors were pessimistic about their chances in 1954 of overcoming the high concentration of procaine present in Seclomycin and hence of satisfying Canadian toxicity standards. They felt that the time spent in Britain on the relatively small Canadian antibiotic requirements was highly disproportionate. From its immediate standpoint the research department was clearly correct, but from a broader viewpoint the position is less clear-cut.

Glaxo found that the Canadian Food and Drug Administration disliked dealing with individual companies when issuing information on regulations for the government tender list, but preferred to deal with trade associations;

businesses such as Glaxo Laboratories which were outside those associations were sometimes neglected, but the Canadian subsidiary could not afford the subscription necessary to join the trade association. It became increasingly clear that until the magnitude of the subsidiary's operations justified local production, it would always be handicapped. Initially the Canadian subsidiary enjoyed an almost clear market in blood plasma for Intradex (reflected in sales worth $22,319 in 1953) but in late 1954, as expected, Connaught Laboratories launched an almost identical product to Intradex, and made large inroads into Glaxo's business by giving free supplies to Glaxo's main customers in Ontario.

In the mid 1950s the subsidiary's pharmaceutical turnover increased, an improvement largely attributable to the success of Dionosil. Estopen was not a success, nor was Estomycin, although that had been expected, because of the side-effects. Herbert Palmer told Hutchinson in 1956:

I have always held the view that we should not make any real progress until we established some manufacturing facilities in the country with all that that implies by way of a readiness quickly to develop those pharmaceutical products which are likely to appeal to doctors in North America. At best, servicing from this country is not an adequate substitute and the two or three thousand miles of ocean between us takes the edge off a sense of urgency.

When I have raised this point, H.J. has been able clearly and easily to demonstrate that our current business in Canada would provide an extremely poor basis for the economic conduct of however small a manufacturing unit we were able to establish and the only way out of this difficulty is, as far as I can see, to acquire an existing business as a going concern in the hope that the products it already has would recover the overheads of the establishment and give us an opportunity of basing further development on something which at least just pays its way.[25]

The Canadian subsidiary had only a very thin marketing coverage of the country as a whole. Hutchinson was keen to extend representation in Newfoundland and Nova Scotia, but given Jephcott's views, this was impossible as selling expenses increased sharply in 1956 and 1957, especially in antibiotics.

In considering how to expand the Canadian business, Hutchinson told a meeting at Greenford in 1957, that he doubted whether the Canadian company had either the personnel or capacity to launch Ostermilk nationwide. The grocery trade would only accept the product if there was a big demand and the sale of dried milk powder was limited in Canada. The main product of Cow & Gate, who had manufactured there from 1931, was evaporated milk. Although Canadian turnover had steadily increased, this was not reflected in increased profits, and Jephcott was pessimistic about those products which the Canadian company was then selling. The previous year's turnover of $330,000 was made up of $210,000 from antibiotics (at an average gross profit of about 40 per cent), $62,000 from Intradex (including $27,000 on government contract), $25,000 from Dionosil and $33,000 from all the remaining products.

Hutchinson felt that prospects were bleak until the product range was extended. While the company had a reasonable share of hospital business for penicillin, on antibiotics generally they lacked a product with wide attraction, despite the promise shown by Crystamycin. Yet when such a product finally appeared in the shape of griseofulvin it seemed to the Canadian executives that the opportunity was thrown away by the granting of licences to American competitors (see chapter 9). In October 1959, Hutchinson wrote to Jephcott:

that we are very disappointed with the turn of events concerning Griseofulvin. We are all of the same opinion that our greatest setback in regard to this product was the handing it over to the Canadian branches of American licencees, each more widely and firmly established in Canada than we are. In the next week or so we anticipate American Home, through Ayerst, will commence their marketing activities of this product. They have as many representatives as both Schering and McNeil added together, and we are less strong numerically than McNeil. This prospect is bad enough, but when I tell you that, in spite of our best efforts, already there has been needless and serious price cutting on the part of Schering and McNeil, you will understand our feeling. This, of course, has compelled us to meet the competition, but where such goings on will end I do not know . . . The granting of licences to Schering and McNeil was most unfortunate, as it takes from out of our grasp an opportunity we have longed for for several years, to get behind something of substance and to put our own company on to a sound basis. The resistance to Griseofulvin is quite marked for no other reason than the cost to the patient and in this regard I am certain that if we had been left alone with the product we could have 'managed' the price to much greater advantage to suit the market than when three of us are involved . . . Why! Even doctors have asked why we handed Griseofulvin to our competitors![26]

The Canadian subsidiary was doing three-quarters of its business in penicillin and streptomycin. The additional turnover had been won with difficulty, nor was it anticipated that it would be easy to keep. As business stood, there was nothing to support local manufacturing operations, which would only result in further losses.

With the merger at home of Glaxo and Allen & Hanburys in 1955, however, the parent company acquired manufacturing facilities in Canada. Allen & Hanburys had started to sell its products in the Dominion, via an agent, in 1897, and during the First World War had built a milk products factory in Ontario, the centre of a rich milk farming area with good rail links. In the 1930s the malt extract plant there had been enlarged. In 1950 Allen & Hanburys had built a new, modern factory near Toronto and in 1953 had added the manufacture of surgical instruments to pharmaceutical products.[27] To rationalise the situation in Canada after the merger, the Glaxo subsidiary's assets were transferred to A & H (Canada) Ltd, a British-controlled company with all but one of its directors resident in London. This new company formed an executive committee of the board, with Hutchinson as President, D. MacLaren of Allen & Hanburys as general manager, and Gullick as sales director for the pharmaceutical division, and with a separate director for the surgical division. Subsequently, Glaxo-Allenburys (Canada) Ltd was formed as a subsidiary of Allen & Hanbury's Ltd. In 1961 Glaxo-Allenburys (Canada) began a programme of improvement of its manufacturing facilities for sterile products, both to meet the requirements of the Canadian Food and Drug Administration and to fill and pack antibiotics and to expand the range of locally manufactured pharmaceutical products.

Sales to Canada from the parent company started to decline with the increasing amount of local manufacture undertaken by the Canadian subsidiary. About 40 per cent of the Canadian company's turnover in Allen & Hanburys and Glaxo products was based on imported goods in packed form and the rest was accounted for by local manufacture, some of which was based on bulk imports of basic drugs, mainly from Glaxo Laboratories.

The first thirteen years of Glaxo Laboratories (Canada) were neither fortunate nor profitable. Although the local management was treated with sympathy and understanding by senior managers in London, at lower levels within the parent company they were treated with less consideration. Hamstrung by the group's worldwide agreements with Merck, they were never provided with the successful novelty products needed to make a real impact on the market. Robbed of a solid profit base in antibiotics, and unable even to cover the country properly with representatives, it was impossible for the subsidiary to succeed. Their predicament was best summarised by Gullick when he wrote to Jephcott in 1957, 'we need more bucks'.[28] However, although the subsidiary did not make a great contribution to the parent company's profitability, nor did it cost a great deal. At least Glaxo (Canada) Ltd had established a presence in the continent which the parent company had otherwise eschewed.

Glaxo in South America: 1945–1962

Glaxo's businesses in South America continued to meet with varying fortunes in the post-war period. The German presence which had represented the most serious competition to Glaxo in the 1930s, was virtually eliminated during the war and it was not until the late 1950s that Bayer and Hoechst started to become active again in the area. In the subcontinent as a whole US influence increased between 1945 and 1962, with a corresponding domination of the market by the big US pharmaceutical corporations. Political and economic instability characterised most of the Latin American republics. Glaxo therefore had to contend with increasing government interference with imports, designed to protect national economies, as well as vigorous US competition. In these circumstances few South American countries were an attractive prospect for the establishment of manufacturing subsidiaries. Nevertheless tariffs and import controls, combined with the sheer distance and difficulties of transport from Britain, forced the reluctant parent company to invest in local manufacturing facilities. But Jephcott's dislike of investing Glaxo's money where the return was uncertain meant that the subsidiaries all suffered a constant lack of working capital. It was difficult too to persuade the most capable managers to uproot themselves and their families to take on responsibilities in politically unstable countries.

In line with the company's policy for its overseas subsidiaries Glaxo's established companies in Argentina and Brazil were re-named; new subsidiaries were formed in Uruguay (1947), Chile (1951), Cuba (1953), Colombia (1957) and Venezuela (1959). By 1962 manufacturing facilities had been established only in Argentina, Brazil and Cuba although plans had been drawn up for Venezuela. Of those Argentina and Brazil were the most significant, for in Cuba apparently promising prospects had disappeared with the revolution.

Jephcott made his first post-war visit to Central and South America in 1950; his subsequent tours were not as frequent as those he made to the countries of the Commonwealth, but he made the journey again in 1953 and 1958. Visits from other members of Glaxo's senior management were also more frequent than in pre-war days. On his tour in 1950, Jephcott concluded that Glaxo's representation in much of South America was weak, evidencing events in Chile as a particular instance. Glaxo's sales there had been high during the war and when Jephcott visited the country in 1950, he was assured that the government was keen to import British antibiotics and insulin to save on US dollars. He and the British commercial secretary at Santiago called on the Minister of Economics and Commerce who received them effusively and they seemed to reach satisfactory terms. But soon after Jephcott had left Chile, the Minister was ousted and a new scheme for the bulk import of penicillin (to be packaged on government account) was developed. An order was placed, at a price Glaxo Laboratories could have met with ease, with an American supplier. The incident reflected not only Glaxo's problems in securing adequate representation across such large areas: it also mirrored the chronic political instability and the proximity and influence of the USA in the subcontinent.

47 The Argentinian company's new factory at Chivilcoy.

Argentina

In Argentina 'the 1950s became a period of retrenchment or of departure' for the British there, whose influence had been so strong that they also suffered 'the vituperation inevitably directly against a dispossessed colonial power'.[29] Against this trend, Glaxo's subsidiary in Argentina expanded steadily. Relations with the parent company were governed by a royalty agreement, drawn up in 1947 and revised in 1950. From then on, royalties of 5 per cent on food products and 10 per cent on pharmaceuticals manufactured locally were payable by the subsidiary to Glaxo in London. C. J. Richardson, Chairman of the company since 1941, had been described by his father to Jephcott in 1939 as 'impervious to a degree and tactless ... when dealing with the British element'.[30] Despite his energy these characteristics seemed increasingly inappropriate and he was superceded in 1948 by Reginald (Rex) E. Petley; the company's name was then changed (in line with Glaxo policy) to Laboratories Glaxo (Argentina) SA Cel.

When the company's lease of its milk-drying factory at Quequen expired in 1948, new milk-drying premises near Chivilcoy, 100 miles west of Buenos Aires, were bought from the River Plate Dairy Company, together with ample land on which to extend its manufacturing facilities. After new buildings were completed at Chivilcoy in 1951, baby foods, including a new one called Acilac, and Glucodin were packed there. With the introduction of Farex in 1952, turnover in food products expanded; in 1949 food represented only 15 per cent of the company's turnover but by 1954 the proportion had risen to nearly a third. Profit margins on food products were squeezed, however, after retail prices were frozen by government decree in 1949.

In the immediate post-war years penicillin, introduced in 1946, was the Argentinian company's best-selling pharmaceutical product. But, as in many other countries, the Argentine government was impatient to establish local productive capacity in pharmaceuticals. In 1950 Glaxo was dislodged from the Argentine penicillin market when import licences for penicillin were suspended so as to support the local productive monopoly which had been granted to E. R. Squibb's Argentine subsidiary. The demand for penicillin far exceeded the productive capacity initially installed, but Squibb not only maintained a high price structure, it also doggedly opposed imports of cheaper penicillin. Glaxo's tenuous position in the penicillin market depended upon the inconsistent official attitudes towards meeting the short-fall between supply and demand. Given the price structure that prevailed in 1950–1952, the company was aggrieved at its exclusion from the business. When, in 1952, the Argentine Ministry of Health announced that only bulk streptomycin could in future be imported, Glaxo quickly arranged to build a streptomycin filling and packing plant in Argentina to safeguard its position.

In 1953 Squibb, nervous about its monopolistic position in Argentine penicillin supplies, asked if Glaxo was interested in buying penicillin for sale under the Glaxo label. Petley's salesmen in Argentina were apprehensive at this proposal, in view of the high reputation of Glaxo penicillin and the inferior quality of locally manufactured Squibb material; but the London office was attracted by Squibb's suggestion so long as standards could be guaranteed and offered to take crude penicillin from Squibb. It was a good stroke of business to get in on the ground floor with antibiotics in Argentina in association with Squibb, the only local manufacturer. Glaxo Laboratories had a better sales organisation than Squibb, who were soon anxious to sell it the maximum bulk raw materials to meet increased sales. As Glaxo's margin of profit was small, it was essential to maintain a high level of sales; Glaxo's total unit sales of antibiotics in 1957 were three times those of 1955.

The Argentine subsidiary was careful not to bind itself too tightly to Squibb as its supplier of penicillin. Glaxo Laboratories never bought more than two months ahead so that if sales fell beneath expectations, it was possible to cancel one month's orders. Petley also bought streptomycin sulphate and dihydrostreptomycin at prices which surprised Jephcott and Herbert Palmer. Whereas in world markets the price of a gram of streptomycin was normally about 50 per cent above the price of a mega of penicillin,

Squibb's prices in Argentina reversed that ratio. For Glaxo there was also the possibility that the association with Squibb would bring other benefits in the future. Herbert Palmer wrote that Squibb's general policy implied 'that those who are prepared to play ball with them may reasonably expect to find themselves in a position of some priority in respect of any future developments of which Squibb or Olin-Mathieson [Squibb's associated corporation] have the patent rights'.[31]

During the years of the Peron regime, privately deplored by Jephcott, he and Glaxo were relieved to find no desire to nationalise industries generally or the pharmaceutical industry in particular.[32] Glaxo's policy was to increase the self-sufficiency of the Argentine company reducing its dependence on imports, so that its operations could continue should political or economic circumstances temporarily sever its British supplies. Jephcott persuaded his London colleagues that, if the return upon Glaxo's investment was to rest mainly upon royalties and dividends, the company must 'exercise exemplary patience'.[33]

The revolution in 1955, which overthrew the Peron regime, changed the perspective for Glaxo. Although privately it was welcomed by the company, the instability which followed in its immediate wake was not. The provisional government had to cope with a major economic crisis featuring inflation and high wage demands, and with complete chaos in public utilities and all government departments. The political disarray was accompanied by a dislocation of foreign exchanges, and the independent operation of both free market and official rates of exchange, together with unpredictable and revised import quotas. Although government policy was to free business as far as possible, in the short term it tried to limit profits to the percentages ruling before the revolution, together with an attempt to freeze prices. Underground opposition to the new administration, with acts of sabotage, created turbulent conditions and Glaxo postponed for a year the major capital investment which had then been under discussion. However, Rex Petley wrote in 1956, 'Don't forget the revolution *must* succeed, otherwise the consequences would be quite unbearable.' He besought patience: 'the task before the Provisional Government is tremendous and . . . the political and economic chaos produced by 12 years of mismanagement and misappropriation of public funds cannot easily or rapidly be rectified'.[34]

In 1956 the issued capital of the company was raised to $9m by capitalising approximately $6m of accumulated royalties due to the parent company. These royalties were unremittable at the dates when they accrued and were fully employed in the business. At the same time a site of 28,000 square metres of land in the industrial area of Munro in the province of Buenos Aires was bought. The new factory completed there in 1960 included manufacturing facilities, analytical and sterile filling laboratories, packing plant, warehouses and administrative offices. It was initially agreed that the parent company should invest £100,000 in the building and equipment, with the subsidiary financing the rest of the expenditure, reckoned originally at £150,000. Part of the remittance from Britain was in the form of plant and equipment which could be imported into Argentina without fiscal duties. Although Jephcott was reluctant as usual to invest further capital without certainty of adequate returns, he felt that the group had no option if it intended to continue business in Argentina. Any restriction of expansion would be 'not only destructive to the Company's future prospects', but what counted equally with Jephcott, 'no less destructive to the work of the staff'.[35]

Glaxo continued to add to its product range in Argentina. Introductions included cortisone products, L-Thyroxine and Cytamen products containing vitamin B_{12} in 1957, Complan and Akotin in 1958 and Grisovin, Fersamal and Cytatrope in 1959. After the merger with Allen & Hanbury, whose small business in Argentina had 'suffered at the hands of a series of none too satisfactory agents', some Allen & Hanbury products such as Dequadin tablets were added to the range. Further extensions at Chivilcoy were planned, with new spray-drying equipment for milk products; they were completed in 1965 at a cost of approximately £150,000.[36] Turnover rose much faster in the late 1950s, and by 1962 was more than four times the value it had been in 1957. Food products represented a quarter of the turnover in 1962, pharmaceuticals three-quarters.

Between 1946 and 1962 Glaxo's subsidiary in Argentina was able to consolidate and expand its activities. By coming to terms with US competition, particularly in the shape of Squibb, the company maintained a share in the penicillin and streptomycin markets, thus underpinning its pharmaceutical development. By 1962 the Argentine subsidiary had made considerable advances towards the self-sufficiency, both in production and finance, judged to be desirable by the parent company.

Brazil

When Joseph Hutchinson, on Glaxo's behalf, visited Brazil during the war, he advised 'a more venturesome' commercial policy. In his judgement, 'Brazil as a country has a tremendous future and probably will occupy one of the most important positions in the Western Hemisphere after the war'.[37] Events up to 1962 did not, however, justify his optimism. The Brazilian organisation had evolved from an agency run from Argentina and despite the formation of the subsidiary company the methods of an agency still predominated in 1950. 'Whilst the volume of business now being conducted by the Brazilian Company is quite substantial, this organisation, except for sales promotion, is by far the weakest we have', Jephcott reported to the Glaxo Laboratories board in 1950. 'There is urgent need to strengthen it.' The local company was 'nothing more than a native Brazilian sales organisation having no prestige or standing in the commercial world'.[38] Antibiotics virtually sold themselves until 1952, since supplies from Greenford were relatively plentiful and competition was not too severe. Salesmen were able to achieve satisfactory results without too much effort and, as they did so well with antibiotics, tended to neglect sales of other pharmaceuticals.

Jephcott visited Brazil as part of his grand South American tour of 1950 primarily to investigate the advisability of local packing and manufacture. He found that the economic and financial issues involved were complex. Pharmaceuticals locally prepared and packed were cheaper than the same products imported: penicillin was subject to 25 per cent *ad valorem* duty, and streptomycin was only temporarily exempt from this by special decree. Many pharmaceuticals (and *all* tablets) paid a high rate of duty and their importation was prohibitively expensive. Local production of pharmaceuticals was undertaken by Brazilian firms and Jephcott was concerned that these manufacturers might press for even higher import duties. Import licences and exchange control were problems, as also was finance. Capital outlay for even modest packing and manufacturing premises was estimated at £70,000. In all, to provide a capital structure appropriate to the turnover of the business and to provide for local manufacture the company needed an injection of funds of £175,000 from its parent, for which Bank of England consent was required.

Even so, local manufacture was considered imperative. Two British and several of the principal American pharmaceutical houses had already embarked on this course and Jephcott was convinced that such a move was unavoidable if Glaxo Laboratories was to maintain its long-term position in Brazil. Further action was deferred until after the presidential elections of 1950, which saw the democratic re-election of Getulio Dornelles Vargas, who had been Brazil's revolutionary dictator from 1930 to 1945. Like many other Brazilian politicians, Vargas 'spoke in riddles, a form of appeal which the Brazilians call *confusionismo* ... perhaps the most important political "ism" in Brazil'.[39] In the subsequent period *confusionismo* befogged Glaxo's attempts at planning in the country.

New strains then appeared in the Brazilian economy. The Korean War had sharply escalated prices of world commodities and Brazil rapidly accumulated large balances of foreign exchange from its substantial exports of primary materials. Instead of conserving these balances, the government indulged in prodigal expenditure on unproductive goods which, coupled with increasing internal inflation, led to Brazilian exports being priced out of

48 The offices of the Brazilian company in 1952.

world markets. By September 1952 Brazil had a huge unfavourable trade balance, with sterling indebtedness exceeding £40 million and dollar indebtedness of about $600 million (of which about one-third was to Germany). In that year the prohibition of imports of packed goods brought the Brazilian Glaxo subsidiary's business to a standstill. Only a limited amount of trading was possible as a result of careful disposals of stocks. ICI, who had a factory at Niteroi, was able to supply Glaxo with some products, but quantity, quality and price proved unsatisfactory. Nevertheless, to provide local manufacturing capacity, Glaxo chose to take over the Niteroi factory from ICI when the latter decided to withdraw from Brazil. The factory had been neglected and a failure on the part of Glaxo's local management to co-ordinate sales and production rapidly led to a crisis there, only solved temporarily by the suspension of production for three months.

By the mid 1950s antibiotic prices had fallen sharply as supplies of locally manufactured penicillin production became readily available. Whereas in 1950 antibiotics had contributed two-thirds of Glaxo's turnover in Brazil, by 1954 they represented only 8 per cent of the total. It was clear to Glaxo that there was little to gain from the antibiotics business and the company therefore looked for other ways to develop the business. In the Brazilian pharmaceutical market, a Glaxo report noted:

Although our products are mainly sold on medical prescription ... there is still a constant clamour for novelties, which seems to be something of a mania with the Brazilians ... we still have the benefit of the excellent reputation which we have established in the past but ... many doctors are being lured away from our lines towards the more complex formulations offered by our competitors.

Journals and newspapers contained numerous advertisements for elixirs containing a surprising range of vitamins and minerals, upon whose quantity claims to product superiority rested. Glaxo noted:

our selling problems in the Brazilian market may be summed up by saying that we are a very highly reputable company trying to sell only ethical products in a non-ethical society ... we should consider how we should adjust our own standards in Brazil so that we can better meet local demands without imperilling our prestige or integrity. Clearly it would be wrong and quite dishonest to offer products which are either harmful or utterly useless, but if for example, there was a great demand for a product containing vitamins A, D, B_1, B_2, B_6 and B_{12}, together with an assortment of mineral salts, should we not offer it, even though the scientific purists might question the efficacy of some of its constituents?

The report argued that Nicorbin tablets, containing four vitamins, which Glaxo Laboratories planned to market in Brazil, would make little headway against popular Brazilian remedies which boasted six or seven vitamins and perhaps ten minerals.[40]

In other countries where competition and falling prices had dislodged Glaxo from a place in the antibiotics business, the launch of specialities such as Estopen and Estomycin had strengthened its position. But in Brazil to follow such a course of action would have posed a new set of problems. The pharmaceuticals had to be imported and Brazil's lack of sterling, currency oscillations and need to reduce imports suggested that it would be difficult to maintain supplies from Greenford. Other product areas were considered. Glaxo considered that veterinary products did not offer a promising market because, despite the size of the agricultural sector in Brazil farming was uncommercialised, customers were widely dispersed, and transport would be difficult in most areas.

Although the Brazilian market for dried milk was enormous, it was dominated by Nestlé, and Glaxo doubted whether it could profitably re-enter the business on any substantial scale. There was an almost universal 'lack of interest in child nutrition', suggesting there would be no demand for other Glaxo specialities.[41]

Moreover, by the late 1950s many of the large US pharmaceutical firms were established in Brazil and competition was consequently much fiercer than in Argentina. Squibb, Pfizer, Merck, Sharp & Dohme, Johnson & Johnson, all employed capital some twenty times the size of Glaxo's operation and their sales differed by the same ratio. A report in 1958 on pharmaceutical companies in Brazil described Glaxo as the most dynamic of British companies active in the country (the others were Evans Medical, ICI and Burroughs although only Evans manufactured locally). But Glaxo's profit trend was 'low', according to the report and as a return on capital employed Glaxo's profit was about half that of the more successfully established US companies.[42]

In 1959 there was a reorganisation of the Brazilian company, starting with the sales staff, where 'expensive and painful pruning' was undertaken. A new President for the company, Idris Lewis, was seconded from the South African subsidiary: Lewis had trained at Cardiff University, and had joined the Greenford Research Unit as a botanist in 1944. After helping to set up operations at Barnard Castle, he had gone out to Johannesburg in 1954. Lewis was appalled by what he found in Brazil. He had great difficulty both in replacing salesmen without relaxing pressure on the market, and in obtaining men of suitable quality. The Rio and Sao Paulo branches were, he wrote:

pitifully weak from the top to the bottom . . . it will be many years before they can be built up to really pulsating entities . . . dismissal indemnities will have to be faced . . . for several years . . . these will become successively greater as time goes on, because we shall progressively be reaching personnel with longer service each time . . . one of the major problems [is] that the older members who should be giving that dynamic lead . . . are those who are most set in their ways of the old order.[43]

He was critical of the factory where 'productivity is abominably and pitifully low' but laid the blame on 'lack of experience and lack of capital in the past',[44] warning that much greater expenditure would be required for the factory to produce economically. Lewis set about reorganising but reported back to the parent company on the difficulties. For example, he noted that in the accounts department there had been 'no set system for control of expenditure on major projects such as launching a new product. I have just introduced a very simple system for this; but it will need the patience of Job and an iron hand to ensure that it works efficiently.'[45] Although turnover had started to rise in the late 1950s, the increase was insufficient to counter Brazilian inflation and in 1962 the subsidiary's position was still weaker than that of the Argentinian company. In London there were doubts about the future of the Brazilian operation, beset with heavy US competition, difficult trading conditions and a history of inadequate management.

Cuba, the Caribbean and Central America

From his base in Cuba, Edward McGough (see page 105) was responsible for all of Central and South America, south of the US border and north of Brazil and Chile. In the late 1940s the area became particularly attractive to

Glaxo as a dollar market and it was visited in 1950 by Jephcott in order to investigate the prospects for further development. He spent six days in Cuba, four in Venezuela, two in Panama, two in Ecuador, and three in Peru, meeting Glaxo's own staff and agents as well as British commercial attaches, bank managers and representatives of the Federation of British Industries. In each country except Peru he found a marked economic dependence upon the USA and violent fluctuations in purchasing power. Jephcott was greatly impressed 'by the complete penetration and domination of US interests, in the supply of capital and consumer goods' in contrast to 'the virtual elimination of British commerce'. In all these countries Glaxo Laboratories 'appeared to be the only representative of the UK pharmaceutical industry'. Despite the intense price competition between US pharmaceutical houses, Jephcott considered it possible to meet 'the urgent necessity for rendering to these markets a delivery service equal to that of competing American houses'.[46] The problems were considerable: price instability for strepto-mycin and penicillin discouraged bulk orders, and exchange regulations virtually precluded consignment sales. Whereas the Americans could deliver in fourteen days, by using the weekly service from New York of the Grace line, the best that could be hoped for from Britain, was six weeks, or ten at worst. Naturally this damaged goodwill and the careful marketing required for new products.

McGough's general policy was to employ agents primarily as distributors, whilst utilising any sales service they were able to give, and to have in each country (which could possibly support it) a representative force responsible solely to the company and working closely with the agent. Groups of countries were the direct responsibility of a European assistant, who was in turn responsible to McGough. Although agents were recruited and trained as quickly as possible, in late 1950 only Panama, Costa Rica, Mexico and Ecuador had them. The only European assistant then employed was training in Ecuador. Nevertheless, Jephcott was satisfied with progress and he judged that the sales potential for Glaxo products in McGough's territory, exclud-ing the West Indies, exceeded one million dollars.

As events turned out this was an over-optimistic view. US competition and Glaxo's own mistakes in trading precluded any large development of business. By the early 1950s throughout the Caribbean, Glaxo had lost all but 10 per cent of the Glucodin business to Cow & Gate 'because we changed the name to Glucodin, apparently abruptly', Jephcott noted during a tour in 1953. 'I can only assume that the careful change from Glucose D to Glucodin which took place at home did not occur out here, possibly owing to the war, and the only name the public knows is Glucose D. We have just made a present of the business to the competitors and it's going to take a lot of getting back.'[47] There was also trouble with weevils gaining access into export Farex packs *en route* from Greenford to the West Indies. Jephcott found in the Caribbean in February 1953, 'that, of recent months, the tendency to purchase locally has been suppressed with a heavy official hand in favour of purchase through the Crown Agents', and warned that 'getting' new products 'past the Crown Agents will be a monumental task'.[48]

In Cuba itself Laboratorios Glaxo de Cuba, SA or Glaxo Laboratories of Cuba Inc, was established in Havana in 1953. Without any production capacity of its own the company worked on a 40 per cent commission basis on sales made for the parent company. In 1954 the final profit was small and in the following year with expenses up and sales down the company showed a net loss. This was not propitious for a company operating as the Area Office for not only Cuba, but also Colombia, Costa Rica, Ecuador, Panama, Peru and the British West Indies. In 1955 McGough suggested that capital investment in Cuba should be increased, initially to improve the packing and thereby wholesaling and distribution. He argued that this would counteract the higher cost of sales and the 'forever increasing difficulties of foreign pharmaceutical firms to operate freely and profitably in markets where excited nationalistic tendencies in the medical and pharmaceutical profession demand "protection", and it would also enable Glaxo to keep abreast of the major US concerns already well established in their backyard'.[49] Increased investment of around $200,000 in a new building and plant for packaging and production was estimated to offer a return on investment of between 6 per cent and 12 per cent. In 1956 the Bank of England consented to Glaxo remitting $235,000 to Cuba and to exporting equipment valued at $15,000, free of payment and the new building was erected in 1957.

A difference of opinion about Cuban prospects between head office in London and the local subsidiary was revealed when McGough proposed a shareholding scheme for his staff. Palmer deprecated the idea:

It would be quite wrong of us to invite Cuban staff to subscribe to shares in the Cuban Company having regard to the fact that the profitability of that Company will, in very large measure, depend upon decisions taken by us in consultation with you as to the prices at which goods will be shipped to your territory from this country . . . it would be foolish of us, if not downright dishonest, to represent to the local staff that by investing money in this subsidiary they had an opportunity of reaping a special reward for their enterprise.

With their experience in the rest of the continent, Palmer and other London managers were particularly pessimistic because the Caribbean area 'like Canada is very near the US and we can waste a lot of money if we try unwisely to compete with the Americans at their own front door with products such as penicillin and streptomycin which today have no novelty and secure no price premium in the market'.[50]

The Glaxo factory in Cuba was barely operating before political disruption in the country started to increase. The subsidiary's sales remained unsatisfactory and by the time Dr Fidel Castro took power in 1959 the worst fears of the pessimists at head office in London about the Cuban operation appeared to be justified. From then on, with the threat of expropriation, most probably without compensation, ever before them, the Glaxo subsidiary ran down its operations. McGough left in 1961 to establish a new area office in Miami and by then Glaxo was only permitted by government order to import four products, insufficient to sustain an adequate turnover. Production largely ceased at the end of 1961, although it took the company some years to extricate itself finally and control of the factory ultimately passed to the Cuban Ministry of Health.

The other central American markets administered, until 1961, from Cuba, proved equally disappointing, included Colombia where a subsidiary had been formed. Small exports of Glaxo baby food to Colombia, especially to the capital Bogota, where a Scottish-born pharmacist became a particular customer, built up a clientele consisting mainly of the richer families of Bogota. A generation later, as these former Glaxo babies became leaders of business, the professions and fashionable society, they became known collectively as 'Los Glaxos', a phrase which became synonymous in Colombia with wealth, health and elegance. It did not, however, sustain Glaxo's business in Colombia and in the late 1950s Glaxo abandoned Colombia.

Although Glaxo had never expected business in South America to offer easy or quick profits, several factors, some prevailing world-wide and others particular to the continent, combined to make it more difficult than anticipated. The growth of nationalism and political and economic instability led to import restriction and high tariffs. The fall in world prices of all forms of penicillin coming as it did so much sooner than expected, led to fierce price competition everywhere and in South and Central America particularly from the US pharmaceutical corporations. They were, in any case, much larger than Glaxo, with greater resources at their disposal and physically closer to the markets. In the period under consideration British withdrawal from investment and influence in South America continued, and in many markets Glaxo found itself the only British participant.

The company can be accused of weak management – indeed, it blamed itself in those terms – but in under-developed economies it was difficult, if not impossible, to find men of calibre and experience, nor generally was the area attractive enough to tempt away those working for the home company. Glaxo's rapid development in pharmaceuticals at home and elsewhere in the world placed strain enough on its personnel resources, and the company was prudent about committing its financial resources overseas.

12

The Commonwealth I: India and Pakistan

On the Indian subcontinent Glaxo's existing subsidiary was strengthened and a new one established in Pakistan in the post-war period. Among Glaxo's subsidiaries, the Indian company, H. J. Foster & Company and its successors, Glaxo Laboratories in India and Pakistan, were foremost in terms of capital employed, turnover and profits (see tables A8 and A9). They were also members of one of the largest and most important expatriate British business communities in the world. Glaxo's experiences there were part of 'an important element in the modern economic history of mainland South Asia, and of the British imperial system as a whole'[1] and these experiences were not limited simply to business activity in the area.

As this chapter shows, 'analysing the history of British expatriate firms in India raises the issue of the role of political factors in business history in a very direct way'.[2] Glaxo's development in India, however, ran counter to that of very many other British companies. Its business was not in decline before independence in 1947, nor did it suffer 'spectacular collapse' afterwards. Indeed the Indian subsidiary was more remunerative than most of Glaxo's other overseas ventures and notably more remunerative than those of other British investors in India in the 1950s and 1960s. Of British multinationals heavily involved in India, in that period several companies including Brooke Bond, ICI, Vickers, Turner & Newall, Tube Investments, Hawker Siddeley and Babcock & Wilcox, had low growth rates. Other companies extensively committed to India, such as Guest, Keen & Nettlefold, British Oxygen, Metal Box and Dunlop, 'did no more than hold their own in relative growth in this period'. Among British companies 'that grew fastest in the 1950s and 1960s, those that increased their capital by a factor of nine or more, only Glaxo and General Electric had major investments in India in the 1950s'.[3]

But India had a greater significance for Glaxo beyond its business in the area. Their local managing director and chairman for twenty years from 1934, E. H. C. Gwilt, was a man of some political and social importance in

49 E. H. C. Gwilt, Chairman and Managing Director of Glaxo's Indian
company.

British India. He was a member of the Central Legislative Assembly from
1939 until independence, and in 1942 he married Lady Thom, widow of the
Chief Justice of Allahabad High Court. Gwilt was, in 1950, elected to the
Bombay Legislative Assembly himself but before that he had enjoyed top
level political contacts with the administration of the last three Viceroys,
Linlithgow, Wavell and Mountbatten. It was through Gwilt's intervention
that Jephcott was invited to India on official war-time missions to advise on
milk powder production and related nutritional needs. As a result of these
visits, Jephcott, with his talent for personal relationships, made contacts of
importance for the future management of Glaxo. Sir Robert Hutchings, who
was Secretary of the Indian Government's Food Department when Jephcott
first visited India as an official adviser later became the member for food and
agriculture on Lord Wavell's Executive Council. Hutchings so impressed
Jephcott that in 1947 he was recruited as an executive Director of Glaxo
Laboratories; henceforth he tried to impart to the company something of the
hierarchical order and administrative system that had sustained British
imperial power under the last Viceroys. Others with experience of wartime
Indian bureaucracy or nutritional problems were also highly placed in the
head-office management of Glaxo Laboratories in the 1950s. Britain's

withdrawal from political control in India held symbolic significance for many, including Jephcott and Tizard. It influenced their thinking and approach in the late 1950s to planning the company's scientific programme and its commercial relations in the rest of the world. Business experience in India emphasised that the world was no longer secure under *Pax Britannica*, and decisions far beyond the subcontinent were influenced accordingly.

The Indian company

During one of Jephcott's official war-time visits to advise the Indian Government, he took the opportunity to discuss post-war Indian development with Gwilt, particularly the latter's recommendation that the Indian company should start milk powder production and the extent to which Indianisation of the subsidiary company was desirable. The City solicitors, Withers, who had an office in Delhi, had given Glaxo strategic advice for the subcontinent which provided the basis for much of their post-war planning although in the event it proved over-optimistic:

India is certain to be rapidly industrialised; markets will expand and there will be a great rise in the living standard. Any Government of India, including the present one, will give greater advantages to manufacture in India, and even greater advantages to companies whenever there is real collaboration with Indians.

Issues of shares to the ordinary Indian public are to be deprecated because, more often than not, the Management has no means of checking the personnel of the Company's shareholders. Shares get into the hands of speculators who are of no assistance, either politically or economically, but a menace. There is always, and particularly at the present juncture, a danger of speculators unloading shares, forced to a false value, on to shareholders who will be dissatisfied later unless dividends are paid commensurate with the higher prices.

Indian Shareholders and Directors having British sympathies and who are politically and economically acceptable and influential, are a desirability. There should be a 'balance' of Indian share-holdings between the differing Indian communities . . . It is desirable to offer Indian shareholders a remunerative investment and to place some restrictions on rights of free transfer . . . Actual control from London is inadvisable and almost impossible for reasons of Income Tax; this entails London acting in an advisory capacity only.[4]

As was the case in a number of other countries, it was felt, both in Greenford and India, that if the company did not show willingness to proceed with pharmaceutical manufacture in India, it might find itself eliminated from the market. New buildings were a priority and in 1946 it was decided to extend the main premises of the Indian company to include additional office space and pharmaceutical manufacturing facilities. Building operations, however, were so protracted that pharmaceutical manufacturing did not begin until 1950. During this interval the nature of the business altered, with the emphasis shifting to the sub-dividing and packing of bulk penicillin, which required further building work. Despite onerous import restrictions, annual turnover grew rapidly in the immediate post-war period to a figure exceeding £2m. by 1950.

To enable the Indian company to plough back profits into the expansion programme, all the shares of Fosters were transferred to the British parent company. This had the effect of enabling the company to avoid the demand of the Indian fiscal authorities that 60 per cent of a company's assessable profit be distributed as dividends. By this manoeuvre capital could be accumulated rather than distributed as dividends and marked the change from an agency business to a manufacturing concern which was of necessity more heavily committed in terms of raw materials and fixed assets. At the same time a Trademark and Consultancy Services Agreement, to last twenty years, was agreed between Glaxo Laboratories and the Foster company, in return for which Glaxo received from Foster fully paid shares to the value of Res 1.5 crores. The Indian company's reserves were capitalised and additional shares were issued for cash, so that total issued capital was increased to Res 2 crores in 1947. One of the main purposes of this reconstruction was to relate the company's issued capital to its earning power, an essential preliminary to the sale of shares to Indian interests judged to be politically desirable. Under the Consultancy Agreement of 1947, the Indian company paid its parent an annual service fee of £7,500 plus all net profit above 7.5 per cent on the issued capital, but limited to 1.5 per cent of turnover for the first five years of the agreement, and 2.5 per cent of turnover thereafter.

Gwilt's connections meant that he was well placed to assess the likely repercussions to Foster's business of Indian independence and the partition which created Pakistan. He wrote to London that the view of the Central Legislative Assembly was that a company with its office in a province of Pakistan was a foreign company. The Provincial government had been informed that foreigners travelling between the Dominion of India and Pakistan should be in possession of valid visas for entry into India. More specifically, the Government of India was examining political measures to protect Indian interests in view of the unilateral action of the Pakistan Government in imposing a duty on raw jute exported from East Bengal to India. Gwilt therefore suggested the setting up of a separate Pakistan subsidiary (see page 289).

When Jephcott visited India in 1947, he found 'the opinion is firmly held that whereas the next two or three years may be fraught with uncertainties and difficulties, which will be . . . perhaps sharply reflected in trading profits, the long-term future in India of organisations such as our own is good, provided we have the courage to sustain the short-term uncertainties whilst actively planning to meet the long-term requirements'.[5] During this visit

Jephcott met the Minister for Industries and Supplies, Raja Gopalachari (who a year later succeeded Mountbatten as Governor-General). At the meeting Jephcott stated that Glaxo Laboratories were willing to consider producing penicillin in India in association with Indian interests. The company would not seek high profit margins but he emphasised the prudence of first scrutinising the economies of penicillin production in India, especially given the adverse climate and the likelihood that many essential raw materials which were not locally manufactured would have to be imported. To the surprise of Jephcott and Gwilt, Raja Gopalachari believed that penicillin production in India should not be undertaken unless there was proof that it would be economic. He stressed that in India the problem was less the number of persons who would benefit from the use of penicillin than the number of doctors who could administer it. Glaxo Laboratories were, nevertheless, nervous that this official attitude might not prevent other persons who were less skilled and less public spirited beginning penicillin production 'as a commercial venture and, having undertaken it, they might obtain government protection for their efforts'.[6] By 1949, however, the Indian Government seemed determined to establish their own local manu-facture and packing of penicillin, undertaking packing in the first instance. Indian political rivalries surfaced, with what Jephcott dubbed 'the Bombay faction' enquiring for crystalline penicillin through Glaxo's Bombay office, while 'the Bengal faction' enquired for crude penicillin through the Indian High Commission in London. With Gwilt's contacts, Jephcott judged it best to support the Bombay interests and pursued negotiations with them. Semi-official estimates in Delhi of the probable future demand in India for penicillin seemed to Glaxo to be grossly exaggerated.

There were other difficulties too. The company had to operate within the government strategy for industrial development enunciated in 1948 (and redefined in 1956) as well as the far-reaching Industrial Disputes Act of 1947. It has been suggested that the 'inadequacy, or peculiarity,' of the framework thus created in the Indian economy may have accounted for the poor growth of some businesses in India.[7] The Industrial Disputes Act made it virtually impossible for any sizeable business to shut down factories or dismiss employees without going through an elaborate process involving exasperat-ing procedures of conciliation and arbitration through procrastinating local authorities. In due course Glaxo's operation became subject to the provi-sions of the Industrial Development and Regulation Act and only narrowly escaped from the ambit of the Foreign Exchange Regulations Act by ensuring that no more than 40 per cent of its shares were owned outside India. Jephcott wrote, in 1949, that Indian officialdom discounted 'the kind of activities which we indulge in by way of secondary manufacture [i.e. processing, packing and filling]', not regarding them 'as importing essential technique and know-how into India: rather does it look upon them as doing the Indian manufacturer out of a job'. He also urged that 'unpalatable as it may seem to Gwilt', the number of Indian staff should be increased and that of Europeans reduced: 'I get the impression that Gwilt is reasonably satisfied if the fellow has a white face and the old school tie.'[8]

The situation regarding licences for the import of raw materials was fluid, and Glaxo regretted that such difficulties occurred so soon after the inception there of large-scale manufacturing. To meet sales demands considerable improvisation was required. Prices also had to be carefully considered. In 1947–1948 the Government of Bombay had taken legal action against the British pharmaceutical company of May & Baker. The Indian officials, considering that the prices of the company were too high, sought to cancel their rights and to take powers for the manufacture of their products. Glaxo considered that it was only the poor briefing of the government's barrister that saved May & Baker, and felt that there was a risk of similar action being taken against Glaxo if selling prices rose too far.

Visiting Bombay in 1949, Palmer found both Gwilt and his assistant, Gardner Lewis, ill through overwork. The factory extension, Palmer wrote, had proved 'a real and persistent headache'. Apart from the usual troubles with licensing and organising supplies, the site manager was 'completely and hopelessly lost', while the European firm of contractors with whom Glaxo had signed the contract had subsequently 'sold out to local interests whose main concern seems to have been profitability rather than honest service'. He continued: 'the organisation has suffered from having to undertake a substantial expansion of physical assets with a poor set of tools and with a staff initially depleted by the formation of the Pakistan Company and, subsequently, bemused by difficulties with which they were not technically competent to deal'. Although Gwilt had many qualities, 'his inability to delegate full authority' had aggravated the situation; 'the more difficulties which have cropped up, the more he has been involved in the details of them – hence the additional strain and the deterioration in mental output'. Nevertheless, Palmer noted, the organisation and installation of the new departments had gone well, and in the circumstances the extension indeed was surprisingly well-built.[9] He added that Indian officialdom was anxious to prevent penicillin from going underground or onto a black market because of inadequate supplies, and Glaxo hoped therefore to have full licensing clearance.

Early in 1950 the name of the Indian company was, in line with company policy, changed from H. J. Foster & Co to Glaxo Laboratories (India) Ltd. At a meeting in Bombay in 1951 between Jephcott and the senior manager of the Indian subsidiary, it was agreed that a doubling of pharmaceutical sales might be achieved within three years. It was therefore agreed to make further extensions to the over-stretched Bombay factory costing about Res 15 lakhs. Despite the difficulties, Jephcott admitted that in India 'in many ways the facilities for tabletting are better than at Greenford'. The tablet department was able to undertake contract work for other companies, as well as producing Glaxo proprietaries. This practice had caused some problems in 1949, when a large contract was offered by ICI for tabletting the anti-malarial drug, Paludrine. ICI had previously considered expansion in India, but were advised by their associates, the Tata group, that such an investment would be inopportune. The Indian government were urging ICI to begin local manufacture of Paludrine, which would entail doing their own tabletting. Jephcott warned Glaxo's Indian subsidiary that: 'In the old days it was a great trick of Woolworth's to find someone who would do a job for them, give him more and more work until they crowded all other customers off his books and then cut the price down until he could not live.' He recommended instead that the Indian company undertake the smaller tabletting contracts offered by Howards. Although in many areas of the chemical industry collaborative agreements were commonplace, traditional suspicion was not altogether eliminated.

Jephcott was even more wary in 1954, warning Gardner Lewis of the dangers of overdependence on one American company, Corn Products, for the supply of dextrose. He referred to the 'fun and games' which had been had in the late 1930s with Corn Products, prior to American Maize coming to Glaxo's rescue, supported by official US action, and cautioned: 'If Corn Products get the whole of your business, they are quite capable of deciding to put a competitor to Glucodin on the Indian market and for one reason or another to deny you supplies of dextrose, so that they shall have a clear run.' To his knowledge, Corn Products had done this in the United States with maize oil, which they supplied to refiners who, after refining, sold it under their own brand names. 'Corn Products decided to enter the market, cut off all supplies and left the erstwhile refiners high and dry', according to Jephcott. 'It is the "skin game" with certain American types amongst them Corn Products', and he concluded, 'He who sups with the Devil had better have a long spoon.'

Glaxo's monthly antibiotic filling capacity had expanded by 1952 to 1,000,000 vials; applications for steel and cement were granted by the Indian Government allowing extension of the premises to attain a monthly filling capacity of 1,600,000 vials. A further increase came at the request of the Indian Government itself which feared a developing shortage of penicillin, so that by 1953 monthly filling capacity reached 2,200,000 vials. This growth occurred in the familiar context of falling world prices for antibiotics, due to over-production interspersed with occasional shortages created by American stockpiling during the Korean War. Meanwhile, packed penicillin products had been removed from Ordinary General Licence (OGL), with the opening of local bottling plants, so that the only competitors to Glaxo India were the other penicillin bottlers, the Indian Penicillin Committee's (IPC) plant at the Haffkine Institute, Bombay, and the plant operated by Dumex (Danish United Medical Export Co) which used material imported from Lovens. However, Glaxo's output was far higher than that of IPC and Dumex combined, giving the company, as Gwilt admitted, 'virtually a monopoly'.[10]

The IPC plant tendered for bulk penicillin in the open market, rather amateurishly, finding themselves over-stocked at times with penicillin bought in at fixed prices as the price fell. By 1952 the IPC were in such a position as a result of a six-month contract signed for the supply of Glaxo (Greenford) bulk penicillin. Although the IPC had hoped to off-load supplies onto the hospital and institutional market in the event of a fall in prices, they had over-estimated the size of this market. Glaxo refused to release the IPC from the contract. 'We would rather see this official body doing a relatively small proportion of the business and consequently having to do it at a relatively high price in order to break even', a local manager wrote. 'In this way IPC becomes directly interested in maintaining a favourable price for penicillin in the Indian market.'[11]

In the process of tendering to the IPC for bulk penicillin contracts, it became apparent that American companies such as Merck were offering penicillin at 7.75 d. per mega whereas Glaxo UK were invoicing Glaxo India at 16.5 d. As Gwilt wrote to Palmer:

Emotion could so easily be whipped up if a charge of over-charging were levelled against us, and though I am aware of the reasons for the differences between the price of penicillin invoiced to us by yourselves and by Mercks to the IPC, it may be difficult to convince those out witch-hunting that the American price is due to overproduction and dumping.[12]

The Commerce Minister had already declared publicly that the prices at which drugs and pharmaceuticals were sold in India were too high. Meanwhile the Indian Company found itself in the paradoxical situation of trying to convince Indian Customs officials that the price as invoiced was not, in fact, too low from the point of view of customs duty, having been recently reduced from 19.5 d. per mega!

The value of drugs imported into India rose from £5.9 million to £11.3 million between 1950 and 1952, prompting the appointment of a Pharmaceutical Enquiry Committee in 1952 to consider both the pharmaceutical needs of India and the savings that could be made by local manufacture. Nearly 80 per cent of the imported drugs were antibiotics, hormones, vitamins, sulpha drugs and other synthetic compounds. The Committee brought pressure to bear on Glaxo India to abandon its own distribution network, feeling that profits from such an operation should not be remitted even indirectly to the parent company. Such thinking threatened the closure of the Calcutta office. Furthermore, the Committee were keen to encourage Glaxo India to allow participation by local investors. Gwilt blamed the Enquiry Committee for further customs harassment:

A planned preliminary to the Pharmaceutical Industry enquiry has resulted in virtually a general attack upon pharmaceutical concerns – British and American – in Bombay. Parke Davis & Co., Eli Lilly and ourselves have been raided by customs and the managing director of [Burroughs Wellcome] . . . tells me that they too are being accused of declaring a shipment of cod liver oil as arachis oil. The latter pays a very much lower rate of duty.[13]

Throughout the Committee's deliberations (1952–1954), the Ministry of Commerce and Industry declined to sanction any new processes under the registration and licensing of Industrial Undertakings section of the Industries (Development and Regulation) Act, 1951. Glaxo India at this stage were seeking permission to import and bottle new antibiotics, such as Estopen, as part of their expansion programme. They became involved in a lengthy wrangle during 1953, trying to prove that their proposed developments did not constitute significant new processes, but were merely simple modifications of existing ones. Disputes such as these were commonplace as private enterprise clashed with central economic planning. In this case the Indian company argued that not only were the proposed developments likely to lead to a foreign exchange saving, they would also utilize appreciable quantities of locally manufactured materials. A further benefit would be the promotion of the development of new techniques leading to the training of further personnel in new techniques, '*without* in any way adversely affecting any overall plan of development which Government may wish to introduce for the drugs and pharmaceutical industry as a whole'.

The geographical distribution of Glaxo India's sales gives a rough idea of the relative importance of the different branch offices. In terms of total sales in 1954, the Bombay Office took first place (£81,200), Calcutta second (£74,900), Madras a close third (£68,100) and Delhi a long way behind (£24,400). The Calcutta branch particularly had expanded rapidly, but the parent company, noting reports of greater political unrest and difficulties with labour in the area, turned down Gwilt's proposals for expansion there. With the exception of 'Glaxo' babyfood, the sales and profits profiles of the individual offices were similar. Antibiotics sales were lower than expected because of fierce competition from the Danish company Dumex. According to Gwilt: 'The gross profit margin on penicillin continues to be high giving some latitude for special discounts and other dubious trading devices resorted to by Dumex, and Squibb principally.' Dumex had made it known to Glaxo India that their policy would be to undercut Glaxo prices for penicillin. Normally some premium would have attached to the Glaxo name, but owing to stock shortages experienced during changeovers in licensing regulations, doctors had begun prescribing generically, leaving the choice to the patient, who invariably chose the cheapest preparation. Glaxo's share of the Indian penicillin market fell from 38 per cent to 31 per cent between 1954–1955 and 1955–1956, although in the same period the total value of the market grew.

New competitors also began to appear in the milk foods area, with Dumex imports capturing 27 per cent of this market, again by under-cutting, although Glaxo managed to maintain a healthy average market share of 65 per cent. Glaxo India were holding their own in sales of vitamin B_{12} which in 1956 represented over 50 per cent of the total market. Glaxo had successfully prevented the entry of competition by careful diplomacy while also negotiating to secure agreements on minimum prices. However, there was always the threat that Merck, whose process Glaxo licensed, would begin their own marketing campaign in India. Glaxo's advantage over Merck was that the Indian company could use any surplus B_{12} in their own proprietary preparations, with the backing of the established sales and distribution network.

Glaxo Laboratories was highly sensitive about its corporate image. A set of unwritten rules existed on marketing, whereby it was permissible for the company's name to be associated with the mass marketing of baby food via various media, but the popular advertising of drugs and proprietaries was eschewed. Jephcott and Palmer were both in favour of discreet lay press advertising at the launch of Codopyrin, but Palmer wrote to Bombay:

Sir Harry particularly asks me to remind you of what happened in the early days of Ostelin in this country when, through the London Press Exchange, a discreet scheme of Press advertising was arranged in order to promote sales of what was then a very novel product. When it was observed that this discreet advertising had absolutely no effect at all on sales, the Advertising Agents suggested that they could do much better if their hands were not tied. They were given the discretion for which they asked and before the second advertisement of the new series had been published everybody in Glaxo was quite certain that our name would be mud with the medical profession if the campaign was allowed to go on ... We feel that your position in India may be very similar in that discreet press advertising for Codopyrin may get you nowhere and you may find that the only way to get value from this medium is to descend to the level of the more blatant Aspirin-type publicity which your better-informed medical public will promptly resent.[14]

Glaxo India therefore relied on the traditional method of marketing drugs – the visits by representatives, sending out samples and advertising in professional journals. By 1956 the company employed sixty-one medical representatives, eight travelling salesmen (for dealers only) and ten salesmen

50 The Madras office at night.

stationed in the principal depot towns. Bombay also boasted a permanent Representatives Training Unit which carried out refresher courses in addition to the initial training.

Another problem, associated with the rapidly growing sales of the Indian company in the early 1950s, was the increasing number of fraudulent preparations appearing on the market bearing Glaxo's name. Such 'spurious manufacture' was not the sole problem of the drug manufacturers, and Gwilt attacked this issue through the Bombay Chamber of Commerce of which he was President in 1953–1954. Infringements were either blatant, involving tampering with products, refilling old containers or actually imitating containers and products or, more subversively, passing off goods made in India as being made in England. One of Gwilt's closest associates in the Bombay Chamber of Commerce, the representative of Unilever, estimated that they dealt with more than 1,000 such infringements in a year.

More critically, Indian climatic conditions exposed physical deficiencies in the sealing of drugs. A major disaster was narrowly averted in 1951, when complaints were received about the looseness of the aluminium caps on penicillin vials. The cause was eventually traced to the rubber bungs, which were half a millimetre too thick, but not before all the stock on deposit in the Indian depots had been recalled. In this case Gwilt's managers were helped by the advice of Metal Box Company experts in Bombay, showing that the creative interchanges between Jephcott and Metal Box's Sir Robert Barlow were replicated lower in the company hierarchy. Packing materials were also important when calculating the economics of milk powder sales. The siting of Metal Box's major tin plate plant in Calcutta influenced Glaxo's decision to build a new milk powder packing plant there. Counter to this normal friendly collaboration, the cost of tin plate and demands for advance payments for supplies strained relations between the Glaxo and Metal Box representatives in India throughout 1953, a situation of potential embarrassment to Jephcott as a member of the main board of both companies.

The Indian Pharmaceutical Enquiry Committee's Report published in 1954 identified areas of specific opportunity for planned increases in local manufacture, 'showing the fields in which newcomers are likely to be welcomed and those in which they are not'. The areas with potential included streptomycin, sulpha drugs, chloroquine and vitamins: the last of these was chosen to spearhead the next stage of Glaxo's Indian development. Their interest was stimulated by the visit of a director of Hoffman La Roche to India in 1955 in connection with his company's proposed new factory to manufacture basic chemicals, principally vitamin A. Glaxo decided that they might be able to drive a wedge into the market, despite the fact that Roche already held 80 per cent of it. There was an expanded demand as a result of an order making the addition of vitamin A to *vanaspati* (vegetable ghee) compulsory. Glaxo had three advantages over Roche in starting to manufacture vitamin A. They had already built up a significant manufacturing, sales and distribution network; the process which the company intended to operate allowed for the building of a dual purpose plant, combining the manufacture of vitamin A with that of cortisone; and the Glaxo manufacturing project used as one of its raw materials lemon grass oil, which was available already in India. Conversely, a major problem was that the optimum capacity for a vitamin A plant would be 20 million mega units, twice the projected annual Indian demand.

In 1957 negotiations began with the Indian Ministry of Commerce and Heavy Industries for the construction of a plant in three stages, starting with small-scale operation in glassware to train the Indian staff and operatives, followed by the installation of a full-scale plant for the production of beta-ionone, the key intermediate, from lemon grass oil. The final stage was the full-scale synthesis of vitamin A and cortisone. The Government were keen to license the Glaxo Indian development, but pointed out that they had been negotiating with Roche on the subject of vitamin A plant for five years and that these talks were nearing fruition. This delay was not only a result of dilatory Indian bureaucracy, but also reflected Roche's desire to keep the Indian government quiescent, while continuing to import and promising the eventual erection of a manufacturing facility. Glaxo's negotiators felt that the Indian government was trying to play the manufacturers off against each other:

The Indian government dealt with ICI and Union Carbide proposals for the manufacture of polythene in very much the same way as they dealt with Roche and ourselves over vitamin A. These companies have been induced each to build a factory substantially larger than the present Indian total requirements. In addition to this they have both had to face substantial Indianisation of the capital for these ventures. The Indianisation of our capital expansion was raised but it was difficult for them to deal with this convincingly in the face of the substantial reserves we have built up and their desire that we should finance at least half this venture from the UK company.[15]

The Indians argued that any excess capacity could be expected, making the adoption of both schemes remunerative in foreign exchange, but a plant working at 10 million mega increased production costs by $\frac{3}{4}$d per mega making exports uncompetitive internationally. The Glaxo team also exerted pressure on the question of import duties, pointing out that the raw materials for the operation of the vitamin A plant were subject to a duty of 27.3 per cent whereas actual vitamin A imports only paid a duty of 14 per cent.

The prospect of two competing vitamin A plants in India displeased Roche, and in July 1957 they approached Glaxo in Britain with a view to reaching 'a gentleman's agreement and not in writing for the disposal of vitamin A in India'. They proposed that the two companies would combine in a joint venture, lobbying the Indian government for the setting up of a single plant to supply the whole of the Indian demand for vitamin A, with Glaxo providing 40 per cent of the required capital while Roche supplied 60 per cent. Roche's agent would be appointed to handle distribution. The British parent company were not impressed: they were certain that it was not in the interest of Glaxo India 'at this late stage to go back to Indian government ... with a proposal that we shall effectively combine with Roche to set up a *de facto* monopoly of vitamin A manufacture in the Dominion'. Palmer predicted 'a very poor reception in Delhi' for such a proposal. 'Our impression is that the private sector in India will only be given reasonable freedom of action if it shows not merely evidence of a desire to expand Indian industry, but also to operate under competitive rather than monopolistic conditions.'[16]

Glaxo in any case enjoyed natural advantages over Roche in vitamin A production, and they were also anxious that under the proposed scheme, Roche might envisage some tie-up of capital with the Indian conglomerate, Voltas. 'Voltas is, to all intents and purposes, a Tata concern and we might well find, in due course, that the 60 per cent holding would become an

Indian majority holding. This, of course, is conjecture only.'[17] Incidentally, it is notable that Roche were remarkably well informed of the contents of the Glaxo proposals. Ultimately Jephcott told Dr Gsell, the Roche emissary, that Glaxo had never, to the best of his knowledge, at any time in its history, joined a cartel agreement, but that it was its custom to observe price agreements.

The delicate situation involving a capital commitment to bottling operations, protected by import restrictions, was complicated in the early 1950s by the prospect of a new government penicillin manufacturing unit set up with international aid, and hence the possible closing of the market to imports of bulk penicillin. Glaxo India certainly had friends lobbying on their behalf against the proposed joint venture between the Indian government, the World Health Organisation and The United Nations International Children's Emergency Fund (later renamed the United Nations Children's Fund). The Ministry of Commerce and Industry would have preferred an association with a commercial enterprise. The Government plant, which was eventually constructed at Pimpri (it opened in 1955) and run by Hindustan Antibiotics Ltd, was described by Sir Maurice Hutton as 'a substantial and extravagantly built unit'. Its annual capacity was estimated at around 20 million mega, roughly equal to the total Indian requirement in 1954. Given the entry at around the same time into antibiotics filling by ICI and several other companies, Hutton judged that the filling capacity of commercial firms surpassed current market requirements and that an expanded government filling plant (part of the Pimpri development) might therefore create idle capacity in other commercial plants, including that of Glaxo. He concluded that it was necessary that even greater attention should be paid to expanding the sales of food products and especially of pharmaceuticals other than antibiotics.

In line with that decision, a new milk-drying factory was erected in the late 1950s at Aligarh, some eighty miles from Delhi. This investment was partly prompted by the withdrawal of Indian government import licences for milk power from Glaxo's Australian factory at Port Fairy. In its first season the Aligarh factory manufactured about 1,500 tons of milk powder, although some problems were experienced. Transport of milk from collecting points scattered over a radius of forty miles was difficult as roads were 'indescribably bad' and, as a result of a new cooperative scheme imposed by the government, initially the milk producers were not well-organised. More importantly, Glaxo India proceeded with their plans for fine chemical manufacture. Phases I and II of the project, working up vitamin A from an intermediate compound, were executed in the factory at Worli, while the purchase of a new site at Thana was being negotiated. The main problem, apart from import licences for capital goods and the purchase of the new site, was staff training. It was estimated that the new fine chemicals project would require thirty technical staff, including ten for research and development, and 100 plant operators. Although prior to this, the majority of the technical staff had received training in England, it was felt that training on this scale would have to be undertaken in India. Wilkins suggested that the Indian Company copy the training method in use in factories at home. It was generally felt that the operation of a dual purpose plant (see page 284) might present additional problems, and the production staff were anxious lest the management should make too much of the flexibility and interchangeability of the two processes in negotiations with the Indian government. One estimate was that a full change-over between the two operations could take three months.

Further problems were met during the pilot stages of the development. The Indian government were unwilling to allow royalty payments for processes which simply involved the working up of intermediate compounds, but Glaxo licensed the process for one of the intermediates, from DPI, a subsidiary of Kodak. Another problem was that the Roche process involved the coupling of two simple molecules, whereas the Glaxo process involved a final treatment of an already complex molecule, the latter carrying a disproportionately high rate of duty; this gave Roche a price advantage.

The Thana stage of the development was seen as a bulk sales project working on relatively low profit margins, funded from the company's cash holdings (around £1m), which would produce additional turnover of £500,000 when the new plant worked at full capacity. The plant was on a site of 37.5 acres, some twenty miles from Bombay, and installation was undertaken by the engineering staff of the Indian company with assistance from specialists seconded from Britain. Advice was liberally dispensed from Greenford. The production engineers issued warnings about the problems of scaling up processes, while Jephcott in turn advised that over-enthusiastic production engineers could get 'carried away with themselves'. The capital to cover the import of capital goods for the project from Britain was provided in the form of a loan repayable with 6 per cent interest. At the new plant all the more important corticosteroids (cortisone, hydrocortisone, prednisone, prednisolone and betamethasone) were completely synthesised from natural products. Glaxo were the first to make all these compounds in India from an imported intermediate in 1958 (hecogenin, derived from the juice of the sisal plant, from which synthesised cortisone was first made by Glaxo scientists in 1954 by a nineteen-stage chemical synthesis). Senna pods from South India were another Indian-grown material converted at the Thana factory into a laxative. Glaxo's vitamin A was also synthesised there by a process of converting lemon grass oil into beta-ionone, developed by

51 Vitamin production at the Thana factory.

Glaxo research workers in England: by 1962, Glaxo India were making over fifty tons of beta-ionone annually, a proportion of which was exported as surplus to India's requirements. The remainder of the vitamin A process, involving many difficult chemical reactions, culminating with the production of vitamin A palmitate and vitamin A acetate, was also carried out at Thana.

The Glaxo fine chemical factory at Thana, opened in 1962, was a landmark in the development of chemical manufacturing in India. With it, Glaxo's Indian subsidiary was assured of its place as the largest in the group: in terms of capital employed in 1962, Glaxo India was slightly larger than the Allen & Hanburys business and the profits it earned showed a better return to the group. Although the business environment in India was often depicted as hostile to foreign investment, it was in fact endeavouring, through a ramified, cautious and sometimes Kafkaesque bureaucracy, to meet different priorities. But within this environment Glaxo performed notably more successfully than many other British enterprises.

Pakistan

Following the partition of the Indian subcontinent, a re-appraisal of Glaxo's business interests in the newly created state of Pakistan was imperative. At a policy meeting held in 1948, Jephcott and Gwilt together laid the foundations of the new Pakistan operation. It was decided to create a new subsidiary, Glaxo Laboratories (Pakistan) Ltd, rather than to continue with a system of branch or agency agreements. More importantly, it was agreed to move the head office from Lahore, which had handled the bulk of the H. J. Foster business, to Karachi, the only port in West Pakistan and the capital of the new Dominion. From the outset it was seen that good relations with the Pakistan bureaucracy would be vital for the success of the subsidiary, especially if manufacturing were undertaken. That would involve applying for import licences for raw materials and lobbying for protective tariffs, both unattainable without personal interviews. The decision to transfer headquarters to Karachi was preceded by the extension of business in the area, following the acquisition of the premises of Foster's former agent, Messrs Ram & Co, in October 1947.

While Gwilt and Jephcott recognised the advantages which would accrue from an early commitment in the new Pakistan state, they were wary of the political and economic uncertainty, and agreed that 'the subscribed capital of the Company will be limited to the barest practicable minimum'.[18] An issued capital of £7,500 (Res 1 lakh) was considered to be ample for the Pakistan company to commence operations. This was also the maximum issue allowable without reference to the controller of Capital Issues, thereby avoiding bureaucratic entanglement.[19] The new company was incorporated as Glaxo Laboratories (Pakistan) Ltd, in 1948. Several executives such as the managing director, R. A. M. Henson and the sales director, W. J. Joy were drawn from Foster's established Pakistan operation. Business in East Pakistan was complicated not only by political instability, but also by its distance from Karachi and attendant transport dislocation. The existing Foster branch in Chittagong had previously been supplied by rail from the Calcutta branch, an arrangement which was impossible following partition. The only alternative was direct shipment to Chittagong by sea, but that was hampered by the fact that the port only had sufficient berthing space simultaneously to accommodate four ships. In other ways conditions in Chittagong were chaotic. Eventually the Pakistan company arranged with the Assam-Bengal Railway Cooperative Society for the Chittagong office to handle propaganda and clerical work, while the railway company handled the storing and distribution of goods shipped through the port.

Another problem at the beginning was the remittance of profits to the British parent company. The Pakistan subsidiary was expected to produce an annual turnover of £150,000 with new profits of about £24,000. Aside from the complexities of exchange controls, punitive rates of tax were threatened on any dividend distribution of profit as a result of the low capital invested (the dividend ratio was approximately 300 per cent). It was impracticable to raise invoice prices to Pakistan, as any disparity between prices charged to the Indian and Pakistan companies for identical goods would have invited hostile attention. The most attractive solution proved to be a combined trademark and consultancy agreement based on a percentage of gross turnover, the model for which was the agreement signed between CIBA and their Indian subsidiary. The actual percentage involved, however, was disputed by the Pakistan authorities, who insisted that the rate of 10 per cent on sales sought as royalty for consultancy and trademarks was not permissible unless the company actually manufactured in Pakistan. In all matters regarding remittance of profits, as Glaxo's legal advisers pointed out, 'The danger to a company trading abroad is that where any part of the control of the business is exercised by a person in the UK, the business can be treated as carried on in the UK and therefore liable to UK taxation.'[20]

By the end of the first fifteen-months trading period the finances of the Pakistan company were causing concern. The net trading profit on sales was inadequate to cover royalty payments and overheads and extra capital was required to fund sales expansion, as stock levels needed to be higher. The board of the parent company considered the capital requirements of the Pakistan subsidiary in July 1949. The original authorised capital had been £375,000 (50 lakhs), with £7,500 subscribed. The parent company later subscribed a further £67,500 (£33,750 paid). The Indian company had made a loan of £86,250 to Glaxo Laboratories Pakistan, 'as a means of employing their surplus funds' and £30,000 remained pending as unremitted profits and consultancy fees.[21] The parent company were reluctant to recommend an increase in the capitalisation of the Pakistan subsidiary, and London did not provide funds even indirectly by deferred payments for goods shipped.

The advantages of beginning local manufacture, initially as a packing operation, were integral to any decision on capitalisation. It was clear that the inauguration of local production would be officially approved, and remove problems over trademarks and consultancy fees. It was also anticipated that considerable savings on customs duty would be made; for instance, milk powder in tins was assessed for duty at 45 per cent whereas imports of bulk milk powder were only subject to 30 per cent. However, such a scheme required the participation of local shareholders, preferably with a large number of local investors each holding a small number of shares so as to preclude the possibility of cohesive minority action coercing the British parent company. Unfortunately the profit figures and balance sheets had little prospect of attracting investment from small shareholders until the factory, for which the money from the issue was required, became operational. In addition, Jephcott foresaw a managerial problem associated with the development of manufacturing in Pakistan. He doubted whether Glaxo's senior managers in Pakistan 'understand what production . . . is all about'.[22]

It was eventually agreed that, even if the issue was heavily undersubscribed, the Pakistan company at least would be able to show that it had tried to interest local investors. In late 1950, after protracted negotiations, the Pakistan government approved the subsidiary's application to increase its issued capital from £7,500 to £375,000 on condition that, in accordance with the government's industrial programme, there was 30 per cent local participation. Glaxo Laboratories accepted this in principle, but wanted to defer it because they wished to secure the maximum number of Pakistan shareholders, 'rather than to have one or two financial interests with, possibly, political axes to grind', and felt that in order to attract a wide range of investors, 'any local issue had best be deferred until the factory had been erected and there was visual evidence of the Company's activities'.

The Pakistan finance department also agreed that the subsidiary company could pay its British parent for the use of trademarks and for technical services in respect of goods manufactured in Pakistan but, while they accepted the company's proposal of 2 per cent of turnover for trademarks, they rejected 5 per cent for research and technical services, asking for the assessment of such service *pro rata* to world turnover. The real 'difficulty', according to Jephcott after his visit in 1950, 'was that of the official fearing to make a settlement lest he lay himself open to criticism', but he felt that the finance department's attitude established 'a very friendly relationship and mutual understanding of our respective difficulties'. He expected that outstanding issues would 'be settled with reasonable promptitude and with as much consideration for use as the circumstances permit'.[23]

The issue was finally made, after much concern over the granting of vital import licences, in 1953, with a 30 per cent local shareholding: for the first time a Glaxo subsidiary became a public company. Jephcott, however, was unenthusiastic: indeed he was privately 'sorry to learn of the success of the Pakistan issue', predicting that 'Henson and the Pakistanis will need to learn the hard facts of business before they are much older'.[24] Palmer was equally apprehensive, cautioning Henson of 'the dangers of the present position, for the continued absence of any licences to import milk foods and antibiotics may well imperil profitability for the balance of this year, and have some rather curious repercussions on the Karachi share market where, even before allotment letters have been posted, there seems to have been some misguided activity in the new security we are about to issue'.[25]

By 1951 Glaxo Laboratories Pakistan Ltd employed twelve sales represen-

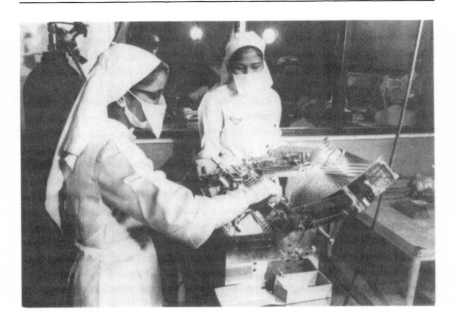

52 Antibiotic filling at the Karachi factory.

tatives in East and West Pakistan. Penicillin had become by far the biggest-selling product for the Pakistan company, representing 34 per cent of all sales. In marketing the drug in Pakistan, the company concentrated its efforts on the sale of crystalline penicillin, with the emphasis on massive dosage techniques, whereas many of the American competitors concentrated instead on preparations with prolonged action. Marketing was vulnerable to fads in medical practice: 'The visit of Sir Alexander Fleming recently was of great interest to medical practitioners throughout W. Pakistan and in his lectures he provided authoritative support for our massive dosage technique and also referred to the new penicillin Estopen which we will be marketing shortly.'[26]

Streptomycin was scarce partly because of increased demand for Glaxo material from the National Health Service in Britain, but more significantly because of the introduction of export licences in the United States for sulpha drugs and antibiotics as a result of the Korean war and the stockpiling of essential drugs. In Pakistan only certain chemists were authorised to hold stocks of streptomycin, while the shortages gave rise to 'quite substantial quantities of dihydro-streptomycin ... being smuggled across the border from India'.[27]

Sales representatives were able to supply vital information on the complexities of local market conditions. One commented in 1951 that 'most of the competition for ostocalcium [a Glaxo preparation] comes from our own preparation Caldeferrum'.[28] Doctors' demands for a wide diversity of pack sizes could not always be satisfied as the company gradually eliminated uneconomic pack sizes and concentrated on only a few for each item. Among vitamin products 'sales of Berin (vitamin B_{12}) solution are much better than tablet sales in East Pakistan because doctors there are very injection-minded'.[29] The East Pakistan representatives were unanimous that there was a substantial household demand for their products, while all the company's salesmen united to plead for more vivid advertising material to vie with the promotional methods of companies like Lederle or Parke Davis. The sales representatives were tightly controlled, with orders to adhere to a set interview devised by Henson.

With the successful raising of extra capital, Glaxo Pakistan was well placed to erect a factory to meet the increased demand. This, however, required further political mediation. Despite the fact that one government department could sanction the raising of capital for a development programme, another could block the scheme from another direction. Henson described the situation as 'a sort of hothouse with the Government anxious to industrialise at all costs and various parties trying to exploit the situation by negotiating monopolies, etc'.[30] The Pakistan government soon found that, without locally available raw materials, the inauguration of industries was costly, and that a measure of tariff protection was desirable where production costs were high. The Pakistanis were unable to command the foreign exchange often required for raw materials and new industries, with the imported raw material often more expensive than imported finished products. As in India, 'one shadow hanging over the whole of the future operations of the Pakistan company was the possibility of a government penicillin factory which would close the Pakistan market to imports of bulk penicillin and effectively annex any established bottling plants'.[31]

The Pakistan Industrial Development Corporation (PIDC) had funds for the joint government penicillin scheme with other contributions from the World Health Organisation and UNICEF. Glaxo Pakistan had already clashed with the PIDC when the latter appropriated the site for the proposed Karachi factory so as to erect a shipyard. Furthermore, the PIDC enjoyed links with other pharmaceutical companies such as the Union Chimique Belge and Heydens. The official justification for building a penicillin plant was to save foreign exchange on antibiotics, but prestige was an almost equally important motive. Once India was committed to a penicillin plant in the guise of the Pimpri project (see page 286), there was compelling pressure for Pakistan to follow suit. The aim of the United Nations was to establish a plant producing the simplest antibiotics which would not compete with commercial enterprise.

Eventually, UNICEF announced an aid programme for Pakistan, including £207,000 ($577,000) for a penicillin fermentation and bottling plant. This grant, a setback for Glaxo Pakistan, was approved despite lobbying by pharmaceutical industrialists at the United Nations against such schemes. The Pakistan company, however, determined to collaborate with the govenment factory and felt assured of its weight as the main foreign pharmaceutical company established in Pakistan. Meanwhile the delay before the government factory became operational left opportunities for the bottling of antibiotics. The manufacturing programme was put into operation as soon as the necessary 'permissions' had been obtained. In the light of the 'complete bogging down' of the government project by mid 1955, without even a site being chosen, Henson felt confident enough to carry the programme through to the second stage, proceeding with applications to manufacture injections, tablets and ointments, and even recommend expansion to include a light chemical plant.[32]

The manufacturing premises (the factory and the new laboratories) were opened at Karachi in 1955. As planned, these included provision for the packing of infant and other foods, the manufacture of certain pharmaceuticals and the vialling of antibiotics. This rapid expansion prompted doubts from London about the change in function from sales and distribution to packing and manufacture. On the subject of cost information from the Pakistan company, at least one executive in London had 'the unhappy impression' that his Pakistan colleagues 'are approaching their accounting difficulties in a somewhat cavalier and light-hearted fashion ... there is a vast difference between a purely selling agency and a production cum selling organisation'.[33] As for the light chemical plant, London head office was singularly unenthusiastic. Both Jephcott and Palmer were reluctant to become involved because of the dependence of such a scheme on imported raw materials and, after discussion, it was concluded that a light chemical plant would represent no more than a costly piece of 'flag flying' in the circumstances.[34]

After the Karachi factory had begun production, Henson turned his attention to the East Pakistan market, and specifically to the possibility of starting local secondary production. He envisaged replacing existing rented premises in Chittagong with a small factory where the filling and packing of milk foods and glucose could be undertaken. East Pakistan already annually accounted for 100–125 tons of milk foods and 300 tons of glucose, rather more than half the totals for Pakistan as a whole, and Henson believed he would get government permission to develop a factory in the East. Jephcott agreed to Henson's idea in principle: 'I get the impression that cash in the till is burning a bit of a hole in Henson's pocket, but I do not mean to imply from this that I in any way depart from my agreement earlier expressed that we should provide manufacturing facilities in East Pakistan.'[35] In addition there were also justified anxieties that Pfizer and Dumex would jointly build a factory in East Pakistan. Later presenting the case for expansion to the London Board, Jephcott supported Henson: 'For a variety of reasons – cost of freight, duplication of stocks and provincial government pressure – we are satisfied that there is justification for planning ... a factory ... in Chittagong.'[36]

The estimated investment involved was 40 lakhs. The provincial government pressure referred to by Jephcott concerned the use of East Pakistan's foreign exchange allocation to pay for the raw materials required by industries in West Pakistan, which would then manufacture goods for East Pakistan. The capacity of the plant planned by Henson was based on doubling or tripling the normal demand in East Pakistan, a rough-and-ready method of reckoning which caused anxiety among the accountants at Greenford. The plans to develop facilities in East Pakistan formed just one aspect of the company's growth in the late 1950s. Partly as a result of pressure from government to manufacture in order to effect foreign exchange savings, partly also as a result of the 'cash in the till', which Jephcott estimated at £225,000, the Pakistan company scrutinised two other investment possibilities.

The first of these was a project for the primary production of milk powder. It seemed likely that the government might impose tariffs on imported milk powder as a step towards the prohibition of all imports if milk drying was established in East Pakistan. Henson mirrored official attitudes in looking enviously at the Indian company, which was investigating the possibility of replacing Australian powder imports. In consultation with a British expert, the Renala district of the Punjab was chosen as the most suitable site for a milk collecting and drying operation. The estimated cost of a plant annually producing 600 tons of powder, saving 3.6d per lb on Australian imports and yielding extra profit of £20,000, was £150,000.

The second scheme was to provide locally manufactured glucose. Two starch producers manufactured for the Pakistan market. Glaxo Laboratories had the options of entering a joint venture with the stronger of the two, Rafhan Starch, or taking over the weaker company, Zeb Corn Products, or using its own expertise to develop a project without local collaborators. At this stage Jephcott wrote: 'I am still of the same opinion that sooner or later Pakistan must refuse to issue import licences [for dextrose], partly on grounds of non-essentiality and partly on grounds of potential local production and I am gravely disturbed at the patent inability of Henson to make up his mind to have a policy on the alternatives.'[37] Zeb Corn was

53 Transport of Glaxo products in Pakistan had to rely on age old methods.

dismissed following investigation which revealed 'such a low rate of technical competence and such a low degree of commercial integrity'.[38] Rafhan Starch were keen to locate a new glucose plant at their site at Sargodha, 100 miles north-west of Renala, so eventually the independent development was chosen, having considered costs, likely political developments and the chances of expanding sales of by-products; two saleable by-products of the glucose process were identified, hydrol (to tanneries and a new rayon factory being built under five-year plan) and corn steep liquor (ironically to the government penicillin factory at Daudkhel). This investment was estimated at £225,000.

It was initially intended to fund this expansion by means of a 'one-for-two' rights issue, increasing the issued capital from £787,500 to £1,181,250, with the balance to be found by the Pakistan company out of its retained profits. However, as a result of pressure from the Pakistan government to undertake more local manufacture of a basic type, the company was forced to include plans for the production of vitamin A, Farex and Stibatin. Several of the existing projects were scaled up as a result of increasing demand, including the milk powder plant and the glucose plant. The result was that by the time the financial aspects of the scheme reached the main board in

1961 the rights issue required to fund the development was proposed as a one-for-one issue to raise a total of £1,320,000 and on that basis the issue was successfully made.[39] Despite the considerable misgivings, Glaxo's operations in Pakistan had expanded rapidly. Fourteen years after its formation, the capital employed gave Pakistan second place among Glaxo's overseas subsidiaries.

In the Indian subcontinent, despite the end of the Raj, over-optimistic predictions from some advisers and the labyrinthine complexities of political regulation, national economic planning and exchange controls, Glaxo, relative to most British companies, flourished.

13

The Commonwealth II: Australia and New Zealand

In both Australia and New Zealand Glaxo's presence had been long established, but the size and strength of the operations varied. Although the subsidiary in Australia grew and by the end of the period it was, in terms of capital employed, the third largest of Glaxo's overseas subsidiaries, its profitability did not rank commensurately. New Zealand, although it occupied a special place in the affections of the parent company, came to represent, not surprisingly, a very small market in the 1950s and 1960s for Glaxo worldwide.

Australia

The immediate post-war period presented many problems in Australia. The subsidiary's scattered premises across Melbourne and at Port Fairy were inconveniently laid out and inadequate for business expansion. Both the Australian and New Zealand governments subsidised milk production for dried powder so that, for example, in 1946, the cost per ton of milk powder delivered at Greenford was £88 from Australia, £97 from New Zealand and £157 from Britain. The threat of the gradual ending of these subsidies had disturbing implications for the group's costs. For the pharmaceutical side, additional accommodation was recognised as imperative for the proper expansion of the penicillin business, but Rupert Pearce, sent out in the late 1930s to run the Australian company, found the utmost difficulty in solving the problem.

During the war Australian penicillin production had begun by a government-owned institution, Commonwealth Serum Laboratories (CSL). Until 1948 CSL's production was confined to surface culture and was dislocated by difficulties with labour and materials, but it dropped its prices sharply with the advent of Glaxo's competition. As the import duty of 25 per cent which Glaxo had to pay on penicillin did not apply to bulk, the company decided in 1947 to create facilities to sub-divide and pack in Australia as

298

quickly as possible. By early 1950, however, CSL presented serious competition. Glaxo's estimates suggested that in 1951 its productive capacity would be sufficient to supply between 60 per cent and 80 per cent of Australia's current penicillin usage, although the company was told by the Director General of Health in Canberra that CSL was in fact supplying only 25 per cent or 30 per cent. It was expected that CSL would continue to meet all Glaxo's price reductions whatever the cost to itself so long as it had the support of the Government. Predictably there was official pressure to give preference to local producers. The Health Department advised some hospitals to direct at least half their penicillin business to CSL, arguing that British supplies would be immediately discontinued in the event of war and that Australia would then have to rely entirely on CSL's output capacity.[1] Glaxo felt that the only way for them to meet these arguments, based on national security rather than commercial considerations, was by holding bulk stores of crystalline penicillin in Australia as an insurance against a failure of supply during an international emergency. Later in 1950 Greenford heard that CSL had approached Merck for assistance in undertaking the production of streptomycin in addition to the limited quantities of penicillin which CSL was already producing. This news determined Jephcott to visit Australia and New Zealand as well as India, Pakistan and Canada, 'to expedite action to make the various subsidiary companies, particularly Australia, self-sufficient at least for purely pharmaceutical operations'.[2]

The detailed report which Jephcott submitted to his co-directors after his return to London was a major strategic statement. He found Australia characterised by marked inflation accompanied by an acute shortage of labour, endemic strikes with concomitant cuts in fuel and power and, superimposed upon the whole, a rapidly mounting re-armament programme. The combination of all these influences made industrial development very difficult, unless firmly supported by a sponsoring authority as an essential part of the re-armament programme or the development of the country's primary services. The Ministry of National Development would not support any Glaxo Laboratories project using critically short building materials when, in their opinion, CSL's existing facilities were adequate to meet anticipated demand. The Ministry exercised an over-riding control over development projects but, according to Jephcott, its activities were necessarily mainly negative, since the number of industrial development projects far exceeded available national resources. As in South Africa (see chapter 14), Glaxo Australia was confronted with the quandary of a small domestic market from which it would be hard to support the costs of modernisation or extensions; but the high level of production costs in Australia and the notoriously expensive and unreliable shipping costs made it impossible to rely upon profits from export. The Australian directors' wish to diversify or expand also had to contend with Jephcott's well-founded caution about capital expenditure.

There were problems, too, with the proprietary infant foods. Glaxo powder, in common with other similar products, was subject to price control at a time of steadily rising production costs. In consequence, the gross margin of profit, after providing for interstate carriage, but before making any allowance for administrative expenses or selling costs, fell to under 3 per cent. As there was a long-established and widespread demand for Glaxo, it was judged unwise to discontinue its sale in order to make additional milk powder available for more profitable export business. Sales of Farex, however, were at a more profitable and satisfactory level, although new competition had appeared from the Australian plant of Cow & Gate. Sales of Farex rose from 1,015,065 lbs in 1950, representing 5.32 sales per new Australian live births, to 1,094,406 lbs in 1953 (5.41 per birth), with only a mild check in growth caused by the import restrictions of 1952 (see page 303).

Australia was, except for one or two relatively simple lines (Minadex, Adexolin Liquid, Ostomalt), wholly dependent upon the supply of packed pharmaceuticals from Britain. Increasingly since 1945 this had resulted in difficulties, either because Greenford could not supply orders promptly or because of the strikes and other eccentricities of the Australian dock workers. As a result, the subsidiary company often laboured under a difficult and unpredictable stock position, which was aggravated by the introduction of a free medicine scheme. At first, the products which might be obtained free were restricted to the so-called life-saving drugs including penicillin, streptomycin and insulin. Subsequently, additions were made at intervals to the list; on every occasion that a product was added there followed a sharp upswing in demand for it. This, superimposed upon a limited and unpredictable stock position, made it difficult if not impossible to deal with orders promptly, while the consequent need to ration customers demoralised the sales promotion staff. In some instances doctors refused to order a Glaxo product because of the inability of chemists to fill the prescription. In the case of vitamin B_{12} preparations the position was even more regrettable, as certain local manufacturers imported B_{12} in bulk from the USA and took the business which properly should have been Glaxo's. With Greenford's cooperation steps were taken to deal with this problem but at a considerable cost in air-freight.

Sales of penicillin progressed rapidly in 1950–1951, but streptomycin's position was less satisfactory. As soon as supplies were available for export, limited quantities were sent to Australia in common with other markets. At the time when Glaxo's production of streptomycin was increasing, the Australian Government, as part of a dollar-saving effort undertaken at the request of the British Treasury, enquired whether Glaxo could supply the whole of Australia's streptomycin requirements, in which event they would no longer issue licences for the import of American material. They received Glaxo's assurances and the use of streptomycin in Australia, as in Britain, became more widespread. Numerous complaints then ensued about the inadequacy of supplies; representations were made to the Ministry of Health, mainly by those who had previously imported the American material, that licences for the import of US material should be resumed. There was some justice in these complaints of inadequate quantities. The current monthly consumption in Britain was about 10 kg per million of population: the amount allocated by Glaxo to Australia represented under 4 kg per month per million of population. In response to this criticism, Glaxo increased the issue to Australia by 50 per cent, in part by drawing on local stocks to a somewhat dangerous extent, in part by shipment of additional supplies from Britain. These latter shipments were only possible by cutting supplies to other markets, but this was felt to be necessary, given the undertaking to the Australian government. Allocation of streptomycin supplies to Australia was given a high priority by Glaxo during 1951.

To remedy the situation, Jephcott, while in Australia in 1951, discussed Glaxo's proposals for an Australian antibiotics factory with two successive Ministers for National Development, Richard (later Lord) Casey, and Sir William Spooner, as well as with the Minister for Health, Sir Earle Page, the Director-General of Health, and the Army's Director of Medical Services. All except the soldier initially couched their replies in guarded or even hostile terms. Both Ministers for National Development faced proposals for industrial development far in excess of Australia's resources and, with the international tension generated by the Korean War, they gave priority to re-armament, following advice received from various Ministers, including the Equipment Control Committee, a war-time council which had just been reinstituted. In addition, both the Ministries of Health and National Development refused to countenance any proposal by Glaxo 'to widen the activities and enhance the industrial status of our Australian subsidiary by undertaking the production of antibiotics in that country', if that entailed penicillin production, 'because it was considered likely to prejudice the Commonwealth Serum Laboratories'. As Jephcott concluded, after several interviews:

Their attitude was clear. They would give no encouragement, indeed would react most unfavourably, to any proposal for erecting another penicillin plant. On the other hand they would favour the production of other antibiotics (streptomycin a little regretfully, since CSL had contemplated its manufacture) and especially of other essential medicinal substances not at present manufactured in Australia.[1]

Jephcott met the Deputy Director of the CSL during his visit of 1951, but the latter was unwilling to give any indication either of the capacity of the CSL plant or of the extent of its operations. Jephcott suspected that schemes had been proposed and indeed that some were already afoot, for increasing CSL's capacity. Apart from the desire of those responsible for CSL's operations to expand their activities to the maximum, the Minister of Health and the Director-General of Health both feared that the opening of a major new plant might result in price competition adversely affecting CSL's operations.

In 1951 with Jephcott's report before them, the London parent company concluded 'that it would be foolhardy to proceed with the proposed antibiotic plant'. In the course of time it swerved from this decision, but for the time being it was rightly convinced that 'to carry out this plan in the teeth of opposition would be to run a grave risk not only of doing harm to our business in Australia but also of incurring heavy capital expenditure in setting up a plant that might not be able to operate owing to the shortages of desirable raw materials and the expansion of the CSL penicillin plant'.[4] Jephcott wrote of his Australian visit in 1951, 'one cannot fail to be impressed with the magnitude of economic, labour and other problems which face the country [but] the resources and potentialities for the future are no less impressive. To a very great extent indeed Australia's problems could be solved were there the preparedness on the part of labour to work whole-heartedly for the future of the country rather than endeavour to secure the maximum immediate benefit for itself.' So far as Glaxo Laboratories were concerned, he saw considerable opportunity for expansion if only the necessary facilities for local production, such as had already been provided in India and New Zealand, were available. The company's organisation needed strengthening, he felt, particularly on the technical and production sides. During and since the war the chemical industry generally in Australia had progressed swiftly, and Glaxo had 'considerable leeway to make up under conditions which are even less favourable than those which existed in the immediate post-war period'. This, of course, required large capital expenditure of uncertain remunerative capacity, at least in the short term, as had been Glaxo's recent experience in Britain. Virtually all Glaxo's products were subject to price control, and it was likely that these controls would be even more widely and severely imposed so that the case for holding wage levels could be established. As a result Glaxo would require a substantial expansion of business if it was to secure a favourable return on investment.

In the difficult conditions prevailing in Australia in the 1950s, 'the inability of management to reach prompt decisions upon what should be done and vigorously to give effect to them' was, in Jephcott's view, partly to blame for the problems of the subsidiary:

the present disjointed nature of the Melbourne organisation is a serious weakness, resulting in delays, waste of time and a degree of general inefficiency ... Pearce is preoccupied with day-to-day affairs and, indeed, is himself often uncertain what should be done. The absence of a senior officer technically competent and with initiative, is all too obvious.[5]

There is no doubt that in his early days at Melbourne, Pearce had imposed thoroughly needed order and routine on the Glaxo business in Australia, and in many respects he was a man of considerable energy. But by the late 1940s he had realised that the technological advances in the business had outstripped his understanding, and although this in itself need not have been an insuperable disadvantage, combined with other factors it became a major obstacle. Immensely pro-British and patriotic, in the manner of certain Australians in the heyday of the conservative politician, Sir Robert Menzies (1949–1966), Pearce had some highly Australian habits. He arrived at his office early, and worked with furious intensity in the mornings, but he was known for his long and festive lunches, which were even the subject of a famous joke in a satirical newspaper. Despite being a man with a decisive manner, he was strangely indecisive in business, and there was a tendency for his decisions to be erratic. Dedicated in his commitment, there is no doubt that he found his job an increasing strain in the 1950s, and that both he personally, and some of his colleagues, felt happier when he retired in 1958. There were other weaknesses among the Melbourne board of directors. A discussion with its chairman in 1951 left Jephcott 'in no doubt that he hadn't the least idea of what our business was all about'.[6] These organisational weaknesses persisted long after the death or retirement of the individuals specified.

In 1952 the Australian government abruptly placed very severe tariff restrictions on the import of all types of goods from the sterling area. The Australian trade balance had fallen so out of alignment that some such action had been expected by Glaxo, but no-one imagined that such severe restrictions would be imposed almost overnight. The Customs Department, which had never been very efficient, was hurled into chaos by the Cabinet's crude decision to put an arbitrary restriction on practically all classes of goods, regardless of whether duty was payable or not. Goods that had previously been admitted free of duty into Australia were subject to a 40 per cent reduction on the 1950–1951 import figure. An 80 per cent cut of future imports was imposed on dutiable goods, on the fallacious principle that a customs duty already existed because similar goods were made locally, and that local manufacturing capacity would therefore be sufficient to meet all

54 R. C. Pearce, Managing Director of the Australian company arriving in London in May 1952 for the Overseas Executives' Conference.

demands, even if the imported article was reduced by 80 per cent. A further category of restrictions on the import of plant had far-reaching implications for Glaxo in Australia.

Pearce's initial reaction was that these controls were so ill-conceived as to be unenforceable for any length of time. The controls were directed against imports from within the sterling area, and made no effort to reduce imports of dollar goods. There was widespread astonishment that life-saving drugs like penicillin featured in the restrictions. Pearce's greatest concern was for the large number of imported materials required to complete Glaxo's new manufacturing and packing building at Villiers Street in Melbourne.[7] Other difficulties soon followed. It became clear that Australian government policy entailed total restriction of Glaxo products unless substitutes were manufactured in Australia and imported stocks were inadequate to ensure continuity of supply. In May, when Pearce visited England for discussions with Jephcott, Glaxo was officially told that it would not receive a penicillin import licence for either bulk or vialled penicillin because CSL had stocks to meet at least six months of Australian needs. In effect, Glaxo was precluded from importing practically all its packed products, and almost all of the ingredients for its limited range of locally packed products. Pearce still could not credit that these restrictions would continue beyond October 1952, by which time Australia would be exporting its primary produce. He doubted that ships would go out empty to collect this cargo, especially as the controls were seriously depleting government revenue.

These grim short-term prospects under the system of import licensing convinced Pearce that Glaxo's future in Australia lay in direct distribution. The wholesale distributors in Australia were becoming more and more Glaxo's competitors, and discounts to wholesalers were costing the Australian company about £75,000 a year. As a result of the 1952 tariff and his discussions with Pearce, Jephcott laid down new principles that, in view of the altered conditions in Australia, Glaxo should try to ensure economical operation, not only in fermentation but in the manufacture of other products not yet available in Australia, using the same individuals and, whenever possible, the same equipment. Profits would remain doubtful until the volume of production was increased, and profitability was seen as a long-term aim over the wide range of products contemplated.

It was agreed to develop an antibiotic production unit at Port Fairy to provide for the manufacture from primary raw materials of penicillin, streptomycin and vitamin B_{12}, and to provide facilities for local small-scale manufacture of liver extracts and radiologicals. From the outset it was realised that the Australian antibiotic unit's costs would not compete with those of the British factories. But, as Jephcott acknowledged, 'Unless we take prompt steps to establish local manufactures, we stand little chance of recovering our liberty of action within this sphere, or of enjoying adequate margins of profit with which to carry out further developments.'[8]

A particular hurdle was the possibility that the Australian Capital Issues Board would reject the Australian company's application for a capital increase, especially so far as that was to be used to finance the fermentation plant (which required a capital investment of £250,000). The Australian company had net profits before taxation and royalties of £100,000 for 1951–1952 (on a capital of £350,000), and in the event, after a delay, the Issues Committee permitted an increase of capital by £500,000.[9] As a result of this development, Glaxo changed its marketing approach in 1954. While continuing to recommend crystalline penicillin as the best material to use, representatives also brought Mylipen to the fore in an attempt to take a larger share of the aqueous procaine penicillin business.

Extensions to the Port Fairy factory, in order to undertake antibiotic production, were completed in 1954, after delays due to changes made by the company in the plans, and in the import of plant and machinery. Despite the specialists sent out from Ulverston to fill key managerial, production and engineering posts, technical problems persisted until the official opening of the fermentation facilities by Jephcott in March 1956. After that visit, Jephcott reported that he was 'far from happy' with the management there.

At the present time I do not think we could make changes which would improve it, but its weaknesses are very apparent. Although Pearce has improved a little, he still continues fearful of allowing others more knowledgeable than himself to have freedom within appropriate spheres lest, by so doing, he shall diminish his own authority. In consequence, decisions are delayed and a degree of procrastination takes place which at times is quite serious.

He praised the work at Port Fairy, but complained that an attempt to 'save a few coppers on the production side at the Welss Street Factory' had produced 'a quantity of such low-grade dextrose containing sufficient copper to cause the rapid rancidity of Glaxo on the Australian market'. He found, moreover, 'no person of adequate weight and knowledge at Port Fairy with any background in milk drying' so that they were in 'danger of the kind of slip-up which would have been excusable 35 years ago and is quite inexcusable today'. Jephcott feared that recent quality problems combined with the

steadily falling demand for Glaxo in Australia . . . may well sound the death-knell of the product, and whilst it was not a highly profitable part of our business, it did make substantial contributions to their overheads, which they certainly cannot afford to lose. I suspect with milk powder we shall have to start all over again in Australia with the introduction of Ostermilk. The mean cheeseparing attitudes which were perhaps unavoidable in the early thirties, and [with] which Pearce was much associated . . . are still to be observed.[10]

His analysis continued in a critical vein:

There is no doubt at all in my mind but that a substantial part of the losses which were incurred between July and September last could have been avoided if there had been management of the right calibre. Fermentation was pressed forward at a time and under conditions when wiser heads would have said – wait, we must get things right before we add to the expense of putting ever-increasing quantities of raw materials virtually down the drain. Out of our experience at Port Fairy we have certainly learnt that whenever overseas we propose to establish any substantial new manufacture which is likely to give rise to problems, not only of a technical nature, but of management outside the scope of the local officers, it is imperative that in these early stages we should have on the spot someone of real management capacity such as certainly did not exist in Australia.[11]

There were further extensions to the Port Fairy factory in the late 1950s, to expand streptomycin production. They were however attended by similar technical problems and the unfavourable reports made by visiting UK personnel on the Australian production and organisation at the time were resented by the Australians. Pearce wrote to Palmer in 'waspish tones'[12] over the scathing report delivered on the Port Fairy factory, feeling that 'two or three of the people that work in this country and who had experience of Ulverston and Barnard Castle, say that ... they could write an equally scathing report on your two factories'. Despite these criticisms the report had acknowledged the difficulties:

our people out there have been doing a difficult job under, what I consider to be in many cases, unnecessarily difficult conditions. They are willing, tremendously enthusiastic and as hard working as people are here, but all their efforts seem to be leading them deeper into the mire and unfortunately there does not at the moment appear to be any sign that the way ahead is any easier ... the Company has to face the fact that although the Port Fairy factory is of an uneconomic size so far as fermentation is concerned, we can, if we do not manage affairs properly, lose more money than is necessary. If ever there was a case for maximum plant efficiency, it is at Port Fairy.[13]

However, Pearce generally accepted specific criticisms mentioned in the reports.[14]

When Griff Hunt, Pearce's heir-apparent, visited Greenford in 1957 the possibility of expanding the range of antibiotics produced at Port Fairy was discussed.[15] He wanted to diversify into penicillin both in order to achieve fuller use of the fermentation facilities and to compete with CSL which held the greater part of this growing market. The latter were also producing Penicillin V, flouting the patents held by Eli Lilly, Distillers and Lovens. Glaxo had signed a licensing agreement with Distillers, however, which precluded manufacture by subsidiary companies. In discussion with Distillers, Palmer sought to reverse this decision, by pointing out that Distillers' best hope of recovering any royalty payment from Penicillin V sold in the Dominion would be to licence the production by Glaxo Australia at a similar rate paid by the parent company (a maximum of 7.5 per cent off sales to the three key patent holders).[16] Pending a decision of Distillers, which was also trying to exert pressure on the Australian Health Department to extract payment from Commonwealth Serum Laboratories, the Australian com-

55 Port Fairy, the fermentation plant in the 1960s.

pany tried for import licences for British-produced Penicillin V. Negotiations assumed new importance following the inclusion of the drug on the Free Medicine list early in 1958. The Australian company were also lobbying, in 1958, for an anti-dumping tariff on penicillin, and explored diversification in fermentation products.[17] Inconclusive talks were held with Bristol Laboratories for the production of Tetracycline in Australia; similarly, collaboration with Pfizer and Lederle on Terramycin and Aureomycin, suggested by the Australian company, came to nothing.[18]

Eventually, the political persistence of Pearce and Hunt was rewarded and a measure of protection granted by the Tariff Commission 'after the most strenuous efforts on Mr Hunt's part, both before the Commission itself and its associated smaller body'.[19] Even greater benefit arose from a rationalisation agreement with the other protected Australian manufacturer, CSL, whereby the company, now known as Glaxo-Allenbury, concentrated on Penicillin G and streptomycin and the Government-owned company on Penicillin B. Together with a redesigning of the plant at Port Fairy these moves strengthened the position of Glaxo in Australia and, after the losses made in 1961–1962 which amounted to £A 88,078, in 1962–1963 the subsidiary made a small profit of £A 7,035.

In their technical, marketing and head office management personnel, the Australian subsidiary contained individuals of considerable enterprise and imagination, of which the feat of commissioning an antibiotic plant at Port Fairy was only one example. But the political environment within which the subsidiary operated was inconsistent and unreasonable, adjectives equally applicable to the senior long-term direction from the Melbourne offices. Given the talent of the employees, and notwithstanding the wider obstacles of the market, the performance of the subsidiary disappointed the expectations of the parent company.

New Zealand

Both under Jephcott and his successors the Palmerston North company kept a special place in the group, which remained mindful of its historical origins, but the small population of New Zealand meant that it was a comparatively insignificant market for pharmaceuticals. For most of the 1950s and 1960s the local manager was a former Greenford detail man, Roy Stagg, who ran the company with considerable individuality. Shrewd, intelligent and dedicated, Stagg was a flamboyant man, with a mischievous streak and a taste for unpredictable or paradoxical behaviour. He relied a good deal on personal hunch, both in selecting subordinates and in taking decisions, and although some of his hunches were inspired, he was unrepentant about those which were not. His self-confidence made him unpopular in his early years in New Zealand, although his charm tended to disarm his critics.

The Palmerston North company was lively, if volatile, under his stewardship, and his behaviour was watched from London with 'incredulity but tolerance'.[20] Jephcott in 1960 described Stagg as 'a very complete individualist' who had failed 'to knot our New Zealand staff together as a team', but relished being surrounded by a 'weird mob'.[21] Griff Hunt, the Australian managing director, similarly commented of Stagg, 'his executives are an odd assortment, but in the main . . . capable. The younger ones are enthusiastic and ambitious, and being so, probably get in one another's hair occasionally'. The factory and office at Palmerston North in the 1960s resembled Greenford 'in the immediate post-war period . . . everyone felt that the Company was going places and that it was quite a lively show'.[22]

In the early 1950s, Glaxo in New Zealand, with its milk powder production and new offices and factory (built in 1947) at Palmerston North, represented the best facilities the company had overseas for the preparation and packaging of foods and pharmaceuticals. The picture reflected by New Zealand, however, was one which was becoming increasingly familiar. Despite the turnover figure for the first six months of 1951 showing an increase of 18 per cent over the previous year, the net trading profit, before tax, had diminished by 7.7 per cent.[23] The reasons were manifold, not least of which was the margin of profit on food slowly and steadily diminishing, as the rising cost of labour was added to the manufacturing costs. The cost of milk powder was troubled by currency fluctuations. When New Zealand decided to revalue in 1948 to bring its currency up to parity with sterling, the increase was a colossal 25 per cent. Repercussions of the change on business generally were expected to be immediate and in certain cases severe, notably on the price of milk powder. In 1947–1948 the average price (fob NZ) of powder received by Glaxo UK from New Zealand was 10.2d per lb sterling. Currency revaluation would raise this to 12.67d per lb sterling. Worse still, current stocks of powder that year amounted to around 600 tons, of which 400 tons was a loan from the Ministry of Food, leaving just 200 tons before use of the new season's powder, at the high price.[24]

Nor was milk powder production, a major part of the whole New Zealand operation, without problems. The unpredictability of the New Zealand weather gave Stagg plenty of opportunity to exercise his penchant for drama. News that drought conditions in early 1955 meant output would be drastically reduced, came as an 'unpleasant shock' to those back in Britain.[25] Two years later, the company suffered 'a sad setback' in their milk supply when thirteen of its suppliers left *en masse*, involving a loss equivalent to 216 tons of powder. This event also raised ghosts from the past, as Stagg reported:

It has been disconcerting to find that, despite the many nice things which are said to us at Suppliers Meetings, there are some long memories, dating back to the days when there was no alternative outlet for whole milk, of a 'take it or leave it', and 'go back to pigs if you want to', attitude by Glaxo.[26]

In December 1956 and January 1957, the milk powder output fell short of budget, but supplies of liquid milk were always difficult to predict. In fact this was of less importance than previously, for by 1957 there was in Britain itself an increasing surplus of milk for manufacture and Glaxo found that the policy of the Milk Marketing Board towards importers of milk powder was based on a not too benevolent neutrality. The company realised that the Board would be unlikely to look favourably upon increased importations from New Zealand.

As far as pharmaceuticals were concerned, the purchase in 1948 of Adex (NZ) Ltd, a company producing vitamin A concentrate and oils from fish liver was part of the parent company's policy to secure its supply of essential raw materials. Adex, however, was dogged by difficulties: the fish were caught from small boats off the Cook Strait and the South Island, and the fishermen were of rather random efficiency. Eighty per cent of the fish liver thus obtained yielded a low vitamin A content, although those of high potency provided 55 per cent of the total vitamin A recovery. Until 1951 Adex operated profitably, and the trading accounts for the six months to the end of December 1950, showed a profit of almost £20,000.[27] In fact, Glaxo (New Zealand) whose own finance was restricted, avoided overdrafts by borrowing from Adex which certainly, up to 1951, always had surplus cash available when needed.[28] Despite satisfactory trading and competent and energetic management, the directors of Adex recognised that the future was

56 The Adex plant in New Zealand.

hazardous: its success was dependent upon acquiring supplies of fish liver, always uncertain both in quantity and quality. Falling prices for these rich liver oils due to competition from synthetic vitamin A also posed a threat. In the short term, a molecular distillation process installed two years earlier, which enabled concentrates of high vitamin A to be obtained even from liver oils of lower potency, helped ease the situation.[29]

But by 1953 it was becoming increasingly apparent that the natural vitamin A market was dead. In the competition from synthetic vitamin A, price was only one factor, albeit the major one. Merck, licensed by Hoffman La Roche to manufacture under patent, appeared to be the chief 'offender' since Pfizer, although similarly licensed, had stayed out of the field. It became obvious that Roche was trying to eliminate competition by a price war. It was equally clear that neither Merck nor anyone else was making any profit at the present level. Adex suffered from additional technical problems such as shortage of equipment, staff and space, compounded by unreliable processes. As Palmer wrote:

Our operations in the Vitamin A field seem to be just 'one damn thing after another'. If it is not the waterside workers' strike, it is fumes and labour shortage at Island Bay on Timanu and, when these influences are not exerting their full effect, apparently the electricity supply proves insufficient.[30]

By 1953 Adex was preparing to go into voluntary liquidation but the matter remained a source of discussion and was not resolved for many years. Adex remained in business, making low profits, by selling its concentrate to Greenford at a price well below that obtaining in world markets and with the help of a contract to supply capsules of vitamin A to UNICEF.[31] Despite

the New Zealand subsidiary's indebtedness to Adex for loans, its role was
not appreciated by Stagg at least. 'I am pretty certain that in so far as Stagg is
concerned, Adex has been out of sight, and in a considerable degree out of
mind subject to the occasions when he has necessarily come into the picture',
Jephcott told Palmer in 1956.[32]

In all its activities the New Zealand subsidiary was bedevilled with
problems and falling profits in the 1950s. The shortage of high calibre staff
throughout the period also remained a constant issue, for reasons Jephcott
discovered for himself on a visit in the mid 1950s:

I found to my surprise and horror that there is no organised training in pharmacy,
and the whole-time instruction of qualified pharmacists in New Zealand comprises a
period of three weeks. This goes far to explain the poor educational standards which
I had observed amongst our so-called qualified pharmacists in New Zealand.

The best of the young New Zealand graduates almost invariably travelled to
Britain for post-graduate work and many did not return. 'If the future of our
business in New Zealand is to be dependent upon New Zealanders whose
training and experience is restricted to that country, the outlook is not too
good', Jephcott concluded.

The New Zealand government in the 1950s encouraged the development
and use of prophylactic products of biological origin against animal diseases
prevalent in the country. By 1959 Glaxo had determined to penetrate this
field and compete with laboratories already in the market. Two New
Zealand veterinary surgeons with British qualifications were hired, and were
trained for vaccine work in New Zealand and in Australia where Griff Hunt
was also considering a similar project. The Veterinary Biological Project,
despite being given priority by Jephcott, was slow in getting off the ground
due to double complications of new buildings and staff recruitment. It also
proved expensive. By 1961 Glaxo (New Zealand) had committed themselves
to the tune of £107,000, and sought another £100,000 from the parent
company, a figure which as Jephcott commented 'will not be the last'.[33] New
Zealand, however, pointed out that the project, when completed, would be
capable of showing a return on the investment of 9.8 per cent p.a. (after tax
and UK royalty) within five or six years. In the closing months of 1961,
Jephcott estimated that additional capital of £100,000 – £150,000 was likely
to be needed overall by the New Zealand subsidiary during that financial
year, with £175,000 projected for mid 1963 and £200,000–£250,000 by 1964.

Developments in this expensive venture became controversial, prompting
Stagg to prepare a somewhat defensive and lengthy memorandum in early
1961. He pointed out that the decision to establish a local veterinary
biological project had emanated from Greenford around 1957. Stagg's initial
reaction to Greenford's decision had anticipated events. 'Glaxo's projected

entry into the New Zealand vaccine field will not be calm and smooth sailing.'[34] 'I was not asked to provide estimates of capital expenditure or profitability until November 1959 when Sir Harry's query, as he may recollect, caused me to make up estimates on the spot ... I had no idea of, and omitted to take into account, cost of plant or farm buildings.'[35] Jephcott received Stagg's comments in 1961 'without any vast enthusiasm', and reprimanded Stagg: 'I am not impressed by your dragging in the Veterinary Antibiotic turnover. That is just a red herring. I am sure you would not suggest for one moment that this biological venture was for the purpose of preserving the antibiotic business.'[36]

In 1960, the requirement had been for a fairly simple building to house various laboratories and offices at an estimated cost of £14,500. By 1961 this had become a much more elaborate scheme with a larger building incorporating separately ventilated suites for Leptospina, Brucella, Salmonella and human vaccines and provision for freeze-drying and filling at an estimated cost of £120,000 (plant £36,000, buildings £72,000 and installation costs of £12,000).[37] Jephcott appeared resigned to the situation and told Pacey 'I am in some measure reassured by your indication that, although the operation may show a loss in the first year or two, there should be a progressive improvement in the profitability, so that a reasonable return will be shown on the investment in a few years' time.'[38] Besides, the project was now so well advanced towards manufacture that to turn back would be both difficult and humiliating for the company.

In 1961 the Department of Health set up a special committee on pharmaceutical benefits, a meeting of which Glaxo was invited to attend. The outlook towards the industry was not friendly, as Stagg told Greenford. 'The general feeling in this country, as elsewhere, is that pharmaceutical manufacturing houses are making too much profit and their products cost too much money.'[39] In New Zealand, as in the US, the public was becoming increasingly aware that heavy medical bills could be greatly reduced by asking the doctor to use scientific (generic) names in writing prescriptions instead of brand names.

Word artists invent the brand names, and often try to make them sound like some other highly successful drug. All this represents not only economic waste but danger ... In a rational society, I would think, the medical profession would arrange for a simple way to get pure, high-quality drugs to the public at a cost not inflated by rival brand promotional activities.[40]

Glaxo's own position with the Health Department had been good; the company was under Price Control Division scrutiny, mark-ups were approved and accounts did not show excessive tax paid profits compared with shareholders' funds used in the business. To answer the critics, Stagg

57 Roy Stagg.

suggested producing information covering the long period in which Joseph Nathan & Co's shareholders lived without or with very low dividends whilst funds were built up to produce the present prosperity.[41] The post-war period was difficult for Glaxo in New Zealand. Despite static turnover and falling profits, however, the company continued to invest in new projects there in the hope of creating a small and efficient subsidiary with a level of business reflecting the size of the country.

14

The Commonwealth III: South Africa

The background and the market

South Africa provides an interesting case of a market in which Glaxo Laboratories made a considerable effort in the 1940s and 1950s, largely at the instigation of Jephcott and under the influence of his loyalty to the Commonwealth Dominions. At that time British multinational investment in South Africa was particularly successful, but political factors and other local characteristics resulted in a gradual diminution of the South African subsidiary's role within the group in the 1960s.[1] The partiality which Jephcott felt for the country, the company and certain of the latter's executives was an important influence in the period before then.

The immense geographical size of South Africa posed constant problems for promotional work and supply throughout this period; moreover, the local market was both complex and idiosyncratic. South Africa's population had risen from about 8.5 million in 1930 to 11.26 million in 1945, and then to 13.7 million in 1955 and 14.9 million in 1960; but in practice this did not represent the size of the market available to Glaxo, for it included a large black population, which could not afford modern pharmaceuticals except when prescribed through state hospitals. As late as 1962 a South African government commission found it impossible to establish the actual total expenditure on medicines in South Africa, because of the confusing patterns of local returns and the fact that 70 per cent of medicines in local use, especially the more expensive types, were imported. The quantities and values of raw and semi-raw products could not be determined.

Tensions in the wholesale trade led to intense and chaotic competition between pharmaceutical manufacturers in the 1950s. By 1959 there were no less than eighty companies competing in this relatively small ethical market, of which thirty-two were South African subsidiaries of foreign multi-nationals (fifteen USA; ten British; two German; two Swiss and one each from Norway, the Netherlands and France), while thirty-three foreign companies were locally represented by agencies or distributors (sixteen USA; six British; four Swiss; three German; and one each from Belgium, Denmark, Ireland and Israel). An analysis of sixteen leading producers in South Africa showed that ethical business, as part of their total pharmaceutical turnover, increased from 57.3 per cent spread over eight companies in 1954, to 70.5 per cent spread over sixteen companies in 1959. Of these sixteen firms, fourteen manufactured or processed their products under licence or patent right agreements; 65 per cent of the raw material used was imported.[2]

Glaxo's presence in South Africa dated back to 1929 and sales of Glaxo products had grown during the war, with the efforts of Bob Brown and Robbie Fotheringham added to those of Glaxo's agent, Menley & James. Glaxo had, however, eschewed one product area. The British Ministry of Food's prohibition of milk exports during and immediately after the war meant that Glaxo were eliminated from this line of business when the post-war South African government introduced import quotas based on war-time market shares. Glaxo realised that it could never regain its previous footings in such products as Ostermilk, and abandoned the market.

From agency to subsidiary

In January 1948 Jephcott paid the first of his visits to South Africa and Rhodesia. He made an extensive tour from Cape Town to Port Elizabeth, Durban, Johannesburg and Bulawayo, meeting agents, hospital authorities, customers, businessmen and officials. As a result of his travels and inter-views, he decided that it was opportune for Glaxo to invest capital from Britain. He judged that the market could best be developed by leaving Menley & James in charge of physical distribution and such local manufac-ture as seemed desirable and economic, while forming a local Glaxo company to be responsible for all promotion to doctors, chemists and hospitals. Even so, it was not until 1957 when he motored from Johannes-burg to Cape Town, that he appreciated the distance between even trivial settlements and the difficulties in organising widespread representative coverage. Jephcott visited South Africa once every two years from 1948 until 1963 and developed a deep affection for the country. He was keenly interested in the fortunes of the local company, although he made a point of demonstrating his trust for the managing director by his own non-interfer-ence. For the local company he was an invaluable friend at court in London. His attitude engendered fierce loyalty: 'he didn't pay American salaries, but people wouldn't leave Glaxo for American salaries because of HJ'.[3]

On Jephcott's return to London, his co-directors accepted his recommen-dations, and Leslie Birchley was appointed managing director of the nascent Glaxo Laboratories (SA) (Pty) Limited. Birchley had started his career with

Glaxo's Home Sales Staff in Liverpool in 1934, and then from 1936 until 1939 he worked in London. He spent the war with the RAF, returning to Glaxo after demobilisation to become area sales executive for the north of England, the post he held when appointed to South Africa.

Glaxo Laboratories (SA) (Pty) Limited began operations in 1948, from three offices in the Menley & James stock depot in a sleazy area of Johannesburg. The new company started with a small staff, consisting of Birchley, as Managing Director, Bob Brown as Sales Director, a company secretary and typist, together with Fotheringham and two other representatives who had come out from Britain. As the company expanded, there was some difficulty in recruiting suitable representatives. 'Local material offering is very mediocre', Birchley wrote in 1951. 'Representatives of a sort are to be had but mostly they are of the unqualified kind with very little pharmaceutical background, who move around from firm to firm. Generally speaking, they are not of the calibre one looks for in a Glaxo representative.'[4]

The South African company was unique among the Glaxo overseas subsidiaries in working through distribution agents. Menley & James were responsible for the actual physical distribution, storage and invoicing of goods, in return for a commission varying with the class of product and customer, but overall averaging approximately 6 per cent of turnover. Because of the geographical difficulties of South Africa, such an arrangement was common among other pharmaceutical companies in that period. The first year of trading was successful, with a turnover more than double the highest previous annual sales of Glaxo products in South Africa. This trend continued in succeeding years and there was a modest growth in staff. Several more local representatives were recruited, together with additional office staff.

Although the rapid increase in the use of antibiotics such as penicillin and streptomycin stimulated the growth of the South African subsidiary, it was a precarious market because over 90 per cent of antibiotic usage was concentrated in the hands of the four Provincial Hospital Authorities and the Central Medical and Veterinary stores, all of which purchased their requirements by open competitive tender. The quantities put out to tender were so high that they attracted bids from virtually every producer in the world, and consequently price competition was intense. It was usually in South Africa that price breaks in antibiotics first appeared, possibly because most of the major pharmaceutical companies were represented in the country, which they considered to be a good credit risk. It became a grim joke among Glaxo executives in South Africa that when they reported losing a big tender for penicillin to a competitor, the price would be received with incredulity in the British headquarters, but that some three months later, London would meet similar low competitive quotes elsewhere in the world.

As a result of the magnitude of these antibiotic tenders, a high percentage of the subsidiary's annual turnover was vulnerable to effects of savage competitive tendering: some years as much as 66 per cent of turnover was thus at hazard. In Birchley's phrase, there was no stability: 'either duck or no dinner'.[5]

Glaxo Laboratories always agreed trade price structures for crystalline penicillin in South Africa with other British distributors and when penicillin prices were reduced in 1950, all the British companies agreed trade prices which were to be firm net prices, with no cash or other hidden discounts. This maintained stable trade prices for over six months. Glaxo Laboratories were not party to the similar arrangements fixing Distaquaine prices, but nevertheless had a friendly understanding whereby their Sectopen prices and the prices of Distaquaine Forte were identical pro rata per dose. This worked well, as all the big American producers like Squibbs or Wyeths sold their dry fortified products at exactly the same trade price levels as Distaquaine Forte and Sectopen and did not try to cut British prices. However, in 1951, British Drug Houses began giving wholesalers a discount of 5 per cent for cash within thirty days, and ICI appointed as 'stockists' the major wholesaler in each large centre of population, to whom they gave a preferential discount of 5 per cent or 7.5 per cent. May & Baker took umbrage at all this, and abruptly reduced their trade prices by about 10 per cent. By so doing May & Baker were not breaking the British convention prices, but Birchley felt 'it is utterly stupid to start a price war at this stage ... on the whole chemists and wholesalers do not welcome unnecessary price reductions since they only mean a lower actual cash profit on each vial sold'.[6] Price-cutting, however, remained a feature of the South African market.

The Wadeville factory

During a visit to London by Birchley in 1952, the establishment of a local factory was discussed. This was a complex issue: Jephcott believed that increasing Afrikaner nationalism created in South Africa the possibility of the sudden imposition of tariff protection. As this would have robbed the South African subsidiary of any ability to compete, he supported the idea of creating a local factory, which could swing into modest production with the minimum of delay. Because the South African company was so heavily involved with penicillin and streptomycin, consideration of the factory was primarily related to these products; but the total market in South Africa and Rhodesia for antibiotics was insufficient to support the smallest possible economic fermentation operation. Primary manufacture, therefore, was only possible if the local producer was assured of securing all business.

58 A. L. Birchley on the right, Managing Director of the South African company arriving in London in May 1952, the first member of Glaxo staff to travel by Comet.

Furthermore, since costs were directly related to scale of manufacture, local users – mainly the government acting through the four Provincial Hospital Authorities – would have had to decide to forsake the advantages of the prevailing system of cut-throat open tendering, with every major world producer scrambling to win business on a price basis, for a structured system of higher prices to support the local producer. This was a large sacrifice to ask of the authorities for the security of making South Africa self-sufficient in antibiotics. A further problem lay in the fact that South Africa was a signatory to the General Agreement on Trade and Tariffs (GATT) which, amongst other provisions, bound signatories to refrain from imposing customs duties on antibiotics.

These problems were debated at length with South Africa's New Industries Committee. Glaxo Laboratories offered either to erect a complete primary fermentation factory, in return for a government guarantee of a monopoly of orders: to work up into finished penicillin from the intermediate, cyclohexylamine salt, which would be imported from Britain; or to organise a secondary sterile packing operation of bulk imported finished antibiotics into dosage forms, with secondary production of suspensions, tablets, ointments and other formulations making full use of local packing materials. Matters were complicated by a joint proposal from Distillers, Squibb and National Chemical Products of Germiston, to manufacture penicillin and streptomycin in a new plant at Germiston. This led officials in Pretoria to treat Glaxo's proposals with more reserve. Because of their GATT obligations and their aversion to giving a monopoly to one company, the South African Government finally indicated that neither of the first two alternatives was viable, and the third alternative was adopted.

Since the hazards of open tendering for antibiotics remained, the factory project required a balanced product range to ensure that use of its facilities was optimised. In addition to secondary production of penicillin and streptomycin, pharmaceuticals such as Adexolin, Minadex, Glucodin, ointments, Cytamen Liquid and ampoules were manufactured, with a roller drying plant for manufacturing Farex included in the factory plans. Initially it was felt that tablet manufacture should be left in the hands of Menley & James, rather than duplicating their production facility in the Glaxo factory. Although the factory project was delayed by protracted negotiations with the New Industries Committee, other progress was made. In 1952 both Jephcott and Palmer visited South Africa to examine possible factory sites. Since roughly half of South Africa's total business was represented by the Witwatersrand complex and the Transvaal, it was agreed to locate the factory on the Reef. A site of over eight acres on the edge of Wadeville Industrial Township was accordingly bought for £8,302 from Germiston Municipality which was thereafter consistently cooperative; it was one of the first municipalities on the Reef to recognise that gold mines had a limited life and it pioneered industrial development within its municipal boundaries.

The move into manufacturing meant that the original capital structure of 1948 (£50,000 authorised, £40,000 issued) was inadequate, and the authorised capital of Glaxo Laboratories (SA) (Pty) Limited was increased in 1954 from £50,000 to £250,000; £100,000 capital was issued, of which £60,000 was allotted to the British parent company in consideration for plant supplied to Wadeville. At the same meeting approval was given to expenditure of £65,000 on the main factory building at Wadeville. By the next year Birchley was warning Jephcott that the ratio of capital employed to turnover was 'uncomfortably close to 1:1 and yet, owing to the peculiar circumstances of this market we are finding ourselves short of working capital, and cannot live without reasonable credit on purchases from the parent company'. The question of the amount of credit allowed by Greenford on goods shipped out was a recurring one for most of the overseas subsidiaries. The liquidity problems in South Africa were in part due to the inevitable delay between the British company shipping bulks and the local subsidiary receiving revenue from Menley & James for the sale of finished products created from those bulks. But, according to Birchley, 'the more important reason' was 'the magnitude of the capital lock-up in raw and packing materials necessary to meet the wild and unpredictable swings of demand so characteristic of this market'. Wadeville's overheads could only be sustained by increasing turnover and throughput, yet Birchley felt that this could only be achieved, 'by having adequate materials constantly on the spot to snap up the business that so often offers literally overnight and yet which cannot be forecast'.[7]

Greenford, in turn, was concerned at the value of invoices outstanding to the parent company; they considered that a subsidiary company should normally take about two months' credit on goods supplied, but in September 1955 the balance on the South African subsidiary's account was £59,773, representing the approximate value of four months' invoices. Birchley was extracting working capital from Greenford in the form of extended credit on goods supplies. Later in 1955, Jephcott agreed with Birchley that the South African subsidiary was short of working capital, but was averse to providing additional capital from Britain for the subsidiary by extended credit on goods supplied, and suggested that they seek overdraft facilities from their bank. When this proved impossible, because of the prohibitive rate of interest demanded, Jephcott agreed that the parent company would make the subsidiary a loan at 5 per cent annually.

During Wadeville's planning phase, the South African subsidiary met another problem. The parent company had purchased Dextran Limited, a British company which produced blood volume expanding products (see page 165). Dextran's overseas associate African-Dextran Limited in South Africa was experiencing serious financial troubles, and had manufactured vast quantities of Dextran of suspect quality, sufficient, if released, to wreck the global market. Shortly after the purchase of Dextran in 1952, Jephcott visited South Africa, where he inspected the local Dextran works. Having investigated the local works' accounts, Glaxo's auditor described them as 'three times insolvent', with all tangible assets, other than stocks, specifically mortgaged, and a long list of unsecured creditors, some for considerable amounts. The inventory was also highly inaccurate. There were well over 35,000 flasks in stock, but there had been little proper sales promotion, either by Dextran or its agents, Crookes. Jephcott reported in 1952, that in Johannesburg:

there is a strong vested interest in the hands of certain doctors for the production and sale of blood plasma.

Outside Johannesburg . . . there is an urgent demand for a product of the Dextran type since blood plasma is not readily available and of uncertain, if not dangerous quality . . . the installed capacity of the Dextran plant far exceeds any South African usage of the product on the most optimistic assessment . . . I am quite definite in my view that to acquire South African Dextran as a company would be to buy a first-class headache, nor can I see the possibility . . . of the judicial managers the South African equivalent of the receivers being prepared to part with it on terms which would have any conceivable attraction to us.[8]

He also had severe criticisms of the site and layout of the factory building (where cheap jewellery was also made). Instead it was decided to buy only Dextran's stock, plants and rights at a price reflecting Glaxo's expectation that it would take three years to liquidate packed stock, so that there would be no need to operate the plant for at least two years. Ultimately the local Glaxo company inspected every bottle, rejected any showing suspended matter, and bought the rest. With the liquidation of African-Dextran, Glaxo bought some of its plant from the factory at Edenvale which, it seemed, might be useful in the proposed Wadeville factory.

Early in 1954 contractors started building operations at Wadeville and handed over the buildings during October of that year; preliminary manufacturing operations began in November. As Jephcott wrote after two years' working, he was 'satisfied that the factory is about as good as we could have conceived for the capital expenditure', although its capacity was in many respects 'fantastically in excess of the load upon it'. He continued: 'On the other hand less capacity would have cost us almost as much.' He found various aspects of the building aesthetically unpleasing, and wrote that 'Birchley has held the reins of capital expenditure so tightly that the office did not reach a reasonable standard of amenity and the echo and intensity of lighting was painful to me'.[9]

Certainly severe economy marked the construction of the Wadeville factory, but for this Jephcott also held some responsibility. 'The one thing I've never learnt to do is spend money', he once confided to Birchley and the tight budgeting of 1954–1955 started an unfortunate tendency at Wadeville. To some managers it seemed in retrospect that the company was too proud of its ability to improvise production without spending money and that some opportunities to invest in new equipment were delayed. In 1954 the only second-hand machinery sent from the British parent company were the roller driers for Farex production, but other equipment from Greenford – for labelling and filling – was new. Pipework, tanks and other pieces were, however, taken from the dismantled African-Dextran factory at Edenvale and used in the new building at Wadeville. Altogether, the financial pressures, and the ingenuity used to circumvent them, were considerable; but for many years – or so it seemed to some people involved in production at Wadeville – the amount of time spent on discussing future investment was in inverse proportion to the amount eventually spent.

In equipping the factory, constant thought was given to the fact that the

Reef is at an altitude of about 6,000 feet above sea level. Meticulous attention to this aspect eliminated all the more obvious snags, yet when the factory commenced its first proving run, the British-made incubator in the Sterility Testing Laboratory steadfastly refused to reach 37°C. It was only after a special capsule for the incubator was air-freighted out from Britain that the factory finally began production. Another snag appeared after the factory had been running for six months when the highveld winter set in with its low humidities. Bulk streptomycin came out from Britain in large aluminium canisters, and after twelve days tossing at sea and another three days jolting on the railways, the canisters had acquired a considerable charge of static by the time they arrived at Wadeville. When the canister was attached to the filling machine in the Sterile Area the streptomycin dropped into the vial and immediately flew back up into the canister. Eventually Wadeville devised methods of getting rid of the static and streptomycin filling thereafter proceeded without hitch.

Although the factory was commissioned in November 1954, the official opening was delayed until February 1955 when Jephcott performed the ceremony. The opening of the first factory in Africa south of the Equator equipped to handle sterile filling and processing of antibiotics received considerable publicity. Of the 'very merry' party after the opening ceremony, Jephcott wrote afterwards, 'the consumption of tea was fair, beer more considerable and gin enormous'.[10]

After commissioning the factory it soon became evident that it was a mistake to keep the sales and administration offices in central Johannesburg. The overloaded South African telephone system could not cope with the demand; Wadeville was a rapidly developing industrial suburb and the telephone cable serving it was wholly inadequate. For those at the head office in Johannesburg, to contact the Wadeville factory was virtually impossible: indeed, it was quicker to drive eleven miles out to Wadeville than to get a telephone call through. Moreover, as Jephcott had predicted at the time of the opening ceremony, hospitals welcomed the local facilities but 'expect[ed] to be able to whistle up quite sizeable quantities at short notice', making it hard 'to regulate stocks or plan production'.[11] In mid 1955 Glaxo Laboratories (SA) (Pty) Limited transferred all its operations to Wadeville and in so doing blazed a trail that most of the pharmaceutical industry in South Africa later followed. At the time its competitors thought Glaxo were eccentric to leave Johannesburg for the wilds of the East Rand, and that to be remote from central Johannesburg would injure business. Glaxo Laboratories, during the next twenty or so years, saw one after another of its competitors build factories in locations from fifteen to twenty-five miles from central Johannesburg and transfer their entire office and administration staff out to these factories.

It was agreed, in January 1955, that for large South African antibiotics tenders, the British company would supply penicillin or streptomycin to Wadeville at prices lower than normal for bulk antibiotics. The factory overheads at Wadeville were 1s. 0d. (5p.) compared with about 8d. (3.4p.) at Barnard Castle, and Jephcott decreed that penicillin (whether the crystalline or procaine) would be replaced at 3.75d. (1.6p.) fob per mega and streptomycin at 4.75d. (2p.) fob per mega. As Birchley wrote in November of that year, 'antibiotic business which, unfortunately, still constitutes nearly two-thirds of our turnover ... owing to the fierce competition ... [is] steadily becoming less and less a source of profit. It is rather like a treadmill, you go harder and harder and get nowhere.' In the four months, July–October 1955, the South African subsidiary sold 60,000 megas more penicillin than in the corresponding period of 1954, yet its sterling turnover in penicillin decreased by 27.75 per cent. Streptomycin sales rose by 202 kilos, which was worth only £5,500. 'Antibiotics business with its extremely fine profit margin is subject to the wild swings of demand necessitating large capital lock-up in stocks.'[12]

The whole economy of the Wadeville factory was founded on antibiotics production, yet its opening coincided with a sharp decline in prices for antibiotics. Other products that could be manufactured there did not yield enough profits to cover overheads. The South African subsidiary's annual turnover in the mid 1950s on products other than antibiotics was about £100,000 with imported products accounting for about 55 per cent of this. There was, by the middle of the decade, a 20 per cent duty on all imported pharmaceuticals except vitamin B_{12}.

During the early years of manufacturing operations at Wadeville, maintenance of workload posed a constant problem. So long as Glaxo Laboratories obtained a good share of the hospital business on antibiotic tenders, the factory facilities were employed. However, when it failed to secure a few big tenders because of price cutting by overseas competitors, it was harder to keep the factory busy. Although manufacture of other pharmaceutical products helped, unfortunately overall turnover in these products did not permit long, and therefore economic, manufacturing runs.

Jephcott sent Birchley a characteristic homily – and one which reflected his views on the overseas subsidiaries – in 1955, after an accountant's report on overhead costs had spread consternation in London and Wadeville. While he did not wish to cast doubt on the competence of the report's author as an accountant, Jephcott wrote:

his report reflects the dangers of which I have long been aware of allowing accountants to run businesses, and I am quite sure you will not allow that to happen. In the commencement of any new operation, until the turnover is built-up to something approaching factory capacity, overheads are a heavy load and, if charged against the first necessarily limited output of a product, would make it so expensive that either your selling price was too high to do the business, or your Sales Manager was under the dreadfully depressing effect of knowing that the more he sold the bigger loss he made.

The answer to your problem is simple to state, but not easy to accomplish . . . It is, first, to keep your overheads down to a minimum . . . and secondly, to expand your turnover until your factory is operating at an economic capacity . . . In addition, everyone who is capable of being spared for a few hours a day or week should be out scratching for business. You have but one source of income – the proceeds of sales – and more sales you *must* have. Now many years ago we faced a similar situation here and all of us put our shoulder to the selling wheel and organised our work so that we could, each one, get out after business. We all learnt a good deal.[13]

But Birchley maintained and reiterated in a letter to the Subsidiary Companies Unit (see page 228) that he could not with any accuracy predict what would be a normal and reasonable stock level of bulks and packed stock in any given quarter, because there was no such thing as a normal or reasonable level of demand.

With the Wadeville Factory we have one and only one great advantage over competitors – service and being able promptly to meet demands. That means having the necessary bulks readily available because . . . our competitors can import packed stock as quickly as we can get in bulks, and it takes us additional time to convert those bulks into packed stock. In other words, we have to gamble all the time where stock maintenance is concerned – it is characteristic of this market that you get the business if you have the stock on hand, if you have not, you miss the business.

'South Africa is a crazy market', he wrote, especially in 'vulture business' when hospitals were forced to make sudden orders for antibiotics after they had awarded their annual tenders to rival manufacturers on a price basis, but before the supplies arrived.[14]

The search for other new business

Nevertheless, Jephcott's advice was noted and the South African company made an effort to diversify. When the Wadeville project was at blueprint stage in 1952–1953, its main purpose was to process and pack antibiotics, with pharmaceutical and food manufacturing regarded as useful secondary operations to broaden the productive basis. Subsequently, in 1955, the slide in antibiotic prices made it all too apparent that margins on antibiotic business and the hazards of competitive tendering for antibiotics offered no sound basis for carrying overheads. These considerations led to a period of inventive effort locally; efforts which were encouraged by Jephcott 'who believed that the men on the spot were in the best position to know what the local market needed'.[15] The subsidiary had to develop its pharmaceutical and food business if it was to grow: the relatively large-volume proprietary

59 Sir Harry Jephcott opening the Wadeville factory in 1955.

products offered a reasonable profit margin, steady and predictable demand, and were not subject to intense price-cutting. The most vigorous sales efforts were redirected towards the food and pharmaceutical retailers and, by 1956–1957, the penalty of success was an accommodation crisis at Wadeville.

Some provincial authorities used large amounts of Bidaylin and called for considerable quantities on open tender under the generic name 'Multi-vitamin Syrup'. A multi-vitamin syrup was formulated which was a palatable and elegant preparation and won several tenders. Eventually Wadeville decided to sell the product to retailers and coined the name Citradex for it. Other Glaxo overseas organisations later marketed the same product. Ironically, when some years later Glaxo Laboratories (SA) (Pty) Limited entered into a Trade Marks Agreement with the parent company they had to pay a royalty for the use of the Citradex brand-name, their own brain child. Other essays into formulation and marketing local ideas were not always successful: Copalcin (an antidiarrhoeal) and Pholco (a cough mixture containing pholcodeine) were products which enjoyed relatively short popularity, but they contributed to factory throughput at a time when it was most needed. More lasting locally produced products were the flavoured varieties of Farex and Glucodin Tablets. Flavoured Farex was an idea eventually adopted by the British parent company and other Glaxo overseas subsidiaries although these companies devised different flavours from South Africa. In other fields, a Veterinary ICD granule for dogs was launched as a canine equivalent of Caldeferrum for humans.

There was regret among some South African managers about the handling of corticosteroids and fears about the arrangements for griseoful-vin (see chapter 9). As Jephcott lamented from Durban in 1959, 'we were ourselves late in the field and, when we had supplies, the overseas companies were given no more than miserable dribbles. As a result, the US competitors, who are particularly strong here, dug themselves in and have an impregn-able position; added to which the dictum from Greenford has been that we must not under-sell the US manufacturer, with the result that hydrocorti-sone products here are fantastically above UK prices, and no worthwhile business can be secured ... If we now supply to our US competitors griseofulvin to outsell our people here feelings will run high.'[16] Another complaint of some managers at Wadeville was that they had insufficient technical training from the English parent company, particularly on the production side.

In 1956 Michael Meyer, a chartered accountant with the subsidiary's auditors, Cooper Brothers & Co, joined Glaxo Laboratories SA as company secretary and chief accountant. It was an important and significant appoint-ment as he later became Financial Director, Deputy Managing Director and ultimately (1974–1985) Chief Executive of Glaxo in South Africa after Birchley. Max Jamieson, who had been Managing Director of Glaxo's agents in South Africa, was transferred in 1955 to the parent company of Menley & James in London, but after the latter's take-over by Smith, Kline & French, returned to South Africa where he was appointed to Glaxo's Board in 1957.

With the advent of Jamieson, the functions in Sales Department were divided. Bob Brown headed a new Contracts Division responsible for all aspects of tendering, including the coordination of price intelligence from all parts of the world, in the field of open competitive tenders. Jamieson assumed responsibility for all promotional activities including the control and direction of the medical representatives and customer relations. Jeph-cott reported in 1957:

Idris Lewis [the production director] is doing an excellent job and is taking a keen interest in the overall conduct of the business as well as the factory. Birchley was warm in the praise of the help he gets. Indeed, it is only with Lewis that he can intelligently discuss his problems for the new company structure has disclosed Brown's weaknesses. Brown is a failure as Sales Director. He exhibits no initiative and will not take a decision on his own responsibility however trivial. He and Fotheringham are ... problems. Neither has capacity above that of a hack representative and both look back with nostalgia to the days before the company existed.[17]

The take-over of Menley & James by Smith, Kline & French had one further important effect on the activities of the South African company, for from the summer of 1957, Menley & James relinquished all agency distribution business. This posed several problems. Geographically, South Africa was a difficult terrain in which to undertake distribution. The main centres of population where the wholesalers operated were widely dispersed, while railway services were poor. To achieve satisfactory distribution, cooperation from wholesalers or insurance against products constantly running out of stock, manufacturers tended to set up stockholding depots to service the needs of wholesalers in the area in the main centres of population – Cape Town, Port Elizabeth, Durban and Johannesburg. Menley & James had done this. Unfortunately, these stockholding depots were required by the provisions of the Medical, Dental and Pharmacy Act to be under the supervision of a qualified pharmacist, whose salary represented a sizeable overhead. Menley & James had been able to spread this overhead between their numerous agencies, but Glaxo could not countenance creating such depots and bearing the entire overheads itself.

Fortunately at this time the railways introduced a new express freight service between Johannesburg and the main coastal cities of Durban, Port Elizabeth and Cape Town. Although its freight charge was 25 per cent above ordinary goods train rates, the railways guaranteed that express goods would reach their destination in three days, by hooking goods trucks on to main line passenger expresses. This enabled Glaxo to devise a new distribution system. Offices were rented in Durban, Port Elizabeth and Cape Town each equipped with a female clerk, a telephone and a postbox. The clerk received orders from the wholesalers in her area by telephone and occasionally by post: each day she made a regular fixed time telephone call to Wadeville during which she transferred the orders to a tape recorder attached to the telephone in the Order Department at Wadeville. The fixed time telephone calls were so arranged as to enable Wadeville to assemble the orders and get them on to that day's passenger or express goods train. Heavier orders went express goods, antibiotics and lighter items by passenger train. This system worked splendidly, so that wholesalers in the coastal towns were full of praise for the service provided. The Glaxo coastal offices held no stock at all and thus could operate legally without a qualified pharmacist in charge. The Company's Stores Controller had for years been employed by the South African Railways in the System Manager's Office, and his expertise was indispensable to the success of the new distribution system.

Between 1955 and 1957 the tender system grew more intense. Streptomycin price reductions by Eli Lilly's local company, in 1956, caused Birchley concern. Instead of giving substantial tenders at six or twelve months intervals and purchasing *ad hoc* any shortfall, South African hospital and other authorities (with the exception of the biggest tenders) began indulging in weekly tenders for even the most trivial requirements (one one occasion Jephcott saw a tender for twelve tablets of soap). Generally prices for weekly tenders were more favourable, with prompt delivery a material element in success, and competition was keen; British Drug Houses, who carried stocks on behalf of Distillers, often secured the business as their larger margins enabled them to have less regard for the price.[18] Further troubles developed in 1958. A fall in copper prices resulted in the Rhodesian Tenders Board buying polio vaccine strictly on price, with the result that the South African Government Laboratory secured all tenders. Glaxo would have had to drop to 2s. 9d. (13.8p.) per cc. in vials to meet them and feared that the South African Government Laboratory would drop the price even further if competition appeared. As Jephcott lamented in 1959, 'I was told whilst in Salisbury, by Government Officials, that this emphasis on price with little regard to quality was proving a severe embarrassment to them but there was little they could do about it.'[19]

The problems of overheads on antibiotics became acute with a continuous narrowing of profit margins and falling revenue. With antibiotics turnover falling, Birchley felt that his company's best prospects lay in the pharmaceutical business, and was disappointed that more new products had not recently come from Greenford. Jephcott replied that, with the Medical Department's continuous pressure for new products of medical interest, 'The Greenford Pharmacy Unit had been bogged down.' Neither the Medical nor Home Sales Departments thought there was 'any chance of rapid development of new pharmaceuticals'; anyway 'it could not be assumed that new pharmaceuticals developed in the UK would be suitable for overseas markets'. Jephcott told Birchley that he believed 'the development of new pharmaceuticals lay in the hands of the markets concerned', especially as local competition was such an important factor. 'The overseas companies must be the prime investigators of such products.'[20] In the postwar pharmaceutical world that was an increasingly impossible burden to lay on a subsidiary company.

In 1960 Birchley suggested that they might have reached 'the psychological moment' to begin local fermentation of antibiotics. 'The Union's gold and foreign exchange reserves have declined quite alarmingly in 1960', he wrote, 'in recent months Government policy has changed markedly towards local industry . . . they are literally falling over backwards to support local manufacturers.' The ever-widening range of dumping duties and increased tariff protection indicated the official policy of increased self-sufficiency, but Birchley confessed, 'I am by no means eager to get into the headaches of fermentation.'[21] While appreciating the possible difficulties if a competitor undertook local primary production of antibiotics, Jephcott was mindful of Glaxo's Australian experience (see page 306), 'where it has been demonstrated to our distress that the carrying out of the antibiotic fermentations at a point remote from the many technical services which are available in the UK, and upon a scale which necessarily greatly enhances the overhead cost, can be an extremely hazardous and very unprofitable activity'.[22] In the South African case, the British parent company calculated that the cost of locally fermented antibiotics would be up to three times higher than the antibiotics' prices of the world's major producers and there the matter rested.

The merger with Allen & Hanburys

There were more pressing problems caused by the parent company's merger with Allen & Hanburys in 1958. Allen & Hanburys (Africa) Limited, which was the A & H subsidiary in South Africa (although it was incorporated in Britain), was their largest overseas operation, and was considered the 'shining star' of their foreign subsidiaries.[23] Founded in the early part of the century to sell Allen & Hanburys' products in the Union of South Africa, the subsidiary gradually developed into an organisation of its own, which, while resembling its parent, had notable differences owing to the circumstances under which it operated and the localised requirements of South African doctors and pharmacists. Therefore, although Allen & Hanburys (Africa) Ltd largely supplied goods manufactured by the parent company, it also made original instruments to the special design of South African surgeons.

A & H was based at Congella in Durban, but conducted its business on lines very different from those of Glaxo in South Africa. Whereas Glaxo's distribution was through wholesalers, A & H (Africa) was virtually a manufacturing wholesaler, whose business largely comprised direct sales to retail pharmacists. Glaxo's business in South Africa was almost entirely in ethical pharmaceuticals, whereas A & H (Africa) apart from its ethical pharmaceuticals, also traded in galenicals, surgical goods, generics and proprietaries as well as wholesaling other people's goods. In addition, A & H (Africa) kept a printing department and supplied chemists' labels and stationery. Although Glaxo had a smaller and less effective sales team, its representatives promoted pharmaceutical specialities exclusively to the medical profession. In contrast, A & H representatives were generalists, who dealt in only a few medical specialities, such as Dequadin. In terms of size of turnover, numbers of staff and capital employed, A & H (Africa) was considerably bigger than Glaxo Laboratories (SA) (Pty) Limited, but in terms of return on capital employed and of pre-tax, net profit before tax, Glaxo was more profitable.

Indeed to Jephcott, and even to some junior A & H personnel, the position of A & H (Africa) was puzzling. With a large indoor staff at Durban and a large sales force, who tirelessly worked to push up turnover by complex and expensive methods, its profits remained exiguous: to some observers it seemed that a major crisis in A & H (Africa) could not have been long postponed if the merger with Glaxo had not occurred. In other respects the post-war history of A & H (Africa) had suffered its unhappy moments, and although successive managing directors included an experienced pharmacist and salesmen of dazzling energy and enthusiasm, in some commercial matters and business routines it was in the grip of inflexible conservatism. The Congella organisation needed rationalisation: its poor profits meant that staff pay was comparatively low, and according to its quality control chemist, the whole operation was 'going to rot'.[24] Finally, although the parent A & H Company in England in many ways exercised closer control of its subsidiaries than Glaxo, it was at the same time far more remote, with less of the personal sympathy that marked Jephcott's relations with Birchley and his staff. This is not to minimise the achievements of Harold Dreebin, A & H (Africa)'s Managing Director, who communicated his sales flair to his representatives, was single-minded in his commitment, and a sedulous and acute reader of scientific and medical journals.

With these fundamental differences, rationalising the two operations so as to secure the greatest overall benefit for the organisation proved arduous. The first step was taken in August 1958, when Birchley joined the board of Allen & Hanburys (Africa) Limited, while Dreebin was appointed to the board of Glaxo Laboratories (SA) (Pty) Limited. This enabled the two chief executives to learn about each other's operations and personnel at Wadeville and Congella. This process of familiarisation was assisted by the inauguration at Congella of monthly Executive Committee meetings along the lines already developed in the Glaxo organisation. At these meetings, which were minuted, management decisions were taken, thus leaving Board Meetings for purely formal business. The Executive Committee meeting also enabled senior staff who were not Board members to share in decision-making.

This question of motivation pinpoints one of the weaknesses of the pre-merger Allen & Hanburys in South Africa. With the company incorporated in England, where policy decisions were taken at the parent company's board meetings, local senior staff lacked the opportunity to show initiative or feel team spirit. Indeed the institution of the Executive Committee revealed a wealth of unused managerial talent at Congella, some of which later played an outstanding role in the future operations of the merged organisation in South Africa. Writing to Palmer from Johannesburg in 1959, Jephcott confessed:

you may be disappointed that I have taken no drastic step here towards integration. To have done so would have wrecked the A & H organisation, caused immense ill feeling, imposed hardship upon a considerable number of persons with 20–40 years' service, and resulted in an immediate financial loss. It could only have been justified were they making losses, and would have been very unacceptable against a background of increasing profitability ... In large measure responsibility for the shortcomings of A & H (SA) rests in London. The fellows out here have been kept in blinkers ... Dreebin told me the other morning that he had learnt something of Company finance for the first time during the talks I have had with him.[25]

Considerable tact had to be shown, not least because Dreebin, as managing director of the older and much better-known company, until the nature of the merger became clear, had confidently expected that A & H would have the ascendancy in South Africa. In the circumstances Glaxo showed exemplary patience which it is doubtful that many other businesses would have evinced. It was for this reason that according to one A & H employee, 'Jephcott, although a man of iron, was absolutely adored by the staff'.[26]

By 1959 the Durban and Wadeville operations had been sufficiently studied for broad conclusions to be reached. In the first place it was clear that, until the two companies were fully merged, there would be little overall benefit to the group. Secondly, the diversity of Allen & Hanburys (Africa)'s activities made it hard to distinguish accurately between profitable, marginally profitable and loss-making activities. It was decided initially to create a merged company to be known as Glaxo-Allenburys (SA) (Pty) Limited, which traded along lines similar to Glaxo Laboratories, distributing through wholesalers in Transvaal, Cape, Orange Free State and South West Africa. In Natal and the Border district, Glaxo-Allenburys continued to trade direct to retailers with whom direct accounts were kept.

As a first step towards merging the companies, Glaxo Laboratories (SA) (Pty) Limited in July 1960 increased its share capital from £250,000 to £750,000 and bought from the British parent company all the assets and liabilities of Allen & Hanburys (Africa) Limited, which ceased to trade and became the property owning company. Glaxo Laboratories (SA) (Pty) Limited then changed its name to Glaxo-Allenburys (SA) (Pty) Limited. Although these steps sound simple, they involved considerable effort in the six months before July 1960. Every product of both companies was re-labelled to reflect the new company name; stocks labelled with the Glaxo-Allenburys name had to be accumulated for release after 1 July, when the separate Glaxo and A & H products were withdrawn for re-labelling with the new company name.

Another major pre-merger task was to educate Glaxo's representatives in

Allen & Hanburys' products and conversely, to put A & H representatives through a crash course in Glaxo's products. When the sales teams were combined, in July 1960, they were equally conversant with the combined range of products sold under the Glaxo-Allenburys' banner. This educative process was not confined to the representative teams: both at Wadeville and Congella, staff were encouraged to stop thinking of Glaxo or A & H, and to begin thinking Glaxo-Allenburys. Soon after the merger, a senior A & H executive at Bethnal Green, wrote that he required a monthly return of all A & H products sold in South Africa for statistical purposes. Birchley, who disliked paperwork, replied regretting his inability to assist because there were no A & H products being sold in South Africa, as the company now sold only Glaxo-Allenburys' products.

With the complete integration of the Glaxo and Allen & Hanburys Companies in South Africa, the Board was reconstituted so as to reflect the new position. Harold Dreebin was already a member of Glaxo Laboratories (SA) (Pty) Limited board, and remained when the company changed its name to Glaxo-Allenburys Laboratories (SA) (Pty) Limited. Arthur Buchan, financial director of A & H (Africa), and Cyril Maplethorpe, managing director of Allen & Hanburys in London, joined the board of the merged company. A little while earlier, Arthur Dawson, who had been a director of Glaxo Laboratories (SA) (Pty) Limited, since its inception in 1948, had resigned on his retirement as Secretary of the British parent company. Idris Lewis, the production director of Glaxo SA, had been seconded to the Brazilian subsidiary of Glaxo group in 1959 (see page 269) and resigned from the South African board in 1960.

The degree of integration achieved by the formation of Glaxo-Allenburys (SA) (Pty) Limited in July 1960 was never regarded as more than interim; active investigations continued into ways and means of improving the efficiency and profits of the new united operation. One step was to shut the inchoate A & H factory project in Rhodesia, which could not compete with the distribution facilities offered by the Glaxo agents in the territory, Geddes Limited, which were by far the dominant wholesalers in Rhodesia. Allen & Hanburys had acquired a factory site in Rhodesia, on which building had not begun, and had sent two representatives to soften up a market where they had no real hold. The project in retrospect seems grandiose for a country with Rhodesia's population, and it is likely that it would have fared similarly to Allen & Hanburys' Nigerian venture, where an impressive building fronted a comparatively insubstantial business. Not only did distribution from the A & H factory cost more than the commission for which Geddes would provide a superior distribution service but, in addition, Glaxo in England owned a 33 per cent stake in Geddes' share capital. The Salisbury property was eventually sold.

Two sections of the Congella business with substantial turnover but doubtful profit were generics and galenicals. The Torch Brand range of products had been built up on the trade in Haliborange Tablets and mainly covered an extremely broad range of generic tablets and liquids, such as every wholesaler carried, together with a few proprietary products. The Torch Brand range was drastically pruned: only a comparatively short list of products with proprietary value was retained and marketed countrywide through wholesalers, a rationalisation which while reducing turnover in Torch Branch products, improved the range's profits.

The business in galenicals was conducted along similar lines to that of every major wholesaler in the country, providing the retailer with exactly what he demanded. Virtually every order was a 'one-off' packing job: if the chemist wanted half a pound of a drug he got it; if the next retailer wanted three-quarters of a pound, he also got it. This was an extremely expensive operation, but one justified by Allen & Hanburys on the grounds of obligation to the public. Despite the forebodings of the Congella staff who had run this trade for years, it was decided to embark upon pre-packaging of all galenicals. A survey was made to establish the most appropriate pack sizes for each galenical; thereafter that drug was available only in pack sizes. This enabled galenical packing to be undertaken on a production line basis and hence properly costed and realistically priced. To Glaxo-Allenburys' relief, retailers accepted the innovation with few grouses. More significantly, other major wholesalers quickly copied Birchley's initiative and within six months every one of them had switched to similar pre-packaging of galenicals.

A survey of the South African pharmaceutical industry in 1962 revealed that of the 27 major companies, Glaxo-Allenburys had 9.6 per cent of total turnover, but spent 15.85 per cent of the total wage and salary bill, and employed 16.7 per cent of total staff.[27] These figures persuaded Birchley that it was essential to consolidate all pharmaceutical activities at Wadeville, especially as the accounts for 1962–1963 disclosed that 50 per cent of Congella's gross manufacturing profit came from fifteen specialities, whose production could be transferred to Wadeville without requiring additional buildings. As this decision scarcely reduced staff numbers it was not wholly satisfactory. The combined capacities of Wadeville and Congella far exceeded foreseeable demand; but there were difficulties in closing Congella without damaging galenical sales in Natal and wholesaling activities in that province. Of the twenty-seven major pharmaceutical firms operating in South Africa, Glaxo-Allenburys was the only one running two separate establishments.

In 1962 Evans Medical was taken over by Glaxo Laboratories in the UK. Fortunately the Evans business in South Africa posed fewer problems than

Allen & Hanburys (Africa), since it was considerably smaller than either that of Glaxo or A & H, and was essentially confined to ethical pharmaceuticals, distributed through wholesalers along traditional Glaxo lines. Evans had few sales staff and owned no property in South Africa. There was no point in bringing Evans into Glaxo-Allenburys (SA) (Pty) Limited as even with the now combined sales staffs of Glaxo and A & H, Glaxo-Allenburys were promoting a huge list of products. It was therefore decided that ESL & W (SA) (the Evans subsidiary) would continue to operate as a separate company although every possible economy would be pursued.

South Africa in 1962

By 1962 the South African subsidiary was, in terms of capital employed, the fourth largest of the Glaxo group's overseas operations; its ranking in return on capital employed, however, was seventh, an indication of the unsolved problems remaining (see page 377). Until the late 1950s the apartheid policies of the South African government, and international reactions to those policies, scarcely intruded upon the conduct of pharmaceutical subsidiaries there. But the tariff protectionism of the Nationalist Government in Pretoria forced foreign business to invest in more local production, and the increasing bureaucratisation of Afrikanerdom also had repercussions on the tendering system and other aspects of sales. The organisation of factory workers also had special requirements, and the fact that blacks were largely excluded on price grounds from prescription of modern chemotherapies affected the economics of distribution in such a large country. By 1957 Jephcott was:

convinced that the standard of living of the native must improve ... the native market afforded both a challenge and an opportunity but its problems will not be solved at Greenford. We shall need to treat them as a research project tackled in the field and be prepared to spend a modest sum annually, say £10,000/£20,000 for a period of years by seconding two or three persons to the market to study the native needs ... to devise products and to experiment in marketing procedures.

But generally in the 1950s the treatment of black Africans, either in a political or medical sense, was not an issue for Glaxo or Allen & Hanburys. This changed after 1960, with the 'wind of change'; the state of emergency which followed the shootings at Sharpeville and the departure in 1961 of South Africa from the Commonwealth. Apart from the financial crisis of 1960–1961 which this provoked in the South African economy, it marked a turning point in the political context of Wadeville's operations: politics gradually became more obtrusive. The new and increasingly delicate relations between business and politics were illustrated by Birchley to Jephcott in 1963. A 'terrific furore' was caused in South Africa by a documentary film 'Sabotage in South Africa' shown on British and American television. It was considered 'most horribly slanted to show S. Africa up in a bad light': Bristol-Myers in America were co-sponsors of the film's broadcast in the USA. 'As a result, the local Bristol-Myers organisation – who naturally have no control over their parent company's advertising – have incurred the most severe displeasure of the S. African government and the damage it has done to their business here is quite incredible.' This incident temporarily affected Glaxo because 'when the storm first broke' the South African Broadcasting Corporation reported that the objectionable film had been sponsored by 'the overseas company of a large Wadeville pharmaceutical firm', which seemed to mean Glaxo, although the situation was later clarified. As Birchley wrote:

The violence of the anti-Bristol-Myers feeling amongst the general public is one of the most astonishing things I have ever encountered . . . dozens of people of both English speaking and Afrikaans speaking sections of the public have told me that under no circumstances will they ever buy another Bristol-Myers product and our representatives report that . . . chemists in all parts of the country have returned all B-M stocks and refuse to sell them. Doctors in many cases now refuse to see B-M medical representatives and I imagine that their prospects of ever getting a Government or Provincial tender in future are remote in the extreme.

Birchley expected that 'Bristol-Myers turnover here will drop by over 50 per cent in coming months and it may well be that their local business has been dealt a mortal blow through no fault of the local executives'. He begged Jephcott that in Glaxo's advertising and sponsorship, 'the utmost care is taken to ensure that wittingly or unwittingly our name is not associated in the slightest degree with any material that might be construed as critical of South Africa, otherwise we could so easily suffer the fate of Bristol-Myers and find our business wrecked overnight'. To this Jephcott replied that he was 'not a bit surprised at the reaction in South Africa . . . amongst certain political groups it is the popular thing to throw bricks at South Africa, and most regrettably; it does not seem to be anybody's business (not even of South Africa) to make the objective unbiased statements as to what South Africa is doing for the African. You have to come to South Africa to hear about that, and the vast majority of those who are very vocal have never been within a thousand miles of the country.'[28] In the event Bristol-Myers' business recovered after a short depression, but this incident typified special difficulties which were an increasing undercurrent in South African business from the late 1950s. Jephcott's sympathies are clear from the Bristol-Myers' incident, but as the South African government became more entrenched and politically isolated, the attitude of some Glaxo senior executives in London to the Wadeville subsidiary became less responsive.

In July 1963 Jephcott resigned as a director of Glaxo-Allenburys (SA)

(Pty) Limited. According to Birchley, from the subsidiary's formation in 1948:

his contribution to any success achieved by Glaxo in South Africa was immeasurable. To those of us privileged to work with him he was a most inspiring leader and his frequent visits to South Africa were always looked forward to by the staff. Sir Harry had an almost uncanny knack of inspiring confidence – no matter how harrassed or hassled he might be with problems, after meeting H.J. and chatting for half an hour about matters in general (not the specific problems) one felt on top of the world and able to achieve anything. His ability to delegate was amazing. With overseas executives, once he had made his choice and appointed the person, Sir Harry put complete and utter trust in him and backed the person to the hilt. Any suggestion of 'back seat driving' from London was anathema to Sir Harry; several times he said to the writer, 'I am not interested in what decisions you take Leslie in South Africa until the year ends in June – then if I'm not satisfied you will hear soon enough'.[29]

While Jephcott remained chairman of the Glaxo group, Birchley's operations were sure of sympathetic although by no means uncritical treatment: but perceptions of the South African investment, and of some individual features of its market, began to change after 1960.

15

Glaxo in Europe

The European continent, and specifically the original six members of the Common Market, provide another key marketing sphere in which Glaxo's performance can be judged. In the inter-war period, Nathans and later Glaxo Laboratories had put some effort into creating sales agencies and other outlets, with success in Greece and Italy, but rather less so elsewhere (see chapter 5). Senior executives in the 1940s felt little affinity with continental Europeans – Jephcott himself was a poor linguist – and indeed in the immediate post-war era of political dislocation and raw material shortages, it was understandable that British industrialists should concentrate on opportunities outside Europe, in the Dominions or elsewhere.

By the early 1950s economic and political conditions in Western Europe were returning to equilibrium; German and Italian growth exceeded British from the early 1950s, as too did French growth from the middle 1950s. But by then Jephcott and most of his senior colleagues in London were too committed in time and resources elsewhere to give much thought to markets across the Channel and North Sea. In mitigation it can be said that the company felt hamstrung by Treasury or Bank of England regulations and that some executives perceived that Britain's low rate of post-war investment had put the country at a disadvantage to continental Europe, both specifically in the pharmaceutical sector and in broader terms of national manufacturing competitiveness. Unusually for a British company, Italy has provided Glaxo's main market on the European mainland. For a crucial decade after the Second World War, it was the only country on the continent to which Jephcott and his executives gave any concerted or systematic attention, and even this would have been reduced had not the meticulous care given to financial matters by the local managing director meant that the subsidiary was strong and self-sufficient in cash terms, and able to generate its own programme of growth.

Glaxo in Italy

There are interesting features of the Italian pharmaceutical market. One is that Italian patients, and hence their doctors, prefer symptomatic to prophylactic medicines. Italians traditionally like to feel and see their medicaments having almost immediate effect, and tend to stop taking their dosages (and perhaps seek other medical advice) if results do not occur within a few days. The second Italian characteristic is a marked preference for treating illnesses at home with medicines, rather than in hospitals. This partly is psychological in origin. The family unit is a strong and enduring bond in Italy, where patients prefer to be nursed by their own relations; moreover, many Italians do not care for the discipline and regulated regimen of hospitals, which some people regard as akin to prison. But in addition to these psychological explanations, there is a solid historical basis for the Italian emphasis on home treatment. It was only after about 1953 that there was any sizeable Italian hospital building programme, and until the 1950s, *faute de mieux*, doctors were compelled by the limited hospital beds available to treat patients at home with medicines. Habits acquired before 1953 have persisted long after the hospital building programme was completed. (Somewhat similar traditions also survive in Spain and Portugal.)

Another critical characteristic of the Italian market has been its patent law. There was controversy in Italy on the patentability of pharmaceutical products and their manufacturing processes from 1859, when Article 6 of the Law on Industrial Patents established that medicaments could not be subject to patent. This law did not expressly extend the prohibition to processes of manufacture, but in practice the Patent Office always refused to issue patents for processes of manufacture of medicaments. A subsequent law of 1934 permitted the patenting of manufacturing processes of pharmaceutical products, while another in 1939 annulled its predecessor, but neither actually operated. The second was, in fact, declared illegitimate by the Supreme Court of Appeal in 1951, a sentence reversed in 1957 by the Constitutional Court, whose judges, however, invited the government to re-examine the question. Increasingly Italy's post-war industrial development, the diplomatic pressure exercised by other nations, and anticipation of the requirements of uniform legislation within the Common Market made a solution to this problem exigent. Unfortunately, the instability of Italian government resulted in all proposals either being discarded in favour of more urgent legislation, or being referred to procrastinating committees in order to postpone controversial action.[1] The unsatisfactory state of Italian patent law had long-term commercial disadvantages for Glaxo. For example, in 1959, when griseofulvin had not long been on the Italian market, Farmitalia, who were also Merck's Italian agents, approached the product's co-licensors, ICI and Glaxo, stating, in effect, that given the state of Italian patent law they could begin griseofulvin manufacture and sale with impunity, but would be prepared instead to take a technical licence from Glaxo, and pay a royalty, while undertaking to restrict their activities to Italy. Glaxo accepted that they were being stretched across a barrel, but were inclined to submit.[2]

It was not until well after the period under consideration in this book that full patent protection was introduced in Italy. Until then there flourished in Italy a range of small and medium-sized pharmaceutical companies, privately owned and controlled by Italians: in some cases a single individual and his immediate family. In 1962 it was estimated that there were 1,200 such companies in existence, of which only about eighty were noteworthy. These naturally had been unable to afford any sort of research department and lived by copying the products of foreign multinationals in a manner which sometimes was little short of piracy. It is against this, rather unpromising, background that the development of Glaxo's Italian business should be seen.

In 1945 the Glaxo Laboratories' board in London adopted the main proposals of a report from Peter Gent (see page 124) recommending that the Italian company (sequestrated during the war – see chapter 6), should be revived, as soon as practicable, if possible with external local shareholders. From the outset Gent saw the political and marketing advantages of trying to internationalise Glaxo, and to increase its ties with indigenous interests in local markets in Europe. His views were heard with respect and often agreement in London, but made little practical impact until after 1963. However, in response to Gent's proposals of 1945, the London board determined not only to rehabilitate the Italian company, but to seize every advantage to expand its activities, despite realising that net profits available to the parent company from the Italian subsidiary would in the short-term be trivial or even non-existent. Both Gent and the London board recognised the advantage that might accrue from being in at the start of the reconstruction of the post-war Italian pharmaceutical market. Thus in December 1945, all the shares in the Italian company were bought back by Glaxo Laboratories for about 6m lire, met out of the accumulated profits in Italy.

It could hardly have been expected that production would resume, after six years, without difficulty. However, a particularly bitter blow was the problem in the winter of 1945–1946 with the quality of the Colloidal Calcium and Ostelin (C, C & O) manufactured. In the pre-war market these products had not only 'contributed in a spectacular and, perhaps, disproportionate manner to the company's financial success, but had played an extremely large part in establishing the good name of Glaxo Laboratories in Italy'.[3] By February 1946 the crisis was such that practically all stocks on the market had to be withdrawn. It proved, however, to be a temporary problem although some Glaxo products, for example Adexolin Liquid, lost their pre-war predominance and market share permanently.

In the summer of 1946 the Italian company resumed its relations with Latteria Piacentina for the supply of roller press milk powder. Latticello (Babeurre) was re-launched on the market in June. Ostelin Forte (milk powder) and Minadex (vitamin product) were also successfully launched. The success of Minadex was 'spectacular, but ... attended by very considerable growing pains', chief among them being the shortage of sugar, one of its chief ingredients, which meant that there were only sufficient supplies for northern Italy and these satisfied less than half the demand. The rising costs of the raw materials for Minadex meant that its profit margin was almost completely eroded.[4] Rising prices were also a characteristic of the Italian economy in the post-war years. Principal retail food prices increased by 102 per cent between August 1946 and September 1947; the national cost of living index rose 2,800 points in the twelve months to August 1947. As in other European countries, the government wrestled with reconstruction with inadequate funds, conditions which encouraged 'the free (or black) market to flourish unhindered'.[5]

In 1946–1947 the Italian company's major marketing success was with Ostelin 800, the unit sales of which increased by nearly 400 per cent over the previous year. It secured first place amongst its competitors (Lepetit, Maestretti and Erba) despite their earlier start. Despite the poor quality of supplies, C, C & O maintained a surprisingly high level of sales. Glaxo penicillin was officially launched in Italy in July 1947. The country had previously relied on United Nations Relief Administration supplies of American penicillin, but when the Rome government set its first import quota, the Italian company obtained a share along with five importers from the USA. Glaxo's share was about 13,000 mega, but it would have been at least double that if, at a critical juncture, an Anglo-Italian commercial agreement had not been signed permitting Italy to convert much of its sterling credit into dollars.

Summarising the position in 1947, Gent claimed that Glaxo Laboratories' prestige 'in Italy is high and the Italian company can be reckoned among the best pharmaceutical houses, but its name is not yet pre-eminent'. He hoped to remedy this but warned that in place of the pre-war 'atmosphere of nationalism and political discrimination', there would be intense and unprecedented foreign competition. 'The Italian Company has no time to lose in developing its resources', he urged; 'one of the most galling of decisions recently taken was to forego material already licensed for import, because lack of production facilities made it impossible to handle the particular product for at least 12 months.'[6]

Even with the limited revival of business, the premises in Via Quirico Filopanti, measuring about 35,000 square feet, were heavily congested. Herbert Palmer visited Verona in 1947, and confirmed that additional space was urgently needed if the subsidiary was to maintain and expand sales of its existing pharmaceutical products and introduce new ones. Some suggestions by Palmer on improvements to layout were adopted, but these only relieved congestion in the immediate term, and it was decided that a new site should be found on which to erect a factory capable of primary production.[7]

In 1948 the Italian subsidiary changed its name, in line with the parent's company's policy, to Laboratori Glaxo SpA. Its capital was increased to 50m lire, partly because of the revaluation of the plant due to depreciation in the value of the currency, and partly to finance the construction of a new factory. The latter was officially opened as part of the programme of the international medical congress held in Verona in 1949. The guest of honour at the opening ceremony was Sir Alexander Fleming, who was attending the congress and who was at the same time made an honorary citizen of Verona; The street on which the new factory stood was subsequently named for him. The opening ceremony was the only occasion that Jephcott personally visited the Italian subsidiary between 1945 and 1953, but the subsidiary's managers visited Greenford and Jephcott placed great trust in Gent. The trademark and consultancy agreements between the English parent and its subsidiary company were signed in London in 1949, when capital was increased from 50m lire to 250m lire, with the issue of 200m lire in shares to the parent company in consideration for the trademarks. However, because of doubts raised by legal advisers as to tax liability, the completion of the issue of these shares was delayed until the following year.

The value of sales reached almost 100m lire in 1950, but Laboratori Glaxo's sales of penicillin were threatened by the Leo company, which was financed on the Italian side by Count Armenisi, proprietor of the *Giornale d'Italia* (a major Rome daily newspaper), principal shareholder of the Banca Nazionale Agricola and a powerful supporter of the Christian Democrat party. Armenisi was the *eminence grise* behind various restrictions introduced by the Italian government during 1950 which many doctors feared would revive the penicillin black market product, especially as Leo's product had not been marketed by November of that year. The demand for penicillin from Laboratori Glaxo was enormous, and in 1951 the company had to introduce a system of rationing on the basis of the previous year's sales.

The locally produced Leo penicillin had secured a firm foothold in the market by March 1951, and although doctors professed to dislike it, there were soon signs of its substitution for both Glaxo and American penicillin. There was also a chronic shortage of streptomycin, but no restrictions were introduced on its importation. An arrangement was therefore made with a

60 Sir Alexander Fleming's visit to Verona in 1949 coincided with the opening of the new Glaxo factory there. Sir Alexander on the left with Derek Maton, Deputy General Manager.

61 Sir Alexander and Peter Gent being greeted by some of the women staff
of the Italian company.

local penicillin manufacturer, who did not make streptomycin, to exchange
streptomycin for penicillin. By 1953, however, Italian production of penicillin certainly, and streptomycin probably, exceeded national requirements,
and the consequent price-cutting made it doubtful whether Laboratori
Glaxo could profitably trade in imported packed streptomycin. As soon as

62 Jephcott visited Verona in September 1953, seen here on the right in conversation with Gent.

the penicillin market collapsed after 1951, Verona and London considered developing primary manufacture of foods and vitamin B_{12}, but decided against it for the time being. The parent company was waiting on events until its hand was forced.

Palmer advised Laboratori Glaxo in 1951 that in place of the lost antibiotics business, the best immediate prospect was to start Italian production of Farex and Casilan (another milk-based food). He based this view on the evidence of the British company's turnover, and the experience of other subsidiaries. He felt it would be impossible for the Italians to sell contrast media or vaccines on a sufficient scale to be profitable; that there was no hope respecting hormones, until Glaxo had bought expertise in the insulin field; that Calciferol was impossible so long as the British company could supply good quality Ergosterol at a reasonable price; and that there were too many production difficulties for other products to be attempted. Gent however considered that Casilan would hold only limited appeal for Italians, and remained very keen for the Verona factory to become the first Italian maker of Calciferol. In retrospect his scepticism that Farex and

Casilan would appeal to Italian taste was justified. In 1952 Laboratori Glaxo began marketing Farex in English packs, accompanied by intense medical propaganda to paediatricians. It was agreed to wait six months for the results of this campaign before committing themselves to a production project. The large public advertising and propaganda that the campaign entailed were alien to the way in which Laboratori Glaxo had always conducted its business.

In fact sales of Farex proved unexpectedly low (five tons in 1953). This was attributed by Jephcott to its high retail price, deriving in turn from the price Greenford charged the Italian company – 38/ – (£1.90) Cif for a 20 lb container, while a retail chemist in England could buy the same weight already packed in 10 oz cartons for 32/ – (£1.60). Hutton, too, was astonished that the Farex invoice price was so high: 'Here we have another relic of this procedure of charging 33.3 per cent on cost, except that in this case it is not on cost ex-factory, but on the cost of placing the goods in the country of destination.'[8] But he opposed Jephcott's suggestion that Greenford should supply Farex in cartons invoiced at production cost as too generous, especially in view of the difficulty of remitting dividends from Italy. Despite the Farex failure, Laboratori Glaxo had large amounts of free cash. By 1953, with an issued capital of 250m lire, reserves totalled 667m lire.

By this time four of the senior executives of Laboratori Glaxo were Italian and three English: H. A. Gent (Managing Director), Dr Cav. Ugo Rinaldi (Deputy), Vittorio Agnesone (sales manager), Derek T. Maton (production manager), G. T. Gardner (chief accountant), Luigi Fresco (secretary) and Enrico Fezzi (medical adviser). This staffing reflected Gent's policy of trying to Italianise the management of the company. Although some Italian executives came to feel that this policy did not move fast or far enough, in fact Gent was both bold and prescient in his pursuit of it, especially in the 1950s. Its effects on the quality and motivation of the Veronese management were clear by the time of Jephcott's retirement: the strength and self-confidence of Italian executives in later periods, in comparison with those of other overseas subsidiaries, was notable, and made a contribution to profitability.

Of the immediate post-war Italian nationals, Agnesone was the first medical representative recruited when the Italian company was formed, and after returning from war service, was made Director of Medical Propaganda, with additional charge of the Sales Department. In 1946 Rinaldi was appointed as assistant manager under Azzini. The brother-in-law of Colasanti, an earlier Glaxo director of medical propaganda, he had been prior to 1940, as a Government official in Rome, 'extremely useful to us in all the relations with the Ministries on official questions, so much so, that even before the death of his brother-in-law, he was paid a retaining fee'. He remained extremely useful to the company. As Gent commented in 1946: 'Rinaldi has a very quick and intelligent brain, good organising ability, wide experience, and perhaps most important of all, a most successful way of handling people. His appointment represents undoubtedly a great strengthening to our staff.'[9] At a time when many of Glaxo's overseas subsidiaries were dogged with manning and organisational difficulties, the Italian company was conspicuous for its success in this respect, suggesting that other British companies consistently under-estimated the wealth of managerial talent available in Italy. Jephcott, who appeared to show no partiality for the Italian company although there existed between him and Gent a close personal friendship, 'was very impressed with the organisation' after a visit in 1953. As he noted at the time: 'Directors and higher executives are very competent and well chosen for their respective responsibilities. At all levels there is obvious loyalty to Glaxo and pride in the organisation. Credit is due to Mr Gent for the excellent morale of the staff.'[10]

By 1956 it was clear that the Verona company, with its existing line of products, was in a rut and needed a broader product base. Greenford prices of certain raw materials, while reasonable by British standards, left Laboratori Glaxo with small profit margins, so much so that in several cases cheaper supplies were available from elsewhere in Italy. In 1956 the Italian company was given a discount of 30 per cent on vitamin B_{12} prices, though other subsidiaries received only 25 per cent, in order that they should have a margin of about 10 per cent on bulk sales. Farmitalia were constantly reducing their price for vitamin B_{12} in Italy, and Glaxo had to follow suit; as a result the margin on bulk sales fell to about 6 per cent, of which a half disappeared as commission. In Gent's opinion:

Farmitalia, producing here, are obviously in a position to go much lower and also our experience indicates that they will do so. They make no secret of . . . their intention . . . to eliminate all competition.[11]

In the event, Farmitalia dropped their prices of B_{12} so sharply that by November 1958, they were established as its main producer and seller in Italy, 'and Gent found it very difficult to get any business in the face of their competition'.[12] There was additional keen competition from Germany and other continental suppliers.

Competition in Italian pharmaceuticals quickened in the 1950s. Squibb, after the success of an aggressive sales policy in antibiotics, transferred its efforts to general pharmaceuticals, with equal impact. It spent heavily on both prestige advertising and specific advertising until the Italian consumer had become 'Squibb minded' by 1956. In contrast, the Glaxo company, although maintaining a small but valuable trade in antibiotic preparations, could not compete on straight antibiotics, while its failure caused it to be regarded as the 'Cinderella' of the major pharmaceutical firms.[13] Instead it was dangerously dependent on Colloidal Calcium and Ostelin sales. By the nature of the business, pharmaceuticals turnover had to support practically the whole organisational cost; food sales still returned a loss although turnover increased. The company's lack of competitive edge was demoralising, Gent felt, especially to the sales staff. The mid 1950s were also a politically tense period for the Italian pharmaceutical industry. There was a strong criticism in parliament and the press, particularly from the Communists, of prices, and Gent privately conceded:

There is some justice in this for with little 'cost consciousness' by doctors, the vested interests of the chemists in high prices, and the inability of the public to judge on price merit, most pharmaceutical firms base their sales tactics of proprietary products on keeping prices up and forcing sales with high-powered and often exaggerated and non-ethical publicity and propaganda expenses. Large numbers of medical representatives are paid on commission: a continual and excessive supply of free samples; a heavy subsidising of innumerable medical congresses, free gifts to doctors, etc.

Gent added that 'The medical profession in its acquiescence to these methods is not wholly free from blame.' With some antibiotics, trade discounts reached 75 per cent, and Gent doubted whether this fierce competition ultimately benefited the final consumer, the public. As a result of public criticism, the public health department introduced arbitrary and inconsistent price controls on pharmaceutical products, and for a time at least Gent complained of procrastinating disputes with bureaucrats following Glaxo's non-acceptance of the prices granted to them.[14]

By the mid 1950s, the Italian subsidiary was obtaining all its penicillin from Leo, at a price almost 40 per cent below the market price, which Gent considered no longer 'unduly high'. In the early 1950s, local producers had 'attempted to keep their prices high enough to cut out those who were engaged in secondary production, but their agreements in this connection had, as might be expected in Italy, broken down'.[15] Laboratori Glaxo still took all its dihydrostreptomycin from Greenford, which required only a low profit from the price it quoted. In December 1956 Greenford's price for streptomycin to the Italian company was 5.36d per gram base, which with one exception was the lowest price charged to any of Glaxo's overseas subsidiary companies. On these streptomycin deliveries, the Italian company made a profit of about 10 per cent, less sales commission. Thus Italy differed from most world markets where the price of a gram of streptomycin base was about 50 per cent above the price of a mega of penicillin.

Italian medical opinion did not favour preventitive medicine, and there was little demand for vaccines: the Italian company was not selling any at the end of 1956. Vaccines were governed by more stringent regulations than other pharmaceuticals, and could not be handled, as imported bulks 'manufactured', i.e. packed locally. Gent therefore wanted to open a locally financed vaccine unit producing Pertussis and Triple Antigen. As to vitamin B_{12}, 'Gent said there was no morality in the market for this material – or for many other raw materials – in Italy.' Price-cutting was 'rampant'. To these laments Jephcott re-affirmed that subsidiary companies 'must be allowed to buy materials in the cheapest market even though these materials were offered by Greenford . . . if we were not to destroy our overseas assets'. Gent contemplated expanding the Italian company's business by extending the range of food products, but feared that it would be 'very expensive' to try to get back into the babyfood market from which they had been forced to retire during the war. In any case, as Jephcott observed, the food business did not yield substantial profits.[16]

Under legislation which became operative in 1955 a discount of 17 per cent was imposed on all payments for pharmaceutical preparations, made by institutions which managed the National Health Schemes; 11 per cent of this discount was borne by the pharmaceutical industry, and 6 per cent by wholesalers and chemists. This was resented by the manufacturers. The industry's attempted defence of itself was, however, handicapped by 'lack of real unison between members of the industry and the continuation of the Antibiotics Trade Discounts War, publicly known and justly censured'. The wholesalers and chemists had a vested interest in the continuation of the trade discounts war and ignored efforts to change practice. There was also apathy and even antagonism from the medical profession, principally because of excessive medical publicity and propaganda to which they were subject. Gent complained:

During the past year the prices we have requested, and demonstrated as reasonable with our cost analyses, have been cut by anything from 15 per cent to 25 per cent. To refuse to accept the cut price means either relinquishing the product or interminable negotiations which seldom bring satisfaction. While admitting the fairness of much of the criticism of high prices of certain pharmaceutical preparations – this cannot be denied when one realises that an antibiotics chemist seldom received less than 50 per cent trade discount – the Government has been heavy-handed in dealing indiscriminately with all sections of the industry. The Government Health Department themselves are not entirely blameless, and often bend before the pressure of certain vested interests. Unfortunately in this type of game we are not so well equipped, and consequently often suffer. This state of affairs which has ruled for the past two or three years will certainly continue. Ours must be a long-term policy to maintain the Glaxo prestige and . . . keep our faith in sound well-proven products at reasonable prices.[17]

By December 1956 there was an agreement in force between the four penicillin producers and Glaxo not to sell below certain prices. Although this benefited Glaxo, contraventions of the agreement were frequent and increasing. The agreement provided the chemist with excessive discounts of between 40 per cent and 50 per cent on face prices, but it did provide reasonable margins.

The company's fortunes continued to fluctuate in 1956–1957. Final turnover of 1,051m lire was lower than forecast as also was net profit at 37m lire. Calci-ostelin, as before, continued to compensate for disappointment in other products: Gent was particularly thankful for Calci-ostelin B_{12} Orale, introduced in February, of which about 130,000 packs with a total value of nearly 35m lire were sold. Although antibiotics exceeded the forecast 28m lire, the margin continued to suffer and gross profit was only up by 4m lire. The veterinary market development also proved slower than anticipated.

There were difficulties too in registering new products. Gent continually faced the problem that prices authorised by the government were slashed to rock bottom, so that the final price barely made the product worthwhile. A good example of this was the registration of Plasmadex in November 1956. For the 1 vial pack of 5 cc. the Italian company sought approval for a price of 830 lire, expecting to be granted 700 lire, calculated to give a gross profit of 67 per cent. Instead it was granted a price of 350 lire, yielding only 35 per cent gross profit. Nevertheless, by 1957 Jephcott felt 'that the Italian company was making its way out of the doldrums' of recent years, albeit at a 'laboriously' slow rate. At a conference in June of that year:

Gent explained that progress in the pharmaceutical business in Italy very largely depended on the ability of the manufacturers to offer new products. To be first in the field with a novel product or presentation meant a great deal. Entirely new products were not susceptible to the same degree of price control as products which merely imitated or varied something that was already on the market; at the same time they had a very great appeal to doctors and patients alike.[18]

As the registration procedure took at least six months, it was imperative for the subsidiary to have information for registration as early as possible, even before a saleable product had been evolved. Although Farex sales did not yet cover expenses, the volume of Farex sales in Italy had at last reached the point at which locally produced material was cheaper than the imported product, and plans were accordingly agreed for Farex manufacturing facilities to be installed.

Throughout 1959 Gent suggested ideas for the expansion of Laboratori Glaxo, not only to meet the challenge of the Italian market but also of the developing Common Market. His proposals for a concerted strategy for major European markets are described below (see page 357), but so far as Italy was concerned, he was equally urgent and fecund in ideas for expansion. Palmer and Gent agreed that for effective coverage of the whole of Italy, fifty salesmen and a product of real novelty were needed; in the meantime Gent wanted Glaxo to build at Verona a steroid plant to produce

hydrocortisone and a small fermentation unit, initially to produce griseofulvin. Although both projects might prove unremunerative, Gent felt they
would develop an effective basic manufacturing capacity. Later it was
decided that, whatever Common Market external tariff on antibiotics was
finally agreed, it would probably cover the extra cost of production in Italy,
although it might be economic to import a crude intermediate from Britain.

Following the merger in Britain in 1958, Glaxo found that Allen &
Hanburys' arrangements in Italy were extremely complicated. The company
was tied to Importex Chimici Farmaceutici SpA by long-term agreements
and a 25 per cent financial interest. It was clearly against Glaxo's interests to
extend the manufacturing operations of Importex, but A & H's agreements
provided Importex with a right to do this, which Importex's energetic
owner, Kropf, might wish to exercise. Jephcott feared Kropf might approach A & H to provide finance for such operations. In the event the
problem was temporarily solved by refusing him licences for new products
from the combined company in England and finally resolved by his
premature death.

Late in 1959 the Italian government introduced the chemical INAM
(Principal National Health Instruction) reform which considerably extended
the list of products qualifying for National Health benefits. This stimulated
sales of certain traditionally static products, and improved the possibilities
of new products once they had been admitted to the list. There was,
however, the burden of the discount of 12 per cent on the face price of
products prescribed under the various health schemes. As from October
1959, there were enforced reductions in the face prices of all products
containing penicillin. A further blow to the company was the exclusion of
griseofulvin from the list of products admissable under INAM. Other plans
had to be changed, too, by the Italian company as a result of the new list. A
planned expansion of the sales of hydrocortisone lotions had to be
abandoned when they were not included in the scheme. Admission to the
free prescription list was also important. In 1960 griseofulvin and Efcortelan
lotion were admitted to the free prescription list of the Italian health service
as the result of eighteen months of work by Gent and his staff. Their success
was largely due to the support of Trabucchi, the then Minister of Finance, a
Veronese who was a fellow member with Gent of the Verona Rotary Club.
Trabucchi was able to support Glaxo precisely because griseofulvin was
produced locally in Verona.

As in other countries, arbitrary action by the government of the day was a
hazard. In 1960 the Italian Government surprised the pharmaceutical
industry by removing import duties on poliomyelitis vaccine, but without
making allowance for stocks already in the country. At the same time the
product life was reduced to six months. Consequently such sales as

Laboratori Glaxo managed to make were at a loss, and the rest of the company's stock had to be written off. In June 1961, Gent once again pushed the view that Laboratori Glaxo should attempt to extend its activities in food products, but Jephcott felt that such an operation would be initially costly, and only moderately profitable in the long-run. Apart from the publicity expenses, it might involve substantial expansion of manufacturing capacity. By that time the company's capital employed (including some cash) was nearing 1,000m lire; issued capital was 500m lire; while reserves and undistributed profits were also almost 500m lire. The following year the issued capital was increased by 250m to 750m lire.

Between 1946 and 1962 Glaxo's Italian subsidiary showed a mixed performance, but one which, in a country beset by inflation and political problems and striving against powerful US competitors, was very creditable. Few British companies established subsidiaries in Italy. One of the few that did was Metal Box and one of its managers noted:

Normal Italian business methods and the attitude of the local authorities are quite foreign to British standards ... it is vital that any foreign enterprise should have experienced, able and trustworthy Italian advisers.[19]

Glaxo, fortunate in this respect, was even more indebted to Peter Gent, who had recruited them. Seen in historical perspective, Gent's stewardship at the Italian company was an outstanding achievement and one which had a profound long-term effect.

Glaxo in the rest of Europe

In March 1957, by their signature of the Treaty of Rome, Belgium, France, Germany, Italy, Luxemburg and the Netherlands created the European Economic Community (EEC). Among other provisions the Treaty provided for the gradual elimination, over fifteen years, of all tariffs and other important restrictions between the six members, the establishment of a common external tariff and the creation of a managed market in agriculture. Glaxo Laboratories watched the development closely, as the company's exports to the members of the EEC had risen in the previous three years from 4 per cent to almost 12 per cent of their total export trade. Much of this increase was due to higher sales of bulk materials, mainly antibiotics and vitamin B_{12} to continental manufacturers. It was in the hope of creating a wider non-EEC European market that Britain joined with Austria, Denmark, Norway, Portugal, Sweden and Switzerland in establishing the European Free Trade Area (EFTA).

The inspiration for closer European integration was mainly political, but there were suggestions that a larger European free market would favour the extension of mass production and result in lower costs per unit of output. In practice, the keen competition offered by national producers on the continent made this a dubious proposition, at least for pharmaceuticals in the short-term, as British companies had limited organisations or marketing structures on the European mainland. Apart from strong local competition, Britain's drug exports to Western Europe were restricted by fiscal and other legislative provisions. Tariffs on drugs and medical specialities varied in the EEC and EFTA countries from between 0 and 12 per cent in Belgium to up to 35 per cent in Germany, and additionally most European countries maintained quota restrictions. There were restrictive registration requirements in France and Scandinavia, price controls in Belgium, Italy, Norway and Sweden, and licensing restrictions under social insurance schemes in France, Italy, the Netherlands and Switzerland. In Belgium imported drugs were subject to compulsory and costly analysis, and the use of trademarks was restricted in Denmark. As a result of these barriers, Glaxo's European structure was embryonic though expanding in 1957.

In France there was no Glaxo agency, although Dextran Sulphate was sold in bulk to Equilibre Biologique (formerly Alimentation Equilibre). There was also an agreement, expiring in July 1960, whereby Clin-Byla had first option on Glaxo's new products for exclusive manufacture and sale on royalty terms in France and its overseas possessions. Clin-Byla was a partnership of long-standing and complex structure, dominated by two families, the Comars and the Midys. The Byla Group, as experts in biologicals, were one of the first companies to market insulin in France. The Comar family had, in 1897, taken over the business of an inventor of proprietary products, Dr Clin, and by the 1930s were selling a wide range of alkaloidal and chemotherapeutic preparations. After agreements between the companies covering two decades, Byla united with Clin-Comar in 1950, with the result that brand names such as Clin-Byla were marketed by the Clin-Comar company.

In Germany, Glaxo Laboratories also had no agency, but vitamin B_{12} was sold in bulk to Dembach-Roussel, Dionosil to another importer, and foods to the British forces in Germany through the Navy, Army and Air Force Institutes (NAAFI). Small quantities of radiologicals and streptomycin were sold in the Netherlands through the company's agent, Philips-Roxane NV, of Amsterdam, which also took bulk deliveries of vitamin B_{12}; other merchants handled small amounts of bulk antibiotics and vitamin B_{12}. A large Danish business consisted mainly of bulk penicillin sold to Lovens Kemiske Fabrik,[20] but Glaxo's Copenhagen agent, Ercopharm, also took small quantities of radiologicals and of Casilan, Eltroxin and streptomycin. In Norway, Glaxo's agents, Nyegaard of Oslo (see chapter 4), took radiologicals, vitamin B_{12} and (on a consignment basis) some antibiotics. Glaxo marketed antibiotics in Sweden via the 'chosen instrument' technique; this kind of joint arrangement, which was legally binding but did not involve Glaxo in investing funds, became commonplace in the 1980s but was unusual at that time. But, generally, Glaxo's senior managers were apprehensive about the detailed working of such arrangements and distrusted joint ventures. For Europe as a whole Herbert Palmer reached the uninspiring conclusion in 1957: 'Rather as a result of past history than because of future prospects, it would be desirable to buy time.'[21]

From the outset in 1957 it was seen as desirable that the Italian company should spearhead the marketing attack on the EEC. The alternative options for Laboratori Glaxo were threefold: to establish local sales offices and organisations in leading EEC markets like France or Germany; to develop its own primary manufacturing; or to ally itself with existing French, German or Italian interests to achieve a viable sales and manufacturing organisation. On ground of cost the last of these alternatives was preferred by the London board, and Peter Gent was keen for Verona to be authorised to lead the group into Europe. But despite the circulation of a series of clearly argued memoranda, setting out the opportunities, there was a reluctance to make any commitment, and by the early 1960, there was still no concerted plan for Glaxo in Europe.

'We have in effect ignored Europe during all the years of Glaxo Laboratories, and there are many valid reasons for this, but do we want to go on ignoring it?' Gent demanded of Fred Wilkins (then Deputy Managing Director of the parent company) in a personal letter of 1959. He advocated a decision to start a company organisation in each of the main European markets, based on a cogent and accurate analysis of the group's position.

As a policy of development of the G.L. empire I can see no alternative. Agencies are a complete anachronism and concessions of rights to other companies, although they can be of very practical value, only end up by assisting the development of someone else's organisation instead of our own. One can argue of course that we should have started this twenty or more years ago, in which case we could have had today a network of companies each at least equal to what we now have in Italy, but ... circumstances were against such a policy at the time, because in addition to the uninviting aspect of pre-war Europe, the rapid development of G.L. itself brought such pressure on the company's total resources that they were perforce utilised in areas of most tranquil promise. The immediate postwar period again offered a great opportunity but there was so much to be done with what we had that it was not unnatural to put aside consideration of what we had not.[22]

But in 1959, so it seemed to Gent, given the creation of the EEC, it was essential to establish Glaxo Laboratories in Europe. 'The time is ripe for such development since resources are greater and the whole stature of the organisation so much more mature', he wrote.

We at least have the happy coincidence of an opportunity presenting itself where strength to grasp it is adequate . . . the first thing to do is to create our own sales and medical propaganda organisation in each main country . . . from the background of a local G.L. Company. We should of course find the introduction of many of the older products very hard going if not impossible, but Glaxo production and research today is of a quality high enough to support a first-class sales organisation in any country, allowing the necessary time for its establishment, and meanwhile the newer products like Griseofulvin provide ready opportunities.[23]

In 1959 Palmer, Austin Bide and Arthur Langridge of the Subsidiary Companies Unit explored the possibility of cooperation with Union Chimique Belge SA (UCB), described as 'similar to, but smaller than, ICI'.[24] The company's diversification into pharmaceuticals dated from the early 1930s, when they had enjoyed privileged access to Belgian colonial markets for anti-malarials and arsenicals. With products ranging from basic chemicals and fertilisers to fine chemicals and pharmaceuticals, by the late 1950s it was known for its technical strength and financial success. Its pharmaceutical division had been relatively recently established, with its research directed at finding new synthetic chemotherapeutic agents in a limited number of fields; its concentration on fermentation, biological and food products had fructified in a series of novel products. UCB was interested in establishing reciprocal marketing agreements with other European manufacturers, and discussed an arrangement with Glaxo Laboratories covering the EEC (excluding Italy) and other countries including Finland, Sweden, Australia, New Zealand, India and Pakistan. The idea was that each company should, in its own best markets, manufacture and sell selected products of its partner under the latter's house-name and trademarks, in such a way that the partner could eventually take over its own lines if it wished.

UCB's approach to European trading, which involved a willingness by Glaxo to offer reciprocal facilities within the Commonwealth, was alluring because it offered the chance of establishing, at lowest cost, a Glaxo sales force in Benelux, France and Germany. The scheme involved negotiations by Palmer, Hurran, Langridge, Bide and Gent, who all supported the idea of an association with UCB. Glaxo's trading agreement with Clin-Byla for France, expiring in July 1960, was one obstacle, but the Board resolved in December 1959 to seek an arrangement with UCB covering the Benelux countries, Belgian Congo and France, but here again negotiations proved laborious and unsatisfactory. 'Six months have passed and we are no nearer to starting sales promotion in the Common Market countries, whereas the situation in Europe is developing rapidly, and almost every day brings news of new ventures', Gent wrote in 1959. The Milan office of the accountants Price Waterhouse, he added, received a daily average of three enquiries from

British and American concerns interested in starting new companies or initiating European joint ventures.[25]

In 1960 Glaxo and UCB set up Glaxo (Benelux) SA jointly as a result of their talks with Union Chimique Belge. Glaxo Laboratories and UCB each subscribed 2 million francs (authorised capital being 5 million francs), but cooperation, which began well, did not develop as originally envisaged, because of the British company's acquisition of Evans Medical. UCB had hoped that, in return for helping to revive Glaxo sales in Benelux, the British would reciprocate by using UCB's facilities in France, thus providing a better spread of overheads in that market and enabling a quicker development of their French sales force. Evans Medical, however, had established a presence, albeit precarious, with a small range of products in France, Evans SA of Paris (with capital of 10,000 new francs, of which Evans Medical and Laboratoires Delagrange SA held 51 per cent and 49 per cent respectively), and Glaxo therefore had little need to avail itself of UCB's French organisation. As a result, by September 1961, UCB had indicated that it would not provide further risk capital for Glaxo (Benelux), and hinted that it would accept the severance of the original agreement. The first year's accounts, covering ten months trading to September 1961, showed a loss of about 2.5 million francs, and Palmer's reports were only lukewarm about the future. Glaxo made a 50:50 agreement with UCB in which Glaxo retained the right to buy out UCB.

In 1961 when the Prime Minister of Great Britain, Harold Macmillan, announced his government's intention to apply for British membership of the EEC, there was much speculation as to how this would affect British industry. Glaxo was one of the companies specified by the *Financial Times* (31 July) as most likely to benefit from national political incorporation into Europe. Opinion within the company was more realistic about Glaxo's status in Europe, but divided as to the merits of involvement in the European Community. Peter Gent, who advocated an outright European commitment, saw more clearly than some that owning a substantial Italian company did not constitute a strong foothold in Europe. As early as 1958, when Beecham Research Laboratories made a breakthrough in semi-synthetic penicillins, Gent wrote that Beecham 'seem to have very close contacts with America but nothing in Europe' and,

if there is even the slightest chance of doing a deal with Beecham for Italy this might be a heaven-sent opportunity for the Italian Company to get into primary production at last. I should have liked to say 'to Europe' instead of 'for Italy', but have we anything to offer in the other European countries?[26]

He felt that British companies would be compelled to fight a defensive action at home against foreign competitors unless they faced continental markets

directly: the commercial risks from membership of the Community had to
be met if Glaxo was to sustain its growth. Gent urged that only by squarely
confronting its European competitors would Glaxo remain an autonomous
company with a decent return on investment.[27] Although the reluctance of
the British directors to integrate the company with Europe contrasted with
Gent's progressive views, he was keenly aware of the perils posed by the
EEC. Even if abolition of tariffs and trade barriers potentially provided
another 170 million customers for Glaxo, it also exposed the company to
competitors whose 'commerce had been developing at a greater rate than
our own in conditions decidedly less favourable than those in which UK
companies had been able to work, consequently menacing our own position
both in the UK market and in the Commonwealth markets where we have
hitherto had a very substantial degree of protection'.[28] In addition to the
difficulties of competing with new rivals on equal terms, there was also the
problem of financing and organising a European group.

Finance was always Gent's *forte*, and he was at pains to try to convince
head-office sceptics that the finance of continental ventures was not an insuperable hurdle. Existing British currency regulations were largely directed
at limiting the export of capital for industrial production ventures and not
at sales promotion organisations. Gent urged that Glaxo should imitate
certain of its American competitors in forming Swiss holding companies to
retain the assets of overseas subsidiaries, a practice which was attractive
because taxes were not levied in Switzerland on profits from foreign
operations so long as they were held abroad. As Gent pointed out, foreign
concerns which formed Swiss holding companies to control their assets
abroad were also entitled to special concessionary tax rates. Loans from
shareholders to such holding companies were also tax free out of profits.
These fiscal provisions enabled cash to be accumulated at a rate impossible
in other countries and created funds for new investment and expansion. In
particular, profits made by one subsidiary could be loaned to another
subsidiary without incurring Swiss tax, as taxes only became payable when
the holding company distributed a profit to its shareholders. As Gent wrote,
'there is nothing underhand about this arrangment and the English banks
have advised their clients quite officially of the facilities which are available'.[29] Low Swiss import duties also enabled trading profits to be accumulated there, and as Gent showed, many of the Italian company's competitors
worked this to advantage.

Gent advised that the Swiss market, almost untapped by the Glaxo group,
'could undoubtedly give highly interesting results if it were worked systema-
tically by an adequate team of our own medical representatives organised
from a group company situated in Switzerland and this work could be
financed during the early non-profit making stages by the income arising

from the sales of bulk products to the Italian company and also the French company, thus reducing the incidence of taxation at least in Italy'.[30] In any case the formation of a Swiss holding company offered an attractive means of financing operations in Europe. With its sound, unrestricted currency, operations in Switzerland enabled a company to retain a high proportion of its profits for reinvestment. It had the advantage over an overseas trading company of profits being freely transferable world-wide and of taxes only being assessed when the dividend was declared to shareholders. In principle, goods could be sold to the Swiss holding company and distributed throughout Europe, and even beyond, keeping all the trading profit and thereby minimising tax.[31]

In Britain the reception of such proposals was cautious. Contrary to Gent's interpretation of affairs, Palmer thought that the Bank of England and the Treasury would be reluctant to see half a million pounds invested on the continent for marketing strength rather than in fixed assets. A transfer of investment from the Italian company into shares in a Swiss holding company was dependent on Treasury consent, quite apart from representing a loss of dividend from Verona.[32] Whether or not this procrastination signified corporate reluctance for the Italian subsidiary to gain in operating or financial autonomy within the group as the nucleus of a new European continental grouping, the sentiment extended beyond the parent company: the Bank of England, as agents for the Treasury, continued to scrutinise and restrict expenditure on subsidiaries outside the sterling area. Although Gent perhaps exaggerated the misperceptions of Whitehall, he was correct to deplore the parent company's hesitancy: 'every postponement of co-ordinated action in Europe makes it increasingly evident that time is not on our side', he wrote, citing speeches by Selwyn Lloyd, the then Chancellor of the Exchequer, in support of this view.[33]

Furthermore, Gent took exception to Palmer's notion that the company was reluctant to take any risks unless there was the 'early prospect of one or two significant products coming along in which we would have an exclusive, or virtually exclusive position'. He remonstrated that:

This attitude will keep us for ever bound in a vicious circle. It has happened in the past and will happen again that when the major product comes along we have not the organisation to exploit it ... for unless we do so we shall always be obliged to farm out in major European markets the very products which could establish the Glaxo name in an unassailable fashion.[34]

In July 1961 Selwyn Lloyd introduced an emergency budget intended to redress the trade imbalance and loss of invisible earnings. Its provisions included the restriction of overseas non-sterling investment to cases which would benefit the balance of payments by a return within eighteen months

and encouragement of the repatriation of overseas earnings. Gent condemned the logic of Lloyd's 'proposals and particularly the exhortation, on
the one hand, to limit dividends and, on the other, to increase remittance of
earnings from abroad'. He felt that the Treasury did not understand the fact
that 'limitation of currency for new investment abroad will automatically
encourage people to make every effort to retain more, and not less, profit
abroad to finance development'. Gent believed that the possibilities of
export from Italy should be investigated in the widest sense, starting with
the European and particularly the Common Market countries. But more
generally, so Gent wrote:

the UK approach to the Common Market makes even more urgent that the Glaxo
organisation should extend itself in Europe and we should be . . . setting up sales
promotion organisations. The location of production is in many cases a secondary
consideration and in any case is a question of economic strategy that must be applied
to the study of each specific project. In Italy . . . our local standing would enable us to
raise capital here for any production venture that economic or other factors indicate
to us as suitable for an Italian location.[35]

He felt that the company should urge the Treasury and Bank of England to
liberalise their policy towards expansion outside the sterling area, particularly given precedents established by Metal Box and Lucas Industries in
obtaining loan capital and exporting currency for development. Subsequently Gent obtained confidential details of Lucas Industries' financial
plans for an effort in the EEC, which he forwarded to London, only to be
told by Jephcott in December 1961:

Quite frankly the problem of financing is not one which worries me: I am much more
concerned with what it is proposed to do and how to do it. Until the programme
carries conviction, I am not prepared to worry my head about the finance.[36]

Aside from financing operations in Europe there remained the problem of
organisation. Gent was convinced that Glaxo's ultimate goal should be to
establish a unified and integrated organisation throughout Europe, even if
this could not be achieved at a stroke. The immediate aim was to stimulate
efforts in Germany, France and Benelux whilst approaching the overall
problem 'not in terms of single markets or even in terms of the Common
Market but rather with the ultimate object of extending Glaxo's activities to
countries comprising at least the Six [of the EEC] and the Seven [of the
EFTA] in which we are not yet established either at all or in any substantial
degree'.[37] Gent proposed a two-fold programme of autonomous subsidiary
organisations in France, Benelux and Germany followed by expanding cooperation, consultation and mutual assistance.

Discussions at senior level within the company demonstrated that a
standardised corporate identity would prove elusive. At the meetings of the

senior European executives of the Glaxo group held in Brussels in 1962–1963, there were vexatious discussions on the naming of company products, and in particular whether to use 'Glaxo', 'Glaxo-Evans', 'Glaxo (incorporating Evans)' or 'Glaxo (*anciennement* Evans)'. Evans enjoyed goodwill amongst the French medical community so that it was unlikely that another foreign competitor would be welcome in the market, but Glaxo's research reputation provided reasons for including its name on the product. Gent, for example, opposed having a 'transitional period' using both names and was eager to have products identified with 'Glaxo' because this would in the long term be beneficial. The remainder of the committee disagreed, mainly because probably not more than 500 of the 28,000 doctors in France, had even heard the name Glaxo. The problem of international standardisation of products was, for British companies at least, acute in the early 1960s. The fact that even today a solution can be less than obvious shows that the Glaxo Group's discussions were far more than personal squabbles.[38]

Conclusion

It was not, as Dr W. J. Reader has pointed out, until the 1960s that 'the post-imperial truth revealed itself ever more starkly', and 'the attractions of Europe grew rapidly brighter with the early blossoming of the EEC. Here was a market which seemed to offer all and more than all that could be found in the old colonial world, and without the political hazards and uncertainties. British businessmen's suspicions of all those foreigners turned into enthusiasm, and the pattern of British investments began to set heavily towards continental Europe.'[39] In the period covered by this history, the major European markets were dominated by the European chemical companies whose commitment to pharmaceuticals was both larger and of greater longevity than that of Glaxo – Bayer, Hoechst, Sandoz, CIBA, Roche and Rhone-Poulenc. Glaxo had a strong base in Italy and steadily rising exports from the UK to Europe in the late 1950s, but the caution which had led the company to minimise direct foreign investment in the post-war period, also dictated delay in the deliberations over taking firmer steps into Europe.

'For British Industry', the Confederation of British Industry concluded in 1966, 'the advantages of trade without hindrance in a larger, dynamically expanding market would provide the opportunity to plan operations on a truly European scale, to grow, to develop and to concentrate in the way that the capital-hungry, research-based industries of today and tomorrow need.'[40] These advantages applied to Glaxo even more than to most companies, yet it was characteristic of the group's difficulties in the early 1960s that, despite excellent analyses by Gent, Langridge and others, the capacity for decisive action was lacking. The CBI and political leaders might welcome prospective British membership of the EEC for its 'revitalising psychological stimulus of free and strong competition' and 'widening of the mental as well as physical horizons',[41] but the reality, as Glaxo's discussions show, was that even a company of its enterprise initially reacted to this prospect with considerable caution.

16

Epilogue

The Glaxo Group in the early 1960s consisted of the business whose growth from its origins as a New Zealand merchanting firm has been traced in this history, along with the multifarious and only partially integrated activities of the companies with which it had merged in recent years. The acquisitions of Allen & Hanburys Ltd and Evans Medical Ltd were followed by those of the Edinburgh Pharmaceutical Industries Ltd in 1962, the British Drug Houses Group Ltd in 1967 and Farley's Infant Food Ltd in 1968. Over the next two decades rationalisation occurred, with the disposal of some subsidiaries involved in activities not related to the Group's primary objective, defined as the discovery, development, manufacture and marketing of prescription medicines.

From at least the time when Glaxo Laboratories became involved with penicillin, the company had identified itself as predominantly concerned with pharmaceuticals, but in 1962 about half of the value of home turnover was still derived from food products, dried milk, baby and infant foods. Over the next two decades Glaxo's strategy and structure changed and the Group's business expanded to a different level. While some expansion was a consolidation of existing operations, some was the result of changing the emphasis within the business and some came from new directions which the Group decided to follow, more particularly the decisions taken in the 1960s to introduce an international strategy and to start basic research.

The development of Glaxo's overseas operations to 1962 has been charted and in the early 1960s half of the Group's total turnover derived from manufacturing and trading overseas, the bulk of which was in the countries of the Commonwealth and South America. While the balance of power in the international pharmaceutical industry shifted in the post-war years to the USA – of the twenty leading companies in the industry, more than half are American – the international nature of the business was increasingly recognised. Mergers and restructuring in the industry have created even

Table 8. *The distribution of Glaxo sales 1965–1989*

	1965 percentage	1985 percentage	1989 percentage
UK	38	16	11
Europe	20	30	27
North America	4	26	41
Central and South America	3	2	1
Africa	7	5	2
India, Pakistan and Middle East	19	8	4
Australia and New Zealand	4	3	3
Japan	—	5	7
Far East	5	5	4
	100	100	100

Source: Sir Paul Girolami: *The Development of Glaxo* (LSE seminar paper 1985, revised and printed by the company, 1990).

larger multinational corporations, active in the major markets which are in the developed countries. Even so, no company has achieved a share of more than about 10 per cent of any major country's pharmaceutical market (except Glaxo which has 12 per cent of the UK market), partly because each company can operate in only some of the more than forty different classes of drugs in the industry. Over the last twenty years the main thrust of Glaxo's marketing and manufacturing overseas has changed with this perception of the situation. The shift from the countries of the Commonwealth, first to Europe where the countries of the EEC constitute the world's largest pharmaceutical market, and then to the second largest market, the USA and Japan, has transformed the geographical distribution of Glaxo's sales, as can be seen in (table) 8.

Glaxo's reluctant steps to expand in Europe beyond its existing Italian subsidiary, taken at the time of Britain's first and unsuccessful attempt to join the EEC, have been chronicled. In the years immediately before and after British entry in 1972, Glaxo had to strengthen its position in other European countries – Germany and France, for example – in order to establish a firm presence in Europe.

Although Glaxo had been trading in Japan since the 1950s it was not until 1972 that the Group, recognising the size of the market there and, belatedly like many other British companies, the 'Japanese economic miracle', decided that it could no longer treat Japan as a residual market. By buying into and building onto the existing agency in Japan, Shin Nihon, and establishing co-marketing agreements with other Japanese pharmaceutical companies Glaxo's operation in Japan grew rapidly. By 1985 sales were five and a

(a)

(b)

(c)

63 (a) Allen & Hanburys' Bethnal Green factory; (b) production of Haliborange tablets and (c) Sterivac production.

half times and the number of people employed there two and a half times what they had been in 1975.

Glaxo's independent entry to the USA market, the largest in the world, was inhibited for many years both by the agreements and licensing arrangements made in the immediate post-war years with major US pharmaceutical operations and by the Group's own realisation of the difficulties and costs of establishing themselves there. In 1978 the decision was taken to buy Meyer Laboratories Inc, of Florida, an organisation with a strong marketing force, which was what Glaxo had lacked in its previous and distant pre-war attempt to break into the American market. Building onto this base manufacturing and development facilities to sustain a presence in the USA was expensive, but led to spectacular growth in a short time. In 1985 sales were forty times and assets employed eighty times larger than in 1980.

In these markets as well as those in which it had been for a longer period well-established Glaxo launched new products, the fruits of research and development both at Greenford and at Allen & Hanburys' research

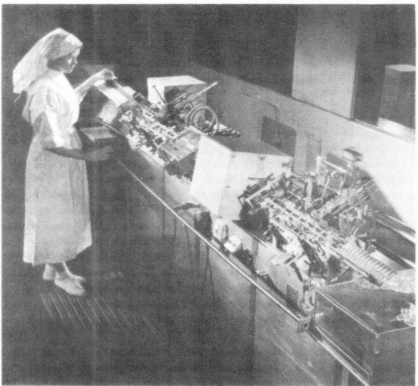

64 Evans Medical had its transport fleet to carry its products from the factory at Speke.

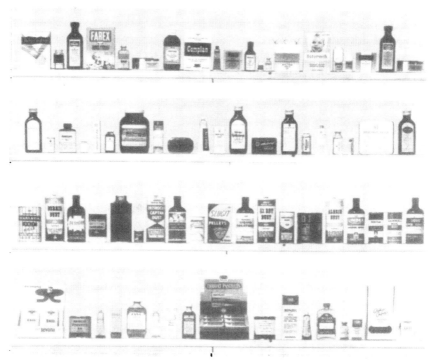

65 Glaxo Product ranges under the names of Glaxo, Allen & Hanburys, Murphy and Evans in 1962.

establishment at Ware. The successful anti-asthma drugs, salbutomal (Ventolin) and beclomethasone (Becotide), came from Ware as also did the anti-ulcer drug, ranitidine (Zantac) which, in 1988, became the first-ever pharmaceutical product to have sales of more than £1bn in one year. At Greenford a range of successful antibiotic cephalosporins were developed. It is of vital importance for a pharmaceutical company to exploit its discoveries in all possible markets both in order to recoup the research and development costs and to finance more research, which will in turn result in further discoveries to sustain and maintain the company's position in the market. Over the last two decades the costs of research and development have spiralled while the therapeutic revolution has apparently peaked and decelerated; in the world pharmaceutical market, ninety-three new medicines were launched in 1961, but in 1980 the figure was only forty-eight. In the developed world the pattern of disease has changed too, with cancer, heart disease and ulcers replacing tuberculosis and malnutrition as the most challenging areas of medical research. They, along with herpes and AIDS, present more intractable research problems.

In the period betwen 1945 and 1962 Glaxo's research policy was discussed constantly, particularly the question of long-term research expenditure as against short-term development work, in a framework of containing research costs. Greater expenditure on basic research was one of the policy decisions of the early 1960s which has taken the Group's business onto a different level. In 1984 Glaxo spending on research was 100 times what it had been in 1964 which, even after allowing for inflation, is indicative of a greater input of resources into research and development. Moreover, the Group's R & D expenditure is no longer confined to the UK: 25 per cent of it in 1985 was outside the UK. The Group's long-term commitment to the Japanese market has been demonstrated in part by a substantial investment in an R & D centre there, which will eventually employ some 300 scientists. The pharmaceutical industry has to maintain a constant search for the most flexible way of carrying out research and development and the problem of how to measure the return on the amount so invested comes under periodic scrutiny not only by the industry but also by government and public bodies. The issue of whether there is an optimum size for the most productive research and development work and if so, what it is, has been a matter of public debate more than once.

It was explored by the Monopolies Commission in 1972 when a bid by Beecham for Glaxo and a proposed defensive alliance between Glaxo and Boots to thwart the Beecham takeover were referred to the Commission. Describing both companies as 'outstandingly successful', the Commission's Report noted that Beecham's pharmaceutical prowess was largely based on one therapeutic class, semi-synthetic penicillins. It was not the Glaxo management's 'expressed distaste for a merger with Beecham on the ground that its image as a thrusting seller of non-ethical medicines and toiletries would damage the work of Glaxo as a well backed scientific company and seller of ethical medicines' that persuaded the Commission. Rather it was the view they took that the size and market power of any merged company was more likely to reduce rather than increase innovation:

Beecham's research interests are relatively narrow, as is also the range of drugs which it sells. The prosperity of such a company is . . . vulnerable . . . [and it has] in consequence, a strong incentive to remedy its potential weakness by broadening the scope of its research. Should Beecham acquire Glaxo . . . the resulting company would be much less vulnerable . . . and some of the research which Beecham might otherwise have done . . . might not be undertaken.

The Commission's conclusion that the merger would not be in the best interests of the British pharmaceutical industry accorded with Glaxo's own view. The period of self-generated growth which followed for the Group has taken it to a higher ranking in the corporate league of the world pharmaceutical industry, giving it greater security against such hostile bids.

That growth took place in a rapidly changing environment and one where the pharmaceutical industry had to contend, like other industries, not only with volatile economic conditions but also with more stringent regulations specific to the industry. The procedures for testing and registering new medicines have, in the interests of greater safety, become more complex and lengthier, thereby reducing the patent life of the product in the market and hence the return the company can expect to make. The testing and registration regulations and the bodies that administer them vary from one country to another, as also do the means adopted by governments to contain or reduce the costs of health care. In Britain, for example, the Voluntary Price Regulation Scheme established in 1957 was replaced with the Pharmaceutical Price Regulation Scheme after the Sainsbury Committee reported in 1967. It is necessary for pharmaceutical companies to grapple with methods of prescription, promotion and pricing which vary widely from country to country.

Glaxo has rightly been considered in recent years to be one of the brightest stars in the firmament of British industry. The success of the Group today, different in size, structure, organisation and nature as it is from Glaxo in 1962, has been built on the foundations laid and the lessons learned by Glaxo Laboratories in the pharmaceutical industry in the years covered by this history.

Appendix: Glaxo statistics

There are no surviving accounts for Joseph Nathan's trading before the business was turned into a company, and those from the company's early years are sketchy. The tables that follow should be taken as indications of trend rather than exact statements of quantity.

Table A.1. *Joseph Nathan & Co 1899–1903*

	Profits £
1899	4,210
1900	9,055
1901	10,757
1902	8,768
1903	10,447

Table A.2. *Joseph Nathan & Co Ltd – 1915–1946*

Year	Issued Capital £	Capital Employed £	Net Profit £	Net Profit Return £
1915	166,140	203,168	9,570	4.7
1916	185,015	226,053	12,400	5.5
1917	189,397	281,672	25,272	15.4
1918	198,860	271,874	32,170	11.8
1919	440,893	540,066	50,481	9.3
1920	448,711	575,308	70,850	12.3
1921	762,050	912,833	63,671	7.0
1922	888,429	957,259	20,176	2.1
1923	1,013,540	1,047,753	11,486	1.1
1924	''	1,056,372	32,118	3.0
1925	''	1,083,065	50,694	4.7
1926*	728,694	771,886	27,167	3.5
1927	731,854	731,854	55,474	7.6
1928	''	803,797	61,216	7.6
1929	''	809,676	65,377	8.1
1930	''	827,741	68,066	8.2
1931	''	821,868	52,311	6.4
1932	''	801,151	28,789	3.6
1933	''	805,673	39,522	4.9
1934	''	828,236	55,563	6.7
1935	''	849,668	74,432	8.8
1936	''	867,836	85,166	9.8
1937	''	886,358	91,398	10.3
1938	''	906,819	90,647	10.0
1939	''	941,144	88,510	9.4
1940	779,635	947,385	87,600	9.2
1941	''	961,270	72,849	7.6
1942	''	985,249	82,942	8.4
1943	''	1,010,583	84,298	8.3
1944	''	1,029,183	77,563	7.5
1945	''	1,058,207	87,988	8.3
1946	''	1,096,541	97,298	8.9

Note: *1926 £286,686 capital written off

Source: Balance Sheets and Profit and Loss Accounts. Authors' calculations of net profit as percentage return on capital employed.

Table A.3. *Glaxo Laborator-ies Ltd – 1936–1945*

Year	Sales £	Net Profit £
1936	683,585	143,569
1937	789,971	257,796
1938	985,440	175,660
1939	1,182,841	230,761
1940	1,391,738	261,586
1941	1,774,560	345,878
1942	2,077,204	397,645
1943	2,499,928	565,627
1944	2,521,292	503,383
1945	2,528,907	512,277

Table A.4. *Glaxo Laboratories Ltd – 1947–1963*

Capital employed, trading profit, net profit, profit percentage return on capital employed

Year	Capital employed‡	Trading profit	Net profit	Percentage return on capital employed‡
1947*	2,637,317	1,663,746	1,139,982	43
1948†	3,455,347	1,628,619	976,101	28
1949	4,591,286	1,960,996	930,247	20
1950	5,010,002	2,711,511	1,237,085	25
1951	7,754,617	3,491,847	1,332,829	17
1952	9,380,813	3,687,034	1,580,425	17
1953	10,436,112	3,071,367	1,580,610	15
1954	11,567,259	2,922,929	1,484,189	13
1955	12,651,002	2,825,527	1,556,501	12
1956	13,895,892	3,002,692	1,765,428	13
1957	16,799,133	3,889,750	1,837,629	11
1958	21,880,808	5,310,166	2,610,566	12
1959	23,853,089	5,387,617	3,017,796	13
1960	27,562,943	6,786,320	3,760,410	14
1961	33,636,492	6,991,301	3,717,801	11
1962	35,469,790	6,754,917	3,342,643	9
1963	39,414,750	7,599,815	3,326,034	8

Notes: * Year ending 30 September
 † 9 months only because of change of year end to 30 June
 ‡ Authors' calculations

Source: Glaxo consolidated accounts

Table A.5. *Glaxo Laboratories, Capital 1947–1962*

Issued capital (£)		
1947–1949	779,635	
1950–1952	1,496,350	1949 reserves capitalised
1953–1954	2,292,700	
1955–1956	3,885,400	1956 share capital reorganised
1957	5,478,100	
1958	6,208,883	
1959–1960	9,783,550	
1961–1962	13,391,867	1962 reserves, nearly £3m capitalised

Table A.6. *Glaxo Laboratories Ltd – home and export sales 1950–1962*

	Home	Export
1950	4,273,710	1,654,477
1951	4,571,171	2,967,184
1952	4,717,000	2,915,000
1953	5,031,000	3,038,000
1954	4,279,000	2,870,000
1955	na	na
1956	5,643,000	3,874,000
1957	7,290,000	4,680,000
1958	8,435,000	5,634,000
1959	12,818,000	5,922,000
1960	13,722,000	6,616,000
1961	19,936,000	7,767,000
1962	20,223,000	8,814,000

Notes: 1958 Includes Murphy Chemical Co. and Irish Co
1959 Includes Allen and Hanburys
1961 Includes Evans Medical

Source: Glaxo board papers 1950–1962

Table A.7. *Glaxo Laboratories Ltd – trading profits and losses of overseas subsidiaries 1951–1962*   (£ sterling)

Year	Argentina	Australia	Brazil	India	Italy	New Zealand	Pakistan
1951	23,700	65,100	91,700	468,700	264,700	82,000	130,000
1952	51,900	59,400	48,500	404,500	170,900	162,000	106,800
1953	15,500	38,000	(38,400)	420,800	88,400	114,100	111,200
1954	89,200	60,800	(117,100)	544,400	17,100	131,000	167,400
1955	63,200	23,500	(17,800)	484,600	36,600	96,600	69,900
1956	62,100	33,000	7,500	704,500	29,200	94,400	214,000
1957	117,300	69,000	5,400	1,006,500	36,400	90,200	212,000
1958	116,000	76,500	7,500	1,225,000	146,000	107,600	330,000
1959	125,536	97,092	3,027	1,321,887	148,363	98,629	337,142
1960	156,959	167,900	(1,800)	1,829,400	141,600	126,800	456,500
1961	170,000	123,000	(9,400)	1,986,000	156,000	134,000	517,200
1962	9,000	108,000	(2,500)	1,850,000	282,000	167,000	546,000

Year	South Africa	Uruguay	Canada	Ceylon	Colombia	Cuba	Ghana	Malaya
1951	28,500	5,300	(9,700)					
1952	32,300	6,400	(2,200)					
1953	34,100	4,700	(7,300)					
1954	35,500	11,400	(9,900)					
1955	9,250	5,100	(5,280)					
1956	21,200	4,300	10,500					
1957	68,700	3,200	5,400					
1958	79,000	4,700	15,000					
1959	29,813	2,820	6,300	41,797	12,921			
1960	25,582	2,300	22,810	43,575	46,200	(3,100)		
1961	99,000	3,000	7,000	31,000	27,000	6,900	(2,600)	60,000
1962	67,000	5,600	16,000	44,000	23,000	7,000	(3,200)	69,000

Note: () indicate losses

Source: Glaxo board papers. 1951–1962

Table A.8. *Glaxo's overseas subsidiaries 1954*

	Trading profit £'000	Total turnover £'000	Percentage of total turnover in each country		
			food	pharms	antibio
Argentina	89	545	31	48	21
Australia	61	549	44	19	37
Brazil	(117)	120	6	86	8
Canada	(12)	70	2	28	70
India	544	3200	33	31	36
Italy	17	466	4	63	33
New Zealand	131	617	19	27	54
Pakistan	167	1140	23	32	45
South Africa	36	307	7	27	66
Uruguay	11	99	0	62	38

Source: Glaxo board papers

Table A.9. *Capital employed and return on capital employed for the Glaxo Group – year ending 30 June 1962*

	Capital Employed £'000	Return on Capital Employed Percentage
Glaxo Laboratories	10,049	24.3
Allen and Hanburys	2,785	28.6
Evans Medical	4,658	13.1
Murphy	996	15.4
Ireland	80	25.0
India	2,922	63.2
Pakistan	1,788	30.6
Ceylon	181	28.7
Malaya	179	31.1
Australia	1,357	7.6
New Zealand	754	22.5
Nigeria (1)	472	(3.6)
Ghana (1)	51	(105.8)
Sierra Leone	24	–
South Africa	941	10.4
Italy	360	83.9
Canada	60	–
Cuba	88	9.1
	£27,745	25.7

Note: (1) Losses were incurred in Nigeria and Ghana

Source: Glaxo board papers

Notes

1 The origins – Joseph Nathan & Co

1. This quotation, and much information in ensuing paragraphs, is taken from Nathan family papers in Glaxo Archives, Box 1.
2. B. Weinreb, and C. Hibbert, eds. *The London Encyclopaedia*, (London, 1983), pp. 396–7.
3. Glaxo Archives, Box 1.
4. Marriage Certificate of J. E. Nathan and Dinah Marks, Glaxo Archives.
5. Sir L. Woodward, *The Age of Reform* (Oxford 2nd edn, 1962), p. 394.
6. F. Broeze, *Steam Navigation to Australia and New Zealand* in *The Journal of Transport History*, volume X (London, 1989).
7. James T. Critchell, and Joseph Raymond, *A History of the Frozen Meat Trade* (London, 1912), pp. 68, 266; Stone, R. C. J., 'The New Zealand Frozen Meat Storage Company', *New Zealand Journal of History*, vol. 5 (1971); P. S. E. Hereford, *The New Zealand Frozen Meat Trade* (Wellington, 1932); R. Perren, *The Meat Trade in Britain 1840–1914* (London, 1978); J. Burnett, *Plenty and Want* (London, 1966), p. 101.
8. Falconer Larkworthy, *Ninety One Years* (London, 1924); Philip Mennell, *The New Zealand Loan and Mercantile Agency Company Ltd* (London, 1894); R. C. J. Stone, *Makers of Fortune* (Oxford, 1973), pp. 21–4; W. H. G. Armytage, *A. J. Mundella: the Liberal Background to the Labour Movement* (London, 1951); T. Lindsay Buick, *Old Manawatu* (London, 1903).
9. For a general view of the New Zealand economy at this time, see C. F. G. Simkin, *The Instability of a Dependent Economy* (Oxford, 1951) and W. J. Gardner, 'A Colonial Economy', in W. H. Oliver, ed., *The Oxford History of New Zealand* (Oxford, 1981), pp. 57–86.
10. Maurice Nathan to Alec Nathan, 1/C/2; see also R. C. J. Stone, *Makers of Fortune*, pp. 19; J. A. Dowie, 'Business Politicians in Action: the New Zealand Railway Boom of the 1870's', *Business Archives and History*, vol. 5 (1965), pp. 32–56; Judith Bassett, *Sir Harry Atkinson* (Auckland and Oxford, 1975).
11. A. H. Ward, *A Command of Cooperatives* (Wellington: New Zealand Dairy Board, 1975); H. G. Philpott, *A History of the New Zealand Dairy Industry 1840–1935* (Wellington, 1937).
12. R. E. Clevely, *Bunnythorpe and District 1872–1952* (Wellington, 1953), p. 51.
13. Auckland *Observer*, 21 January 1882, quoted Stone, *Makers of Fortune*, p. 40.
14. L. M. Goldman, *The History of the Jews in New Zealand* (Wellington, 1958);

obituary of J. E. Nathan, *Jewish Chronicle*, May 1912. We are grateful to Dr A. P. Joseph for his help on Jewish genealogy.
15. Quoted Sir Harry Jephcott, *The First Fifty Years* (Ipswich, 1969), pp. 55–6.
16. Glaxo Archives, Box 1.

2   The Nathans and proprietary foods 1903–1918

1. J. C. Drummond and A. Wilbraham, *The Englishman's Food* (London, 1959), pp. 299–303, 373–9.
2. Edmund Cautley, 'The Use and Abuse of Proprietary Foods in Infant Feeding', *The Practitioner*, vol. 82 (1909), p. 583.
3. F. Coutts, *Report to Local Government Board on an inquiry as to Condensed Milks, with special reference to their use as an Infants' Food*. New Series, No. 56 (HMSO 1911), p. ii.
4. Cautley, 'The Use and Abuse of Proprietary Foods', p. 584. See also Mrs G. C. Frankland, 'Boiling Milk', *Nineteenth Century*, vol. 40 (1896), pp. 454–60.
5. Cautley, 'The Use and Abuse of Proprietary Foods', p. 584. For a resume of the aetiology, bacteriology and treatment of summer diarrhoea, see Leopold Mandel, *The Practioner*, vol. 73 (1914), pp. 390–9. See also F. W. Forbes Ross, *Intestinal Intoxication in Infants* (London, 1897) and his letter in *Lancet*, 1 October 1904, pp. 979–80.
6. C. Killick Millard, 'Dried Milk as a Food for Infants', *British Medical Journal*, 29 January 1910, pp. 253–4.
7. R. P. T. Davenport-Hines, 'F. S. Oliver' in D. J. Jeremy and C. Shaw, Eds, *Dictionary of Business Biography*, vol. IV, (London, 1985), pp. 488–92.
8. Glaxo Archives, Box 1.
9. Clevely, *Bunnythorpe*, pp. 55–68.
10. Alec Nathan, memorandum of 29 March 1917, Box 1/D.
11. On the manipulation of concepts of imperialism in business advertising, see John Mackenzie, *Propaganda and Empire* (Manchester, 1984).
12. Clevely, *Bunnythorpe*, p. 57.
13. Alec Nathan, memorandum of 29 March 1917, Box 1/D.
14. *Daily Express*, 16 March 1904; see also Anon., 'Three Month in the London Milk Trade', *Economic Review* (1894); C. Hassard, 'The Milk Trade from Within', *ibid.*, vol. 15 (1905); P. J. Atkins, 'London's Intra-Urban Milk Supply c. 1790–1914', *Transactions of the Institute of British Geographers*, vol. 2 (1977); P. J. Atkins, 'The Retail Milk Trade in London c. 1790–1914', *Economic History Review*, vol. 33 (1980).
15. Reminiscences of S. Jacobs who joined Joseph Nathan & Co. in 1898, Glaxo Archives, Box 1.
16. Alec Nathan, memorandum of 19 March 1917, Glaxo Archives.
17. Albert Naish, 'The Sheffield Dried Milk Scheme', *British Medical Journal*, 29 August 1908, p. 571.
18. *Ibid.*, p. 573.
19. Joseph Nathan & Co., Board Minutes.
20. W. J. Reader, *Metal Box, A History* (London, 1976), p. 24.
21. *Ibid.*, p. 92.
22. Alec Nathan, memorandum of 19 March 1917.
23. Among the proprietary foods on the market, Biogene was soluble, tasteless, odourless casein, free from starch and sugar. The Prideaux Company made one

of Glaxo's direct competitors, Lacvitum as well as Lacta and an adulterated form
of casein, Casumen, which was marketed as a flake-like powder mixable with
ordinary food and drinks. It was combined with other foods in the form of
arrowroot, chocolate, cocoa, cornflour, biscuits, bread and macaroni; with the
addition of water, a weak alkali and saccharin, it could be used as a diabetic
milk. Casein was also combined with ammonia under the brand name of
Eucasin; with sodium, as Nutrose; with 5 per cent of sodium glycerophosphate
as Sanatogen; and with 20 per cent of albumose (derived from egg albumin) as
Sanose. Another form of dried casein was Allenburys No. 1 Food, produced by
Allen & Hanburys, a dry powder made from cow's milk, with the excess casein
removed, and the deficiency in fat and sugar corrected; it was starch-free and
useful as a temporary infant food in the first three months of life.

Other proprietary foods for infant feeding included condensed milks with
malted flour (Allenburys No. 2 Food; Horlick's Malted Milk; John Bull No. 1
Food); condensed milks with partly malted flours (Manhu; Milo; and Thein-
hardt's Infantina); and condensed milks with unchanged flour (Anglo-Swiss).
Benger's Food was a mixture of cooked wheaten meal and extract of pancreas;
Garnrick's Soluble Food was composed of dessicated milk, malted wheat flour,
lactose and pancreas extract. There was also a wide range of carbohydrate
foods, which were sometimes recommended for judicious use with milk after the
third month of life. Carbohydrate foods were sub-divided between those with
the starch practically unchanged (Neave's, Ridge's, Opmus, Albany, Robinson's
Patent Barley and Groats, Scott's Oat Flour, Chapman's Flour, etc.); partly
malted foods (Allenburys No. 3; Cheltine Infant's Food; Coomb's Malted Food;
Hovis No. 2; John Bull No. 2; Moseley's; and Savory & Moore's); and finally,
complete malted foods (Mellin's; Horlicks; Paget's Malted Farina; Hovis
Babies'; Cheltine Maltose; Diastased Farina; Racia).

Among the pre-digested or peptonized milks there were the Allenburys
peptonizing powders, Fairchild's zymine powders and peptogenic milk powder,
Savory & Moore's condensed peptonized milk, and pre-digested varieties such as
Loeflung's peptonized milk and Backhaus's milk. Paget's Milk Food Company
sold sterilised milk which had been modified in its relative component percentages, and a variety of preparations were sold under the misnomer of facsimile
human milk. The least obnoxious of these were Frankland's Artificial Milk made
by adding cream and whey to whole milk, Somatose Milk and Rieth's Albumose
Milk.

24. F. Van Allen, memorandum of 29 April 1909.
25. Alec Nathan, memorandum of 19 March 1917.
26. John Armstrong, 'Hooley and the Bovril Company', in R. P. T. Davenport-
    Hines, ed., *Speculators and Patriots* (London, 1986), pp. 18–34.
27. Francis J. H. Coutts, *Report to Local Government Board on Dried Milks, with
    special reference to Infant Feeding* (London, 1918), p. 19.
28. Alec Nathan, memorandum of March 1917.
29. Alec Nathan, to Joseph Nathan, 22 December 1909.
30. Alec Nathan, memoradum of March 1917.
31. *Ibid.*
32. *Ibid.*
33. *Ibid.*
34. *Ibid.*
35. J. E. Nathan & Co, Board Minutes, 1916.

36. Later immortalised as Miss Meteyard in Dorothy Sayers' novel *Murder Must Advertise* (London, 1933).
37. Alec Nathan, memorandum of 19 March 1917.
38. Coutts, *Report on Dried Milks*, p. 69.
39. *Ibid.*, pp. 70–3.
40. See Jose Harris, 'Bureaucrats and Businessmen in British Food Control 1916–19', essay in Kathleen Burk, ed., *War and the State* (London, 1982), pp. 135–56; Sir Stephen Tallents, *Man and Boy* (London, 1943). For specific studies of British food control during the First World War, see W. H. Beveridge, *British Food Control* (Oxford, 1928); E. M. H. Lloyd, *Experiments in State Control at the War Office and the Ministry of Food* (Oxford, 1924); *Food Production in War* (Oxford, 1923); E. F. Wise, 'The History of the Ministry of Food', *Economic Journal*, vol. 39 (1929).
41. J. M. Winter, 'The Impact of the First World War on Civilian Health in Britain', *Economic History Review*, vol. 30 (1977), pp. 487–507. See also Deborah Dwork, *War is Good for Babies & other Young Children* (London, 1987).
42. Sir Harry Jephcott, *The First Fifty Years* (Ipswich, 1969), p. 106.

3   Boom and depression for Glaxo and the Nathans

1. Alec Nathan to Wellington Office, 9 August 1919, Minehead box, Glaxo Archives.
2. Alec Nathan, Memorandum of March 1917. Glaxo Archives.
3. Jephcott, *The First Fifty Years*, p. 91.
4. *Ibid.*, pp. 92–3.
5. *G.L. Staff Bulletin*, January 1947.
6. J. Nathan & Co, New Zealand, to South Western Co-op. Milk & Trading Co, Port Fairy, 6 July 1922, D1/5.
7. *Economist*, 21 June 1919.
8. Jephcott, circular of 5 January 1956. D1/1/30.
9. A. Nathan to Archibald Sandercock, 21 August 1919, Minehead box.
10. A. Nathan to Moll, 20 August 1919, Minehead box.
11. F. Nathan to Louis Nathan, November 1922. D1/5.
12. *Ibid.*
13. A. Nathan to J. Nathan & Co, August 1919, Minehead box.
14. A. Nathan to Wellington Office, 9 August 1919, Minehead box.
15. F. Nathan to Louis Nathan, November 1922. D1/5.
16. F. Nathan to J. Nathan & Co, 28 February 1923, D1/5. Prince's wife was also David Nathan's sister-in-law.
17. Nathan and Pacey to F. C. Randall, 4 June 1926. D1/5.
18. Louis Nathan to London Office. 10 August 1925. D1/5.
19. Alec Nathan to Wellington Office, 22 January 1929, D1/5.
20. *Ibid.*, 20 June 1929, D1/5.
21. Unsigned memorandum of 23 July 1929, D1/5.
22. Alec Nathan to Wellington Office, 22 November 1929, D1/5.
23. Pacey to London Office. 22 September 1930, D1/5.
24. *Ibid.*, 22 December 1930, D1/5.
25. Fred Nathan to London Office, 9 September 1930. Pacey to London Office, 22 September 1930, D1/5.
26. Alec Nathan to Fred Nathan, 26 October 1931, D1/5.

27. Alec Nathan to Pacey, 2 September 1936, Joseph Nathan & Company papers, Wellington.
28. F. C. Randall to Wellington Office, 14 March 1929, D1/5.
29. *Ibid.*
30. Alec Nathan, memorandum enclosed in Randall to Wellington office, 17 February 1930, D1/5.
31. Fred Nathan to London Office, 13 March 1930. H. E. Pacey to London Office, 28 April 1930, D1/5.
32. London to Wellington, 31 July 1934, D1/5. 964.

4 Diversification into pharmaceuticals: Glaxo Laboratories Ltd

1. A. L. Bacharach, *Science and Nutrition* (London, 1938), p. 73; see, for example, Maria Theresa Earle, 'The Feeding of the Young', *National Review*, vol. 43 (1904), pp. 793–9, and Report and verbatim minutes of evidence to Sir Almeric Fitzroy's inter-departmental committee on physical deterioration, Cd. 2175 of 1904.
2. W. R. Betts, *Life of Sir John Bland-Sutton* (London, 1956), p. 50.
3. See W. L. Braddon, *The Cause and Prevention of Beriberi* (London, 1907).
4. *Lancet*, 1 March 1919, vol. 169, p. 363.
5. Harry Jephcott and A. L. Bacharach, 'The Anti-Scorbutic Value of Dried Milk', *Biochemical Journal*, vol. 15 (1921), p. 137.
6. Sir Edward Mellanby, 'An Experimental Investigation on Rickets', *Lancet*, 15 March 1919, vol. 196, pp. 407–414.
7. House of Commons Debates, 2 December 1919, vol. 122, col. 204; see Francis Watson, *Dawson of Penn* (London, 1950), pp. 149–59; Christopher Addison, *Politics from Within*, vol. II, (London, 1924), pp. 221–32.
8. *Chemistry and Industry*, 1 October 1966, p. 1652; *Proceedings of Society of Analytical Chemists*, vol. 4 (1967), p. 67.
9. Bacharach, *Science and Nutrition*, p. vii.
10. Jephcott, *The First Fifty Years*, p. 111.
11. Jephcott and Bacharach, 'Anti-Scorbutic Value', p. 139.
12. See his paper, 'The Estimation of Lactose by the Polarimetric and the Gravimetric Methods', *Analyst*, vol. 48 (1923), pp. 521–8.
13. *Analyst*, vol. 48 (1923), pp. 529–35.
14. Published in *Proceedings of World's Dairy Congress*, vol. 2 (1923).
15. Dame Harriette Chick, Margaret Chick, Margaret Hume and Marjorie Macfarlane, *War on Disease: A History of the Lister Institute* (London, 1971), p. 160.
16. *Lancet*, 3 January 1925, p. 27, and 3 September and 24 December 1927.
17. Sir Frank Hartley, *Pharmaceutical Journal*, 3 June 1978.
18. Chick *et al.* *The Present State of Knowledge Concerning Food Factors 1919–1932* (London, 1933), p. 155. For a brief sketch of nutritional research between the wars, see Lord Boyd-Orr, *As I Recall* (London, 1966), pp. 85–122.
19. Steenbock papers, Glaxo Archives Box 1. 9/11/13/1.
20. W. Aykroyd, *Vitamins and other Dietary Essentials* (London, 1936), p. 49.
21. *Ibid.*, p. 62.
22. *Ibid.*
23. Fred Nathan to London Office, 11 April 1929, D1/5.
24. The constituents of Tisdall's original blend were Wheat Middlings 53 per cent, Rolled Oats 18 per cent, Cornmeal 10 per cent, Wheat Germ 15 per cent, Bone

Meal 2 per cent and Yeast 1 per cent. Glaxo's adapted formula for Farex as used from 1932 until March 1933 differed in several respects: Wheat Flour 80.25 per cent, Ground Wheat Germ 15 per cent, Bone Meal 2 per cent, Alfalfa 1 per cent, Dry Yeast 1 per cent, with an addition of 00.75 per cent of vitamins A and D. The whole mix was finely ground so that the product could be fed through a rubber teat. There were initial problems over taste: the British palate found alfalfa slightly alien, especially as there was only the blandness of wheat flour to hide it. Subsequent research showed that oats and maize made Farex less insipid and masked the taste of alfalfa. A modified recipe was therefore introduced in March 1933, comprising: Wheat Flour 53 per cent, Oat Flour 18 per cent, Maize Flour 10 per cent, Wheat Germ 15 per cent, Bone Meal 2 per cent, Dry Yeast 1 per cent and vitamin supplement 1 per cent.

25. Jephcott to Tisdall, March 1935. Glaxo Archives.
26. Board memorandum, March 1935. Glaxo Archives.
27. Glaxo Laboratories Ltd, review of 1937–1938, Green Box Accounts.
28. M. Robson, unpub. PhD thesis 1989, chapter 1, p. 38.
29. Glaxo Laboratories Ltd, review of 1937–1938. Green Box Accounts, Glaxo Archives.
30. *Ibid.*
31. *Ibid.*
32. We are grateful to R. P. Amdam and K. Sogner who are researching the history of Nyegaard & Co for this information from their preliminary paper April 1991, a copy of the Glaxo/Nyegaard Agreement of December 1936 and J. E. Jorpes & B. Strandell, *An Early Attempt at Isolating the Antianaemic Principle in Liver*, Acta Medica Scandinavica, vol. 168, fasc. 4, 1960.
33. Alec Nathan's Notebooks; Glaxo Archives.
34. Jephcott to S. Harvalias, 11 December 1934, A4/5.
35. Jephcott to Alec Nathan, 10 September 1934, A4/5.
36. R. Clifford-Turner, *Gold on the Green* (Greenford, 1985), pp. 26–7.
37. *Ibid.*, p. 38.
38. *Ibid.*, p. 37–8.
39. Glaxo Archives. D1/5.
40. Pacey to London Office, 27 June 1931, Jacobs to Wellington Office, 2 July 1931, Pacey to London Office, 11 July 1931 D1/5.
41. Sydney Jacobs to Wellington Office, 16 July 1931, D1/5.
42. Sydney Jacobs to Wellington Office, 27 April 1933, D1/5.
43. Glaxo Archives, Alec Nathan's notebooks.
44. Glaxo Laboratories Ltd, review of 1937–1938. Green Box Accounts.
45. A. Nathan, working instructions, 1936, Glaxo Archives.
46. *Ibid.*
47. A. Nathan, memorandum 1929, Glaxo Archives.
48. See Stanley Chapman, *Jesse Boot of Boots the Chemist* (London, 1974), Judy Slinn, *A History of May & Baker*, (Cambridge, 1984) and Geoffrey Tweedale, *At the Sign of the Plough*, (London, 1990).

5   Early internationalisation and the growth of overseas markets 1909–1939

1. Alec Nathan, memorandum 1919, Glaxo Archives.
2. R. P. T. Davenport-Hines, 'Glaxo as a multinational before 1963' in Geoffrey

Jones, ed. *British Multinationals: Origins, Management and Performance*, (Aldershot, 1986) pp. 142–3.

3. Alec Nathan, Memorandum of March 1917. (Emphasis in original.)
4. D. C. St. M. Platt, *Finance, Trade and Politics in British Foreign Policy 1815–1914* (Oxford, 1968), p. 352; see Charles A. Jones, 'Great Capitalists and the Direction of British Overseas Investment in the late nineteenth century; the case of Argentina', *Business History*, 22 (1980), pp. 152–65.
5. Trinder Capron to Anstey, 19 December 1919, Glaxo Archives, Green Box 15.
6. Sir Robert Michell, Annual Report for Bolivia for 1928, dated 1 February 1929, paras. 197–200, PRO FO 371/13466.
7. Sir Charles Bentinck, despatch 25 of 28 February 1929, PRO FO 371/13507. See R. P. T. Davenport-Hines, *Dudley Docker* (Cambridge, 1984), pp. 69, 213; R. P. T. Davenport-Hines, *Markets and Bagmen* (Aldershot, 1986), pp. 9–14.
8. D. C. St M. Platt, *Latin America and British Trade 1806–1914* (London, 1972), pp. 159, 207, 212.
9. C. C. Richardson to F. C. Randall, 27 February 1935. SCUM/2/A/1.
10. Richardson to Jephcott, 24 June 1936, 15/4.
11. Richardson to Jephcott, 26 August, 21 October, 5 November, 1937, SCUM/2/A/1. Jephcott to Richardson, 15 November 1937.
12. Jephcott, 1934, Glaxo Archives.
13. Jephcott, 1934, Glaxo Archives.
14. Richardson, 1941, Glaxo Archives.
15. Alec Nathan, 1914, Glaxo Archives.
16. Jephcott to Ayerst, McKenna, Harrison, 3 December 1937. 18/1/11.
17. Jephcott, Report of 24 June 1935. 18/1/11.
18. Jephcott to Hutchinson, 4 March 1936. 18/1/11.
19. Hutchinson to Jephcott, 9 and 16 October 1941. 18/1/9.
20. Hutchinson to W. W. Law, October 1941. 18/1/9.
21. Sir Alfred Mond, *Industry and Politics* (London, 1927), p. 274.
22. Glaxo Archives 1914.
23. Alec Nathan, Report on Australian business, 11 March 1935, Green Box 16.
24. Fred Nathan to Louis Nathan, 1922.
25. Alec Nathan, report on Australian business.
26. Information from interviews with Jim Perry, Paddy Smith, Ray Donahue, Arthur Fox and Bob Jennings, Port Fairy, 15 and 16 March 1984.
27. Private information.
28. A. Nathan, February 1930 D1/5.
29. Jephcott, *The First 50 years*, pp. 98–9.
30. Fred Nathan to J. Nathan & Co, 28 February 1923. D1/5.
31. J. B. Pillow, quoted diary of Dr G. E. Morrison, 5 September 190 Mitchell Library, State Library of New South Wales.
32. A. Nathan, memo enclosed in Randall to Wellington Office, 17 February 1930, D1/5.
33. Fred Nathan to London Office, 13 March 1930. Harold Pacey to London Office, 28 April 1930. D1/5.
34. Alec Nathan to Wellington Office. 20 June 1929. D1/5.
35. Unsigned memo of 23 July 1929, D1/5.
36. Jephcott to Alec Nathan, 12 March 1934, Green Box 16/17.
37. *Ibid.*
38. Alec Nathan memorandum 1919. On scraps of paper see Christopher H. D.

Howard ed., *The Diary of Sir Edward Goschen 1900–1914*, (London, 1980), pp. 298–302.

39. Marquess of Dufferin and Ava, quoted William L. Langer, *Diplomacy of Imperialism*, (London, 1951), p. 109.
40. Randall to M. J. Nathan, 2 October 1929. 19/4/5.
41. Randall, memorandum of 11 November 1929. 19/4/5.
42. Randall, memorandum of 11 November 1929, 19/4/5. On Snia Viscosa, see Donald Coleman, *Courtaulds* vol. II (Oxford, 1969), and Geoffrey Jones, 'Courtaulds in Continental Europe 1920–45', in Jones, ed., *British Multinationals: Origins, Management and Performance*, (Aldershot, 1986), pp. 120, 123, 131–3.
43. Randall, memorandum of 11 November 1929, 19/4/5.
44. Randall, memorandum of 11 November 1929, 19/4/5.
45. Frederick Randall, memorandum of 11 November 1929, 19/4/5.
46. Harvalias to Jephcott, 2 November 1934, A4/5.
47. Sir Sydney Waterlow, Annual Report on Greece for 1936, p. 14. PRO FO 371/21147.
48. Harvalias to Jephcott, 2 November 1934.
49. Jephcott to Alec Nathan, September 1934, A4/5.
50. Despatch 19 of Sir Sydney Waterlow (Athens), 6 April 1937, and Annual Economic Report for Greece in 1936, dated April 1937, PRO FO 371/21143.
51. *Ibid.*
52. *Ibid.*
53. Harry Jephcott to Alec Nathan, 19 November 1936, A4/5.
54. *Ibid.*
55. *Ibid.*
56. *Ibid.*
57. *Ibid.*
58. Sir Sydney Waterlow's Annual Report on Greece for 1936, PRO FO 371/21147.

6 Glaxo Laboratories and the hinge of fortune: the Second World War

1. J. C. Drummond and Anne Wilbraham, *The Englishman's Food* (London, 1959), pp. 448–9. For a wider perspective on British wartime food control, see E. M. H. Lloyd, *Experiments in State Control at the War Office and the Ministry of Food* (Oxford, 1924): W. H. Beveridge, *British Food Control* (Oxford, 1928) and R. J. Hammond, *Food: History of the Second World War*, United Kingdom Civil Series, 2 vols. (London, 1955).
2. Accounts 1939, Glaxo Archives.
3. Clifford-Turner, *Gold on the Green*, (Greenford, 1985), p. 46.
4. *Ibid.*, p. 47.
5. Glaxo Press Release. n.d. (late 1950s). Glaxo Archives.
6. L. F. Haber, *The Chemical Industry 1900–1930*, (Oxford, 1971), pp. 133, 135.
7. J. Slinn, *A History of May & Baker* (Cambridge, 1984).
8. W. J. Reader, *ICI A History*, vol. II, (Oxford, 1975).
9. Haber, *The Chemical Industry 1900–1930*, p. 184.
10. See Michael Robson, 'The Pharmaceutical Industry in Britain and France 1919–1939' (unpub. PhD, London University, 1989). See also J. Liebenau, ed., *The*

Challenge of New Technology: Innovation in British Business Since 1850 (Aldershot, 1988).

11. For an account of Bennett and the Wellcome Foundation during war-time see A. Rupert Hill and B. A. Bembridge, *Physic and Philanthropy: a History of the Wellcome Trust 1931–1986* (London, 1986), pp. 47–66.

12. M. Robson unpub. PhD, London University, 1989, p. 16.

13. Sir Frank Hartley, 'TRC in Retrospect and Prospect', unpublished paper of 1946, Glaxo TRC B/I.

14. Hartley, *ibid.*, p. 8.

15. *Ibid.*

16. The best accounts are *Lancet*, 24 August 1940; David Masters, *Miracle Drug* (London, 1946); Ronald Hare, *The Birth of Penicillin* (London, 1970); Sir Ernst Chain in *Proceedings of the Royal Society* (London, 1971); David Wilson, *Penicillin in Perspective* (London, 1976).

17. W. J. Reader, *ICI*, vol. II, pp. 458–9; R. P. T. Davenport-Hines' entry on Lord MacGowan in D. J. Jeremy and C. Shaw, eds., *Dictionary of Business Biography*, vol. IV (London, 1985), pp. 21–7. Carol Kennedy, *ICI The Company That Changed Our Lives*, (London, 1986), pp. 127–9.

18. Wilson, *Penicillin in Perspective*, p. 217.

19. TRC Board meeting, 1 September 1942.

20. Wilson, *Penicillin in Perspective*, p. 224. See also *Glaxo Bulletin*, June 1946.

21. Sir Harry Jephcott to Anthony Jephcott, 2 November 1943, Jephcott papers Whangarei, New Zealand; Sir Anthony Jephcott, interview, 6 April 1984.

22. Peacock to Jephcott, 8 January 1945, HJ 23.

23. Jephcott to John L. Smith, cablegram 4 April, 1945, J23.

24. Glaxo board meeting 20 March 1945.

25. Wilson, *Penicillin in Perspective*, p. 227.

26. Board meeting, 1 May 1945.

27. Board meeting, 29 May 1945.

28. Glaxo Archives.

29. On Hoadleys, see *Australian Dictionary of Biography*, vol. IX (Melbourne, 1983), pp. 312–314.

30. Geoffrey G. Jones, *The History of the British Bank of the Middle East*, 2 vols. (Cambridge, 1986 and 1987).

31. Sir Claremont Skrine, British Consul at Mashad 1942–1946, *World War in Iran*, (London, 1962), p. 74. Elizabeth Monroe, *Britain's Moment in the Middle East 1914–71* (London, 1981); Sir Dennis Wright, *The Persians Amongst the English: Episodes in Anglo-Persian History* (London, 1985).

32. Frances Bostock and Geoffrey Jones, *Planning and Power in Iran: Abol Hassan Ebtehaj and Economic development under the Shah* (London, 1989).

33. Evans, Fripp, Deed & Co to Glaxo, c/2.

7   Pharmaceuticals triumphant 1946–1962

1. Glaxo Board Minutes, 27 June, 1946.

2. Sir Penderel Moon, *Wavell: the Viceroy's Journal* (London, 1973), p. 34; Clifford-Turner, *Gold on the Green* (Greenford, 1985), p. 87.

3. Moon, pp. 34, 53.

4. A. N. Whitehead, *The Aims of Education* (London, 1929), p. 69.

5. Harry Jephcott to Rupert Pearce, 21 November 1939.

6. Jephcott to Pearce, 16 December 1938.
7. Jephcott to Herbert Palmer, 29 August 1939.
8. Annual Report and Accounts, 1947.
9. Jephcott, confidential memorandum on trading and finance, OEC (53), 1, SCU (M), 10.
10. Jephcott to Sir M. Hutton, 4 February 1953. D1/1/30.
11. Sir Maurice Hutton, memorandum of 19 January 1950, EB (50) 10.
12. Memo, February 1953. D1/1/40.
13. Sir H. Jephcott, 'The Glaxo Research Organisation', in Sir John Cockcroft, ed., *The Organisation of Research Establishments* (Cambridge, 1965).
14. On Tizard generally, see Ronald W. Clark, *Tizard* (London, 1965) and the account by Sir William Farren and R. V. Jones in *Obituaries of Fellows of the Royal Society*, vol. VII (London, 1961), pp. 313.48.
15. Sir Henry Tizard, 'The Strategy of Science', *Chemistry and Industry*, 16 August 1952, p. 788.
16. *Ibid.*, p. 789.
17. Sir Harry Jephcott, 'How Much Research?', *Research*, vol. 5 (1952), p. 2.
18. *Ibid.*, p. 3; interview with Dr Tom Macrae, 7 November 1984.
19. Tizard, 'Strategy of Science', pp. 790–2.
20. Jephcott, 'How Much Research?', p. 3.
21. Memorandum submitted by Glaxo Laboratories Ltd to the Guillebaud Committee, 28 October 1953.
22. ICI and Wellcome evidence to the Guillebaud Committee.
23. W. D. Reekie, *The Economics of the Pharmaceutical Industry* (London, 1975), p. 23.
24. Glaxo archives, Dextran files, Glaxo Board Minutes 25 July 1952.
25. Reekie, *The Economics of the Pharmaceutical Industry*, pp. 7–8.
26. Glaxo Archives, BM. 58/43.
27. L. Hannah, *The Rise of the Corporate Economy* (London, 1983) pp. 144–7.
28. M. Robson, The Pharmaceutical Industry in Britain and France 1919–1939, unpub. PhD (London, 1989).
29. For an excellent account of A & H's history, see G. Tweedale, *At the Sign of the Plough*, (London, 1990).
30. H. Jephcott, draft notes. n.d. Glaxo archives.
31. *Ibid.*
32. Hannah, *The Rise of the Corporate Economy*, p. 129.
33. Jephcott, draft notes.
34. Chairman's speech to A & H directors: 16 November 1959, H. J. papers, packet 43.
35. *The Story of Evans Medical, 1809–1962* (Evans Medical, Liverpool 1962).
36. Notes on the meeting of 5 January 1961 by I.V.L. Fergusson 1961.
37. *Ibid.*
38. I. Fergusson to Evans managers, 9 January 1961.
39. Glaxo Board Papers. EC (62) 110.
40. Glaxo Board Papers EC (62) 103, Home Sales Department, Trading Summary for 1961/2.

8   Research and development: a strategy of science?

1. Memorandum on research policy for consultants' meetings 20 February 1946, B1/1.
2. *Ibid.*
3. *Ibid.*
4. *Ibid.*
5. A. L. Bacharach and F. A. Robinson translated Zechmeister and Cholnoky, *Principles and Practice of Chromatography* (London, 1941).
6. W. F. J. Cuthbertson, and G. Lester Smith, 'Recent Work on the Anti-Anaemia Factor', *Glaxo News*, vol. 2 (1944), p. 100; see *Nature*, vol. 161 (1948), p. 638. See also Emery, 'The Story of Penicillin, Streptomycin and vitamin B_{12} 1940–51', Glaxo Archives.
7. Board Minutes, 29 January 1946.
8. Interview with Dr Tom Macrae, 7 November 1984.
9. Sir William Farren, and R. V. Jones, in *Obituaries of Fellows of the Royal Society*, vol. VII (London, 1961), pp. 313–48. One senior member of Glaxo's research staff wrote to Tizard: 'you certainly do me good . . . I always have at least one jolt during questioning of myself or others': quoted Clark, *Tizard*, p. 405.
10. Sir Henry Tizard 'The Strategy of Science'.
11. Macrae interview.
12. Research and Development Minutes (hereafter R.D.Mins.). (52) 1, p. 2–3, 5; see also R. D. Mins. (52) 2, p. 2.
13. R.D.Mins. (52) 4, p. 1.
14. R.D.Mins. (53) 1, p. 1; see also Mins. (53), 2.
15. R.D.Mins. (53) 1.
16. R.D.Mins. (53) 2, p. 2.
17. *Ibid.*
18. *Ibid.*, p. 2–3.
19. Jephcott to Palmer, 2 November 1951, 16/17.
20. *Ibid.*
21. R.D.Mins. (52) 4.
22. Walter Sneader, *Drug Discovery: The Evolution of Modern Medicines*, (Chichester 1985), pp. 90–2.
23. Jephcott to Palmer, 28 September 1955.
24. *Ibid.*
25. Jephcott, 'The Glaxo Research Organisation', p. 160.
26. Walter Sneader, *Drug Discovery.*
27. F. B. Smith, *The Retreat of Tuberculosis 1850–1950* (London, 1988), pp. 194–203. L. Bryder, *Below the Magic Mountain: a Social History of Tuberculosis in Twentieth Century Britain*, (Oxford, 1988), pp. 243–5, 264–5. Davenport-Hines, 'Blaming the Ill', *Times Literary Supplement*, 29 April 1988.
28. R.D.Mins. (53) 1.
29. R.D.Mins. (53) 9.
30. R.D.Mins. (55) 1.
31. Jephcott, 'The Glaxo Research Organisation', p. 153.
32. R.D.Mins. (55) 8, p. 5.
33. *Research*, 5 (1952): 1–4.
34. R.D.Mins. (55) 8, p. 6.

35. R.D.Mins. (55) 15, p. 2–3.
36. W. J. Reader, *ICI A History*, vol. II (Oxford, 1975), p. 460.
37. R.D.Mins. (55) 3.
38. Jephcott to C. W. Maplethorpe, 17 October 1959, Glaxo Archives HU 43.

9   The development and commercial exploitation of griseofulvin

1. R.D. (52) 2, p. 3.
2. Transactions of the British Mycological Society, 1949.
3. Brain, Wright, Stubb and Way, 'Uptake of Antibiotic Metabolities of Soil Micro-organisms by Plants', *Nature*, 1951.
4. R.D. (55) 9, p. 2–3.
5. R.D. (55) 3, p. 3.
6. R.D. (55) 9, p. 3. 'Notes', p. 6.
7. Quoted in Hanson to Walker, 19 June 1958; Hurran to Walker, 17 June and Walker to Palmer, *et al.*, 18 June 1958, D1/3/1.
8. Bide to Jephcott, *et al.*, 27 June 1957; Bide to ICI, 1 May 1957, D1/3/1.
9. Hanson to Walker, *et al.*, 7 May 1958, D1/3/1.
10. Hurran to Uvarov, *et al.*, 4 June 1958, D1/3/1.
11. 12 February 1958; see also Walker to Ungar, 14 August 1957, and Ungar to Walker, 19 August 1957, D1/3/1.
12. 20 May 1958, D1/3/1.
13. Minutes, 14 May 1958, D1/3/1.
14. Vol. 182, p. 476, *Experimental Ringworm in Guinea Pigs: Oral Treatment with Griseofulvin.*
15. Vol. 182, p. 1320.
16. Vol. 70, p. 949.
17. Palmer to Sexton, 20 June; Walker to Hurran, 17 June; Hurran to Palmer *et al.*, 18 June; Hanson's comment, 18 June: Hanson to Walker, *et al.*, Fantes to Campbell, 23 June; Walker to Palmer, 25 June 1958, D1/3/1.
18. Bide to Palmer, 31 October 1958, D1/1/3.
19. Howell to Uvarov, 11 November 1958; Also Hanson to Walker, 30 July 1958, D1/3/1.
20. Blank to Campbell, 13 November 1958, D1/3/1.
21. *Ibid.*
22. *Ibid.*
23. Turner to Bide, 26 November 1958, D1/3/1.
24. Bide to Palmer, 10 December 1958, D1/2/2; see Palmer to Wilkins, 31 December 1958 and 8 January 1959; Palmer to Tishler, 7 January 1959, D1/3/1.
25. Bide to Carey, ICI 22 January 1959, D1/2/2, F.1.
26. *Ibid.*
27. McKenzie to Bide, 26 January 1959, D1/2/2. Griseo (1).
28. Palmer to Wilkins, *et al.*, 14 January 1959, D1/3/1.
29. Meeting Minutes 25 March 1959: Hurran to Wilkins, 26 March 1959 D1/3/1.
30. C. 24 March 1959, D1/3/1.
31. Walker to Wilkins, 19 May 1959, D1/3/1.
32. R. P. T. Davenport-Hines, *Sex, Death and Punishment* (London, 1990), p. 195.
33. Francis Brown to Austin Bide, 27 January 1959.
34. *Ibid.*
35. Brown to Palmer, 17 June 1959, D1/3/1.

36. Palmer to Wilkins, 15 January 1959, D1/3/1.
37. 'Griseofulvin, An International Symposium', 5 January 1960, D1/3/1.
38. Medical Commentary No. 105, November 1959; Campbell to Palmer, *et al.*, 11 December 1959, Report, D1/3/1.
39. Palmer to Morgan *et al.*, 16 April 1959, D1/3/1.
40. *Ibid.*
41. Hurran to Campbell, 21 October 1959, D1/3/1.
42. ICI to Morgan, 2 June 1960; ICI to Wilkins, 24 March 1961; Lindon to Jephcott, *et al.*, 10 May; Thompson, ICI to Wilkins, 1 March; Wilkins to Thompson, 11 April 1960; 'Collaboration between ICI Pharmaceutical Division and Glaxo Laboratories Ltd, on Griseofulvin', D1/2/2. ICI Agreement.
43. Macrae to Lees, 6 March 1962, D1/3/1.
44. Keen to Wilkins *et al.*, 8 July 1965, D1/3/1.

10   Glaxo Laboratories and the international development of the pharmaceutical industry

1. W. D. Reekie, *The Economics of the Pharmaceutical Industry*, (London, 1975); B. G. James, *The Future of the Multinational Pharmaceutical Industry to 1990*, (Associated Business Programmes, 1977).
2. Christopher A. Bartlett, 'How Multinational Organisations Evolve', *Journal of Business Strategy*, vol. 3 (1982); R. P. T. Davenport-Hines, 'Glaxo as a Multinational before 1963', in Geoffrey Jones, ed., *British Multinationals: Origins, Management and Performance* (Aldershot, 1986). For other references to Glaxo as a multinational, see David Shepherd, Aubrey Silberston and Roger Strange, *British Manufacturing Investment Overseas* (London, 1985), and Mark Casson, 'Contractual Arrangements for Technology Transfer: New Evidence from Business History', *Business History*, vol. 28 (1986), pp. 20–3.
3. Bartlett, 'Multinational Organisations', pp. 22–3. On the crisis-torn multinational development see the case-studies of Vickers, Dunlop, etc. in Jones, *British Multinationals*, and Peter Hertner and Geoffrey Jones, eds., *Multinationals: Theory and History* (Aldershot, 1986).
4. Bartlett, 'Multinational Organisations', p. 23.
5. *Ibid.*, p. 24.
6. Robin Higham, *Britain's Imperial Air Routes 1918–1939* (London, 1960); Martin Daunton, *Royal Mail* (London, 1985).
7. On the problems of control in multinational enterprise see Jones, *British Multinationals*, pp. 48–50, 52–4, 62–8; Hertner and Jones, *Multinationals*, pp. 105–8.
8. Harry Jephcott to Ernest Samuel, 3 January 1933, Green Box 18.
9. Hertner and Jones, *Multinationals*, p. 102; Maurice Corina, *Trust in Tobacco* (London, 1975); Sherman Cochran *Big Business in China* (Cambridge, Mass., 1980); Geoffrey Jones, 'The Gramophone Company: an Anglo-American multinational, 1898–1931', *Business History Review*, vol. 59 (1985), p. 98; Mira Wilkins in R. P. T. Davenport-Hines and Geoffrey Jones, eds., *The End of Insularity!* (London, 1988); Jurgen Osterhammel, 'British Business in China 1860s to 1960s' in R. P. T. Davenport-Hines and Geoffrey Jones, eds, *British Business in Asia since 1860*, (Cambridge, 1989).
10. Bartlett, 'Multinational Organisations', p. 24.
11. Jephcott to C. C. Richardson, 3 June 1941, 15/4.

12. W. B. Reddaway, *Effects of United Kingdom Direct Investment Overseas* (London, 1967–1978).
13. W. J. Reader, *Metal Box, A History* (London, 1976).
14. Jephcott to Herbert Palmer, 8 February 1959 D1/1/30; Jephcott, memorandum of 5 May 1953, SCU (M) 10.
15. Susan Strange, *Sterling and British Policy* (London, 1971); L. S. Pressnell, 'The End of the Sterling Area', *Three Banks Review*, no. 121 (1979); Sidney Pollard, *The Wasting of the British Economy* (London, 1982).
16. F. J. Wilkins to Palmer, 25 September 1952, D1/1/31.
17. Jephcott to Mace, 30 June 1955, SCU (M) 2A/B.
18. Glaxo Archives, Board Papers, 1949 and 1960.
19. Jephcott, confidential memorandum on trading and finance, DEC (53) 1, SCU (M) 10.
20. Glaxo Archives, Board Papers 1954.
21. Minutes of meeting on Argentina, 29 May 1956, D1/1/19.
22. Mace, memorandum on consultancy agreements, 1953, SCU (M) 10.
23. R. E. Petley to Palmer, 5 December 1954, SCU (M) 2A/B.
24. Doris Jephcott to her mother, 23 March 1921 (quoting Pacey, a New Zealand director), Jephcott family papers, Whangarei, New Zealand.
25. Mark Casson, 'Entrepreneurship and Foreign Direct Investment', in P. J. Buckley and M. Casson, eds., *Economic Theory of the Multinational Enterprise* (London, 1985). We are grateful to Mr T. A. B. Corley of the University of Reading for alerting us to the neglect of entrepreneurship in economic theories of foreign direct investment.
26. Jephcott to Palmer, 29 August 1939.
27. Sir Maurice Hutton to Sir Robert Hutchings, 6 June 1952, D1/4/2/2.
28. Bartlett, 'Multinational Organisations', pp. 24–5.
29. Jephcott, Report on African Tour, 8 March 1959, quoted Davenport-Hines, 'Glaxo as a Multinational', p. 161.

11 Across the Atlantic: North and South America

1. Palmer to Jephcott, 22 January 1953, D1/1/30; Chapman, Stanley, *Jesse Boot of Boots the Chemist* (London, 1974), p. 200.
2. Jephcott, board memorandum of 28 April 1947. See David Caute, *The Great Fear: the anti-communist campaign under Truman and Eisenhower*, (London, 1978). For an earlier attitude to drugs being obtainable from other sources (in this case Indian opium from China), see diary of Sir Edward Hamilton, 11 April 1891, British Library Add. Ms. 48655; other references to strong right wing feelings among US pharmaceutical companies, especially after the Kefauver hearings, are in the section on Eli Lilly in Waldemar Nielsen, *The Golden Donors* (New York, 1985), pp. 285–99.
3. Interview with Dr Tom Macrae, 7 November 1984.
4. Jephcott to Palmer, 30 January 1953, D1/1/30.
5. Jephcott to Wilkins, 1 January 1954, D1/2/3A.
6. Jephcott to Sir Maurice Hutton, 11 February 1953, D1/1/30.
7. Hector Walker to Jephcott, 25 September 1956, D1/2/3A.
8. Jephcott's papers, diary, New York 1955.
9. Jephcott to Palmer, 14 April 1954, D1/1/30.

10. F. J. Wilkins, report on visit to Merck of 30 November to 2 December 1954, D1/1/31.
11. *Ibid.*
12. *Ibid.*
13. Palmer to Carl Anderson, 9 December 1954, D1/1/52.
14. Palmer to O. F. Morgan, 27 June 1956, D1/1/52.
15. Jephcott's papers, diary, New York 1955.
16. Palmer to Hutchinson, 15 December 1954, D1/1/19.
17. Palmer to Jephcott, 11 March 1955, D1/1/30.
18. Palmer to Jephcott, 14 February 1956, D1/1/30.
19. Wilkins to Palmer, 24 February 1959, D1/1/31.
20. Joseph Hutchinson, memorandum on Canada, 28 March 1950, D1/1/19.
21. J. T. Marsh, memorandum on the Canadian market and British suppliers, 1950, D1/1/19.
22. Jephcott, report to Glaxo Laboratories Board, 13 March 1953.
23. Jephcott to Palmer, 25 January 1953, D1/1/30.
24. *Ibid.*
25. Palmer to Hutchinson, 28 February 1956.
26. Quoted in Jephcott to Palmer, 22 October 1959, D1/1/19.
27. W. D. M. C. Huston and E. C. Cripps, *Through a City Archway: The Story of Allen & Hanburys, 1715–1954* (London, 1954), p. 255. See also Geoffrey Tweedale, *At The Sign of the Plough* (London, 1990).
28. Laurie Gullick to Jephcott, 27 November 1957, D1/1/19.
29. A. Graham-Yooll, *The Forgotten Colony* (London, 1981), p. 243.
30. C. Richardson to Jephcott, 2 November 1939, 15/4.
31. Palmer to Jephcott, 14 February 1956, D1/1/30.
32. Jephcott letters D1/1/19, D1/1/30.
33. *Ibid.*
34. Petley to Palmer, 3 February and 5 March 1956, D1/1/19.
35. Jephcott to Palmer, 14 March 1956, D1/1/30.
36. Herbert Palmer to R. G. Petley, 27 February 1958, D1/1/21.
37. Joseph Hutchinson to Jephcott, 11 September 1942, 18/1/11.
38. Jephcott to Glaxo Laboratories Board, 25 April 1950.
39. *The Times*, 25 August 1954.
40. W. Sable, Memo 9 May 1955, D1/1/19.
41. *Ibid.*
42. 'Banas' Industrial Relations Report November 1948, D1/1/21.
43. Idris Lewis to W. J. Hurran, 1 December 1959.
44. Lewis to Hurran, 14 October 1959, D1/1/21.
45. Idris Lewis to W. J. Hurran, 14 October 1959, D1/1/21.
46. Jephcott to Glaxo Laboratories Board, 1950.
47. Jephcott to Glaxo Laboratories Board, 1953.
48. *Ibid.*
49. G. McGough to I. Townsend, 22 August 1956, D1/1/22–3.
50. Palmer to McGough, 23 May 1957, D1/1/22–3.

12 The Commonwealth I: India and Pakistan

1. B. R. Tomlinson, 'British Business in India 1860–1970', in R. P. T. Davenport-Hines and Geoffrey Jones, eds., *British Business in Asia since 1860*, (Cambridge, 1988), pp. 160–1.
2. *Ibid.*
3. *Ibid.*
4. N. T. Williams of Withers to Jephcott, 12 July 1944, 16/3/3.
5. Jephcott memorandum of 26 March 1947, SCU (M).
6. Jephcott memorandum of 26 March 1947, SCU (M) 8.
7. B. R. Tomlinson, 'British Business of India', pp. 160–1.
8. Jephcott to Palmer 1 December 1949, D1/1/14A.
9. Jephcott to Palmer, 7 October 1949, D1/1/14A.
10. Gwilt to Palmer, 27 January 1953, D1/1/17, p. 2.
11. Palmer to Haryott, 4 September 1952, D1/1/17.
12. Gwilt to Palmer, 27 January 1953, D1/1/17, pp. 2–3.
13. Gwilt to Jephcott, 25 April 1953, D1/1/17.
14. Palmer to Haryott, 25 September 1952, D1/1/17.
15. H. Jephcott, 'Roche Products Vitamin A in India', memo 31 July 1957, D1/1/17.
16. *Ibid.*
17. Gardner-Lewis to Palmer, 16 July 1957, D1/1/17.
18. Memorandum on setting up Pakistan subsidiary, 19 January 1948; Box SCU (M) 7.
19. E. L. C. Gwilt to A. Sandercock, 14 February 1948, Box SCU (M)/7; Pakistan Subsidiary Company Meeting, 2 March 1948, Box SCU (M)/7.
20. Pakistan Subsidiary Company Meeting 2/3/48, Box SCU (M)/7; Berkoff (N. Williams and Col.) to H. C. Mace, 13 April 1948, Box SCU (M)/7.
21. H. C. Mace to H. Jephcott, 8 June 1949, Box SCU (M)/7; Capital requirements of Pakistan Company, BM 49/40.
22. Glaxo Laboratories (Pakistan Company), BM 49/50; Jephcott to Palmer, 27 January 1951, green 16/8.
23. Jephcott, report to Board on Pakistan, 8 January 1951.
24. Jephcott to Palmer, 19 February 1953, D1/1/30.
25. Palmer to Jephcott, 12 February 1953, D1/1/30.
26. Medical Representatives Conference, 23 March 1951, SCU (M)/7.
27. *Ibid.*
28. *Ibid.*
29. *Ibid.*
30. R. A. M. Henson to Jephcott, 15 July 1955, SCU (M)/7.
31. Report on India, Pakistan and Ceylon by Sir M. Hutton, 30 April 1954.
32. Hutton to Jephcott, 19 September 1954, D1/1/18; Henson to Jephcott, 15 July 1955, SCU (M)/7.
33. Craig to Palmer, 20 January 1954, D1/1/18.
34. Pakistan Company Meeting, 14 June 1957, SCU (M)/7.
35. Jephcott to Palmer, 5 September 1958, D1/1/18.
36. Glaxo Laboratories Pakistan Ltd, BM 58/51.
37. Jephcott to Palmer, 15 October 1958, D1/1/18.
38. Henson to Palmer, 6 October 1958, D1/1/18.
39. Pakistan Company capital requirements, BM 60/92; Pakistan, BM 61/118.

13   The Commonwealth II: Australia and New Zealand

1. R. A. Langridge (Export Department) to Palmer, 7 March 1950, D1/1/14A.
2. Glaxo Laboratories, Board Minutes, 22 December 1950.
3. Jephcott, memorandum on Australian Project, 21 November 1951, BM 51/63.
4. Jephcott, report to Glaxo Laboratories Board, 1951, BM 51/17, BM 51/63A.
5. Ibid.
6. Jephcott to Palmer, 4 February 1951, Green 16/8.
7. Pearce to Jephcott, 24 March 1952, D1/1/14A.
8. Jephcott, report of overseas tour, 19 October to 15 December 1952.
9. Minutes of Conference of 29 May 1952, D1/1/14A.
10. Jephcott to Palmer, 12 April 1956, D1/1/30.
11. Ibid.
12. Wilkins to Palmer, 31 May 1957, D1/1/14A.
13. W. F. Manning to Palmer, 29 March 1957, D1/1/30.
14. Pearce to Palmer, 31 May 1957. Ibid.
15. 'Australian Company' – minutes of a meeting held at Greenford, 20 November 1957. Ibid.
16. Palmer to Hunt, 27 May 1958. Ibid.
17. Pearce to Palmer, 27 March 1958. Ibid.
18. Palmer to Pearce, 25 August 1958. Ibid.
19. 'Report on visit to Australia and New Zealand, November/December 1964', 6 January 1965. H. W. Palmer, BM 65/13. D1/1/71.
20. Mace to Stagg, 14 February 1963. Ibid.
21. Jephcott to Hunt, 6 May 1960.
22. Hunt to Jephcott, 21 June 1960.
23. BM 51/19.
24. Jephcott to Executive Board, 25 August 1958, SCU (M) 19B.
25. Stagg to Mace, 7 February 1955, SCU (M) 9B.
26. Stagg to Hurran and Mace, 16 August 1956, SCU (M) 9B.
27. BM 51/18.
28. BM 51/19, p. 3.
29. The distillation plant had been installed with help from Distillation Product Industries, a division of Kodak. D1/1/15.
30. Palmer to C. C. Debell, 12 May 1952. D1/1/15. Investigations at Island Bay factory, Wellington, 1952–1953. Ibid.
31. Memo from Stagg to Greenford, 29 August 1961. SCU (M) 9/A/2.
32. Jephcott to Palmer, 12 April 1956, D1/1/30.
33. Minutes of Meeting 11 November 1959; memo from Staff, 26 November 1959, BM 61/61. D1/1/15.
34. Stagg to Hurran, 18 January 1957, SCU (M) 9/A/2.
35. Glaxo Laboratories (NZ) Ltd. Memorandum to Directors, veterinary biological project, 13/4/61, SCU (M) 9/A/2. Note: this memo is not signed by Stagg.
36. Jephcott to Stagg, 27 February 1961, SCU (M) 9/A/2.
37. W. C. J. Coughtrey to Stagg, 9 March 1961. Ibid.
38. Jephcott to Pacey, 29 May 1961. Ibid.
39. Memo from Stagg to Greenford. 28 August 1961. Ibid.
40. Quoted by Stagg in memo to Greenford, 28 August 1961, from Vance Packard, The Waste Makers (London and New York, 1961).
41. Memo from Stagg. Ibid.

14   The Commonwealth III: South Africa

This chapter owes much to the unpublished memoir written by Leslie Birchley and kept at Parktown, Johannesburg. On a visit to South Africa in 1985, we found that few historical materials from the period before 1963 had been preserved at Wadeville.

1. Jones, Geoffrey, ed., *British Multinationals: Origins, Strategy and Performance* (Aldershot, 1986), pp. 16–18.
2. Report of the Snyman Commission on the Pharmaceutical Industry in South Africa, 1962, p. 108.
3. Interview with Leslie Birchley, 28 January 1985.
4. Birchley to H. C. Mace, 15 January 1951, SCUM/6.
5. Interview with Leslie Birchley, 28 January 1985.
6. Birchley to Subsidiary Companies Unit, 26 June 1951, SCUM/6.
7. Birchley to Jephcott, 18 November 1955, SCUM/6.
8. Jephcott to Palmer, 4 September 1952, D1/1/30.
9. Jephcott to Palmer, 26 February 1955, D1/1/30.
10. Jephcott to Palmer, 26 February 1955, D1/1/30.
11. Jephcott to Palmer, 26 February 1955, D1/1/30.
12. Birchley to Jephcott, 18 November 1955, SWCUM/6.
13. Jephcott to Birchley, 15 August 1955, D1/1/15.
14. Birchley to H. C. Mace, 3 November 1955, SCUM/6.
15. Birchley South African Newsletter, September – October 1950, D1/1/15.
16. Jephcott to Wilkins, 4 February 1959, D1/1/30.
17. Jephcott to Palmer, 26 February 1957, D1/1/30.
18. Jephcott to Palmer, 26 February 1959, D1/1/30.
19. Jephcott to Palmer, 22 January 1959, D1/1/30.
20. Minutes of Greenford meeting of 2 December 1944, SCUM/6.
21. Birchley to Jephcott, 8 December 1960, SCUM/13.
22. Jephcott to Birchley, 22 December 1960, SCUM/13.
23. Interview with Leslie Birchley, 28 January 1985.
24. Interview with Arthur Fallam, 29 January 1985.
25. Jephcott to Palmer, 8 February 1959, D1/1/30. See Jephcott to Palmer, 26 February (from Lagos), D1/1/30: 'A & H are masters of laying on the physical aspects of being important and then assuming that they are, as individuals, important'.
26. Interview with Arthur Fullam, 29 January 1985.
27. The Snyman Commission 1962. Information from L. Birchley.
28. Jephcott to Palmer, 8 February 1959, D1/1/30.
29. Birchley to Palmer, 5 March 1958, D1/1/15.

15   Glaxo in Europe

1. The Fanfani government finally produced a draft patents Bill, which however did not reach Parliament before the elections of 1963. This Bill proposed to extend the application of industrial patents to new medical products and to new processes of the manufacture of medicaments; it excluded sera and vaccines both for human and veterinary use, together with their manufacturing processes. The duration of a patent was to be ten years. The law proposed that the description

of a new process of manufacture should refer to a single well-defined and reproduceable process, not based on chemical formulae in generic terms or with variable constituents; each process could give rise to a maximum of three product patents, and if the new process led to further medicaments it would be necessary to apply for as many patents of the new process as of the medicaments obtainable. An important provision of the proposed law was the permission given to the Ministry of Health to issue special non-exclusive licences – with compensation to the patent holder – for the patented products or processes, whenever this was necessary to insure the quality of the products, their production in sufficient quantity and at appropriate cost, or in any other circumstances where the interests of public health required.

2. ICI's griseofulvin licensee in Italy, Vismara Terapeutici, was the pharmaceutical branch of a family business of pork meat purveyors, Francesco Vismara, which produced salami and other food derived from pork meat. Vismara had developed its pharmaceutical business after 1945 and had approached Glaxo shortly after the war with the object of a joint venture in penicillin production. Its original pharmaceutical speciality was extracting hormones and other substances from pig organs (thyroid, liver, adrenals, etc.), but latterly it undertook research and production of synthetic hormones and other drugs, particularly anti-viral substances. The parent company had issued capital in 1964 of 1,000m lire, while Vismara Terapeutici had a comparable position to Glaxo in the Italian market; the group ranked among the fifty biggest companies in Italy. They had ties with ICI.

3. H. A. Gent, Report of September 1946, Gent Papers. Privately held.
4. *Ibid.*
5. *Ibid.*
6. H. A. Gent, Report of 31 August 1947, Gent Papers.
7. *Ibid.*
8. Jephcott to Hutton, 11 September 1953. Hutton to Jephcott, 15 September 1953, D1/1/19.
9. H. A. Gent, Report of September 1946, Gent Papers.
10. Jephcott, BM 53/47.
11. Gent to Palmer, 19 November 1957, D1/1/19.
12. Wilkins to Palmer, 19 November 1958. Ibid.
13. Glaxo Archives. Gent papers.
14. Hutton to Jephcott, 15 September 1953, D1/1/19.
15. Minutes of Meeting of 14 June 1956, Gent Papers.
16. *Ibid.*
17. Papers accompanying 1955–1956 Budget.
18. Minutes of Conference 24 June 1957.
19. W. J. Reader, *Metal Box. A History*, (London, 1976), pp. 196–7.
20. Despite the fact that Lovens were selling bulk penicillin to the East Asiatic Company in India and undercut the prices charged to Glaxo India by the parent company for similar bulk supplied.
21. H. W. Palmer, Report to GL Board on European Free Trade, 26 October 1957.
22. H. A. Gent to F. J. Wilkins, 7 March 1959, Verona Papers.
23. *Ibid.*
24. Palmer, Report to G. L. Board on European Trading, 30 June 1959; see Palmer, Report to G. L. Board on European Trading, 29 October 1959.
25. H. A. Gent to J. W. Hurran, 1 December 1959.

26. H. A. Gent to Palmer, 19 November 1957, D1/1/19.
27. H. A. Gent to H. Jephcott and H. W. Palmer, 14 September 1961.
28. Gent, Memorandum to European Executives Meetings, 9 May 1963, Verona Papers; information from Commendatore Gent, 1984.
29. *Ibid.*
30. The Swiss market, of course, was not large, and was dominated by Sandoz, Roche and CIBA.
31. H. A. Gent to Palmer, 29 September 1961.
32. Palmer to H. A. Gent, 3 October 1961.
33. H. A. Gent to Palmer, 27 November 1961.
34. *Ibid.*
35. H. A. Gent to Jephcott, 30 August 1961, Verona Papers.
36. Jephcott to Gent, 11 December 1961, Verona Papers.
37. Gent to Jephcott, 13 December 1961.
38. Minutes of the Third Meeting of Senior Executives of the Glaxo Group, 21 June 1963.
39. W. J. Reader, *Metal Box. A History*, p. 204.
40. Confederation of British Industry, *Britain and Europe: an industrial appraisal* (London, 1966), p. 2.
41. *Ibid.*, pp. 2, 8.

Select bibliography

Books and articles

Abrahamian, Ervand, *Iran between Two Revolutions* (Princeton, 1982)

Addison, Christopher, *Politics from Within*, 2 vols. (London, 1924)

Anon., *The Story of Evans Medical* (Liverpool, 1962)

Armstrong, John, 'Hooley and the Bovril Company' in R. P. T. Davenport-Hines, ed., *Speculators and Patriots* (London, 1986)

Armytage, W. H. G., *A. J. Mundella: the Liberal Background to the Labour Movement* (London, 1951)

Atkins, P. J., 'London's Intra-Urban Milk Supply c. 1790–1914', *Transactions of the Institute of British Geographers*, volume 2 (1977)

'The Retail Milk Trade in London c. 1790–1914', *Economic History Review*, volume 33 (1980)

Auckland Observer, 21 January 1882

Australian Dictionary of Biography, volume IX (Melbourne, 1983)

Bacharach, A. L., *Science and Nutrition* (London, 1938)

'The Estimation of Lactose by the Polarimetric and the Gravimetric Methods', *Analyst*, volume 48, (1923)

Bartlett, Christopher A., 'How Multinational Organisations Evolve', *Journal of Business Strategy*, volume 3 (1982)

Bassett, Judith, *Sir Harry Atkinson* (Auckland and Oxford, 1975)

Betts, W. R., *Life of Sir John Bland-Sutton* (London, 1956)

Beveridge, W. H., *British Food Control* (Oxford, 1928)

Bostock, Frances and Jones, Geoffrey, *Planning and Power in Iran: Abol Hassah Ebtehaj and Economic Development Under the Shah* (London, 1989)

Boyd-Orr, Lord, *As I Recall* (London, 1966)

Boyd-Orr, Sir John (later Lord), 'Nutrition in Relation to Education, Agriculture and Medicine', *Health and Empire*, volume 12 (1937)

Braddon, W. L., *The Cause and Prevention of Beriberi* (London, 1907)

Bryder, Linda, *Below the Magic Mountain: A Social History of Tuberculosis in Twentieth Century Britain* (Oxford, 1988)

Burnett, J., *Plenty and Want* (London, 1966)

Casson, Mark, 'Contractual Arrangements for Technology Transfer: New Evidence from Business History', *Business History*, volume 28 (1986)

'Entrepreneurship and Foreign Direct Investment' in P. J. Buckley and M. Casson, eds., *Economic Theory of the Multinational Enterprise* (London, 1985)

Cautley, Edmund, 'The Use and Abuse of Proprietary Foods in Infant Feeding', *The Practitioner*, volume 82 (1909)

Chapman, Stanley, *Jesse Boot of Boots the Chemist* (London, 1974)

Chick, Dame Harriette, Margaret Chick, Margaret Hume, and Marjorie Macfarlane, *War on Disease: A History of the Lister Institute* (London, 1971)

Clark, Ronald, W., *Tizard* (London, 1965)

Clevely, R. E., *Bunnythorpe and District 1872–1952* (Wellington, 1953)

Clifford-Turner, R., *Gold on the Green* (Greenford, 1985)

Cochran, Sherman, *Big Business in China* (Cambridge, Mass., 1980)

Cockcroft, Sir John, ed., *The Organisation of Research Establishments* (Cambridge, 1965)

Coleman, Donald, *Courtaulds*, volume II (Oxford, 1969)

Confederation of British Industry, *Britain and Europe: an industrial appraisal* (London, 1966)

Coutts, Francis J. H., *Report to Local Government Board on an inquiry as to Condensed Milks, with special reference to their use as an Infants' food* New Series, No. 56 (London, 1918)

Critchell, James T., and Joseph Raymond, *A History of the Frozen Meat Trade* (London, 1912)

Davenport-Hines, R. P. T., 'Glaxo as a Multinational before 1963' in Geoffrey Jones, ed., *British Multinationals: Origins, Management and Performance* (Aldershot, 1986)

Davenport-Hines, R. P. T., ed., *Markets and Bagmen: Studies in Marketing and British Industrial Performance 1830–1939.* (Aldershot, 1986)

Davenport-Hines, R. P. T., and Geoffrey Jones, eds., *British Business in Asia since 1860* (Cambridge, 1988)

Dowie, J. A., 'Business Politicians in Action: the New Zealand Railway Boom of the 1870s', *Business Archives and History*, volume 5 (1965)

Dufferin and Ava, Marquess of, 'Speech at the Hospital for Sick Children' in Henry Milton, ed., *Speeches and Addresses of . . . Dufferin* (London, 1882)

Drummond, J. C. and Anne Wilbraham, *The Englishman's Food* (London, 1959)

Dwork, D., *War is Good for Babies and other Young Children* (London, 1987)

Farren, Sir William and R. V. Jones, on Sir Henry Tizard in *Obituaries of Fellows of the Royal Society*, volume VII (London, 1961)

Gibb, Sir Alexander, 'The Opportunities for British Industry in the New India' in Sir Adrian Baillie and the Marquess of Dufferin and Ava, eds., *India from a Backbench* (London, 1934)

Goldman, L. M., *The History of the Jews in New Zealand* (Wellington, 1958)

Graham-Yooll, A., *The Forgotten Colony* (London, 1981)

Haber, L. F., *The Chemical Industry 1900–1930* (Oxford, 1971)

Hammond, R. J., *Food: History of the Second World War*, United Kingdom Civil Series, 2 volumes (London, 1955)

Harington, Sir Charles, *The Thyroid Gland* (Oxford, 1933)

Harris, Josie, 'Bureaucrats and Businessmen in British Food Control 1916–19', essay in Kathleen Burk, ed., *War and the State* (London, 1982)

Hartley, Sir Frank, *Pharmaceutical Journal*, 3 June 1978

Hereford, P. S. E., *The New Zealand Frozen Meat Trade* (Wellington, 1932)

Hertner, Peter and Geoffrey Jones, eds. *Multinationals: Theory and History* (Aldershot, 1986)

Higham, Robin, *Britain's Imperial Air Routes 1918–1939* (London, 1960)
Hill, Rupert A. and B. A. Bembridge, *Physics and Philanthropy: a History of the Wellcome Trust 1931–1986* (London, 1986)
Hounshell, David A & John Kenly Smith, *Science and Corporate Strategy: Du Pont R & D, 1902–80* (Cambridge, 1988)
Huston, W. D. M. C., and E. C. Cripps, *Through a City Archway: The Story of Allen & Hanburys, 1715–1954* (London, 1954)
James, B. G., *The Future of the Multinational Pharmaceutical Industry to 1990*, (Associated Business Programmes, 1977)
Jephcott, Sir Harry, *The First Fifty Years* (Ipswich, 1969)
'The Glaxo Research Organisation' in Sir John Cockcroft, ed., *The Organisation of Research Establishments* (Cambridge, 1965)
'How Much Research?' *Research* volume 5, (1952)
Jephcott, Sir Harry and A. L. Bacharach, 'The Anti-Scorbutic Value of Dried Milk', *Biochemical Journal*, volume 15 (1921)
Jones, Geoffrey, *The History of the British Bank of the Middle East*, 2 vols. (Cambridge, 1986 and 1987)
'The Gramophone Company: an Anglo-American multinational, 1898–1931', *Business History Review*, volume 59 (1985)
Jones, Geoffrey, ed., *British Multinationals: Origins, Management and Performance*, (Aldershot, 1986)
Kennedy, Carol, *ICI. The Company That Changed Our Lives* (London, 1986)
Kohn, Marek, *Narcomania* (London, 1989)
Larkworthy, Falconer *Ninety One Years* (London, 1924)
Liebenau, Jonathan, *Medical Science and Medical Industry* (London, 1987)
Lloyd, E. M. H., *Experiments in State Control at the War Office and the Ministry of Food* (Oxford, 1924)
Food Production in War (Oxford, 1923)
Mackenzie, John, *Propaganda and Empire* (Manchester, 1984)
Masters, David, *Miracle Drug* (London, 1946)
Melville, Arabella and Colin Johnson, *Cured to Death: the Effect of Prescription Drugs* (London, 1982)
Mennell, Philip, *The New Zealand Loan and Mercantile Agency Company Ltd* (London, 1894)
Millard, C. Killick, 'Dried Milk as a Food for Infants', *British Medical Journal*, 29 January 1910
Mond, Sir Alfred, *Industry and Politics* (London, 1927)
Monroe, Elizabeth, *Britain's Moment in the Middle East 1914–71* (London, 1981)
Moon, Sir Penderel, *Wavell: The Viceroy's Journal* (London, 1973)
Naish, Albert, 'The Sheffield Dried Milk Scheme', *British Medical Journal*, 29 August 1908
Newsholme, Sir Arthur, *Fifty Years in Public Health, a Personal Narrative with Comments* (London, 1935)
The Last Thirty Years in Public Health, Recollections and Reflections on my Official and Post-Official Life (London, 1936)
Nielsen, Waldemar, *The Golden Donors* (New York, 1985)
Osterhammel, Jurgen, 'British Business in China 1860s to 1960s' in R. P. T. Davenport-Hines and Geoffrey Jones, eds., *British Business in Asia since 1860* (Cambridge, 1989)
Perren, R., *The Meat Trade in Britain 1840–1914* (London, 1978)

Philpott, H. G., *A History of the New Zealand Dairy Industry* (Wellington, 1937)
Platt, D. C. St. M., *Finance, Trade and Politics in British Foreign Policy 1815–1914* (Oxford, 1968)
    Latin America and British Trade 1806–1914 (London, 1972)
Pollard, Sidney, *The Wasting of the British Economy* (London, 1982)
Pressnell, L. S., 'The End of the Sterling Area', *Three Banks Review*, No. 121 (1979)
Reader, W. J., *Metal Box, A History* (London, 1976)
    ICI. A History, volume II (Oxford, 1975)
Reddaway, W. B., *Effects of United Kingdom Direct Investment Overseas* (London, 1967–8)
Reekie, W. D., *The Economics of the Pharmaceutical Industry* (London, 1975)
    'Drug Prices in the U.K., U.S.A., Europe and Australia', *Australian Economic Papers* (June, 1984)
Robson, Michael, 'The Pharmaceutical Industry in Britain and France 1919–1939' (unpub. PhD, London University, 1989)
Scott, H. S., 'Nutrition and Education in the Colonies', *Health and Empire*, volume 13 (1938)
Shepherd, David, Aubrey Silberston and Roger Strange, *British Manufacturing Investment Overseas* (London, 1985)
Simkin, C. G. F., *The Instability of a Dependent Economy* (Oxford, 1951)
Skrine, Sir Claremont, *World War in Iran* (London, 1962)
Slinn, Judy, *A History of May & Baker* (Cambridge, 1984)
Smith, F. B., *The Retreat of Tuberculosis 1850–1950* (London, 1988)
Sneader, Walter, *Drug Discovery: The Evolution of Modern Medicines*, (Chichester, 1985)
Stone, R. C. J., *Makers of Fortune*, (Oxford, 1973)
    'The New Zealand Frozen Meat Storage Company', *New Zealand Journal of History*, volume 5 (1971)
Swann, John P., *Academic Scientists and the Pharmaceutical Industry: Cooperative Research in Twentieth Century America* (Baltimore and London, 1988)
Tallents, Sir Stephen, *Man and Boy* (London, 1943)
Tizard, Sir Henry, 'The Strategy of Science', *Chemistry and Industry*, 16 August 1952, p. 788
Tomlinson, B. R., 'British Business in India 1860–1970' in R. P. T. Davenport-Hines, and Geoffrey Jones, eds., *British Business in Asia since 1860* (Cambridge, 1988)
Tweedale, Geoffrey, *At the Sign of the Plough*, (London, 1990)
Ward, A. H., *A Command of Cooperatives* (Wellington, 1975)
Watson, Francis, *Dawson of Penn* (London, 1950)
Webster, Charles, *The Health Services since the War: Problems of Health Care, the National Health Service before 1957* (London, 1988)
Weinreb, B. and C. Hibbert, eds., *The London Encyclopaedia* (London, 1983)
Wilson, David, *Penicillin in Perspective* (London, 1976)
Winter, J. M., 'The Impact of the First World War on Civilian Health in Britain', *Economic History Review*, volume 30 (1977)
Wise, E. F., 'The History of the Ministry of Food', *Economic Journal*, volume 39 (1929)

Periodicals

Analyst
British Medical Journal
Business History
Economist
Glaxo News
Health and Empire
Lancet
Nature
Practitioner
The Times

Index

Lightning Source UK Ltd.
Milton Keynes UK
UKOW01f1422030317

295811UK00001B/213/P